Withdrawn

MARGARET SANGER
Her Life in Her Words

MARGARET SANGER
Her Life in Her Words

Miriam Reed, Ph.D.

Foreword by Margaret Sanger Lampe

BARRICADE
BOOKS

Fort Lee, New Jersey

Published by Barricade Books Inc.
185 Bridge Plaza North
Suite 308-A
Fort Lee, NJ 07024
www.barricadebooks.com

Library of Congress Cataloging-in-Publication Data

Reed, Miriam, actress.
    Margaret Sanger : her life in her words / Miriam Reed.
        p. cm.
    Includes bibliographical references (p.) and index.
    ISBN 1-56980-255-6 (casebound) -- ISBN 1-56980-246-7 (pbk.)
    1. Sanger, Margaret, 1879-1966. 2. Sanger, Margaret, 1879-1966--
Correspondence. 3. Birth control--United States--History--20th century. 4.
Women's rights--United States--History--20th century. I. Title.

HQ764.S3R43 2003
363.9'6--dc21

                                                              2003040416
Printed in the United States of America
First Printing

Table of Contents

Part III: The Conservative Radical

Appendices

Document Index

Foreword

by Margaret Sanger Lampe

Miriam Reed has gathered many of Margaret Sanger's words into a remarkable story about her courage and ideals. She has researched and read most of the papers of Margaret Sanger. She has captured her essence and her drive, and our family is very grateful that she has done this. The words of Margaret Sanger ring out today as powerfully as they did in the early 1900s and bring to life for all who read them a sense of those times.

As one of her three granddaughters, Nancy, Anne, and me, and one of eight of her grandchildren, Stuart's two daughters, my sister Nancy and I; and Grant's six children, Michael, Peter, Alexander, Stephen, Morgan, and Anne, we hoped we could share with you what she was like to us. Each of us remembers different things about her, but all of us remember a grandmother who came into a room and lit it up, told stories of her travels, and was constantly on the move.

She was a redhead, which she maintained with the help of the beauty parlor for most of her life. She was small and soft-spoken and had a beautiful voice. When she talked to you, you were the most important person in the room, and she concentrated on every word you said. Her eyes never wandered throughout the room, as often happens to all of us. She loved children, dogs, and good food, parties, people, and life. She was active and traveled constantly, speaking to groups throughout the world. One month she would be in Hawaii, the next month in India, the third month in New York or Santa Barbara or San Francisco. She had many friends and was a great correspondent.

She was a very hard worker, and one of my sister Nancy's and my early memories is of "Mimi" sitting on her enclosed porch in Tucson, Arizona, answering her mail. There was always a stack of mail for her to answer, and she did it every day. We lived next door and walked across our lawn to her house to have a second breakfast with her, or hear a story of her travels, or dance to the music being played that morning. She prepared her speeches and remarks with great thought and was always nervous before a presentation, which she felt was the sign of a great speaker. "If you are not nervous, your presentations are usually flat," she said.

Around 1949, she suffered a heart attack in our cabin in the White Mountains of northern Arizona. Our father, a doctor, rushed her to a small hospital and got her stabilized. She was always a bit frail after that incident, and we were always checking up on her. Mother was the one who really looked after Mimi and was very patient with the demands of her mother-in-law. As we grew older, we also pitched in to make sure she was well and comfortable.

Our father, Stuart, was her oldest son. He never knew where his mother was going next. He would say, "Mother, can we have dinner next week?" and she'd say, "No, I'm off to London." He would ask her to slow down, and she did exactly as she pleased.

Her parties in Tucson were fabulous. If she was serving a Japanese dinner, all the guests removed their shoes and donned socks as they entered her home, drank sake, and sat on the floor for dinner. If the menu called for an Indian curry, you can be sure it was hot. We would take our friends to visit Mimi often, and she would create plays for us to present to the neighbors. Mimi was always the star, and we had great fun rehearsing our roles. In addition, a party always followed the play.

We were lucky to live next to her and to meet the interesting people who came to see her. She always shared us with them, and it was a wonderful way to hear about the issues of the day. We met Helen Keller; Nehru's sister, Madam Pandit; John D. Rockefeller, Jr.; and Mrs. Stanley McCormick, who funded the research for The Pill. In addition, we met artists, musicians, political leaders, and Elizabeth Arden. She and Mimi would stand on their heads each morning to bring the blood to their faces, before eating yogurt and wheat germ for breakfast.

Mimi loved Champagne, daiquiris, flambéed desserts, and great big salads that she made at the table. She loved life.

The serious side of her and her courage is well documented and can be found in the Library of Congress and at Smith College. She never threw any papers away, sending a year's correspondence to the library or to Smith each January. Her life and letters are there for all to see.

She made us proud, strong, and independent, and we feel she made a larger contribution to women and children than any other person in the twentieth century. She made us realize that if you believed in something, you must speak out and try to help.

As H.G. Wells said, "When the history of the twentieth century is written, Margaret Sanger will be its heroine." She had a vision, helped the women of the last century come into their own, and gave children healthy mothers who stayed alive and cared for their families.

Enjoy!

Margaret Sanger Lampe
December 2002

A Note to the Reader:

This was supposed to be a very lean book, but once I got deeply into the work, I discovered so many things that begged to be said that the endnotes became very long. I hope for some they may be as fascinating as I found them. The placement of the thumbnail biographies has its own peculiar logic: whenever an individual is mentioned in more than one chapter or belongs to our "general" background knowledge (however that can be defined), that individual's dates and identification is given in the Biographies in the Appendices. If the individual is mentioned in only one chapter, dates and a note are given in the endnotes to the chapter.

General Introduction

On January 18, 1954, Margaret Sanger responded to James J. Corbett of Detroit, Michigan.[1] Corbett was writing an introduction to his pamphlet "Babies," and with the intention of mentioning Margaret Sanger in his introduction, wanted to know how she wished to be remembered. She replied,

> About myself, for which I thank you, why not mention that I coined the term birth control, that I organized the American Birth Control League, I established and edited the magazine *Birth Control Review* and turned it over to the League when I resigned. And then I carried on a seven-year campaign in Washington to change the federal Comstock law. That I organized the first World Population Conference in Geneva in 1927, which 300 scientists attended and that organization is now called the Population Union, and is composed mostly of scientists and demographers.[2] I started the first birth control clinic in the U.S., and it is perhaps the only birth control organization in the world today that is entirely conducted under medical auspices.[3]

Yet merely to recall these accomplishments—along with so many others not mentioned here—impressive as they are, deprives the reader of a deeper acquaintance with a most remarkable woman and the world in which she lived. As Sanger herself said at another time, she hoped only "to be remembered for helping women."[4] All of her accomplishments were for this one purpose—to help women—and throughout her lifetime that basic purpose never varied. "Over and over, I tell the story," she said, "until it must be engraved on the clouds in the sky and the breezes that blow."

From the time of her student days in Claverack College, her concern was for women, and soon enough her demands were to be specific: Let woman decide for herself if and when she is to have children. Let the coming of the children be spaced so that the mother has physical health, emotional strength, and sufficient funds to care for the child. Let every child be wanted!

Margaret Sanger never forsook her fight to help women, never flagged in her efforts to make contraception freely available to women. The short prose selections in this collection have been chosen to familiarize the reader with that fight, with the consistency of her stand, and with the woman herself who engaged in it.

She swept onto the world stage with a charming and youthful appeal. Margaret Sanger was a beautiful, charismatic woman, who retained her beauty and her youthfulness until late in life, her charm even to the last. At eighty, she entertained 150 archaeologists visiting Tucson. "Enthroned on a small settee, regal in a hostess gown, crowned with her copper colored curls, she enthralled her guests as she chatted with them in groups of twenty."[5]

Gentle, self-retiring in manner, her person delicate and petite, she was a disconcerting presence to those who expected a powerfully built, militant woman, one whose physical appearance would exemplify the aggressiveness of the powerhouse that was the Birth Control leader. Instead, reporters talked of her "gentleness." "One is astounded at her youth, prettiness, gentleness, mild soft voice. One is reminded of Botticelli's Judith, a gentle, springlike maid who treads the hills as if she danced."[6] An earlier *New Yorker* article says, "She seems about as dangerous as a little brown wren....The magnetism which she unquestionably has is the kind that shines out from inside."[7] "A small woman, inconspicuous except for the beautiful auburn hair piled lavishly on her head, sat in an office on lower Fifth Avenue the other day and talked almost timidly about how a movement she started has spread over the world," began one published interview.[8] Recalled Harold A. Content, the prosecuting attorney in the Brownsville clinic case, "What did surprise me . . . was to meet so reserved, and, if I may use a word that has gone out of style, so refined a lady."[9] "I did not expect to find the beautiful, refined lady that I did see when Mrs. Sanger interviewed me. I recall to this day the . . . kindness of her eyes," said one of her workers.[10] Harold Hersey, an early biographer, warned that behind the demure, gentle guise was pure steel.

With her intimates, she was known for her intense gaiety and for intently listening to the speaker. Professionally she was known for her impeccable business dealings. Never did she sell her position as the world leader of birth control for endorsements or profit. Testimony to that integrity came at a party where she was attempting to raise much needed funds for one of her many causes. A doctor came up to her, shook her hand, and said, "I have a special admiration for you, Mrs. Sanger. I've always wanted to shake the hand of a woman who's made millions for others and is still passing out a tin cup for pennies for her own movement."[11]

Her speaking manner, like her appearance, came also as a surprise. "Her success as a speaker arose from a moving sincerity, an innate charm, and a complete mastery of her subject."

> When speaking, Margaret Sanger does not raise and lower her voice or wave her arms. She does not use phrases as fireworks. She steps forward after the usual introduction, beginning in a calm manner and ending the same way....'One can always speak if what one has to say is of consequence,' she says.[12]

She did not enjoy good health, and much of her early life was spent fighting tuberculosis; much of her later life was taken up with a variety of other illnesses. After her heart attack in 1949, she was never truly well again, but nothing kept her from her work. And everything in her life experience came together to prepare her for her work, as she herself recognized.

> As I look back on my life, I see that every part of it was a preparation for the next. The most trivial of incidents fits into the larger pattern like a mosaic in a preconceived design.[13]

The larger pattern began with a radical for a father; a mother too often pregnant; with Margaret's middle place in the family as the sixth child of eleven—a place that provided older siblings to assist her, but the work of younger siblings to tend to; with poverty that prevented her from studying to become a doctor. But only as a nurse would she come to understand the problems of mothers and childbirth. Only as a mother would she know what it was to bear and love and lose a child and thus relate so affectingly with all mothers. The pattern of preparation continued: her first trip to England, where she found mentors; her return to New York at the propitious moment; her marriage to the generous Noah Slee; the fortunate judicial decisions; later, the schism with the American Birth Control League, which left her free to implement the National Committee on Federal Legislation for Birth Control—all the events of her life patterning a life that was to contribute so much to women everywhere.

But she was also intuitive, and early on she glimpsed her future:

> I saw the path ahead in its civic, national, and even international direction—a panorama of things to be. Fired with this vision, I ... wrote and wrote page after page until the hours of

daylight....Though I did not know exactly how I was to prepare myself, what turn events might take, or what I might be called upon to do, the future in its larger aspects has actually developed as I saw it that night....A new movement was starting.[14]

Her intuition sprang from a deep spiritual quality that many recognized in her.[15] Her spirituality was an important part of her life and work—an inner source that sustained and nourished her.

To know a woman of such complexity is best approached through reading her own words. To that end, writings from the stages of her life have been arranged in this volume in chronological order, each selection preceded by an introduction that gives the reader some background information. Grouped under the three phases that marked her life course, the three parts of this volume coincide neatly with three distinct periods of world history: the years to World War I, the two decades between the world wars, and the years following World War II.

Sanger was indeed the "rebel," an agitator, whose early upbringing as the daughter of a freethinking father culminated, in the years before World War I, in membership in the Socialist Party, IWW picketing, and publication of seven issues of her newspaper, *The Woman Rebel*.

She was the politic "reformer," to whom the years of World War I and after brought an understanding of the social processes shaping country and culture, who then promoted birth control through the *Birth Control Review* and formation of the American Birth Control League. Still her message was the same, whether it drew on her anger at child labor, her abhorrence of abortion, or the need to recognize and discuss, without prudishness, sexual activity in marriage as a healthy expression of loving feelings.[16]

She was finally the "conservative radical," the widow of a millionaire, living in "retirement" in Tucson, far from the world centers of New York and London, who continued to decry overpopulation, who made possible the world's first contraceptive pill, who built the foundation of an international family planning organization—the International Planned Parenthood Federation, that lives in 2003 on the world stage, an important arm of the United Nations.

We do not propose a Margaret Sanger without warts. She was a complex, driven woman, determined—or stubborn, if you prefer—a sort of perpetual motion machine, who intermixed and channeled the drive of her mission and shame over her humbling beginnings into a entrepreneurial career of world beneficence—this possible because her incisive perspicacity seized on the underbelly of a matter and nailed the drastic remedies needed; she would never settle for palliatives. Time and the development of events would show that she was dead wrong about some things. If, in her sagacity, she recognized the threat that overpopulation would be to the planet, she was, as well, a woman of her own time, and so she accepted the flawed arguments and skewered data of the eugenicists; she insisted that a child should not be nursed beyond the age of one year, and she was a pacifist even during World War II—positions also taken by many of her contemporaries who were serious, thinking people.

In her personal life, she was autocratic: "To disagree was to digress."[17] She was high-handed and would brook no competition. She had numerous affairs, while married. She was often accused of failing to give credit to coworkers in the field.[18] She strangely and falsely embellished hard facts, a residual of insecurity that tugged at the edges of a life of grand accomplishments.[19]

But she made a difference. All over the world, she changed the lives of women and their children. She returned to women their ultimate power and to children the possibility of the most important thing life could give them: the assurance of being wanted.

Margaret Sanger came with a mission. Once she recognized her mission, she never deviated from the work of its fulfillment. "All my life," she said, "I have acted on an inner voice, and when that speaks to me, it speaks wisely and never fails me."[20] With this edition, Margaret Sanger speaks for herself in words that reveal her humanity and attest to the sincerity of her purpose.

PART I:
THE REBEL

1. Introduction to the Rebel

Accoding to Margaret Sanger's own words, she was, even as a child, a rebel, and although her later tellings would sometimes reshape the facts, we can probably accept her tales of youthful rebellion as true. While still a pudgy little girl, she dared to tread along the dangerous ties of the railroad bridge that spanned the Chemung River. She forced herself to jump onto a haystack thirty feet below, and during her boarding school years at Claverack College, when everyone else was for gold, she took the side for silver. When she decided on a thing, she made a stubborn determination her closest ally until it was done.

That stubborn determination fortified not only Margaret Sanger's ambition and self-interest, but also her compassion, sensitivity, and desire to make the world a better place. After she and Bill Sanger moved their family to New York City in 1911, Margaret certainly could have nursed for better pay if she had nursed for the wealthy. But she chose to stay in Lillian Wald's nursing service, and she nursed in the tenements of New York's Lower East Side, where poverty was at its most extreme and the concomitant population density one of the highest in the world.

Such population density was compounded not only by floods of immigrants, but by a high birth rate, this aided and abetted by the absurd state and federal Comstock laws, which since 1873 had made contraception advice and devices illegal and straightforward language pertaining to sexual matters legally obscene. The physician or layman who dared to abrogate these laws by spoken or written word, in person or through the U.S. mail, faced heavy fines and imprisonment. Without exception, by law, contraception, other than abstinence, was forbidden, even to the woman for whom pregnancy meant death.

It was, therefore, completely in character that in 1911, as a nurse in the tenements of the Lower East Side of New York City, Margaret Sanger would rebel against the Comstock laws. The birth of that rebellion is related in the "Mrs. Sachs story," a story that has been questioned both as to its veracity and in its details. But whether a modified composite or an isolated incident, it smacks of veracity, and it bears retelling as the germination of the rebel phase of Margaret Sanger's career.

According to the "Mrs. Sachs story," Sanger was sent for one day by Mr. Sachs. Mrs. Sachs, once again pregnant, deep in the struggle alongside her hard-working husband to provide for their three living children—the youngest but a year—had attempted an abortion and had been found "prostrate on the floor amid the crying children when her husband returned from work."[1]

For three weeks, Margaret Sanger nursed this very sick mother, and when Mrs. Sachs became better and asked how to avoid another pregnancy, the doctor laughingly told her, "Tell Jake to sleep on the roof."

Sanger was as horrified by this response as was Mrs. Sachs. Several months later, Sanger and the same doctor watched Mrs. Sachs die after a five-dollar botched abortion. Afterward, Sanger walked the streets for hours, immersed in grief at the unnecessary death and at her own ignorance that had contributed to it. Returning home, exhausted, Sanger went to a window, looked down on the dimly lit city, and saw in the darkness a panorama of the misery and mass problems below her:

> too many children; babies dying in infancy; mothers overworked; baby nurseries; children neglected and hungry—mothers so nervously wrought they could not give the little things the comfort nor care they needed; mothers half-sick most of their lives—"always ailing, never failing"; children working in cellars; children aged six and seven, pushed into the labor market to help earn a living.[2]

With the breaking of the dawn came Sanger's realization that these "mass problems seemed to be centered around uncontrolled breeding," that the source of all this misery was too many children. Then and there, she determined to be done with superficial cures, with palliative work forever. She resolved

> that women would have knowledge of contraception....I would tell the world what was going on in the lives of these poor women. I *would* be heard. No matter what it should cost. *I would be heard.*[3]

Slowly, she was heard, at first among the Socialists, where she found kindred spirits and her first publishing opportunities, along with attention from Anthony Comstock himself. When the Socialists proved too conservative, Sanger turned to the Industrial Workers of the World (IWW), the Wobblies, and in working with Big Bill Haywood for the Lawrence and Paterson strikers, she found an ally and, for a time, an outlet for her rebellious spirit. But the failure of the Paterson strike led her to appreciate more fully the burdens borne by the women.

> In the great industrial strikes, urged by the Industrial Workers of the World and the revolutionary Socialists, I saw that the greatest suffering fell upon the women and children. They were the starved, the shivering, during those long days and nights when the agitators were busy urging the factory workers to hold out against their employers. And in not a few cases these starving women were not only forced to hear the pitiful whining of the children for something to eat, but within their frail and enfeebled bodies an unborn child was making ever-increasing demands upon an under-nourished system.[4]

Her disillusionment with male politics and her concern and anger at the misery of women sparked *The Woman Rebel*. With the seven issues of her brash monthly newspaper, Sanger baldly confronted the government, spearheading the demand of the public for their right to information on contraception.[5]

Such confrontation, as all early on assured her, was doomed from its beginnings and the grand jury indictments were inevitable. Fleeing the certain jail sentence that would have followed, Sanger spent a year in Europe, a year that brought both a difficult estrangement from her children and the education she needed to go forward with her work. She returned to America, still the rebel, but with a clearer sense of the scope of her mission.

Although Margaret Sanger had more support that she sometimes cared to acknowledge and although there were others who contributed to the Birth Control movement, it was her charisma, and, finally, her determination, her unrelenting, one-pointed focus on birth control and birth control alone that turned the Birth Control movement into a potent force, one that slowly eroded the Comstock laws to make birth control legal and contraception freely available. The rebellion of one determined, outraged woman was to change the lives of all women all over the world.

2. Early Years

It was "a strange, hard, barren life," recalled Margaret Sanger of her girlhood in Corning, New York.[1] But if her girlhood was hard, it was at the same time the perfect preparation for her lifework that was to come. She grew up accepting as normal a way of life that defied the status quo.

Her father, Michael Higgins, was a rich thinker, but a poor provider, a stonecutter who alienated the Catholic Church, the chief customer for his stone angels and monuments, with his support of atheists and liberal thinkers. Michael Higgins was known for his gentleness, for enjoying a drink, for his pleasant voice, and, as his daughter would be, for a gay, infectious sense of humor. Though not formally educated, he supported establishment of the public library in Corning. He read and discussed the ideas of the most progressive thinkers, the radicals, of his day, feeding his family large doses of, among others, Henry George, the economist who promoted a single tax, and William Ingersoll, the atheist and early advocate of artificial contraception and woman's rights.[2] He read the classics aloud to the family: *Gulliver's Travels, Aesop's Fables, Progress and Poverty*, Edgar Allan Poe, Shakespeare, along with a one-volume history of the world and treatise on phrenology.[3] Never one to indulge in senseless anger, Michael Higgins channeled his outrage at social injustices and the horrific working conditions of the average wage earner into practical activism. In 1889, when Margaret was ten years old, Michael Higgins was an aggressive organizer for the Knights of Labor,[4] supporting a bitter and protracted workers' strike at the Corning glass factories, where a ten-hour day brought a man $2, even as a shorter day in nearby Findley, Ohio, paid—for the same work—$4.[5] Michael regularly goaded his children into challenging their unexamined assertions and conclusions. Hearing Margaret pray for "our daily bread," Michael demanded of her, "Is God a baker?"[6]

For as long as she could remember, Sanger knew her mother as ill, with a cough so severe she was sent leaning against the wall for support. Anne Higgins had tuberculosis, an illness that was aggravated by her many pregnancies. In addition to the eleven live births, Anne Higgins endured seven miscarriages, and for the last ten years of her life, she lay in bed, ill with tuberculosis, each year newly pregnant.[7]

As the sixth of eleven children, Sanger was familiar with the endless demands of running a house and the cleaning and cooking for a family of six children that quickly grew to eleven. As a middle child, she was old enough to help bathe a newborn baby brother and to assist with the care and worries of the younger children. In her noisy, overcrowded home, ever churning with the incessant demands of big and little children, her mother always coughing, always pregnant, scrimping to feed and clothe all those bodies—in the midst of this was her father, endlessly talking, reading aloud to her mother and to the family, espousing his radical ideas and arguing progressive solutions to anyone and everyone who would listen. "To him, the search for truth was all important."[8]

"Father could have had a good business if he had been a businessman," recalled son Bob Higgins. "However," Bob continued,

> he was more interested in making speeches, introducing someone who was discussing socialism, et cetera. Many a time one of us would have to come down the street to Clark's Shoe Store and yank him out of an argument or discussion to come back to his place and sell a monument to a waiting customer.[9]

Despite his being an improvident provider, her mother adored her father as much as he did her, and their relationship was an exceptionally loving one. But the intellectual vitality and loving warmth of that relationship did not obviate the poverty that dogged the lives of the family and the girlhood of Margaret Sanger.

Sanger was especially fortunate in having two older sisters: Mary, the oldest and "the most saintlike woman who walked the earth," and Nan, third in line, who had taught herself German and wanted to see Margaret attend Cornell University.[10] The two sisters scraped together sufficient funds to send Margaret to Claverack College and Hudson River Institute, an excellent Methodist preparatory school, college accredited, not far from Hudson, New York, and there Sanger flourished.[11]

Although Sanger was a scholarship student, working part-time to afford her schooling, she was never a "poor" girl. She was never sullen or angry or depressed, rather she was remembered as "given to gales of laughter." In an interview, Amelia Stewart Michell, a school chum at Claverack, extolled

Margaret's gay spirits, her optimism, and her ability to draw to herself willing assistance for any chore she had on hand. Working her way through Claverack, in "the dish room" as Sanger called it, other students, not on scholarship, were all too willing to help her. Sanger was exceedingly popular, admired by both boys and girls, who sought her out and shared with her their most intimate confidences. She was an excellent student, always reading, devouring books, receiving good grades. She dreamed of attending medical school at Cornell and of becoming a doctor. Sanger claimed that, even at Claverack, her ideas were "advanced." Her friend, Amelia, noted only that "one gathered instinctively that [Margaret] had her own visions, deeply hidden behind those clear, bright eyes." But best of all, Margaret was at ease with herself, danced divinely, and had a robust sense of humor.[12]

During her girlhood, Sanger developed a disciplined, inquiring mind and a no-nonsense approach to life, an ability to cut through to the core issues. Later personal writings admit to times of confusion and doubt, but she never conveyed this to others. Instead, she always had a sense of herself and always knew how to defend herself and to think for herself. It was to serve her—and her cause—and the cause of all women—well in the years to come.

The Manuscript
"Girlhood" is the title on the opening page of this undated and incomplete manuscript (the last page ends in midsentence), but it is referred to as "Memoir" by the Library of Congress archivist. The second half of the manuscript of "Girlhood" is not included here. It tells of the then Margaret Higgins leaving Claverack, taking on a brief stint as a teacher in southern New Jersey—a job for which she was little suited—this cut short by the necessity of returning home to nurse her tubercular mother, dying after those eighteen pregnancies at the age of fifty.[13] Margaret remained briefly at home with her grieving father, but within six months took off to White Plains, New York, where she had been accepted as nurse probationer at the newly founded White Plains Hospital.

Reprinted here is the first, especially interesting, half of "Girlhood." Sanger was probably in her late forties when she wrote "Girlhood," no doubt in preparation for her autobiography. All of "Girlhood" is incorporated, with minor interpolations, into Sanger's first full-length autobiography, *My Fight for Birth Control*, published in 1931.[14]

It is interesting to consider the events that Sanger selected for recall in these few pages of "Girlhood." Whereas the later *My Fight* opens with a long and admiring description of her mother followed by a long description of her father, in "Girlhood," Sanger mentions her mother only twice, both times in passing as an explanation for the family's choice of housing. After that first brief mention of her mother appears the long paragraph that describes, in detail, Corning's well-off mothers, who led comfortable lives with their few children. Nor does she discuss her father in "Girlhood," though she does mention letters from her father, letters that held valuable ideas for a paper she was writing at Claverack on historical women.

Sanger has much to say about Claverack, which she attended for two years, not the three that she claims. Apparently, her sisters were unable to find funds to support the third year. But much here has the ring of truth. Margaret devotes a full paragraph to the discerning Claverack principal, Arthur H. Flack, from whom she acknowledged she learned much. She also writes at length about her very first girlfriend, whose parents, in marked contrast to those of Margaret, gave their daughter the time to study and the money for small luxuries.

Even as a girl, Sanger did not suffer fools. She walked out of the classroom of a teacher who sneered at and bullied her, and Sanger refused to involve herself with a profession—acting—that judged her abilities by the size of her legs. These incidents chosen for "Girlhood" catch the clearheadedness and lack of sentimentality, the rebelliousness, the independence of thought that propelled Sanger throughout her life and made possible her accomplishments. Most especially do the chosen incidents convey Sanger's social awareness and sense of place, her early understanding of the great gulf between the small wealthy families and the large poor families in the town of Corning—and all that entailed.

Girlhood[15]

c. 1926

During the early years of childhood we lived on the outskirts of the city. Mother's health was not good and we built a house among the pines, hearing that pure air was good for "lung trouble."[16] The city of Corning is known for the manufacture of glass. Its fame has gone far for its beauty of design and texture. The huge factories are built on the flats bordering the Chemung River. Thousands of men and women, girls and boys, work there. Three generations have toiled their lives away making chimneys, electric bulbs, and other articles for our daily needs.[17] The city is in the Chemung Valley, with rolling hills running far up Stuben County [sic] to the Lake District. The city is divided by the river, and in my memory all the workers and poor people of the factory lived on the flats near the river surrounding or near the factory, while the owners and people of wealth lived on the hills away from the dirt, noise, and poverty. I noticed, too, that the people down below had large families, many children, while those on the hills had few.

Part I: The Rebel

Very early in my childhood I associated large families with poverty, toil, unemployment, drunkenness, cruelty to children, quarreling, fighting, debts, jails, and the Catholic Church.

The people who lived on the hilltops owned their own homes, had few children, dressed them well, kept their houses and their yards clean and tidy. Mothers of the hills played croquet and tennis with their husbands in the evening. They walked hand in hand with their children through the streets to shop for suitable clothing. They were young looking mothers, with pretty, clean dresses, and they smelled of perfume. I often watched them at play, or I looked through the gate in passing. I was often invited to spend Saturday afternoon with children on the hill, and played games with them, told fairy tales, and invented stories for their amusement.

Now at last we were to move away from the woods on the outskirts of the city. We were growing up. Mother's health was not getting better from the pine woods. The house we had built for six little children was far too small for older ones.

We were to move up to town, not in the same district with the pretty mothers and few children, but on the western hills where there was air, neighbors, and a larger house. We moved. A new life began for us all. I had the first girl friend I had known; together we confided our innermost secrets. She was reticent, proud, and Irish. I always marveled at her poise. She read the books and magazines of fashion, manicured her nails regularly, discounted romance, laughed and poked fun at the priests in their gowns, but went regularly to Mass every Sunday. Together we attended the nearby school. Her home study was a serious matter. When that was necessary, no other work was required of her. Home study in our house was impossible. There were always children to be put to bed, to be rocked to sleep, feet and hands to be washed; then the older members of the family used the one room in the house to tell and discuss their doings. How could lessons be learned in such an atmosphere? It was impossible. I kept up in my studies simply because I liked them and learned them easily.

I was growing into womanhood and had been promoted to the highest grade in Grammar School. The teacher was one of these small important persons who liked to get the laugh on others to keep it off herself.

Someone had given me a new pair of gloves, nice soft ones, the first pair I had ever worn. They were hard to pull over the fingers, and yet I wanted to wear them. I tarried outside and pulled and stretched them over the hands. I walked into the schoolroom about three minutes late. The teacher glanced up and saw me walking leisurely into the classroom. She made me the target for attention. "Oho, Miss Higgins, so it's you. Have you deigned to come to school this afternoon? I wonder at it. Ah, new gloves!" etc. etc. She went on and on until I reached my seat and removed my gloves and sat waiting for her to stop. She started off again—but before she got the next sentence out of her mouth, I was out of the door. I had packed up my books in a determination to leave school forever. I walked straight home to mother and announced I was through with school. I'd never go back again. Here was a fixed determination like that to attend the matinee several years before.[18] I knew nothing on earth or in heaven could change me. I'd go to jail. I'd go to work, I'd starve and die, but back to that school and teacher I would never go. It was so settled in my mind that I would not discuss the cause with anyone. The cause of it all seemed so silly.

The family became alarmed. Mother was glad enough to have me home for a while to help her with the thousand cares. I was capable, quiet, thorough, and strong. I could get through an amount of work in no time. A family council was called. I was questioned as to my future. Did I think I knew enough to do anything in life? Did I think I had an education? Could anyone get anywhere without one? Was I prepared to earn my living? How? When? Questions were hurled at me. Taunts and insinuations and threats of factory life were in the air. I did not care. I would not go back to that school. I had only a few months to finish and go to High School. It made no difference if it had been but an hour. I would never go back.

The outcome of it was that I was to be sent away to boarding school at Claverack, New York.[19] It took the place of high school and preparatory school. There one could prepare for Cornell College. Great rejoicing! A new world to discover! Claverack College and Hudson River Institute was one of the oldest co-education schools in the country. It was nestled in the Catskills Hills, about three miles from the City of Hudson.

Prof. Arthur H. Flack was the Principal of the school, a man whose influence has spread over countless young lives. He made it possible for me to attend school by allowing me to work part-time for my board. The family paid the tuition, and my oldest sister gave me the necessary clothes and books and other requirements.

It was all so new and strange. The girls I met did not come up to the visions I had had of them. They seemed plain, uninteresting, regular, without flair, initiative, or imagination. I was lonely and homesick, but I never wanted to return home. Within a few months I was into the thickest of activities, dances, escapades, teas, long walks in forbidden lanes.

I spent three years at Claverack, three full and happy years.[20] I was interested in social questions. I was ardent for Suffrage, for woman's emancipation.[21] The paper I wrote was to be read in Chapel on Saturday morning. News of it spread about. Boys shouted at me in class, drew pictures of women smoking huge cigars, wearing trousers and men's clothing. I studied and wrote as I never had before. I sent long letters to father, getting facts of Women's Suffrage, facts of Women's History. Oh, what letters in reply!

All about Helen of Troy, the battle of Nebuchadnezzar, Ruth, Cleopatra, Poppaea, Queens, Women Authors, Poets, and Mothers. It was a great essay. I stole away to the cemetery and stood on the monuments over the graves and said every word aloud. Again and again, each day I read in the quiet of the dead.

After suffrage I took up the silver question of Mr. Jennings Bryan. No one else knew anything about it. They were all for gold, so I took the other side and studied and worked on a debate. I gradually became known to have advanced ideas; only serious boys paid attention to me, and the girls came to me in all their sorrows and woes. In recitation and acting I excelled. My teacher said I'd make a good actress, and that was all I wanted to set the goal. I went home on vacation and announced I was going on the stage. Shocks and disapproval were evident. Father pooh-poohed the idea, but my sister Mary, the most saint-like woman who walked the earth, agreed with me as to my ability and said I should go to the Dramatic School as soon as I finished Claverack, that she would apply at once to Charles Frohman and I should try as an understudy to Maude Adams. Great hopes! Splendid aspirations! A wise sister!

Money was saved, application made, pictures taken in various poses, with and without hats. A return letter from the School Management came, enclosing a form to be filled in with name, address, age, height, color of hair, eyes, and skin. All went well, but when I was asked to give the size of the legs, both right and left leg, not only the length, but the size of ankle, knee, calf, and thigh, I was left cold. Enthusiasm for the stage vanished. I returned to finish the last year at Claverack and to prepare for Cornell [University], where I planned to study medicine. It was not that I did not know the size of my own legs. I did. Those were the days when cigarette pictures of actresses, plump and well-formed, came in every "pack." We in the gymnasium compared our legs and criticized our shapes and those of others. That was mutual and friendly and intimate. But to see that personal and intimate information go coldly down on paper and be sent off to strange men, to have your legs, ankles, and hips valued as something apart from the owner of them, was like cutting yourself into parts. I could not see what legs had to do with being a great actress. I expected to have to account for the quality of my voice, for my ability to sing, to play, for grace, agility, character, morals, and for my experience in and ability to love. None of these qualities seemed important to managers who were to train one to become a second Maude Adams. I did not fill in the printed form, nor send the photographs. I just put them all away and turned my desires to more serious studies where brains, not legs, were to count.

3. Socialism

While caring for her dying mother, Sanger had begun "to delve into books about nursing to gain information on the care of the sick."[1] After her mother's death, she went on probation for nurse's training at White Plains Hospital in New York State, and two weeks after acceptance, she became head nurse in the women's ward.[2] She faced grueling work demands in a less-than-modern facility,[3] but continued her voracious reading and made obstetrics her main interest.[4] She thought about why mothers had so many children, and she mentioned her concerns to her nursing colleagues.[5]

In White Plains Hospital, in the face of such a heavy workload, Sanger was fortunate to be under humane and principled medical practitioners: Dr. W. H. Sherman, founder of the hospital, and his assistants were known as civic-minded men who felt a sense of obligation to the community and to their patients.[6] Not only did they serve as models for the best in doctoring, but when Margaret's health broke down under the strain of work and study, Dr. Sherman gave her excellent care during her quite serious illness and the subsequent operation to remove tubercular lymph nodes in her neck.[7]

Nurses' training led indirectly to meeting William Sanger, a handsome, intense architect, who fell madly in love with her, and who in the summer of 1902 took her out one Sunday for a ride in the country. When they returned, they were married. A year later, their first son, Stuart, was born. But Margaret's tuberculosis persisted, and for the next few years, she was quite ill and for a time in a sanitarium. Thus, their second son, Grant, did not come along until five years after Stuart's birth, but within another twenty months of Grant's birth, Margaret's long-desired daughter, Peggy, was born.

By then, the Sangers had built and were living in their own home in

Hastings-on-Hudson, a bit of suburbia friendly to young professionals and their young children, just north of New York City, overlooking the Hudson River. In Hastings, the children could run freely, and Stuart could come out of his back door in the morning and shout "Hi!" giving his "signal to all the world" that the day had begun."[8]

Although Sanger claimed in her autobiographies that "housekeeping with its endless details was never drudgery to me," in her later years, she was known for hating housework, nor was she content, at least after Peggy was born, with the suburban lifestyle—this pretty much confirmed by what she did with the rest of her life and by her comment, "After my experience in 'the midst of life' as a nurse, it seemed to me that this quiet withdrawal into the tame domesticity of the pretty hillside suburb was bordering on spiritual stagnation."[9]

The "tame domesticity" was not to last. The years during turn-of-the-twentieth-century America were the Golden Age of Radicalism, and the brutal labor conditions imposed by rich and powerful employers were being vigorously fought by freethinking radical groups—the IWW Wobblies, anarchists, Single Taxers, Syndicalists, Populists, Progressives, Socialists of all stripes. The Socialists in particular were having good success. By 1912, some two thousand Socialists were holding public office, Victor Berger from Wisconsin held a lone Socialist seat in the U.S. House of Representatives, and in the 1912 presidential election, Socialist candidate Eugene V. Debs won 6 percent of the presidential vote.

One day, probably in 1910, while some work was being done near their Hastings house, Sanger overheard the foreman chastising his crew for their indifference to the labor struggle. She began talking to him. He was a Socialist, and he gave her clippings from the Socialist newspaper, the *New York Call*. According to Bill Sanger, who had himself long been interested in Socialism, suddenly, Margaret

> was transformed. She devoured every article and book she could lay her capable hands on—she attended meetings and lectures—she got to know the leaders of the Social and Radical Labor movements—she plunged into welfare work. Gone forever was the conservative Irish girl I had married; a new woman, forceful, intelligent, hungry for facts, tireless, ambitious and cool, had miraculously come into being.[10]

By 1911, both Sangers were active Socialists.[11] They had sold their house in Hastings-on-Hudson, moved to New York City, and had joined the New York Socialist Party Local No. 5 in Harlem, famous for its radicalism. Bill Sanger ran for alderman on the Socialist ticket and lost. Margaret Sanger was elected "Organizer" for the Woman's Committee of the Socialist Party and paid fifteen dollars per week.[12] Son Stuart was enrolled in Will Durant's class in the Modern School, held for the radicals' children at the Ferrer Center, a cultural center with reading rooms, lecture hall, and library, housed in an old brownstone at 63 East Tenth Street.

The Ferrer Center had grown from the efforts of anarchist Emma Goldman ("the most dangerous woman in America," according to law enforcers) and her lifelong chum, Alexander Berkman, best known for his attempted assassination of Henry Frick.[13] Goldman, a riveting orator, had been lecturing coast to coast on anarchism since before 1900, speaking in some years to as many as seventy-five thousand.[14] Along with lectures entitled "Free Love," "The Philosophy of Anarchism," and others on the works of Ibsen and the modern drama, she offered one titled "The Limitation of Offspring." The last had grown out of her brief experience as a nurse, when she encountered firsthand the desperation of poor, overburdened women too often pregnant.[15] Goldman warmly supported Sanger's beginning work in birth control at the Ferrer Center, and later, after Sanger published *The Woman Rebel*, Goldman promoted and sold that outspoken piece at her lectures.

But *The Woman Rebel* did not appear until 1914. In 1911, Margaret, along with her son Stuart, was "enrolled"—she less formally—in the Ferrer Center, attending their adult offerings. She studied and heard lectures. At first, she said little, but listened intently and, once again, is remembered as reading, constantly reading, an attentive listener, never pushing herself forward, drinking in everything.[16] At the Ferrer Center, she made friends and encountered people profoundly concerned for the state of American society and its great inequities. As they searched for answers through their art, their literature, their research, thinking people such as Will Durant, Eugene O'Neill, Robert Henri, Upton Sinclair, John (Jack) Reed shared their findings and their thoughts, giving lectures and holding classes and discussions at the center.[17]

Sanger became especially involved with the most important radical labor leaders—Elizabeth Gurley Flynn, Carlo Tresca, Big Bill Haywood (among others), who became regular visitors to the Sangers' New York apartment. And much as her father had done, Margaret became an active worker for radical causes. But instead of her father's discussions at the corner shoe store, Margaret began lecturing on birth control and women's issues at the Ferrer Center in New York City to an audience that was educated and committed, many of whom were to be lauded, become successful and famous, or depending on one's political point of view, branded notorious.[18]

Margaret was fortunate in having Bill's mother living with them at this time. In 1911, Stuart would have been eight, Grant three, and Peggy about a year; Peggy was only nine months when "To Mothers—Our Duty" appeared in the *Call*. Subsequent articles appearing in leftist newspapers, the *Call*, *Il Proletario,* and *Solidarity,* under Margaret's name confirm the intensity of her feelings and hint at the extent of her radical activity. But her family was struggling for income. Bill, both a Jew and a Socialist, was a questionable hire at a time when Jews were "not the right people" and to be a Socialist was just a bit disreputable. Moreover, Bill was an artist who really wanted to paint. By 1911, Margaret Sanger had returned to nursing.

As a girl, Sanger, had known poverty. But working as a nurse in the New York Lower East Side, Sanger became acquainted with a poverty such as she had never known. Her shock at this real poverty and the conditions it engendered was genuine. Here she was among

> the submerged, untouched classes, which no labor union, no church nor organization of a highly expensive organized city ever reaches and rarely tries to reach....Ignorance and neglect go on day by day, children born to breathe but a few hours and pass out of life, pregnant women toiling early and late to give food to four or five children, always hungry, boarders taken into homes where there is not sufficient room for the family; little girls eight and ten years of age sleeping in the same room with dirty, foul smelling, loathsome men; women whose weary, pregnant, shapeless bodies refuse to accommodate themselves to the husbands' desire find husbands looking with lustful eyes upon other women, sometimes upon their own little daughters, six and seven years of age.[19]

At least three columns appeared in the *New York Call* under Sanger's name in 1911, all describing life in the Lower East Side in much the same vein.[20] As Sanger wrote elsewhere,

> As a maternity nurse in the slums and tenements of New York I had been brought face to face with conditions that made the so-called sacredness of motherhood a term of unspeakable irony. Pregnant women—drunken husbands—hungry children, children born to a heritage of disease, filth, crime—this was the order of the day. As one pregnancy followed another, a family sank deeper into the mire. And always denied contraceptive knowledge by their doctors, these women were driven to other means. On Saturday evenings before the office of a cheap abortionist they lined up, each waiting her turn.[21]

Amid the plethora of Stuff and the Comfort that parades as reality in this twenty-first century America, the horrors of living in early twentieth-century America among the ill-paid lower working classes is, today, almost impossible to imagine—men working twelve hours a day seven days a week, children under twelve working fourteen hours a day, yet wages insufficient for rent and food; two and three people sleeping in shifts on one bed; crowded, dark rooms in buildings with one toilet for three floors of apartments.

Margaret described for the *Call* the typical day of a laundry worker.

One man, a shirt ironer, said he had a family of five; he had to get up at 5 AM. The children were asleep when he went away; he took ten minutes for his lunch, usually less time for his supper; dragged himself home at 11 o'clock at night to find the children asleep again, and so on until Sunday when he in turn to gain strength for the working week to come, had to sleep most of that day.[22]

There was no need for employers to pay decent wages or to tolerate an eight-hour workday. Labor was plentiful. "Immigration to the United States rose from 229,000 arrivals in 1898 to more than 800,000 in 1904." Not only did the hordes keep coming "at an average of about a million a year over the next decade," but they had many children—usually unhealthy children, yet children whose bodies could toil well enough at menial tasks and who could be paid cheaply.[23]

Employers took advantage of this, and the wealthy prospered. While the poor lived so miserably, the one percent of the American population comprising the rich filled their teeth with diamonds, outfitted pet poodles in $15,000 diamond collars, and dispensed cigarettes wrapped in $100 bills.[24] The wealth of the wealthy was unimaginable, the poverty of the poor beyond description. And Margaret Sanger wanted to do something about it.

The Manuscript
This was one of Sanger's earliest published pieces, and she is wholeheartedly supporting the Socialist Party ("We should join the party" [there is but one, the Socialist party]). Yet her foremost sympathies are with mothers and their children, as they would be throughout her future career as the proponent of birth control.

At this point, her marriage with Bill Sanger was beginning to unravel. In her mention of "the male element" and "the question of 'duty,'" the reader picks up the undercurrent of a seething, ongoing spousal argument.

We hear a great deal from the male element about "Woman's

Duty." The question of "duty" seems to be a stickler, and seems to confine itself to woman only.

Scornful references in the opening paragraph to "fashion," "bridge," and "diversion" betray Sanger's frustration with the "tame domesticity" that, for her, marked her life in Hastings-on-Hudson. The great gulf between the "bridge mothers" and the mothers working in the mill and factory was no different than that between the small wealthy families on the hill and the large poor families on the flats of Corning that Sanger had seen as a child and describes in "Girlhood." The weekly book discussions with other Hastings' mothers and the occasional visit to Manhattan were insubstantial fare when so much misery and wrong needed to be righted.

In "To Mothers—Our Duty" Sanger points out the real problems, sets out solid statistics to back her statements, and offers intelligent solutions.

To Mothers—Our Duty[25]
The *New York Call*, March 26, 1911

In this day and age, when women are striving to their utmost to compete with their sisters in matters of dress, fashion, in "bridge," or anything which offers amusement or diversion from the old routine of our mothers' day, we hear a great deal from the male element about "Woman's Duty." This question of "duty" seems to be a stickler, and seems to confine itself to woman only.

This "duty," so called, means that women should remain at home, not necessarily to drudge—not at all—for among those women referred to above, the servant question forms a large part of their conversation; but "duty" means the care of the home, of the children—the problem of feeding them carefully (even scientifically), of making their little bodies strong and robust, in fact, of giving them a good foundation mentally and physically—for life. . . .

We women can build them up, these bodies and minds, build them up to our highest expectations and then push them out upon a world whose system is greed, exploitation, graft, and scientific robbery.

Can we expect these morals to stay built up in these corrupt surroundings? As this case is an ideal one, so it is an exceptional one; let us turn, then, to one which is no exception.

This is the case of the most abused, most dejected, most imposed upon class of mothers which our social system presents to us, and their number is legion.

Here we find the little mothers at 8, 9, and 10 years of age; here we see them already at work carrying responsibilities of the home, factory, or mill; education is a thing apart from this child, childhood yearnings are crushed, childish joys are barred here, There is time for but one thing—work. Work through childhood, through girlhood, and womanhood.

We follow this child-mother up to the marriage day and find she has given her childhood, girlhood, womanhood, her strength, her very life to the factory or mill for an existence, an existence which the owner of the factory would not allow his horse or dog. Her face is pale and pinched with that haunting look of poverty; it never changes—she is born, lives, and dies with that look. She is married at night after the day's work, that she loses not one day's time.

On, on in the same monotonous way; on, on, waiting for the end.

There's no time for her to think of the little one's coming; she must work only the harder because of its coming.

After months of worry, toil, privation, and physical exhaustion, this child, too, is born. Let us see what this woman gives to society. Her child is undersized, underfed, weak, sickly, and ofttimes deformed. It, too, has paid the price of birth; it has given its little strength with every heartbeat that it may be born, and now it is here, cheated and swindled of its birthright.

Women, arouse yourselves! If you are not so unfortunately placed, it is but a trick of circumstances. . . .

Again, I say: Women, awake, awake to this system and help these downtrodden women back to their homes, back to their little ones, back to that which belongs to every mother—the care and love of her offspring.

By the way, do we ever hear of the male element, who so strongly advocate "home duty" for the "bridge" mother, advocate home duty for these women? It is only the "bridge" women's children who need the care and attention of the mother, evidently.

Let us turn to the mother we have just beheld with her new-born infant. What is to be done with this subnormal piece of humanity? Does it not need even more care and attention than a normal child? But what does it get? Dire poverty drives this mother back again to the factory (no intelligent person will say she goes willingly). It is the fear of the loss of a job, debts, and another mouth to feed that compels her to leave this newborn infant in the care of any one who has the room to keep it. Any friend or neighbor who works at home can take care of this little waif.

We all know the type—hard working, ignorant, with scarcely time to attend to the actual needs of her own.

The little one is placed here among the filth and debris of the workshop. It grows through babyhood and childhood motherless, fatherless, and moral-less.

Of course, there are other alternatives, such as the charity kindergartens, but always the mother on the industrial field is cheated of love and care of her offspring.

In this age of Christianity, in this advanced twentieth century, when science has discovered the methods of breeding the finest horses and dogs, when science has turned its searchlight upon every form of plant life, upon the different parasites which tend to destroy plant life, what has it done toward extricating the parasite poverty, which destroys humanity? Senator Owen, of Oklahoma, said recently,

"We spend $500,000 to exterminate the insect that eats the cotton plant....We have millions for conservation of the forests. Our Senators and Representatives jump to their feet the minute one mentions raising the tariff on wool or on steel, but we can get no such interest when it comes to saving human lives."

Look at the health report for the past three years and see the loss of children in New York City alone:

Year	Under one year.	Under two years.	Under five years.
1908	16,231	20,462	24,141
1909	15,976	20,716	24,519
1910	16,213	20,560	24,266

Or 48,420 little infants under one year of age and 72,926 children under five, all in three years. What a shameful slaughter! What a cowardly and selfish people to allow these modern Herods, Poverty, and Ignorance, deliberately and silently to do away with this army of innocent and helpless babies!

Why should these countless fathers and mothers, almost one million times greater in number, surrender to these few monster exploiters—to this Capitalistic System which bases its existence on the fiendish exploitation and ultimate murder of these children? . . .

If man would do his duty to human beings, as well as he does to Things, we [would] have no need of leaving the little ones to the care of strangers all day. We would have no need of giving our babies' lives to the factory before they are born. We would have no need of seeing our little ones grow up in mental, moral, and physical starvation. We would have no need of suffering the awful pangs of seeing them go out of the world so soon, pangs which are so much keener than those which bring them here. All these and a thousand other sufferings and evils could be stamped out if man would do his duty.

There are two steps toward progress in this universe—organization and specialization. Mothers, let us not consider we are progressing. Let us not consider we have done our duty, until we have first organized. Then let us specialize in attacking and stamping out this social system.

We must organize—all women who have one vestige of love in our hearts for children, all women who have interest in the progress of humanity, all should organize, but not alone.

We should organize under a banner that advocates our cause. We should join the party (there is but one, the Socialist party) which solves the problems of each and every grievance of these working women and children.

First, we should demand through this party absolute equality of the sexes.

Second, to put back the mothers, or the prospective mothers, into the homes, and give her a pension sufficient to keep herself and child. I can hear wails of protest concerning this last demand, on the ground that it will make vagrants of the fathers or will give them more time and money for saloons. All I can ask is that you look into this, find out what has been done, and the results you will find will remove that argument completely. It has been the experience of those interested in this, that when a man feels his burdens partly lifted, he is mentally and physically better fitted for life's work.

Third, to support and educate the children, and by support we mean clearly to feed and clothe them, until they are at least 16 years of age.

Fourth, to keep every child, regardless of race, color, or creed, in this United States out of all factories, mills, and all industrial fields which tend to dwarf the physical or mental development of the children.

Last, to pull down completely this system, which mangles and stunts the minds, morals, and bodies of our boys and men; to fight his awful viper, which undoes all our life's work, to crush and stamp it out forever. This, mothers, is a duty which must go hand in hand with our everyday duties, or our life's work will be all for nothing.

PART I THE REBEL
4. Early Sex Education

When Sanger contributed "To Mothers—Our Duty" to the *New York Call*, it ran on the Woman's Sphere page, edited by Anita C. Block. In Block, Sanger found a kindred soul, for in 1911, both Block and Sanger were ardent supporters of Socialism and the workers' struggle. Both deplored, as well, the prudery that surrounded the discussion of sex.

Sanger had discussed sex with her own children, explaining to them the facts of life through stories drawn from nature. From 1908 to 1910, with only twenty months separating the births of Grant and Peggy, Sanger was either pregnant or caring for an infant at a time when Stuart, Sanger's oldest son, was five, six, and seven. Stuart's queries would have been satisfied by the stories in "How Six Little Children Were Told the Truth."

Sanger's stories apparently answered the queries of other Hastings' children, as well. A neighbor of Sanger's recalled many a talk she and Margaret had on the raising of their children. Later, as their boys grew older, several Hastings' parents organized a boys' club, and on Saturdays, in turn, different parents were on duty to play ball with the boys or to take the children for a walk in the woods to study nature. (The neighbor also recalled what a blessed time it was "for those of us who were not on duty.")[1]

Thus, Sanger may already have had in hand a manuscript or its draft when she arrived in New York, for she had been working on her writing while living in Hastings.[2] Once in New York, she gave to the *Call* the series of columns that offered her approach to sex education for children. The columns appeared in the Woman's Sphere page on consecutive Sundays from October 29 through December 17, 1911.

Anita Block welcomed Sanger's columns on sex education with enthusiasm. In preparing readers of the *Call* for the series, "the importance of which cannot be overstated," Block states,

> There has been for a long time nothing so encouraging as this determination all over the country to stop regarding the working of sex as a dark secret and to bring out into the open light of day all things connected with those phenomena that should be the glory of mankind, but that have been polluted into its scourge.[3]

Block emphasizes that Sanger's approach to sex education is not based on theory, but on "her ACTUAL EXPERIENCE [*sic*]."

> Mrs. Sanger herself told six little boys the truth about themselves and their parents and how they came to be here, and so she occupies the rare position of being able to tell other mothers not only what they should do but what she herself did do.[4]

Certainly, the tone, the setting, the intelligent, obedient children of "Six Little Children" belong to "the tame domesticity of the pretty hillside suburb" such as Hastings-on-Hudson must have been. But the honest information Sanger offers was, in 1911, anything but tame. Sex was then too vulgar, too dreadful, to be spoken about openly. In 1911, as Sanger herself pointed out, "There was not even a language in which to discuss these questions."[5]

But discuss them she did. Growing up in a family of eleven children; seeing her mother through her many pregnancies and miscarriages; living with her father's freethinking, independent values; working as a practical nurse, often in obstetrics—all these gritty life experiences prepared Sanger well for a down-to-earth attitude about sex.[6]

In 1916, "Six Little Children" was revised and became a booklet, *What Every Mother Should Know or How Six Little Children Were Taught the Truth*, offering a small source of income, but more importantly, presenting Sanger as an authority on early sex education and on motherhood and further asserting her cutting-edge leadership on social issues pertaining to women. Her little book, which was well accepted throughout the years, ran into many editions, the latest appearing in 1950.

The Manuscript

In 1911, even Sanger was somewhat cautious in her approach to sex education for children, and occasionally her language may sound precious to twenty-first century ears. "Six Little Children" opens with the story of the family of "Mr. and Mrs. Buttercup" and then tells of the Toads, the Birds, and finally the Mammals, beginning with the straightforward terms "pistil" and "stamen" and using "ovum" and "fertilization" when talking about the

Mammals. All of the stories are factual, well researched, carefully structured, and child friendly.

The column reprinted here is, as indicated, a conclusion to the series and in some ways an anomaly, for along with a discussion of sexual matters, Sanger has much to say about the subjection of women and their difficult role in human history—this subject somehow becoming a large part of a concluding column on sex education for children! Otherwise, in keeping with the earlier columns, this final column offers general, sensible advice. Insofar as masturbation was concerned, however, Sanger was still a product of her time, and her attitude reflects it. Thus, her readers are strongly, though somewhat obliquely, advised of its dangers.[7]

Conclusion, "How Six Little Children Were Taught the Truth" [8]
New York Call, December 17, 1911

The great object which Bobby's mother had in mind was to make these teachings of such a nature that the children would be impressed with the truth that they are only PART of nature's great and wonderful plan.

They were reminded again and again of the stages of life—plants, frogs, birds, and mammals; of the millions of years it took to bring about these wonderful creatures and that at the top of the list, perfect, intelligent, and supreme, stands man. Man, the most complex of all and the most perfect. What responsibilities are at his door! . . .

Their own bodies were a subject that took months to cover in study. They were shown charts of the human figure (both sexes), and all parts of the body were named in the same way as parts of the flowers were named. Parts of the organs of reproduction were called by their names in telling of the works each part performed. No special stress was laid on the naming of these parts, but simply, casually, as one would speak of the various parts of the eye, or any other organ. In the same manner, they were told of the harm done to their bodies in handling or touching any one part unnecessarily. If the eye, ear, or nose was dug into, we would surely greatly injure ourselves, perhaps losing the use of that organ for the rest of our lives. The generative organs are no exception in this. To tamper with this most wonderful part of nature's machinery means not only darkness, dullness of intellect, stupidity, physical and mental weakness, but ofttimes disables a little child for life. . . .

As all the children were still too young to go into the details of either menstruation or venereal diseases, it was considered best to dwell on the early tribes of man on up to marriage and to wait for future developments before going further. The tree dwellers and cave dwellers were already familiar stories to them. The fact that people lived together very closely; that the woman had great freedom in choosing the man whom she wished to be the father of her child, even as freely as the animals chose their mates; that in this freedom great mistakes were often made such as that for a period some mothers chose their sons or brothers or fathers to be the father of the new little one; that after a time it was found that this was very injurious to this new little child, for he often could not walk, or talk, and was weak and sometimes a cripple—and more often died very young.

So the chiefs of these tribes got together and said this must not be, for if this continued, there would be no strong young men or women to till the soil or fight off the animals, wild beasts, or the enemy. Then a law was made that only those of the different tribes or families should choose each other for the parents of the future children, and here the lesson of the Buttercups came in—that often Mrs. Buttercup would reject the pollen from the stamen in her own house, but would accept the pollen from another buttercup house and become fertilized with that.

The part the two sexes took in different ways to strengthen and develop the race seemed of great interest to the children.

The work of hunting and fishing was left to the men of the family, while equally important work, that of cleaning and cooking the food, was for the women. Men spent much time in making tools and weapons. They were able to save much time and energy when the bow and arrow was invented, for instead of taking all the time to creep upon a beast or enemy with a knife or sharp stone, [they] could remain at a distance and do the same work. Thus, men got a little more leisure time. With every new invention their labor and energy was saved, but it took much longer for labor-saving inventions for the woman to come into use.

Gradually, the marriage form came into existence, as these new tools and weapons became more valuable. Men wanted these to go to their very own children, so a law was passed, and the man could choose any woman he wanted to have for the mother of his children by getting consent from the captain or chief of the tribe. If he received this consent, then she, the woman, must live with him, love and honor him (no matter what he did), and obey him in everything. Absolute submission was the law for the wife. If she objected to this and ran away, she was cast out and was beaten. Other tribes had the same laws and dared not take her in, so she was left to die. If she did not like her husband and took another for the father of her child, she was often not only cast into prison but either stoned to death or burned at the stake.

Naturally, after years of this treatment, she became submissive and so dependent on man for her living that she dared not express herself aloud, merely as her husband allowed her to do so. If she was very beautiful, she was not made to work, but the prisoners of other tribes who had been captured were made to work for her. Often the captain or chief had several wives, but the wife was allowed only one husband....

The children were never talked "AT," but always "WITH." They were allowed to talk freely, and once or twice when the older children seemed a little conscious on taking up the matter of their own bodies, yet after a few minutes as the other children joined in the conversation they, too, forgot or overcame the embarrassment, and all went well.

The children were told frankly that some mothers did not like their children to know these things, that like the fairy tales and the story of Santa Claus, the mothers liked their children to believe that the stork brought them, or some other fairy tale. They were told that these things were NOT TO BE TALKED ABOUT WITH OTHER CHILDREN; and any time any child wished to know any thing about himself or any question whatever to come to the mother or father, but NEVER to other boys or girls. These children were taught the necessity for the excretions of the body—that in order to have good health, the used up waste food must pass out of the body or it would become poison and the boy or girl become sick and die. There was no hurry in telling anything to the children. Most of this information was told on walks in the woods, or at times when they seemed to want to know. One story leads to another, and before long the children's questions will bring everything from you which you wish to tell.

The result of these teachings has been commented on by the school teachers of these children, who say they are so truthful, clean-minded, frank, and open about all things that it is a pleasure to know them.

Every mother can teach her children the truth if she only knows it herself and has the right attitude toward it. She can elaborate on this plan or outline as much as she wishes, but she must get down to the child's world in order to make her teachings impressive and successful. The one unpardonable sin on the part of a mother is to let her children learn the truth elsewhere than from her own lips.

5. IWW and the Lawrence Strike

In the winter of 1913, the progressive labor movement was enjoying great success. According to the *New York Call*, on January 15, the general strike of the Socialists was "now on," supported by an "unparalleled total of 200,000 workers."[1] The next day, another 30,000 waist workers answered the "Waist Strike Call," walking off their jobs, singing while doing so. The general strike—a strike by all workers in all industries—was spreading to the hotel workers, to the miners, to other cities.[2] It was the sort of defiant activity that Margaret Sanger applauded.

But by 1912, Sanger's enthusiasm for the Socialists had thinned. Earlier that year, she had attended a strike meeting of women laundry workers in her Socialist organizer position, asking the women strikers to support legislation that would improve their hours and wages. One of the women stood up to her and said, "Oh, that stuff! Don't you know that we women might be dead and buried if we waited for politicians and lawmakers to right our wrongs."[3] And Sanger had to agree. On January 25, she left the Socialist Party—but not the labor movement.

Sanger identified with the common workers. But the middle-class-oriented Socialists had a relatively conservative agenda and were most interested in backing skilled labor.[4] Under the influence of Socialist Democratic Party president Eugene Debs, the Socialists had been supporting woman's suffrage, even marching in the 1912 woman's suffrage parade, but most of the Socialist male leadership were not about to support radical feminist demands and preferred that women remain in their traditional sexual roles and adhere to a traditional division of labor.[5]

Nevertheless, the Socialists regularly cooperated with the IWW, to whom Margaret would next turn, and who were considered to be far more radical and far more militant than the Socialists. The IWW, the Industrial Workers of the World, known for unknown reasons as the "Wobblies," were not interested in "political action," in petitions or negotiation. They were willing to engage in "direct action"—the term describing a political act that aggressively confronted the power of the state, and the IWW was a union open to both skilled and unskilled men; to all women; to immigrants of first and second generation; and to people of color, including Asians.[6] Most threatening to employers, capitalists, and the government (and possibly most appealing to Sanger) was the IWW advocacy of fair pay for all workers through abolishment of capitalism and the wage system.

Probably Bill Sanger introduced Margaret to Big Bill Haywood, the prominent IWW founder and leader, when Haywood, at Bill Sanger's invitation, came to speak at their Local No. 5. Margaret became a great admirer of Big Bill, although Haywood, a large, burly man who appeared capable of violence, deplored violence and did not himself advocate violence.[7] But the Wobblies' more radical reputation appealed to Margaret, who by this time felt so strongly about the ugly lives borne by tenement workers and mothers.

According to Margaret, when the Lawrence workers struck the Massachusetts wool mills on January 12, 1912, the Wobblies "tossed" her into their ranks. Well, scarcely "tossed." Sanger's writings in radical publications identify her a comrade as outraged and radical as the best of them, certainly as one who believed in taking direct action.[8] In 1916, Sanger would take direct action and challenge the Comstock laws by opening her birth control clinic in Brownsville. All in all, it's hard to accept that Margaret Sanger could ever have been "tossed" into anything.

The Lawrence Strike of the woolen mill workers had its genesis in a new law that reduced the hours of allowed work for women and children from fifty-six to fifty-four per week.[9] This was annoying to the mill owners; women and children comprised more than half of the workers and could be paid the least. To compensate for the loss, the mill owners (who had been paying dividends of 8 to 12 percent, along with other dividends and surpluses to stockholders) reduced the wages of all workers proportionately.[10] At the same time, the mill owners speeded up the looms so that the output would remain the same.

On January 12, 1912, a group of workers went to pick up their wages and discovered the pay cut. They were, to put it mildly, unhappy. They exploded in a fury, rushing through the entire building shouting, "Strike!" emptying into the street, and shortly, some twenty-five thousand wool workers were on strike, marching, singing, picketing, and surrounding the factory buildings with their newly devised impenetrable human chain of arm-linked bodies to deploy the entrance of scabs.

By February, the strikers' funds and morale were low. Of particular concern to the strikers were their children. The children were going hungry. Haywood, taking the idea from successful strikers in Europe, arranged to have the Lawrence children sent to New York City, turning to the Ferrer Center to spread the word that temporary homes were needed for the strikers' children.

Sanger, as a professional nurse and a trusted comrade, was depended upon to examine and escort the children from Lawrence, Massachusetts, to New York City. The rail trip in early February with the first group of 119 children went well. When they arrived in New York, the children were greeted by a warm and enthusiastic crowd of five thousand. The strikers' supportive radical community and the Ferrer Center had recruited more takers than children, and the publicity had become extensive.[11] When later that month Wobblies workers attempted to relocate a second group of children, the police stormed the train station at Lawrence, blocked the children from boarding the train, and arrested and clubbed both mothers and children. The subsequent outcry triggered a congressional investigation led by Socialist Congressman Victor Berger from Wisconsin, and Margaret Sanger, along with fifty others, went to Washington, D.C., to testify before the House of Representatives hearing.

Sanger was immediately noticed as the well-spoken, attractive witness, whose fetching photo as the "nurse of New York" appeared in the *New York Herald*. Major papers reported on the congressional hearings, noting that Mrs. Taft, the president's wife, had attended them, and the public read as well chilling tales of wool mill workers' children, without woolen clothes of their own, ill fed and ill clothed in the bitter winter, being attacked with their mothers at the rail station by policemen.[12]

The wool mill owners could not withstand mobilized public opprobrium. On March 12, American Woolen Mills capitulated, shortly followed by the other Lawrence mills. With the two-month strike, the workers had won all their demands: 5 to 20 percent pay raises and overtime. Throughout New England, mill owners were forced to raise wages—though even with the raise, mill workers' wages remained pitiful.

The Manuscript

In this excerpt from the Hearings held by the House Committee on Rules, Mr. Foster is Martin D. Foster (1861-1919), a Democratic Congressman from Illinois, and Mr. Stanley is Augustus O. Stanley (1867-1958), also a Democrat, representing Kentucky.

The Strike at Lawrence, Massachusetts
Statement of Miss Margaret Sanger
Massachusetts Hearings before the Committee on Rules of the House of
Representatives on House Resolutions 409 and 433, March 2-7, 1912

Mr. Foster. You say you are a trained nurse?

Miss Sanger. Yes, sir.

Mr. Foster. And what was the physical appearance of these children that you
took to New York? You know something about how they should look; were
they properly nourished?

Miss Sanger. Well, the condition of those children was the most horrible
that I have ever seen.

Mr. Foster. Tell the committee something about how they looked.

Miss Sanger. In the first place, there were four little children who had chick-
en pox that we kept there; we would not allow them to go away; and then
one of the children had just gotten over chicken pox, and the father begged
us to let the child come; he had one 2 years old and another 3 1/2 years old,
I believe, and he begged us to let those children come, because he was a widower and had no wife or anyone to take care of these children; he left them
with the neighbors during the day. So I took these little children, and we isolated them on the way to New York, and when we got there they were
placed under the doctor's care. All of these children were walking about
there apparently and not noticing chicken pox or diphtheria; one child had
diphtheria and had been walking around, and no attention paid to it at all,
and had been working up to the time of the strike. Out of the 119 children,
four of them had underwear on, and it was the most bitter weather; we had
to run all the way from the hall to the station in order to keep warm; and
only four had underwear.

Mr. Foster. You say only four had underwear?

Miss Sanger. Yes.

Mr. Foster. What was the character of their outer clothing; was it woolen?

Mr. Stanley. Were the people working in a woolen mill?

Miss Sanger. Yes, sir.

Mr. Stanley. Where they make underwear?

Miss Sanger. Yes, sir.

Mr. Foster. How about the outer clothing?

Miss Sanger. It was almost in rags; their coats were eaten off as though they were simply worn to shreds.

Mr. Foster. Was it woolen clothing?

Miss Sanger. No, sir, I do not think any one of them had on any woolen clothing, that is, to my own knowledge.

Mr. Foster. What was their color? Did they seem to be well nourished?

Miss Sanger. They were very much emaciated; every child there showed the effects of malnutrition and all of them, or almost all of them, according to the doctor's certificate that night, had adenoids and enlarged tonsils. They were all examined at the station. We had a little time in the morning, and they were examined before they left.

Mr. Foster. They all looked thin and pale?

Miss Sanger. Yes. I would like to say that when they had this supper, it would bring tears to your eyes to see them grab the meat with their hands and eat it.

Mr. Foster. They ate the meat as though they really enjoyed it?

Miss Sanger. Yes, decidedly.

Mr. Foster. And you say that there were only four out of the 119 that had any underclothing?

Miss Sanger. Yes, sir, and it was the bitterest weather we have had this year.

Mr. Foster. And the outer clothing was ragged?

Miss Sanger. In rags. I think perhaps 20 of them had overcoats.

Mr. Foster. What kind of shoes did they have?

Miss Sanger. Almost on the ground, except some of the older girls, who had been working in the mills, they had better shoes; but the little ones, who had to depend on others, were in a most deplorable condition.

Mr. Foster. Did they have on woolen stockings?

Miss Sanger. I do not think any of them had a bit of wool on their bodies.

Mr. Foster. And yet working in woolen mills?

Miss Sanger. Yes, sir.

6. The Comstock Laws

While the working lives of the poorest of the wage earners were being ground out of them by the factory and mill owners, their reproductivity was being carefully protected by the moralistic Anthony Comstock. Comstock had been originally bankrolled by the YMCA. Later his stalwarts were the New York Society for the Suppression of Vice, the NYSSV, and with such support he had been able to author the Comstock laws that prevailed at nineteenth-turn-of-the-century America.

Rushed through Congress in "hot haste" just before its close in 1873, the federal Comstock law made it a crime to manufacture, sell, or send through the U.S. mails any obscene article, including any article that was intended to prevent conception or any printed matter that offered information on preventing conception. The resulting "obscenity" was punishable by a fine as great as $5,000 and/or a jail sentence up to ten years. Under this draconian edict, no exception was made for use of the mails by licensed physicians (nor was the health of the woman ever considered).[1]

After passage of his bill by Congress, Comstock was appointed by Congress as special agent of the U.S. Post Office Department and given the power to enforce his federal law, with the right to open mail and seize contents and the right to apprehend and arrest wrongdoers. Many states, including New York, then passed their own mini-Comstock laws, and Comstock was deputized by the state of New York to protect the morals of New York and to censor the press. Thus, Comstock had wide-ranging powers.

Unfortunately—or fortunately—Comstock's staff of six men to police the entire United States of America and the state and city of New York was as inadequate as Comstock's mindset was limited. The largest purveyors of contraceptives—such as millionaire Samuel Colgate of Colgate and

Company, for twenty years president of the NYSSV—were regular and wealthy and respected church members. When respectable and millionaire church member Colgate advertised the contraceptive benefits of Vaseline, a product of Colgate and Company, in a wide-ranging campaign during the 1870s, Colgate was conveniently ignored. Those who appeared less respectable were not. While selective, Comstock's reach was long, and on those whom it would fasten, such as the small entrepreneurial businessman, it was merciless.[2]

In the face of these conditions, the wealthy and the middle class continued to secure contraceptive means, but the most poor and the uneducated immigrants had neither leisure nor money to search out device or advice. Doctors refused to give information on contraception (to other than their friends), and the only method of birth control for the poor was illegal abortion, which was just barely affordable, with its often-unfortunate aftermath of death or a near-death illness from infection followed by long-lasting disability.

Comstock's attitude toward birth control reflected, though somewhat more self-righteously, that of the upper and middle classes: "natural" methods—*coitus interruptus* and abstinence—were tolerated (probably because Comstock could not figure out any way to stop them), but any birth control method using "devices" smacked of smut and vice, was naturally associated with prostitution, and was an "obscenity." This attitude then was codified into the laws bearing his name. Comstock and his agents often posed as desperate adults in need of contraceptives, concocting heartrending stories ("My wife, a mother of ten children, desperately ill, terrified of another pregnancy...") to prevail with small businesspersons. When the story was swallowed and the incriminating article brought forth, the seller was arrested. In this way, Comstock was to entrap Bill Sanger in December of 1915 into finding and handing over a copy of *Family Limitation*.

In truth, although Comstock boasted of innumerable convictions, his success rate was slim; but the threat of his laws reinforced the Victorian legacy of prudery and kept people uneasy. While many challenged and circumvented the Comstock laws, ignorance was generally sustained and a hypocritical respectability enthroned.[3]

Comstock was avid that contraception, neither the word nor its discussion, should appear in print. With such nonsense the more sensible Anita Block had little patience: on April 23 and 30, 1911, Block featured in the *New York Call* a two-part article, "Women and Reproduction," in which she supported her statement, "Women have a right to determine for themselves whether they desire to assume parenthood."[4]

In keeping with this point of view and with the success of "How Six

Little Children Were Told the Truth," Block continued her support for an open discussion of sexuality and promised a second series of columns by Margaret Sanger in the *Call*, this series titled "What Every Girl Should Know."⁵ Once again, Block primed readers for the forthcoming columns, forestalling objections from the less modern readers by reminding them, "We want to keep girls, who do not know the nature and meaning of their sex impulses, from being victimized by weak and unscrupulous men....Where are our readers to get such information...if not here?"⁶

"What Every Girl Should Know" sets out very clearly all the things a girl should know about her sexuality, from puberty through menopause. Letters immediately flowed into the *Call*. Most were grateful and approving: "Every reader owes Margaret Sanger a debt of appreciation"; "fine and sensible articles"; "my sincere congratulations"; along with a request for "What Every Boy Should Know." But others were appalled: One woman "blushed"; another was "very sorry indeed that the *Call* should be so polluted to have to be banished from our home circle."⁷

Anthony Comstock was so appalled that when he spotted this column discussing venereal disease, he immediately censored it. As distressing as was the mention of contraception, descriptions of venereal diseases were, apparently, in the eyes of Comstock, equally abhorrent and fell into the category of obscene literature. As Comstock said in another context, "This cursed business of obscene literature works beneath the surface and like a canker worm secretly eats out . . . moral life and purity."⁸

In response to the censorship, the *Call* printed down the space allotted for the February 9 column,

What Every Girl
Should Know
N
O
T
H
I
N
G
By order of the
Post Office Department

Public outcry was overwhelming. Articles and letters of protest filled the columns of the *Call*; the German Socialist daily, *Volkszeitung*, printed its denunciation; Representative Victor Berger, the Socialist who had backed the Lawrence Strike congressional hearings, introduced a resolution calling upon Congress to investigate the Post Office censorship of publications.[9] In the face of such a storm of public protest, the censored column was finally published in the *Call* a month later.

The Manuscript

Margaret Sanger had had her first encounter with the angry old man, the formidable Anthony Comstock. But Margaret was to have the last word: The U.S. government officially reprinted her material for World War I troops.[10] Later, material from *What Every Girl Should Know* was found in pamphlets issued by the War Department, the Navy Department, the YMCA, the YWCA, the U.S. Public Health Service, and the American Social Hygiene Association.

In 1927, *What Every Girl Should Know* was revised and reissued as *What Every Girl and Boy Should Know*, subsequently translated into numerous languages, and continued to be republished until 1980.

What Every Girl Should Know: Nothing
(The Censored Article)
Part III: Some Consequences of Ignorance and Silence[11]
New York Call, March 2, 1913

Prominent medical authorities claim that syphilis was not known in Europe before the discovery of America. Others equally as prominent hold that it has existed for many centuries in Europe, but was confused with other diseases such as leprosy. It makes little difference to the girl or boy today just how long or from where it came. The point we do know is that it is here in our homes and workshops, and we should know what it is like and how to avoid it. . . .

Syphilis is an infectious disease caused by a special microbe which is acquired by contagion or heredity.

It is chronic in course, varied and intermittent in character, and the length of time it remains in the body is indefinite.

It is so widespread that no country in the world is free from it, neither is any organ of the body exempt from its ravages.

Let us take a young man accustomed to promiscuous sexual intercourse, who cohabits with a syphilitic woman. He notices nothing wrong for about five weeks, when he becomes aware of a pimple on the sexual organs, to which perhaps he pays little attention. This grows and becomes hard at the base and is ulcerated on the top.

About ten days after the appearance of the ulcer (or chancre), the boy notices that the glands of the groins begin to swell, but as there is little or no pain attached, he still pays no attention to this.

After three, or sometimes four, weeks, the ulcerated opening heals, but leaves the hard lump under the skin. In two or even three months after the time of infection, the first general symptoms appear. His bones ache, he is mentally depressed, slightly feverish at night, and a rash appears upon his body and sore spots in the mouth. These symptoms usually decide him to consult a doctor, who finds him in the second stage of syphilis. This condition lasts usually about two and a half years, the rash often lasting a short period and leaving, but to return again.

The blood and ulcers on the body contain the poisons of the disease, and for three or four years the poison CAN BE TRANSMITTED by contagion or by heredity.

The third stage is the most destructive, especially to the nervous system, for this disease is recognized as the greatest factor in organized disturbances of the nervous system.

It not rarely is the cause of cerebral and spinal meningitis; paralysis of the legs; paralysis of one side of the body; and that most helpless and terrible disease, locomotor ataxia; softening of the brain; and many other diseases, which affect the spinal cord and which are seldom ever cured. The majority of those diseased are left with physical or mental infirmities, rendering them public charges. . . .

In women, too, the first symptoms are not so characteristic as in men. She may pay no attention to the chancre for a month. Even if she does feel aches in her bones, she thinks she is run down, or she thinks she has malaria; even the rash does not alarm her, and often only repeated miscarriages will be the only symptoms she can remember of the early stage. She may continue for years before the disease reaches the third stage. This is not always so, for in every individual the disease differs in character and duration.

Gonorrhea and syphilis differ in many ways. For instance, the former shows itself in a week or ten days after infection, where syphilis shows no signs for five or six weeks.

Gonorrhea is considered a social danger because of its effect upon the sexual organs, often rendering them sterile. Syphilis is also a social danger, but it has a direct effect upon the offspring and upon future generations because its effects are visited upon the child. . . .

There seems to be no doubt that, if the disease receives the proper treatment, there is every hope for the individual to live a normal life. Fournier, a French authority, says,

"Personally I could cite several hundred observations concerning syphilitic subjects who, after undergoing thorough treatment, have married and became fathers of healthy, good-looking children." . . .

In concluding this series of articles, I cannot refrain from uttering just a word about the relation of the entire subject I have been discussing to the economic problem. It is impossible to separate the ignorance of parents, prostitution, venereal diseases, and the silence of the medical profession from the great economic question that the world is facing today. It is here ever before us, and the more we look into the so-called evils of the day, the more we realize that the whole structure of present day society is built upon a rotten and decaying foundation. Until capitalism is swept away, there is no hope for young girls to live a beautiful life during their girlhood. There is no hope for boys or girls to build up strong and sturdy bodies. There is no hope that a woman can live in the family relation and have children without sacrificing every vestige of individual development. There is no hope that prostitution will cease, as long as there is hunger. There is no hope for a strong race as long as venereal diseases exist....Soon . . . women [will] rise in one big sisterhood to fight this capitalist society which compels a woman to serve as an implement for man's use.

7. Life as a Radical

During the winter of 1913, the Greenwich Village radicals lived a heady, inspiring moment in time. Labor organizers and professionals, artists and artistes, highbrows and working class mixed as never before. A year earlier, a group of highly educated young radical feminists had formed Heterodoxy, a luncheon club, which included author Charlotte Perkins Gilman, heiress Mabel Dodge, and labor leader Elizabeth Gurley Flynn. *The Masses*, no longer a conservative Socialist magazine was being edited by Max Eastman under the banner "No Respect for the Respectable." In January 1913, Mabel Dodge began holding "Evenings" at her sumptuous Village apartment, where gathered Anarchists, Wobblies, artists and writers from *The Masses*, feminists from Heterdoxy, Socialists and radicals of all persuasions, and intellectuals from the Ferrer Center, who came along too, from uptown East 107th Street, to the Village to engage, discuss, and argue. Revolution was in the air. A euphoric rebellion against conservatism, whether in the arts or in politics, had spilled over from the IWW success in Lawrence.

Later called the "Bread and Roses Strike," the wool mill workers' 1912 uprising in Lawrence, Massachusetts, had been a remarkable interlude when mill workers speaking as many as twenty-seven different languages came together in an extraordinary self-imposed democratic organization. Keeping their spirits high with their constant marching and strengthening their sense of unity by singing, each in their own language to the common melody, the mill workers, both men and women, had maintained their morale in the face of ongoing harassment by local police, the state police, twenty-two militia companies, the National Guard, and hired thugs. It was, wrote Big Bill Haywood, "the most significant strike, the greatest strike that has ever been carried on in this country or any other country."[1]

That the worker demands had been met by "this greatest strike" presaged to the idealistic radical community the birth of a new, egalitarian society. Suddenly, all dreams seemed possible. There was every reason to continue the work of agitation and strikes; American society might yet be transformed into one in which workers were paid fairly.

In January 1913, while a Socialist-led General Strike was developing in the garment industry of New York City, the Paterson silk mill workers in New Jersey were faced with increased loom assignments and decreased wages. The Paterson workers, who knew their own worth, had respect for themselves and their craft. They began their strike in the same self-organized democratic manner as had the Lawrence strikers and, impressed by Haywood's popularity with the workers and his past success with building morale in Lawrence, they invited Big Bill to come to Paterson.

Sanger, equally committed, equally enthralled, left her writing and nursing assignments and came to Paterson, as well. Caught up in the vision of a new world order, a new life for the hordes of sickened mothers and children she ministered to in Lower East Side tenements, Sanger threw herself wholeheartedly into the fray. Working closely with Elizabeth Gurley Flynn, Sanger, too, was picketing, organizing, and speaking at the women strikers' Tuesday meetings, where her advice on family limitation was welcomed and appreciated. From the moment of her first maiden speech, Carlo Tresca recalled, that, even though the emotional drain was terrible, Margaret's presentations were powerful and effective.[2] And as she had in Lawrence, she assisted in transporting strikers' children to New York City out of Paterson.

The Paterson mill owners had substantial capital; the time that only money can buy; a backlog of goods; ongoing manufacturing operations in Pennsylvania; and support from the local courts, local police, and the newly assigned state troopers. The strikers, who had none of the above, were, as spring came on, facing hunger and, more accurately, starvation. Yet they hung on.

The protracted strike of the Paterson workers attracted, besides Margaret, many from the Ferrer Center, intellectuals who were neither workers nor unionists, but visionaries who dreamed of a more egalitarian society. The visionaries included journalist John Reed, who conceived the idea of a pageant to be performed by the striking workers. It would be a means to make known the struggle of the workers and to reinforce strikers' morale, and it was planned for a June 7 Saturday night performance at Madison Square Garden in New York City.

The pageant was to feature the silk mill workers playing themselves and would set out for the public the truth of the strikers' story. The art of performance would be married to the workers' reality, and this honest portrayal, it was believed, would counter the omniscient press articles that sided consistently with the manufacturers, describing the strikers and the IWW as outlaws and a threat to American society. In addition, with an understanding of the reasonableness of the workers' strike, moral support and needed funds would come from the larger worker community as well as from the general public.

For three weeks, the Sanger apartment was headquarters for the pageant preparations. Margaret worked on the Strike Pageant Executive Committee that included Bill Haywood and John Reed and worked, as well, side by side with Wobblies and eager volunteers, sparing nothing of herself to make the pageant a reality. On the night of the performance, Margaret was a leader in the parade that wended its way to the armory for the opening of the pageant.

The pageant was, indeed, an extraordinary event, a stupendous drama with a cast of one thousand performers, the workers playing themselves— a theatre experience "without parallel in the world," said the *New York Call* reviewer. Hundreds of IWW members, who were admitted free, had walked from Paterson, West Hoboken, the Bronx, Brooklyn, and College Point to Madison Square Garden to be in the audience. The audience was surely as extraordinary as the performance, and the pageant was an inspiring experience for those on both sides of the proscenium.[3]

But while the pageant was a powerful work of art and an example of the how those from all classes and diverse backgrounds could join together to create great art, it excited only limited interest beyond those not personally involved. Certainly, no new support for the strikers or helpful funds appeared.

Unlike Lawrence, the Paterson strike generated no congressional hearings, no national publicity, no pictures of attractive nurses, no quotes from sympathetic presidents' wives, no heart-wrenching stories of mistreated children. Great theater did not have the reach of a sentimental, widely distributed news story. After a smattering of newspaper descriptions by those who saw and were impressed by the pageant, coverage of the Paterson struggle dwindled, news of the strike faded away, as did the strike itself, while the silk workers, destitute and near starvation, without the help of funds or food, were over the summer driven to return to work at whatever cost.

As she acknowledges in her 1931 autobiography, "No one could have been more serious and determined than we were in those days," and the failure of the strike left Margaret "thoroughly despondent."[4] With its failure, she was forced to recognize the futility of penniless protest. It took longer for her to recognize the futility of pure outrage, yet longer for her to cloak her outrage adroitly, but in the failure of the strike she saw a "fitting conclusion" to her life as a radical organizer.[5]

Spent and disillusioned, Margaret took her children to Provincetown, Massachusetts, for a summer of sand and sea. Many of the radicals were summering there as well, including Big Bill Haywood, who had come, over-worked and exhausted, for rest and recuperation. With the ocean breezes blowing, the friends talked their way through the summer. Intermittently, Margaret left Provincetown to research practical contraceptive information in East Coast libraries. To her distress, she found nothing, certainly nothing that allowed women, rather than the men, to be in control of their fertility. When at one point during the summer Sanger expressed her frustration over the dearth of contraceptive information, Haywood, who had spent time in Europe, suggested to Margaret that she should go to France and see for herself birth control in practice.[6]

Eleven years earlier, Bill Sanger had wooed Margaret with his dream of living and working as an artist in Paris. With the passing of his mother from cancer in the fall and proceeds coming from the sale of their Hastings house, Bill and Margaret were free in October to sail to Europe. In France, Margaret saw birth control in practice: small, happy families and mothers able to enjoy motherhood.[7] She learned there of practical contraceptive methods, means handed from mother to daughter, though never from a physician. But once she saw what she had come to see, she saw no reason to stay. In December, she and the children returned to New York. Bill stayed on in Paris to paint and live the life of the artist, but long before he was back in New York in the fall of 1915, Margaret was involved in what was to be one of her many extramarital affairs, and their marriage was well over.[8]

The Manuscript

The chief threat to the success of the Paterson strike were the unorganized silk workers who were employed in factories newly opened in Pennsylvania—a shrewd move by the silk manufacturers who foresaw that the consolidation of their mills in Paterson was leaving them vulnerable to such things as workers' strikes.[9]

In an attempt to organize workers in Pennsylvania, Margaret Sanger was sent by Haywood to Hazelton, Pennsylvania, to picket the critical and unorganized Duplan Silk Mill. Promptly, Margaret and all the picketers were arrested. Sanger's night in jail produced this lively piece of reporting given below, along with a scrapbook page of newspaper clippings that, to this day, sits in the Library of Congress, belying Sanger's account as one who was "intrigued by this new political and economic radicalism—yet...never a part of it."[10]

Au contraire, she was so much a part of it that, once in Hazelton, she was arrested twice within the week. In the newspaper accounts Sanger is reported as taking a swing at a Hazelston Alderman and threatening to "slap" his face.[11] As Sanger later noted, carefully referring to "one" rather than to herself, "One hardly had any social standing at all in radical circles unless one had…brushed up against the police, or had served at least a few days in jail."[12]

Despite later denials of her involvement, Sanger identified herself completely with the workers and their cause, as seen by her writing "we" were on the picket line, "we" were placed in filthy cells. Sanger's prose below unwittingly betrays her deep emotional investment in the strike and all that it stood for.

With the Girls in Hazelton Jail
New York Call, April 20, 1913 [13]

When eighteen girls of the Duplan Silk Mill of Hazelton, Pa. were put into a patrol wagon and thrown into filthy cells a week ago last Tuesday morning, we all questioned ourselves closely to think what we had done. We had been on the picket line, walking along quietly, when two mounted policemen called out to us, "Stop!" Then they added, "We'll take them all in."

The acting Mayor tried the cases and charged us with "loitering on the streets." The officer said we had loitered after he had told us to stop. However, we all took our time to serve from three to eight days—those walking with me got five days, like myself, while second offenders got eight days.

We were placed in filthy cells, two and three together.

The cells are about eight feet long and five feet wide. Half of the length is taken up with a sheet-iron bench on which the inmate sleeps. In the corner is a toilet, which is flushed once a day. The walls are sheet-iron, covered with paint.

Through the bars every morning at 11 o'clock comes the lone loaf of bread, which must serve until the next morning at the same time. Two cups of water must serve as washing and drinking water. No basin is provided for washing purposes; no blankets or covering of any kind; no comb, brush, soap, towel, or anything for the ordinary decency of the prisoner is allowed her. Nor may any food from outside be carried within.

Before being tried before the judge, we were all thrown together in the cell corridor. The girls pounded on the gates for a drink of water. The keeper gave a pitcher of water to the girls, and they all drank hastily, until one of them spied a large dead roach in the bottom of the pitcher. Closer examination showed the pitcher to be filthy inside as well as outside.

One girl held it high over her head and said, "Girls, do we drink from a pitcher like this?"

"No!" shouted the rest in chorus.

Bang! On the stone floor went the pitcher, crashing into dozens of pieces.

The spirit of the girls was beyond everything ever known in that town before for cheerfulness and defiance. Heretofore, it has been a terrible disgrace to go to the "lock up." But all this has changed in these few weeks, and the girl who serves her time on bread and water is considered a full-fledged fellow worker.

All night long, the boys and girls pounded upon the iron walls of their cells and sang revolutionary songs for the benefit of the Mayor, police, and political bosses who lounge about in the adjoining room.

They did not miss their mark either, for the papers printed glaring accounts of the abusive and revolutionary language of the prisoners.

An influential lawyer was now called upon in Wilkes-Barre. No lawyer in Hazelton would take the strikers' case except a Socialist lawyer, and the authorities ignored his every act. When the tools of the mill bosses heard this, they decided to keep their dirty work hidden by freeing all those who had been arrested.

Before doing so, McKelvey, the political boss, detective, and Alderman in one, went to the girls and boys to ask if their fathers were voters and said he was using all his influence to have them freed. (He is up for Mayor.) But the girls told him they wanted none of his mercy nor influence and preferred to serve their time out rather than accept favors from him.

For that they were kept in the cells a few hours longer. In fact, they refused to come out, until the lawyer came in for them and said they had committed no offense and were free.

The next morning they were on the picket line again at 6 o'clock, but the authorities don't want them in jail again; they want money, and that is what the boys and girls won't give.

While we were locked up, the stench from the toilets became so strong that the girls called to an officer to flush them. He refused to do this, and so the prisoners decided to let the loungers in the adjoining room have some of the odors. They, accordingly, emptied the toilets with the assistance of their tin cups into the cell corridors, which all run into the Mayor's office. The officers came running in and asked what in heaven's name they were up to now! Several officers at once cleaned out the place, scrubbed and disinfected the floors, and those of the girls who could sleep in the sheet-iron beds turned in for the night.

Roaches and bugs infest the cells, and as you are about to get friendly with these, a huge rat comes upon the scene to fight it out with you about that loaf of bread.

The girls decided they'd rather be friends with the rats and give up the bread than show any fear to the officers. Nevertheless, a rat is a rat to a woman.

The fight is still on. The girls [say] they have learned more in eight [days] than they have learned in all their lives before and they are not going to stop learning. Life in the silk mill was heretofore a bore, and work was drudgery. It will not be so again. The girls say they see now that there is a fight on for the working class, and they are in that fight. There is something now to work for, to live for. It is the fight to emancipate the worker from wage slavery.

8. Confronting the Government:
The Woman Rebel

Sanger had long been aware that while the working-class men suffered the indignity of pitiful wages, their women, working long hours both in and out of the home, whether pregnant or nursing, along with their hungry, uncared-for children were the ones who suffered most grievously. With this in mind and once returned from Europe to New York, no longer a visiting nurse and no longer working for the IWW, Sanger began her very own radical activity on behalf of women. She took money from her "dwindling bank account" and began publishing a monthly newspaper with which she intended "to test out public opinion on the broad issues of economic and feministic principles," which is to say, she published a newspaper that would draw to her cause a like-minded community and at the same time confront government enforcement of the Comstock laws.[1] *The Woman Rebel* was defiant, blatant, radical, and extreme, strongly feminist, and it showed the influence of Emma Goldman.[2] In an unpublished manuscript, Sanger recounts the early publishing days of *The Woman Rebel* in the winter of 1914.[3]

The office of *The Woman Rebel* was located in my living room, which also served as playroom and nursery for my three small children. We were living out at the northernmost tip of Manhattan, out "where the open spaces begin," so far north on the most overcrowded island of the world that even the Broadway subway trains manage to burrow their way out into the sunlight and fresh air.

I had chosen that obscure and hidden-away neighborhood, when we had returned from Europe, a few months previous, because it was the best place I could find for my children. Within a week they were playing happily with the other children of the neighborhood; within two, the mothers of the neighborhood were telling me their troubles. Within a month, some of the women I had cared for as a visiting nurse on the lower East Side had learned of my return and were making the long subway journey to the Dyckman section to tell me their troubles. For some inexplicable reason mothers have always chosen me as confidante and counsellor. Yet always, told in a dozen different accents, stammered out inarticulately though without shame or reticence, their story had been the same one—the poignant heartbreaking tragedy of conscript motherhood, the piteous confessions of women worn out and crushed by the incessant travail of childbearing.

Almost against my will these women appealed to me for help, had selected me to free them from the chains of their slavery, the bondage of unwilling maternity. I could not, day in and day out, listen to these stories, these humble tragedies, and remain smugly satisfied with the cosy comforts of my own little home and family....

These experiences led to the founding of my little monthly [The Woman Rebel], which expressed with white-hot intensity my growing conviction that the mothers of the race must be empowered to decide for themselves when they shall fulfill the supreme function of motherhood. Children must be brought into this world by choice and not by chance. Such was the challenge expressed in The Woman Rebel. In its columns, for the first time in human history, were printed the now world-famous and endlessly discussed words: Birth Control.[4]

Writing some years after the fact, Margaret reshaped her life story into a single-minded campaign for birth control, but the reality in 1914 was somewhat different. "The Aim" of The Woman Rebel, as stated in its initial March issue, in the opening essay of the same name, was to spark a revolution, "to stimulate working women to think for themselves and to build up a conscious fighting character."[5] The fight was not only to be one against "slavery through motherhood" and ignorance of the "prevention of conception," but with equal ferocity to attack prostitution, sexual prudery, marriage, middle-class morality, wage slavery—all things that enslaved women. And by women, Sanger meant working-class women.

Sanger had no patience at all with the middle-class feminists—the "New Feminists," she called them. In the same March issue, she wrote of two mass meetings of these middle-class feminists at the Cooper Union. Discussions there over the "right to work," the "right to ignore fashions," the "right to keep her own name"—rights that identified the middle-class woman's movement—seemed to Sanger banal compared to the right of the working-class woman to a decent wage and to contraception.[6]

In keeping with her plan to challenge the Comstock laws and to demand freely available contraceptive information, Sanger also included in this initial issue a short piece titled "The Prevention of Conception," in which she notes that a law exists "forbidding the imparting of information" on conception. She then demands, "Is it not time to defy this law?"[7]

Naturally, with its inclusion of the word "conception," *The Woman Rebel* was immediately targeted by Anthony Comstock, fulfilling one of Sanger's original goals, that of confronting the government. And Comstock, having the year before censored Sanger's column in the *Call* on venereal disease, was, no doubt, on the lookout for this particular firebrand rebel. Under the Comstock laws, the Post Office (and Comstock) immediately banned the March issue of *The Woman Rebel*, as subsequently they would the May, July, August, and September-October issues. Later, Sanger would learn that the cause of the first ban was, indeed, the article "The Prevention of Conception," though at the time the postmaster would not specify a reason, and in the April issue of *The Woman Rebel*, Sanger could only assume the reason for censorship:

> The Postmaster did not like the first number of the WOMAN REBEL....He advised her not to send any more copies through the United States mails....In order to comply with the rules and regulations of the government, the WOMAN REBEL may be forced to become indecent and to advocate a total ignorance of Sexual Hygiene for woman.[8]

"Sexual Hygiene" was a euphemism for contraception, and, of course, Sanger continued to send copies through the United States mail. After the bans, even when the mailing list reached two thousand and additional copies sent free to radical labor organizations, swelled the mailing to five thousand, Sanger and her volunteers found that by stuffing their copies in small batches into post office boxes scattered throughout the city, their mailings would go through. "Sometimes," recalled Sanger in her 1938 *Autobiography*, "daylight caught me, with one or more assistants, still tramping from the printer's and dropping the copies, piece by piece, into various boxes and chutes."[9]

Throughout the publishing of the seven issues of *The Woman Rebel*, Sanger continued to connect the birth control movement solely with the workingwoman's cause.

> If the WOMAN REBEL were allowed to publish with impunity elementary and fundamental truths concerning personal liberty and

how to obtain it, the birth control movement would become a movement of tremendous power in the emancipation of the working class. The attempted suppression is thus primarily a blow at the entire working class of America, intended for no other purpose than to retard the economic and spiritual emancipation of working men, women, and children.[10]

In the June *Woman Rebel*, Sanger set out the stance that she would later take for all women, workers or not.

A woman's body belongs to herself alone. It is her body. It does not belong to the church. It does not belong to the United States of America or to any other Government on the face of the earth. The first step toward getting life, liberty and the pursuit of happiness for any woman is her decision whether or not she shall become a mother. Enforced motherhood is the most complete denial of a woman's right to life and liberty.[11]

The Women Rebel not only challenged the Comstock laws, but lambasted any injustice Sanger happened upon, "A little sassbox," she later called it. "I paid the printer's bill and worked day and night at making it as red and flaming as possible," "a scathing denunciation of all organized conventionalities."[12]

"Organized conventionalities" were easily come by. In the spring of 1914, the radical community at the Ferrer Center was collecting relief supplies for survivors of the Ludlow massacre and for the miners who were continuing to hold out in their strike against Rockefeller's Colorado Fuel & Iron mining company. When Sanger happened upon the Ludlow massacre—one of the most despicable incidents in labor history—she had her say on the front page of the May *Woman Rebel* in her below essay, "Cannibals."[13]

Miners employed by the Rockefeller-owned company were exploited at every turn. They were forced to rent their homes from the company, which owned them. Miners had to buy their own tools from the company, and they had to pay, in advance, for preacher's, school, and blacksmithing fees. Prices for everything were 25 percent higher than prices outside the camp, yet the miners were regularly shorted on the amount of coal they brought in. Miners were not allowed to join a union.[14]

In September 1913, immediately after the strike against these brutal conditions was called, the more than eleven thousand miners and their families were thrown out of their company-owned homes into a raging blizzard. They walked—in the blizzard—to nearby noncompany land in

Ludlow, where the United Mine Workers Union had set up tents. Throughout the fall and winter, the tent colony was relentlessly attacked by Rockefeller's hired gunmen, who shot continually into the settlement using Maxim guns. By spring, the tenacity of the miners' resistance resolved the Rockefeller company to decisive measures.

On April 20, 1914, the National Guard began machine-gunning the strikers. This went on for fourteen hours. The guard then torched the miners' tents. The settlement was destroyed, and twenty-one people were shot or burned to death, including two women and eleven children; one man was shot fifty-four times. Before the subsequent outbreaks were finally ended by entrance of federal troops into Colorado, sixty-six strikers or their family members had been killed. Still the miners held out for another fifteen months. In the end, hunger and the national changes that preceded World War I forced them to return to work with none of their demands met.[15]

The Manuscript
Sanger's outrage at the massacre is over the top (these were, after all, still her salad days). Justified as it was, her outrage would not change the Rockefellers or the government, but the bitterness of tone in this *Rebel* essay displays how strong was her sense of injustice, how sincere her sensitivity to the unwarranted sufferings of others. The energy of this essay points, as well, to her determination to remedy the world's ills and foreshadows a life that was never content with mere words, but steadfastly employed action.

Cannibals
The Woman Rebel, May 1914
Compared with the diseased, perverted, hypocritical ghouls of American "civilization," cannibals strike you as simple, healthy people who live in an earthly Utopia. If they feed and fatten upon the charred flesh of human beings, cannibals at least do not hide behind the sickening smirk of the Church and the Y.M.C.A.[16] They are open, frank, and straightforward in their search for food. They eat their victims outright. They do not use the charred skulls and skeletons of women and children as the foundation of institutions that will hide the cries and shrieks of the tortured, or attempt to kill the nauseating stench of their bloody breath by vomiting forth the perfumed hypocrisies of the Baptist Church—words of peace on earth and goodwill toward men.[17]

Cannibals are not so cowardly that they must employ Maxim guns in the wholesale slaughter of men, women, and children. They do not employ starving sneaks to burn the evidence of their nightmarish appetites or fear themselves to look upon the disemboweled and dismembered corpses of the men, women, and children who are sacrificed to promote great works of charity and philanthropy.[18]

Cannibals, you see, are uncivilized, primitive folk, low in the scale of human intelligence. Their tastes are not so fastidious, so refined, so Christian, as those of our great American coal operators, who have subsidized the State of Colorado and treat the President of the United States as an office boy—these leering, bloody hyenas of the human race, who smear themselves with the stinking honey of Charity to attract those foul flies of religion who spread pollution throughout the land.

Have we workers been inoculated with this foul pollution of the spirit, this poison that is being spread by the Young Men's and Young Women's Christian Associations, and by those churches which are subsidized by the murderous masters of America?

Certainly we have if we do not boycott the Baptist Church and its allies, those "Christian Associations," which are subsidized by the Rockefellers and other criminals in order to kill the spirit of the workers of America.

Certainly we have been if we remain silent or inactive in the campaign against the poison of the "religion" that is weakening and killing the spirit of the American workers.

Working women! Keep away from the Y.W.C.A. as you would from a pesthouse. It is based upon the slavery and torture of the workers of America, upon the bodies of toilers who have been killed in the mines and factories, and upon the bodies of those who have protested against being so murdered—shot down by Maxim guns and burned up with Standard Oil. These substantial buildings have been built by those Christians who riddled the bodies of women and children with bullets when they attempted to escape from a burning pit to a place of safety. It is they who are conferring favors upon you, in order to rob you of your freedom.

They want to inculcate in you the stupid spirit of submission to their mastery. They want to feed you upon the vapid innocuities of religion. They want to make you keep books with their God. They want to keep you in stupid ignorance of your own body, so that you, too, will some day be forced to breed children who can perform their horrible wholesale murders for them—who will shoot down all men and women and children who may dare question their mastery and their tyranny. They will force you to breed the cowards who murder those who are willing to die for freedom rather than to live in slavery.

But remember Ludlow! Remember the men and women and children who were sacrificed in order that John D. Rockefeller, Jr. might continue his noble career of charity and philanthropy as a supporter of the Christian faith. Steer clear of those brothels of the Spirit and morgues of Freedom!

9. Continuing the Confrontation: *Family Limitation*

In August 1914, Sanger met the results of confronting the United States government. Early one morning, she was awakened by "an imperious ringing of the doorbell." When she opened the door, two agents from the Department of Justice thrust a document into her hands, which began, just slightly, to tremble. Margaret had been indicted by the grand jury on nine counts for publishing obscenities and advocating assassination, the latter charge stemming from the article "A Defense of Assassination" in the July *Woman Rebel*, the former because such *Rebel* articles as "The Prevention of Conception," "Abortion in the United States," and the announcement of the formation of the first United States Birth Control League had offended authorities (i.e., Anthony Comstock).[1]

Once arraigned on August 25, Sanger began to consider the possibility of prison and how to provide for the care of her children. At the same time, she was besieged with advice from families and friends, most of whom believed she was either mad or having a nervous breakdown. She was not to be deterred by their solicitousness, however; she had important things to do.

All the women who had read or heard of *The Woman Rebel* and all who had written to her for advice on contraception were to be answered. Drawing on the information she had garnered in France, she wrote *Family Limitation*, a small pamphlet outlining various contraceptive methods. But when she tried to have it printed, interviewing some twenty printers, she found not one who would touch her manuscript, so clearly was it in violation of the Comstock laws. Eventually, through the Ferrer Center, she met a Russian émigré, big, burly Bill Shatoff, who had printed similar material for Emma Goldman. Shatoff worked after hours when the shop was supposed to be closed, setting the type for the printing of one hundred thousand copies of *Family Limitation*—a sixteen-page "lewd" and "lascivious" pamphlet that offered illegal information on contraception. But that was only the beginning of what was involved.

> Addressing the envelopes took a lot of work. Night after night the faithful band labored in a storage room, wrapping, weighing, stamping. Bundles went to the mills in the East, to the mines of the West—to Chicago, San Francisco, and Pittsburgh, to Butte, Lawrence, and Paterson. All who had requested copies were to receive them simultaneously.[2]

When her court date came up in October, Sanger requested an extension. It was curtly refused. Instead, the court informed her that her case would be heard immediately, on the following morning at ten o'clock; and by the time of that pronouncement, it was four o'clock in the afternoon. Convinced that she faced a prejudiced court (she was said to have received word from an unknown source that her sentence had already been decided) and knowing that time in federal prison could be indeterminate and would not allow her to be active and accomplishing her goals, Sanger faced a crucial decision.[3]

> If I was to have a decent defense prepared the only thing I could do was to set sail for Europe, prepare my case adequately, stay until the war was over, and return then to fight it out in the courts....The train for Montreal would leave within a few hours....Had I a right to leave the children without seeing them just once more? Peggy's leg was swollen from vaccination, and this kept worrying me; it almost upset my life....The hours of that memorable night of doubt could well be called a spiritual crucifixion. The torture of indecision.... I knew there was no turning back once I boarded that train.[4]

Meanwhile, in Europe, Sanger's growing fame had preceded her. The Malthusian League, the group working in England for birth control and family limitation, was excited about her work. As Oliver M. Johnson of the league wrote,

> The first intimation the Malthusian League had of Mrs. Sanger's work for the cause of family limitation came in the middle of 1914. In June of that year, Dr. Drysdale, [president of the League], received from America...a copy of a new monthly journal...edited by Mrs. Margaret Sanger.
> To our astonishment, the paper was mainly an argument for

family limitation. Various sociological topics were discussed, but article after article dealt with the question of family limitation, viewed from different angles, and suggested as the essential reform required for the solution of many social problems. Knowing the state of American law on the subject of mailing contraceptive advice, we were surprised and delighted at the courage and frankness of the woman who dared to advocate so openly such an unpopular cause (though the paper, of course, contained only "practical information" and was presumably within the law)....

Two more issues of this journal reached us and then no more, and we learned afterwards that it had been suppressed and the copies confiscated by the United States Postal Authorities.

In November 1914, the Malthusian League office received a telephone message...that Miss B. Watson, from the United States, was in England and wished to get into touch with the Malthusian League. He added that Miss Watson was being indicted for the publication of her paper, *The Woman Rebel*, and that her name was an assumed one. So "Miss B. Watson" was none other than Mrs. Margaret Sanger, the plucky editor of *The Woman Rebel*, who had fled her country to gain time to prepare her defense!

The full extent of her pluck we did not know until afterwards when we learned that on hearing that she was to be prosecuted for articles advocating family limitation, she determined to give the authorities some real cause for complaint and, before leaving America, had managed to get into circulation from a number of centres all over the States 100,000 copies of her newly written pamphlet, "Family Limitation," which described contraceptive methods in detail.[5]

Sanger had indeed managed well, having prearranged with her volunteers to mail, simultaneously, at a signal from her, all copies of the earlier stamped and addressed *Family Limitation* pamphlets. Once at sea, three days after leaving Montreal, Sanger sent a cable and the signal ordering the mailing. And now, having sent through the U.S. mails specific information on contraception—not a mere request for or discussion of such as had appeared in *The Woman Rebel*—now Sanger had, in truth, broken the Comstock laws, fulfilling her intention to make information on contraception freely available to women.

The Manuscript

Sanger notes in *Family Limitation* that instructions are put in the "simplest English, that all may easily understand." And she includes a touch of the

Rebel with remarks directed to "comrade workers" and the comment, "The working women can use direct action by refusing to supply the market with children."

In the main, Sanger offers common sense information and advice, some practical, some that could be questionable, such as the recommendation to douche with Lysol.[6] She gives recipes for other douche solutions and specific instructions on how to douche. She explains the what and how of condoms, the pessary (diaphragm), the sponge, and exact measurements of ingredients for vaginal suppositories, She includes line drawings of a fountain syringe, a French pessary, and a cutaway line drawing of the womb and vagina.[7]

No doubt the latter was what so offended Anthony Comstock that, after having tricked Bill Sanger into handing over a copy of *Family Limitation* and then arresting him in January 1915, Comstock said, "Young man, I have been in this work for twenty years, and that leaflet is the worst thing I have ever seen."[8]

At Bill's trial, Judge Swann agreed with Comstock. Leaning forward on the bench, the judge said, "This is simply awful!" And Judge McInerney, who sentenced Bill, said,

> In my opinion the pamphlet is both indecent and immoral. It is not only contrary to the laws of the State, but contrary to the laws of God. Any man or woman who would circulate literature of this kind is a menace to the community.[9]

Such conservatism was typical and quite in line with the thinking of many Americans, and especially the churchgoers, at that time. Even most of Labor—Eugene Debs was the exception—wanted nothing to do with women's rights, let alone birth control. Only the extremists and the most liberal, the Socialists women's groups, the anarchists—particularly Emma Goldman and her manager, Ben Reitman—and Haywood's IWW, supported Sanger. They not only spoke out for birth control, but actively disseminated its literature.[10]

Within the next few years, following World War I, the progressive labor movement was to be swept from the American landscape. The political climate of repression made it, at the least, unpopular, at the most, hazardous, to be associated with the cause of labor and radical or progressive ideals in any way.

Thus, in later editions of *Family Limitation*, Sanger expunged any mention of "workers" or "comrades" or "exploit." The "awful" pamphlet proceeded to circulate for more than twenty years. Sanger's advice, some of it at least, must have been effective, for she later received many letters from mothers who had *not* become pregnant after reading *Family Limitation*.[11]

Introduction
Family Limitation (1914)[12]

There is no need for any one to explain to the working men and women in America what this pamphlet is written for or why it is necessary that they should have this information. They know better than I could tell them, so I shall not try.

I have tried to give the knowledge of the best French and Dutch physicians translated into the simplest English, that all may easily understand.

There are various and numerous mechanical means of prevention which I have not mentioned here, mainly because I have not come into personal contact with those who have used them or could recommend them as entirely satisfactory.

I feel there is sufficient information given here, which, if followed, will prevent a woman from becoming pregnant unless she desires to do so.

If a woman is too indolent to wash and cleanse herself and the man too selfish to consider the consequences of the act, then it will be difficult to find a preventive to keep the woman from becoming pregnant.

Of course, it is troublesome to get up to douche. It is also a nuisance to have to trouble about the date of the menstrual period. It seems inartistic and sordid to insert a pessary or a suppository in anticipation of the sexual act. But it is far more sordid to find yourself several years later burdened down with half a dozen unwanted children, helpless, starved, shoddily clothed, dragging at your skirt, yourself a dragged-out shadow of the woman you once were.

Don't be over sentimental in this important phase of hygiene. The inevitable fact is that unless you prevent the male sperm from entering the womb, you are going to become pregnant. Women of the working class, especially wage workers, should not have more than two children at most. The average working man can support no more, and the average working woman can take care of no more in decent fashion. It has been my experience that more children are not really "wanted," but that the women are compelled to have them either from lack of foresight or through ignorance of the hygiene of preventing conception.

It is only the workers who are ignorant of the knowledge of how to prevent bringing children in the world to fill jails and hospitals, factories and mills, insane asylums and premature graves.

The working women can use direct action by refusing to supply the market with children to be exploited, by refusing to populate the earth with slaves.

It is also the one most direct method for you working women to help yourself *today*.

Pass on this information to your neighbor and comrade workers. Write out any of the following information that you are sure will help her and pass it along where it is needed. Spread this important knowledge!

A Nurse's Advice to Women

Every woman who is desirous of preventing conception will follow this advice:

Don't wait to see if you do *not* menstruate (monthly sickness), but make it your duty to see that you *do*.

If you are due to be "sick" on the eighth of August, do not wait until the eighth to see, but begin as early as the fourth to take a good laxative for the bowels, and continue this each night until the eighth.

If there is the slightest possibility that the male fluid has entered the vagina, take on these same nights, before retiring, five or ten grains of quinine with a hot drink. The quinine in capsule form is considered fresher, but if this is taken do not use alcoholic drinks directly after, as it hardens the capsules, thus delaying the action of the quinine.

By taking the above precautions, you will prevent the ovum from making its nest in the lining of the womb.

Women of intelligence who refuse to have children until they are ready for them keep definite track of the date of their menstrual periods. A calendar should be kept, on which can be marked the date of the last menstruation, as well as the date when the next period should occur.

Women must learn to know their own bodies and watch and know definitely how regular or irregular they are: if the period comes regularly every twenty-eight days (normal) or every thirty days, as is in the case of many young girls.

Mark it accordingly on your private calendar; do not leave it to memory or guesswork. Only ignorance and indifference will cause one to be careless in this most important matter.

A very good laxative (though it is a patent medicine) is Beechams Pills. Two of these taken night and morning, four days before menstruation, will give a good cleansing of the bowels and assist with the menstrual flow. Castor oil is also a good laxative.

The American Physicians may object to this advice because Beechams Pills are a patent medicine. But until they are willing to give open advice on this subject, we must resort to such as the least harmful, until such time as they do.

If a woman will give herself attention BEFORE the menstrual period arrives, she will almost never have any trouble, but if she neglects herself and waits to see if she "comes around," she is likely to have difficulty.

If the action of quinine has not expelled the semen from the uterus and a week has elapsed with no signs of the menstrual flow, then it is safe to assume conception has taken place.

Any attempt to interfere with the development of the fertilized ovum is called an abortion.

No one can doubt that there are times when an abortion is justifiable, but they will become *unnecessary when care is taken to prevent conception.*

This is the only cure for abortion.

There is current among people an idea that conception can take place only at certain times of the month. For instance, ten days after the menstrual period, and four or five days before the next period. This is not to be relied upon at all, for it has been proven again and again that a woman can conceive at any time in the month. Do not depend upon this belief, for there is no reliable foundation for it. There is also the knowledge that nursing after childbirth prevents the return of the menstrual flow for several months and conception does not take place. It is well not to depend upon this too much, especially after the fifth or sixth month, for often a woman becomes pregnant again without having "seen anything" or without her realizing that she has become pregnant. She thus finds herself with one at the breast and another in the womb. Use some preventative.

Again, it is believed that conception cannot take place if the woman lies upon her left side at the time of the act. It makes no difference which side she lies upon; she can become pregnant if the semen is not prevented from entering the womb.

Perhaps the commonest preventive, excepting the use of the condom, is "coitus interruptus," or withdrawal of the penis from the vagina shortly before the action of the semen. No one can doubt that this is a perfectly safe method; and it is not considered so dangerous to the man as some authorities have formerly viewed it, but it requires a man of the strongest will-power to be certain that he has withdrawn before any of the semen has been deposited in the vagina. It is very difficult to determine exactly whether this has been done. The greatest objection to this is the evil effect upon the woman's nervous condition. If she has not completed her desire, she is under a highly nervous tension; her whole being is perhaps on the verge of satisfaction. She is then left in this dissatisfied state. This does her injury. A mutual and satisfied sexual act is of great benefit to the average woman; the magnetism of it is health giving. When it is not desired on the part of the woman and she has no response, *it should not take place.* This is an act of prostitution and is degrading to the woman's finer sensibility, all the marriage certificates on earth to the contrary notwithstanding. Withdrawal on the part of the man should be substituted by some other means that does not injure the woman.

10. Exile and Europe

S anger arrived safely in England—without a passport—whereupon the English official greeted her with, "England is at war, Madam. You can't expect us to let you through."[1] But, somehow, with help that she never could nor never would divulge, Sanger was let through. After a short stay in Liverpool, where she attended Fabian Club meetings, she made her way to London and to the British Museum to research and prepare her defense.[2] In this unpublished manuscript, she movingly recalls her arrival in London.[3]

Under ordinary conditions, London presents none too hospitable a face to lonely American visitors. The first winter of the war it was veritably and literally, dismally, depressingly, "the city of dreadful night"—cloaked in the blackest darkness to protect itself from possible air-raids, tense with suspense and hysteria, scrutinizing the face of every visitor, who was suspected of being a spy in the service of the enemy,[4] London with its "souless solitudes immense," its "ranged mansions dark and still as tombs," struck a steely terror to my soul, and brought vividly to my feverishly homesick imagination the stern mandate of Dante's "Abandon all hope, ye who enter here."[5]

In the uttermost depths of homesickness, every fibre of my body and soul crying out for my three children, from whom I had never before been separated, my strongest impulse was indeed to abandon all hope; and an overwhelming temptation almost impelled me to take the next boat back to New York. True, it would mean prison; but it would take me back to the children as well.

But even if I had surrendered to this impulse, it would have been impossible, since the submarine blockade hopelessly complicated the booking of Transatlantic passage. For the same reason, it was next to impossible to send for the children, as I had first planned.

There is a courage that is born of despair, a courage unflinching and concentrated in purpose. Such courage came to me, a lonely refugee in a dingy lodging house in Bloomsbury, as I pondered over this dilemma.[6] It came to me just as the flickering flame of my first hope was on the point of being sniffed out in that chilly, cheerless atmosphere. In a sort of illumination I realized that here in London I would acquire the aid necessary to triumph over the federal indictment. In a flash I saw that the support that had been withheld in America would be given in England, the age-old home of free speech and freedom of ideas.

That very day I met the Drysdales, who for two generations had carried on the battle of Neo-Malthusianism, as Birth Control was designated in Great Britain.[7]

Oliver M. Johnson, who wrote of the satisfaction of the Malthusian League on learning of *The Woman Rebel*, recalls also the first meeting between Sanger and the league.

We . . . invited [Mrs. Sanger] to visit Dr. Drysdale's office in Queen Anne's Chambers, Westminister, for the Malthusian League at this time had no separate office, nor was its name upon the door—such as the prejudice even in this country against neo-Malthusianism. On the appointed afternoon we awaited with curiosity and also a little apprehension, the visit of the "Woman Rebel," but we were hardly prepared for the surprise given us by the soft-voiced, gentle-mannered, altogether charming "rebel" who tapped at the door at four o'clock and was ushered into the inner room, where Dr. Drysdale and Dr. Dunlop were waiting to receive.[8]

Picking up with Margaret's account of those first London days,

With characteristic generosity, the Drysdales—Alice Vickery Drysdale; her son, Dr. C.V. Drysdale; and his wife, Bessie—called the attention of a number of the most high-minded writers and thinkers to my case. Not only did they all unhesitatingly respond, but men and women, I had never thought it would ever be my good luck to meet, received me with the utmost cordiality. Beneath London's forbidding exterior, I discovered the warmest, most democratic hospitality, quick of response and understanding of one's motives and ideals. They took me under their wings. They went out of their way to get data necessary for my defense. The foundations for some of the deepest affections and lifelong friendships were laid in those trying days when, despite the rigors imposed by the war upon English society, their unfailing kindness won my undying gratitude.

They sent me to Holland armed with letters of recommendation, to study with the heroic Dr. [Johannes] Rutgers, who had so successfully established birth control clinics in that country. My studies took me not only to Holland, but to France and Spain as well, where I found out how the pioneers of the movement had combated superstition and prejudice of the type I must face on my return to America.

Upon my return to London, [it was] now no longer a city to fear, but to embrace almost as a second home.[9]

In England, Sanger was to receive her finishing education, so to speak. Exposure to European humanistic ideas broadened her outlook. In England, she learned of Nietzsche, whose philosophy was to affect her so profoundly; heard Emmeline Pankhurst speak; and listened to the knowledgeable Fabians. In England, she found the guidance and the mentors that she most needed, and from them she gained the sophistication that enabled her to go forward most effectively with her life and her work. She was taken under the wing of the Drysdales, wise and practiced challengers of the status quo, and, of special importance, she met Havelock Ellis, the learned physician whose seven-volume *Studies in the Psychology of Sex* had moved the discussion of sexuality into a social science.[10] From Ellis's work, Sanger drew the professional basis for her own work. In Ellis she found a kindred spirit who confirmed her own views of sexual activity as a sacred, spiritual force. In Ellis she found a teacher who suggested readings, took her to museums, deepened her appreciation of the liberal arts and humanities. She repaid him with an abiding affection and, eventually, abundant financial support that continued to the day of his death.

In England, not only did she make political and emotional connections that would inform her future public and political policies, but when England and the Drysdales opened to her the doors of the Holland clinics under Johannes Rutgers, Sanger saw how professional attention from trained personnel could teach women to care for themselves more effectively, thereby ensuring safer and surer birth control. She learned from Dr. Rutgers's careful clinic records how birth spacing ensured healthier mothers and babies. Most importantly, in the example of the Holland clinics, Sanger found her model for the future of birth control care in America.

The Manuscript

These excerpts from Sanger's London diary show her deeply vulnerable and, at the same time, searching, pondering. Without the daily demands of three young human beings to worry over, suddenly Sanger has time to think her own thoughts and explore the world through the educational opportunities that are presenting themselves, time to feel her way into her own self-hood. No longer was she attending intense, beer-drinking, radical meetings in a low rent New York apartment.[11] In England, Sanger is ushered into the cultured and conservative world of the tea-drinking Drysdales. "One finds the English very polite . . . very tolerant," she notes. Sanger has time for research at the British Museum, time to go the National Gallery, to see "lovely tapestry brick houses," "flower gardens." It seems" she writes, "almost good to be alive"; yet on another page, "How lonely it all is."

London Diary[12]
1914

Liverpool, November 14. Arrived at the Adelphia Hotel 11 AM. No trouble at Customs as I had only one bag. Mr. Girling helped me to a cab & I found myself winding thru dirty streets greatly like all streets surrounding docks in all cities.[13]

The Adelphia is a palace, fairy-like, plus exceeding comfort. It rained all day. The wind blew. The sound of its howling came thru the windows & down the chimney, until homesickness crept over me like my first days at boarding school. I knew it would not do to "set and think" as the Quakers say, so I set off to find the Clarion Cafe - advertised in Blatchford's Clarion.[14]

I found it at 30 Lord St but no one to be there until 6 PM. In the meantime, I wandered about the business sections & tried to adjust my mind to the prices of clothing marked in the windows so that I might have some idea of the dollars & cents I was likely to deal in. Clothing prices very much the same as N.Y. shoes, hats etc. all the same. Not any cheaper.

At 6 PM I went again to the Clarion Cafe & found the Fabians have their Clubroom there & meet every Tuesday night for discussions. I was invited to tea with several of the members & remained for the discussion....Looked over the register. Found Big Bill [Haywood's] name . . . G.B. Shaw, H.G. Wells, & many other thinkers.

The Club is cozy and homelike. The Comrades welcome us all....

No mail for me yet, but I trust some shall arrive tomorrow to give me an idea of how Peggy & Grant are.

Liverpool is a quaint & clean city. Its lovely tapestry brick houses I like. There is an evenness & quiet settled feeling about the place, as if the people expected to remain where they are for time everlasting. The people seem comfortable, not over-dressed or stylish.

The poor look poor all over - out of their very souls poverty speaks....

War talk is everywhere - It is a relief to read the frank sane statement made by Ramsey McDonald M.P....The City is not greatly affected by the war. Business said to be slow, but things assume the same appearance as usual. Women all back to knitting socks, mitts etc. again.

One finds the English very polite in speech & actions. Very tolerant in listening, too. A dark day - rainy this Sunday, too. I walked about to see church architecture. The Cathedral which is not expected to be finished for 50 years did not look so splendid.[15] As all about it is closed I could not tell. Much talk here of German spy system. I wonder if it is not more the general characteristics of the German to always observe & remember to be accurate in detail etc. which naturally makes his information valuable, without an intention of being a spy or even an intention of using such information. They do the same in U.S. yet no one thinks of calling them spys.[16]

Liverpool. Nov 18th 1914. This is Stuart's birthday - How little I tho't eleven years ago today I should be here, and he where he is, but no doubt eleven years more will bring stranger facts to light....

Yesterday...went into the peasant houses of Wales. Mainly smelting workers....All lovely quaint little stone cottages containing two or three rooms - huddled closely together. Very few windows - stone walks & walls - flower gardens - slow, deliberate, simple folk. Coming back, we stopped off at Chester - another quaint old English town.[17] Houses built out over the walks and a promenade running through the first stories about the main streets. Only an hour there and as it was already night - little more could be seen. Bought a South African lucky chain for Peggy (2S). The day before (16th) Mrs. Scott and Dr. Scott and I visited some of his city patients in Liverpool.[18] How shabby & poverty looking the women are. Someway it seems as if all the old clothing of forty years ago has been kept in use in England. All patched & mended & ragged - still continues to be worn in Brymbo, Wales[19]...miles & miles of wandering roads winding & hard. Very few carts - & all very quiet.

I met Malatesta - small dark personage with splendid head & eyes, which look thru one. It must have been difficult for him to understand my English. He is a silent reticent one, with a feeling of suspicion hovering over him. How different from the Spanish Portet - full of vigor, confident - quick to understand.

In Liverpool, I went to hear a lecture on Nietzsche and was simply inspired & enthused. It was given by a young minister at the Unitarian Church on Hope St. The most splendid & understandable rendering of Nietzsche I ever heard.

In London to the British [Museum] each day. To the National Art

Gallery on Sunday, but so few pictures being exhibited closed off & stored away....

On the 10th I called at the Malthusian League Queen Anne's Chamber to see Dr. Drysdale. Mrs Drysdale was there - Dr. B. Dunlop - Mrs. Stella Brown & a few others. We had tea together & talked of this work & the consequences. Mrs. Drysdale is charming. It did seem to me I had known them both & seen them often –

No mail for nearly two weeks....I hope to get up a lecture on Individualism soon as soon as I get this next work off. A pamphlet.

What a queer thing is faith. To have faith in one. What does it mean - simply that that person shall remain stationary in a certain idea or thought or emotion - that he shall not progress further but remain stagnant in that one particular thing in which we have our faith.

How easily to upturn all these old words upon which so much false sentiment has been built.

It seems almost good to be alive. There is time to get acquainted with one's self, to reflect, to meditate, to dream. There is so little time these days for memories - it's a luxury to have time for anything but work.

Dec. 16th 1914. A very cordial letter from Mr. Havelock Ellis today inviting me to call. I look forward to it with interest.

A letter from Rob. J.R., Ethel & Chas.[20]

Ah, what a strange people inhibit this world. Think as I do and it is "good" but to differ is "wrong."

I have this day cast the dye. I have written Bill a letter ending a relationship of nearly over 12 years.

I cannot seem to write or think connectedly yet. However it will come later.

Dec. 17th. Last night I went to. . . Kingsway Hall   Emmeline Pankhurst was in the chair. Her tone was good. Her intellect clear & sensible. She reminded me of Charlotte Perkins Gilman. She seems like a good General & a maker of good generals. I wonder at her "patriotism" & have a sneaking suspicion it is a tactic rather than a feeling.

Such splendid looking girls in the making she has around her - faces bright, jaws well set, determined. Even the free stride many of them have in walking shows their trend of mind.

Many of them dainty of dress & frail of body, but nearly all I saw had conviction & courage & determination on their faces. Of course, Mrs. Pankhurst is their God but perhaps it is too early to take from them all things which give them support, but it will come later - if not this generation perhaps the next. Women & men must be a god unto themselves. They must cease worshipping at the shrine of other egos & look into their own and develop & nourish it.

In the afternoon I went to a lecture. . . where . . . Drysdale spoke on the cause of the War.

He spoke freely & full of his subject, laughs a great deal in his address, which is good. Proved the growing population of Germany demanding an outlet & the War had to come. Russia is the next to be feared, he said, & when the population begins to decrease, then & only then will there be signs of Internationalism. . . .

How lonely it all is. Could any prison be more isolated? Could one be more alone or more lonely in "solitary" than wandering about the world, separated from the little ones you love, from their childish prattle, caresses, whisperings & quarrels & also from the other ones & things & friends one has & one understands. It is not only the languages which separates "comrades"; it is psychology.

I live & long to get to hear a lecture on Nietzsche. I believe a message to the makers of his teachings is the next greatest step to take.

Yesterday I sent a letter to Bill S parting the ways of our life together. He will not be surprised. I know for the past year he has been prepared for it. Only I am very slow in my decisions. I can not separate myself from my past emotions quickly. All breeches [sic] must come gradually to me. It took me so long to get a Church out of my system. Then Socialism - likewise Society. etc. etc. So in everything.

Dec 22, 1914. Today I went to Brighton to call on Havelock Ellis. Tall, lovely, simple man with the most wonderful head & face & smile. He opened the door in answer to my knock. We had no difficulty in feeling comfortable. It was four o'clock, & he lighted two candles on the mantle. These threw a soft light on to his features, which gave him the look of a seer. We had tea, which he prepared & carried into the room, his workshop, where we sat by the open fire & talked.

Wonderful mind, with an easy, not in a hurry rush at all - such a relief to find.

It seems to be the men who do the most creative & productive work who are also the simplest & easiest to meet & understand.

He talked of the trial on his book Inversions & gave me a copy to read also. His copy of Karazza to take.[21] Thinks the method advised in Karazza splendid if man is able to do it. Spoke openly & freely on this subject, which was a relief.

There is a shyness & reticence about him of the student & the simplicity of a great soul & mind.

I count this a glorious day to have conversed with the one man who has done more than any one in this Century toward giving women & men a clear & sane understanding of their sex lives & of all life.

I am wondering what the kiddies are doing. It's early Christmas eve. I sit here alone by the dying fire & think of them and wonder & dream.

11. A European Education

When Margaret left America to flee to England, Stuart, her first born, turned eleven years old and was attending boarding school, Grant was six, and Peggy four and a half. Olive Byrne Richard, Ethel Higgins Byrne's daughter and Margaret's niece, recalls Margaret as being a loving but preoccupied mother "patting little children on the head in passing," and Margaret later admitted that she was not one to sew on missing buttons.[1]

Margaret had other forces tugging at her. In Hastings-on-Hudson, Sanger had had a life-changing experience, a great "awakening" she called it, which occurred on the very night she and Bill and Stuart moved into their house in Hastings that Bill had designed and built.[2] For weeks previously, Bill and Margaret had worked together leading a beautiful glass window— their "rose window," they called it. On the night they moved in, the rose window newly installed, the rooms no doubt still smelling of fresh paint, a fire broke out, and the rose window and part of the house were destroyed. Sanger afterward wrote that, curiously, as she watched this devastation,

> I was certain of a relief, of a burden lifted, a spirit set free....Somewhere in the back of my mind I saw the absurdity of placing all of one's hopes, all of one's efforts, involving as they did heartaches, debts, and worries, in the creation of something exter- nal that could perish irretrievably in the course of a few minutes. Subconsciously, I must have learned the lesson of the futility of material things. My scale of suburban values had been consumed by the flames, just as my precious rose window of leaded glass had been demolished.[3]

As her indifference to material things grew, Sanger became more ideal-istic, more driven, and ambitious (as noted, Peggy was only nine months old when Sanger's first article appeared in the *Call*), and though Sanger's health was never robust, her energy was extraordinary. She had grown up with a father who had enjoined her to leave the world better than she had found it.[4] Once she discovered Socialism and the unfairness of the world beyond Hastings, she became infused with a strong sense of mission and the need to assist the most vulnerable members of our society—impoverished women and children. Such a sense of mission leaves its possessor little incli-nation to dote on the tedium of domestic concerns.

At the same time, Sanger adored her children and, away from them in England, she missed them desperately. Her feelings are described in *My Fight for Birth Control*.

> My three children were to develop in divergent ways. Their child-hood years seemed to speed by, so swift was their growth. At the time of my great awakening they were just at the ages when they were most interesting and adorable—four, six and ten years. Owing to my own frail health I had spent much time with them planning their lives, reading and playing with each in his turn. They were all so individual, so different, that each was a study. Stuart, the oldest, was sturdy, active, athletic, reasoning, daring and logical. He seemed one who had been born into life to test and prove himself. Grant, the next child, five years younger than Stuart, was the artist type—loving, affectionate, original. He was the embodiment of a talent come to express itself. Peggy was the most independent child I ever knew, was positive, accurate, truthful, mischievous, laughing. She was born to do, to act, to lead. She had the qualities of a per-son of power even at the age of five. Peggy was blonde as Grant was dark, daring as he was cautious, leader as he was follower. They seemed to complement each other in every way. They spoke in terms of "we" always from the time Peggy talked at all.
>
> My life seemed to begin and end in their development and growth. My activities and interests and work outside seemed only for the purpose of completing and perfecting their lives. I was never slavishly domestic, but I was inclined to be slavishly maternal....
>
> [Spring of 1913] found me still seeking and more determined than ever to find out something about contraception and its mys-teries....Seek it I would. If it was in existence, it should be found, I would never give up until I had obtained it, nor stop until the work-ing women of my generation in the country of my birth were acquainted with its substance. I was so settled in this determination

that I ceased to worry further about the details of how this should be brought about. . . .

The effect of this conviction, however, began to have a tremendous bearing upon my personal life. My three lovely healthy children were full of life, vigor and happiness. They were glorious examples of wanted children, mentally and physically. Gradually, however, there came over me the feeling and dread that the road to my goal was to separate me from their lives, from their development, growth and happiness. The feeling grew stronger and stronger within me.[5]

Subsequent events confirmed Margaret's intuitive feelings. From faraway Spain, Margaret sent the affectionate letter below to Stuart. And what was Margaret doing in Spain? In the unpublished "Two Words" manuscript, she says that she went to France and Spain, "where I found out how the pioneers of the movement had combated superstition and prejudice of the type I must face on my return to America."[6] Perhaps. But the trip to Spain might be better explained by her acquaintance with Lorenzo Portet, whom she met in Liverpool shortly after arriving there.

Lorenzo Portet must have been a true soul mate. Sanger describes him in her 1931 autobiography in superlatives. He was by all accounts a fearless individual, "the biggest <u>mind</u> in Europe," a radical after her own heart, one who shared her deepest ideals, beliefs, and values. They shared, as well, many friends in the radical community.[7]

Portet had been a close associate of Francisco Ferrer, the very individual for whom the New York City Ferrer Center had been named. In retaliation for his attempts to lead the Spanish peasants out of the Middle Ages by educating them in modern ways, Ferrer was shot by the Spanish government. Portet immediately organized demonstrations that led to an international protest and so became himself well known. Ferrer had left his entire fortune to Portet that Portet might continue Ferrer's work of educating Spain. This, Portet was doing, establishing and running a publishing house in Barcelona for publication and distribution (read smuggling) of scientific literature from Italy, France, and England throughout Spain.

When Sanger met Portet, just after she arrived in Liverpool, he was teaching at the University of Liverpool. He and Sanger apparently enjoyed an immediate rapport. Sanger describes Portet as "a rare individual . . . an unusually brilliant companion, a loyal inspiring friend," a man of "fiery spirit."[8] Later, Portet offered Sanger a job in Paris as a translator, and in 1917, he was in Paris, awaiting Sanger. But World War I intervened, and before she could join him, he died, suddenly, in the summer, at the age of fifty-seven of tuberculosis.

But for the winter of 1915, Portet had received permission from the Spanish government allowing him a brief return, and Portet and Sanger traveled together to Spain. From Sanger's diary comes the glimpse of a happy, stimulating time for them both. Even while it was ongoing, however, the affair was bittersweet, for Sanger, as involved as she was in discovering her own life, in exploring an exciting love affair, was aware also that her children were in another's care.

The Manuscript

Though Margaret was a working mother away from her children during much of their growing up, Stuart always recalled with affection his mother's warmth and vivacity.[9] When his own two daughters were growing up, they lived in Tucson in a house next to that of their grandmother, whom they visited regularly, and which perhaps compensated for the many years Margaret missed in the lives of her own children.

My Darling Stuart[10]
March 29, 1915

Barcelona

My darling Stuart,

I have not heard from you for a long time. Did you ever get the dollar bill I sent you in a letter from England?

The nice box of writing paper you sent me for Christmas I want to thank you for it, dearest Sunny Jim.

Last Sunday I saw a bullfight. I'll send you a picture of one of them. They have them here in Spain every Sunday. The people go to Church in the morning and to the bullfight in the afternoon. Six bulls are killed during the spectacle, one after the other, and usually three horses to every bull. The men are not hurt at all. But you would not like it because it is not only cruel but it is not a good sport even. The men do not fight the bull at all, only tire it out with banners until it is nearly exhausted, then kill it with a sword.[11]

The people here always put off everything until later on. They are easy going in their living, but hot tempered and quick to love and hate. They are very very polite, but more than the French, but if you will take your geography you will see that the French are their nearest neighbors, and naturally people live more like their neighbors do.

I have not been to the South of Spain & can not go this time, but I hope the next time I come you will be able to come too & we will go South nearer to Africa. The Ferrer Schools are here & Francisco Ferrer lived here & began his schools here & was imprisoned here in a prison which stands high on a mountain fortress—the mountains & prison are called Monjuick. It is there where the Catholic Church has tortured the people of Spain—tortured them to death because they would not belong to the Catholic Church—& so with Ferrer he wanted to educate the children of Spain & teach them to believe in science & think for themselves & because of this he was shot. I went to his grave & tho't of you & was proud that my Stuart had attended the first Ferrer School in America.

There are so many beggars here & so many blind people here that it half spoils the beauty of the place.

Well my darling Lutey, tell me all that you are doing—

Ill give you my address in London & you can write to me directly.

This is Easter week—next Sunday being Easter. The people here make little trees of palms & hang colored balls & trinkets on the palm trees as we do on Christmas trees.

I expect to leave England for Canada or U.S.A. next month & shall hope that father can arrange for you Grant Peggy & I to camp near some Lake or river in Canada—we will have a nice summer.[12]

Give my love to Mrs. Winn & tell her I am going to answer her nice & kind letter very soon.[13] I am busy as can be. My love to you Sweetheart & a thousand kisses on the "nosey posey."

As ever
Mother

12. Death and Acclaim

Bill Sanger, having been found guilty of Comstock's charges, refused to pay the alternative of a fine and was completing his thirty-day jail sentence when, on October 6, 1915, Margaret sailed into the docks of New York City. Insofar as birth control was concerned, Margaret Sanger returned to a much different America than the one she had left a year before. During the twelve months that Margaret was away, public opinion on birth control had shifted markedly, in no little measure because of the strong support given it by Socialist women's groups and other women radicals.

Sanger's indictment in August 1914 had sparked immediate concern from the Progressives, bringing offers of help and support from all over the United States. Elizabeth Gurley Flynn in the Northwest, Eugene Debs nationally, and just about every liberal Socialist figure came forward to speak in Sanger's favor. Many in the radical community saw the importance of birth control to workers' lives and were distributing Sanger's pamphlets.[1] By 1915, a number of local birth control organizations had been established.[2]

The years immediately preceding World War I saw a shake-up in the basic belief systems of America, and the support of the radicals for birth control was but one flume in the onrushing surge of a changing national consciousness, part of an awakened morality and an increased awareness of individual rights that railed against poverty, encouraged the rise of unions, demanded prison reform, and spoke out for freedom of speech and civil liberties. Art and literature were being permeated by the modernism of Ibsen, which jostled the straitened prudery of those Victorians who would rather *not* discuss the evils of capitalism, sex, and women's rights. All these energies came together to catapult Sanger onto the stage of progress in the role of birth control pioneer.

Other events put Margaret and birth control in the public eye. Bill's trial in September had been dramatic and media worthy. Outrage at Comstock's sneaky behavior had drawn the radical community to fill the courtroom during Bill's trial, and disgust with the self-righteousness of the judge brought protests so boisterous that the courtroom was ordered to be cleared.[3] Meanwhile, the influential *New Republic* was backing birth control with its editorials, and in May of 1915, birth control supporters held a well-attended meeting at the New York Academy of Medicine.[4]

News about Margaret Sanger along with requests for funds to assist her were regularly published in *Mother Earth*, Emma Goldman's monthly journal, which was read not just by fellow anarchists, but by a broad and general audience. Goldman and her associates passed out Sanger's pamphlets and sold copies of *The Woman Rebel* at Goldman's lectures, sending Sanger all of the proceeds. After Sanger's indictment, Goldman increased her support of Sanger and the cause of birth control to both their advantage, for as Goldman wrote Sanger, "Not one of my lectures brings out such crowds as the one on the birth strike and it is the same with *Woman Rebel*. It sells better than anything else we have."[5]

By late 1915, public interest in birth control was no longer confined to liberals and leftists. Despite the entrenched conservatism of church and government and the disdain of the medical establishment, the middle and upper classes were coming out in favor of birth control or at least in favor of debating it heatedly. Birth control was a rousing cause célèbre, supported by more than just the radical community.

For instance, *Pictorial Review*, a beautifully typeset ladies' journal dedicated to current fashion and leisured women's concerns, held a "Birth-control Contest: The Most Remarkable Discussion Ever Held By Any Magazine." In the October 1915 issue had appeared letters from a man and a woman, both of whom had explained with reason and balance why limiting future offspring allowed them to care best for their respective families. The editors of *Pictorial Review* had invited future letters from its readers to be entered into a contest with prizes for the best. "Other contests brought forth letters by the hundred. The problem of birth-control brought forth its thousands," wrote the editors, justifying the importance of their current contest.

During this same time, the *New York Times* would not even print the words "prevention of conception"; that a popular magazine of the upper-middle class would print the words "birth control," discuss it, and hold a contest featuring it evidenced the extent of general public interest and acceptance.[6]

The middle and upper classes to which Sanger had been so indifferent during her *Woman Rebel* days were taking Sanger's cause seriously. On her return to America in October, Sanger's federal trial for those nine indictments had been rescheduled for January 18, 1916, and now those very women whom she had disregarded were arranging a fundraising dinner for her.

The dinner was held on the eve of her trial, on January 17, at the prestigious Hotel Brevoort, truly, in 1916, the "best" hotel in New York City.[7] Attendees included, among others, members of Heterodoxy, the educated socialist women's group which had earlier found Sanger too outspoken,[8] including the author Charlotte Perkins Gilman; Mary Ware Dennett, whose National Birth Control League had only a month earlier refused to help Sanger; and individuals from the most influential and esteemed ranks of society: lawyers, physicians, judges, and those in high places, men with degrees from Harvard, Yale, and Princeton and women who had graduated from Wellesley, Radcliffe, and Vassar.

It was a moment of triumph for Margaret Sanger, but during the time of this sudden acclaim came great heartbreak. Highly intuitive as she was, Sanger could not always understand the meaning of the feelings that came to her. She described some of what she had experienced while she was abroad:

In England I had a premonition——at first vague but gradually becoming more vivid. It was a vision barely conscious that came to me sometimes in my hours of sleep or when my mind was otherwise occupied. I can only explain this strange phenomenon by saying that through my mind there would flash a date—November 6. The "six" was larger than the month, a numeral like those on a large office calendar. I looked forward to that date sometimes with exultance—I was sure that on that day the case against me would be dropped. At other times, I was filled with terror at the prospect of that date. What would it bring?

I came back to America before then [on October 6]. Shortly afterwards, my little daughter Peggy became desperately ill. She rallied, seemed on the way to regain her childish health and spirits. There was another attack—inflammation of the heart. I fought to save her life. All other thoughts vanished from my mind in the long vigil at her bedside, the hopeless appeal to specialists, and then the blotting from my consciousness of everything except the heartbreaking struggle of this valiant little soul against death. I hardly knew when the end came, until the hospital nurse spoke to me and tried to lift me to my feet. Then I asked a strange question:

"What is the date today?"

"November sixth. Why do you ask?"[9]

It was a heartbreak Sanger never got over. In 1931, she wrote,

Deep in the hidden realms of my consciousness, Peggy has never died, but has continued to live; and in that strange mysterious place where reality and imagination meet, my little girl has grown up to womanhood. There she leads an ideal life untouched by harsh realities, immune to those influences which deform normal mortals.[10]

Sanger was returned to work by the thousands of letters she received from old subscribers to *The Woman Rebel,* many of those letters from women who, too, had lost children, and who recounted in their letters to Sanger their heartbreak. Their grief moved Sanger out of her own sorrow.

Inevitably, I was swept back in the battle....That grief ate inward, leading to the pit of melancholia. So that when I renewed my battle, it was not primarily to help other mothers as to save myself from lonely sorrow. For my sons were now away at school. My husband, after our long separation, was as passionately and devotedly interested in art as I was in the regeneration of the race through birth control. We had drifted apart; neither of us could possibly go back and resume a life of modest suburban domesticity. So that gradually our marriage, one might say, died of inanition, and finally a quiet divorce was arranged.

Meanwhile, those two little words, "Birth Control," had swept through the press from the Atlantic to the Pacific.[11]

The Manuscript

Despite the increased support and the widespread publicity that was now coming in, Sanger was hard pushed for hard cash. She needed money to live on and money for lawyers. In January, shortly before the fundraising dinner at the Brevoort, she sent out the fundraising letter that follows.

To my Friends and Comrades[12]
January 5, 1916

TO MY FRIENDS AND COMRADES:

I returned to this country on October 6th, four days before William Sanger was released from jail. On the sixth of November, my little daughter died from pneumonia.

A few days after my arrival, I informed the United States Attorney of my presence, asking him if the indictments issued against me a year ago were still pending, inasmuch as the issue on which I was indicted—birth control—has been so thoroughly discussed during the past year in the various journals and magazines throughout the United States, and also inasmuch as no editors or publishers have been indicted. He replied that the indictments were still pending. The case was called for trial at the end of December and postponed until January 4th. It is now set for Tuesday, January 18th, and will positively be tried on that date.

The opportunity was offered me to plead guilty, thereby ensuring my release after payment of a small fine. I refused to do this, because the whole issue is not one of a mistake, whereby getting into jail or keeping out of jail is of importance, but the issue involved is to raise the whole question of birth control out of the gutter of obscenity and into the light of human understanding.

The present indictments are based on twelve articles published in *The Woman Rebel*, eleven of which discuss birth control. The twelfth is a philosophic defense of assassination. My case differs from William Sanger's in this respect, that these indictments do not (in my opinion) violate the law. No question of distributing information in regard to the prevention of conception is at present involved.

I shall go into court on January 18th without an attorney, because I cannot find any lawyer whose mental attitude toward this case is right.

I appeal to you to give me your moral and financial support at this time. Write letters to Judge Clayton, of the United States District Court, Post Office Building, New York City, before whom the case is to be tried. Write letters to newspapers. Hold protest meetings and send resolutions to your Congressmen and to the President of the United States. Raise funds for publicity. Address all communications to me at 26 Post Avenue, New York City.

(Signed) Margaret Sanger
January 5, 1916.

13. Time in Prison

After being indicted in 1914 by the grand jury for publishing obsceni-ties, Margaret Sanger did not go to trial in 1916. The trial was post-poned so many times that the now well-known comment was made, "The Sanger case presented the anomaly of a prosecutor loath to prosecute and a defendant anxious to be tried."[1] Letters were written, including one sent to President Wilson from England signed by names as prestigious as those of H.G. Wells.[2] Important people in America raised their voices as well, and there was a strong and vocal consensus against continuing the per-secution of Margaret Sanger. Finally, on February 18, 1916, the government entered a *nolle prosequi* in the case, declaring that "the indictment was two years old and that Mrs. Sanger was not a disorderly person."[3]

Great rejoicing followed, her friends and family relieved that the danger had passed, Margaret jubilant because now she was free to go on with her work and to do so on the wave of unbridled media attention. Bill Sanger's dramatic trial; the groundswell of public interest; the heartbreaking death of five-and-a-half-year-old Peggy; the widely distributed and soulful photo of Sanger and her two young sons; the attention of the elite; the well-attended dinner at the prestigious Hotel Brevoort; the backing of Heterodoxy and of the National Birth Control League; and finally, the many trial postponements and the publicity that ensued—all this had been extremely newsworthy. Taking advantage of this valuable media attention, in early April of 1916, Sanger set out on a nearly four-month speaking tour of America.

Public speaking terrified her—the "dreadful task of speaking," she called it.[4] Despite her successful experience as a Socialist organizer speaking to large groups of women during the Paterson strike, Sanger "was still as terrified of speaking as in the beginning," and an approaching lecture left her distressed and depressed.[5]

Nevertheless, fortified by pure grim determination, on April 7, 1916, Sanger set out across the nation, leaving in her wake all kinds of reactions and plenty of controversy. While some excoriated her—"vile, obscene matter," "The barnyard morality of the Sanger woman should find few sympathizers in any decent community"—hundreds were turned away from her lectures. Others were politely shocked. Mrs. Herman Lindauer, chairman of the Reform Committee of the Chicago Women's Club, noted, "I examined some of her literature. It was too brutally frank for us. Mrs. Sanger is a splendid and admirable woman, but a little too strong for Chicago."[6]

Where she was not "too strong," Sanger left behind birth control leagues. Sanger visited more than nineteen cities and spoke to at least fifty-two audiences. She was forbidden to speak in Akron, Ohio; locked out of her theater in St. Louis; and arrested in Portland, Oregon. Regardless of the official constraints, she spoke everywhere to packed houses. By the time she returned to New York, she was a national celebrity and ready to set up the first of her envisioned string of birth control clinics.[7]

Every since my studies under Dr. Rutgers in The Hague, my ambition had been to inaugurate the first birth control clinic in America. I planned a clinic based on the model of the fifty-two highly successful clinics conducted throughout Holland under the supervision of Dr. Rutgers.

These Dutch clinics, which had been started as early as 1881 and which in 1898 had received a Royal Patent of public utility, had impressed me as the finest type of maternity centre and had proven their worth in reducing the rate of infantile mortality in Holland.

I began to look around, to search for suitable quarters in some poorer section, where I might help the less fortunate mothers and conduct the clinic without fear of being molested by enemies of the movement. I wished, if possible, to avoid publicity. Finally, in one of the congested outlying districts of Brooklyn, at 46 Amboy Street, Brownsville, I found a place that pleased me.

But I was without funds to finance this project. "The time is not ripe for such a step, even to test the constitutionality of the law," I was advised. Such an attitude always arouses my impatience and spurs me to immediate action; the time is always ripe to combat injustice. I have noticed that for those people who compromise by the excuse "The time is not yet ripe," the time never does arrive for decisive, courageous action!

"It will and must be done!" I retorted, refusing to admit that I lacked the two hundred dollars necessary to sign the lease, pay the first month's rent, to buy the proper equipment, and to engage competent assistants.

"I shan't give up the idea," I asserted stoutly. "I must go on believing in it and wait until the money comes."

That very day, a special delivery letter came to me. I opened it; and a check for $200 fluttered out. With it came a note explaining that it was a contribution voluntarily offered "to carry on your splendid work." Such inexplicable coincidences are perhaps the very things that make life so much stranger than fiction, where I understand they are frowned upon. It enabled me to open that clinic in Brownsville, and it had the most far reaching and unexpected consequences.[8]

Sanger's claim here that she wished to avoid publicity is at odds with the facts. She had always planned to challenge the government on this very issue of legalizing clinics to offer safe contraceptive advice. She was quoted in newspapers, during the summer and after her national lecture tour was over, as saying that she planned to open a clinic.[9] When she finally did open the Brownsville Clinic in Brooklyn on October 16, she wrote the newspapers and the police and alerted them to the opening. Naturally, she was shortly arrested. As she continues with her story,

We were discovered [sic] by the newspapers, and a few days later we were raided by the police. But this attempt at suppression proved a boomerang. As a protest against the arbitrary spirit in which she was sentenced to thirty days on Blackwell's Island, my sister [Ethel Byrne], a graduate nurse who had volunteered to help me, began her hunger and thirst strike. For eleven days the press reported her condition, and the public was aroused to a high pitch of indignation.[10] A protest meeting filled Carnegie Hall to the doors and resolutions passed calling upon the authorities to release the heroic prisoner.[11] At the end of eleven days, during which time the words Birth Control and all that they signified reverberated from coast to coast, Governor Whitman signed a pardon and ordered the immediate release of my sister.[12]

As the price of Ethel's pardon, Margaret promised Governor Charles Whitman of New York that Ethel would never again be involved in working for birth control. It took Ethel a full year to recover from her self-imposed hunger strike, and in her later years, Margaret became less than gracious in acknowledging Ethel's contribution.[13] Subsequently, Ethel became a highly respected professional anesthesiologist and a devout Communist, the latter causing a certain amount of trouble for her grandson, to whom she sent regular mailings of the *Daily Worker* while he was studying at, first, Andover, and later, Harvard. Margaret paid her own price for her choice of life as the rebel and reformer.

> Widely criticized as I was for our militant methods of agitation, for defying the police, choosing to go to prison rather than to compromise, fighting to prevent the police from taking my fingerprints, such agitation was the most effective way of making the American public conscious and aware of the inconsistency and the barbarism of laws that aimed to prevent open and serious discussion of a problem of vital importance to every living man, woman, and child.[14]
>
> Without this 'dramatization' of my campaign, public interest would have soon sunk back into apathy. There was an excitement and adventure in this agitation—the suspense and thrill of a profoundly moving play, as though one were being lifted out of the monotonous pace of everyday life into the pulsating rhythm of a great symphony. Yet as time passed, I discovered that I must pay the price for the exaltation of this great adventure. After being lifted to the crest of the wave, suddenly I would find myself plunged into the deepest disappointment. I suffered from continual calumny of those who denounced me, who ridiculed my efforts, or who cast aspersions on the sincerity of my motives.
>
> My soul was weary from this never-ending battle against misunderstanding, prejudice, superstition. At such times I asked myself whether the compensations were worth the heart-breaking sacrifices that life had exacted of me. Would it not have been better—so I queried myself over and over again—if I had remained satisfied with the tame homely pleasures of married life, closing my eyes to the miseries and tragedies of less fortunate mothers than myself, joining the usual bridge clubs, reading the latest novel or serial, going to the movies or an occasional theatre?[15]

But on January 29, 1917, these options were no longer available to Sanger. When, under pressure from her attorney, the judge offered to dismiss her case if she would promise to "behave" in the future, she responded, "I can't respect the law as it stands today."[16] This time, she was sentenced to thirty days in jail. After the publicity surrounding her sister Ethel's hunger strike (Ethel was also the first woman to be force-fed in the United States, much to the glee of the media), the state no doubt thought it wise to treat Sanger verrrrry gently. Thus, the immediate question when she arrived at the prison from one of Sanger's jail mates, "You'se eats, don't ou?" To which Sanger replied, "As long as the food is eatable."

Sanger was given a relatively comfortable situation at Queen's Prison, allowed to receive and to answer her mail and, as she herself noted, able to take advantage of the enforced seclusion and catch up on her correspondence. Her prison experience left her ever after supportive of prison reform, and it became the one reform other than birth control that she publicly espoused. She was, needless to say, a very happy woman upon her release.[17]

Queens Prison Diary[18]
1917

Feb. 8th, 1917. First Day. Queens County Penitentiary. Only a few minutes after the reporter left me at the workhouse - I was taken into the hospital or Doctor room to be examined & finger printed. I refused both.

Then taken back to Mother Slattery's room & all my possessions returned to me[19] - I was passed over to a woman & man placed into a wagon & driven some length down the Island in front of the Penitentiary. We then got on the boat & came to N.Y.C. 57 St. I think not a word as to where I was being taken - Alice in Wonderland I truly was.

After various changes on cars- came to Long Island City to Queens County Penitentiary Warden - a nice sympathetic chap - met me asked me about lunch & hoped I was not going on a hunger strike which I said no - not unless I was forced on one from bad food. Introduced a very motherly matronly woman to me & sent up some lunch.

Put me into cell 210, where Josephine Blank is also nearby in same corridor.

Josephine is a very interesting type - a half wild nature irritated by chains & bars. Naturally intuitive, high tempered & quick. Outspoken to an unpleasant degree at times.

Has no use for men or many women - but drinks a "bit" once in a while. A kind big hearted woman considered "off" but I think very intelligent.

Afternoon drags slowly - & supper bread & molasses & tea seemed tasteless - Locked in at 6 PM - lights out 9 o clock Other woman in corridor works for warden & only came in at 7 o clock So days alone with Josephine.

Wednesday. Cells open at 7, but bells rung at 6 o clock - breakfast oatmeal & salt milk & coffee - two slices bread (unbuttered) Cleaning cells - a walk in air. Talked with little colored girl "Liza" who knew of Mrs. Sanger & called out "You'se eats, don't ou?" dinner of stew & bread - afternoon four letters - called to Warden's room to be finger printed - told him I objected to being classed as a criminal. Supper of - tea bread stewed peaches.

Women like Warden McCann & matron[20] - Atmosphere here very different from Workhouse or Raymond St. Jail.[21] Women are not treated as well as men though - Not allowed papers - or to send out for anything which men are allowed - No visitors only two a month. All letters read going & coming which is an outrage.

Thursday. Hominy & coffee (no sugar ever) - walk - talked to semi-negro woman - dope field. Indefinite sentence. Horrible liberties a State takes with human lives - for a "crime" of drink - or dope which should be considered diseases– a court has a right to sentence her for one day to three years. Women look pathetically around the ground to see if the men prisoners have left stubs of cigarettes around – Tragic - to see human beings forced to so low a level. -

Some lovely looking girls here - dope mainly Dinner meat potatoes, corn meal pudding - No knives or forks & only one large spoon - Letter today & telegrams. Again question of fingerprints[22] -Warden very decent about it all. No visitors.

14. The First Birth Control Clinic

M argaret Sanger spent thirty days in jail for opening the Brownsville clinic in Brooklyn, but the victory was ultimately hers. Though the decision handed down by Judge Frederick E. Crane from the Court of Appeals in 1918 affirmed Sanger's guilt, it recognized the right of physicians to give contraceptive advice "for the cure or prevention of disease," with "disease" defined as that which caused pain or sickness. Under the Crane decision, with "disease" defined so loosely, physicians were now legally permitted to give information on contraception, which in turn meant that Sanger could open a birth control clinic—legally—if it were staffed by a physician.

The Manuscript

In this article below that Sanger wrote so many years after the 1916 Brownsville Clinic trial and which was published in February 1960 by *Together* magazine, Sanger recalls the events leading up to her jail sentence and the fortunate Crane decision. Sanger also mentions another piece of good fortune: the Committee of One Hundred. This committee had been put together by the liberal philanthropist Gertrude Pinchot, who brought the energy and monies of those in her select circle, including the Junior Leaguers and their ilk, to protest the Brownsville clinic arrests and to raise funds for Sanger and her cause. It was the Committee of One Hundred that had organized the highly publicized protest meeting that "filled Carnegie Hall to the doors" and that raised additional monies to support Ethel and Margaret during the Brownsville trial. Many of these same women of the committee had been involved in organizing the earlier fundraising dinner at the Hotel Brevoort.

In 1960, Sanger no longer mentions Ethel's hunger strike; Ethel had died in 1955. But Sanger's lively account below of the establishment of the first birth clinic and the courtroom scene that followed gives the reader good insight into the person that was Margaret Sanger and the times she survived.

Why I Went to Jail[1]
Together, February 1960

It was a crisp, bright morning on October 16, 1916, in Brooklyn, N.Y., that I opened the doors of the first birth control clinic in the United States. I believed then, and do today, that this was an event of social significance in the lives of American womanhood. Three years before, as a professional nurse, I had gone with a doctor on a call in New York's Lower East Side. I had watched a frail mother die from a self-induced abortion.[2] The doctor previously had refused to give her contraceptive information. The mother was one of a thousand such cases; in New York alone there were over 100,000 abortions a year.

That night I knew I could not go on merely nursing, allowing mothers to suffer and die. No matter what it might cost, I was resolved to do something to change the destiny of mothers, whose miseries were vast as the sky. It was at the beginning of my birth control crusade. Although the practical idea of giving contraceptive information in clinics set up for that purpose in Holland had met with governmental approval, the New York State Penal Code declared that only a physician could give birth control information to anyone—and only then to prevent or cure disease. Always this had been held to mean venereal disease.[3] I wanted the interpretation to be broad enough to protect women from ill health as the result of excessive child bearing and [for them] to have the right to control their own destinies.

As I was not a physician, I would have no legal protection whatsoever if I gave birth-control information to anyone. But I believed that if a woman must break the law to establish a right to voluntary motherhood, then the law must be broken.

I had been a nurse, and my birth-control studies in Holland, where clinics had been operated for 38 years, had qualified me to give contraceptive instruction. My sister, who was also a nurse, could assist me.

Dare I risk it?

I did.

As long as I had to violate the law anyhow, I concluded I might as well violate it on a grand scale by including poverty as a reason for giving contraceptive information. The selection of a suitable locality was of the greatest importance.

The Brownsville section of Brooklyn in 1916 was a hive of activity. Although dingy and squalid, it was crowded with hard-working men and women. An enthusiastic young worker in the cause came from Chicago to help me. Together we tramped the streets one dreary day in early fall, through a driving rainstorm, to find the best location at the cheapest terms. I stopped to inquire from an official of a free milk station about vacant stores.

"Don't come over here." "We don't want trouble." "Keep out." These and other pleasantries were hurled at me as I darted in and out of rooming houses asking advice, hoping for welcome.

Finally, at 46 Amboy Street, I found a friendly landlord, a Mr. Rabinowitz, who had two first-floor rooms vacant at $50 a month. This was all the money we had (sent from a friend in California) to finance the clinic.

We bought the necessary furniture as cheaply as we could. And Mr. Rabinowitz himself spent hours painting until the rooms were spotless and snow-white. "More hospital looking," he said.

We had printed about 5,000 handbills in English, Italian, and Yiddish. They read,

"Mothers! Can you afford to have a large family? Do you want any more children? If not, why do you have them?

"Do not kill, do not take life, but prevent. Safe, harmless information can be obtained of trained nurses at 46 Amboy Street, near Pitkin Avenue, Brooklyn.

"Tell your friends and neighbors. All mothers welcome."

With a small bundle of these notices, we fared forth each morning in a house-to-house canvass.

Would the people come? Nothing could have stopped them!

My colleague, looking out the window, called, "Do come outside and look." Halfway to the corner they stood in line, shawled, hatless, their red hands clasping the chapped smaller ones of their children.

All day long and far into the evening, in ever-increasing numbers they came, over 100 the opening day. Jews and Christians, Protestants and Roman Catholics alike, made their confessions to us.

Every day the little waiting room was crowded. The women came in pairs, with friends, married daughters, some with nursing babies clasped in their arms. Women came from the far end of Long Island, the press having spread the word, from Connecticut, Massachusetts, Pennsylvania, New Jersey. They came to learn the "secret" that was possessed by the rich and denied the poor.

My sister and I lectured to eight women at a time on the basic techniques of contraception, referring them to a druggist to purchase the necessary equipment. Records were meticulously kept. It was vital to have complete case histories if our work was to have scientific value. We also gave many of the women copies of *What Every Girl Should Know,* a brief booklet I had written earlier.

Tragic were the stories of the women. One woman told of her 15 children. Six were living. "I'm 37 years old. Look at me! I might be 50!" Then there was a reluctantly pregnant Jewish woman who, after bringing eight children to birth, had had two abortions and heaven knows how many miscarriages. Worn out, not only from housework but from making hats in a sweatshop, nervous beyond words, she cried morbidly, "If you don't help me, I'm going to chop up a glass and swallow it."

I comforted her the best I could, but there was nothing I would do to interrupt her pregnancy. We believed in birth control, not abortion.

But it was not altogether sad; we often were cheered by gayer visitors. The grocer's wife on the corner dropped in to wish us luck, and the jolly old German baker, whose wife gave out handbills to everybody passing the door, sent us doughnuts. Then Mrs. Rabinowitz would call to us, "If I bring some hot tea now, will you stop the people coming?" The postman delivering his 50 to 100 letters daily had his little pleasantry, "Farewell, ladies, hope I find you here tomorrow."

On the ninth day, a well-dressed, hard-faced woman pushed her way past the humble applicants, gave her name, flaunted a $2 bill, payment for *What Every Girl Should Know,* and demanded immediate attention. My colleague had a hunch she might be a detective and pinned the bill on the wall and wrote, "Received from Mrs. —— of the Police Department, as her contribution."

Hourly after that we expected trouble. It came the following afternoon at closing hour. The policewoman again pushed her way through the group of patiently waiting women and, striding into my room, snapped peremptorily, "You, Margaret Sanger, are under arrest."

Three plain-clothes men from the vice squad promptly appeared. They herded our women patients into patrol wagons as though they were the inmates of a brothel. Women began to cry; the infants in their arms began to cry. The clinic soon became a bedlam of screams. The raiders confiscated our 464 case histories, a highly unethical act since the reports were confidential intimacies. They also took our pamphlets.

It was half an hour before I could persuade the men to release the poor mothers, whom I assured the best I could that nothing would happen to them.

Newspapermen and photographers joined the throng. It was a neighborhood where a crowd collected by no more gesture than a tilt of the head skyward. This event brought masses of people into the streets.

I was white-hot with indignation and refused to ride in the Black Maria.[4] I insisted on walking the mile to the Raymond Street jail, marching ahead of the raiders, the crowds following.

I spent the night in jail in so filthy a cell I shall never forget it. The mattresses were spotted and smelly. I lay in my coat, struggling with roaches, crying out as a rat scuttled across the floor.

It was not until afternoon that my bail was arranged. As I emerged from the jail, I saw waiting in front the woman who had threatened to swallow the glass; she had been there all the time.

I went back at once to reopen the clinic, but Mr. Rabinowitz came running in to say he was sorry—the police had made him sign ejection papers on the ground that I was "maintaining a public nuisance." In Holland the clinics were called "public benefactions."

Again I was arrested. From the rear of the Black Maria, as we rattled away, I heard a scream. It came from a woman wheeling a baby carriage. She left it on the sidewalk and rushed through the crowd and cried, "Come back and save me!"

The crusade for birth control was actually under way—with jail terms and hunger strikes and also with popular demonstrations in our behalf. As I reached the depth of despair and public humiliation, something like a miracle occurred: Help and sympathy sprang up on all sides. Legal aid was proffered. Doctors now rallied to my aid. A group of sympathetic and wealthy women in New York promptly formed a Committee of One Hundred for our defense. Sympathizers even held a mass meeting in Carnegie Hall.

My trial began in Brooklyn on January 29, 1917. About 50 mothers, some equipped with food and pacifiers and extra diapers for their babies, came to court. Timid and distressed, they smiled and nodded, trying to reassure me. Mingled with them were the smartly dressed members of the Committee of 100.

It surprised me that the prosecution should be carried on so vehemently. To me, there seemed to be no argument at all; the last thing in my mind was to deny that I had given birth control advice. I had deliberately violated the letter of the law. But my lawyer, Jonah J. Goldstein, was trying to get me off with a suspended sentence.

One by one the Brownsville mothers took the stand. "Have you ever seen Mrs. Sanger before?" asked the District Attorney.

"Yes. At the cleenic."

"Why did you go there?"

"To have her stop the babies."

"Did you get this information?"

"Yes, dank you, I got it. It wass gut, too."

For days, the legal arguments went on. At last, one wintry day, Judge John J. Freschi banged his fist on the desk. "All we are concerned about is the statute," he exclaimed. "As long as it remains the law," he asked my attorney, "will this woman promise unqualifiedly to obey it?"

He turned to me, "What is your answer to this question, Mrs. Sanger? Yes, or no?"

The whole courtroom seemed to hold its breath.

I spoke out as emphatically as I could. "I cannot promise to obey a law I do not respect."

The tension broke. Women shouted and clapped. The judge demanded order. When it came, he announced, "The judgment of the court is that you be imprisoned for 30 days."

A single cry came from a woman in the corner. "Shame!" It was followed by a sharp rap of the gavel, and silence fell. The trial was over.

The next afternoon I was taken to the Queens County Penitentiary in Long Island City.

I can remember the inmates—pickpockets, prostitutes, thieves—somehow they had heard about me and the birth control movement. One asked me to explain to them about "sex hygiene." When I asked for permission to do so, the matron said, "Ah, gawn wid ye. They know bad enough already."

But I persisted and got my way. I also taught some of the girls to read and write letters. And I kept up with my own writing, planning ahead the birth control movement.

The next step? To appeal to the highest court possible.

I was released on March 6. No other experience in my life has been more thrilling than that release. When I stepped through the big steel-barred doorway that gray day, the tingling air of outdoors rushed against my face. In front of me stood my attorney, my friends, and co-workers; their voices lifted in the martial strains of *La Marseillaise*. And behind, from the windows of the penitentiary, were the faces of newly made friends, and they, too, were singing for me.

The case of the Brownsville birth control clinic began its journey through the courts. It was on January 8, 1918, that the momentous decision came. The New York Court of Appeals sustained my conviction, but Judge Frederick E. Crane's liberal interpretation of the law had the effect of permitting physicians to give contraceptive information to a married person for "health reasons." "Disease" was now to include everything in the broad definition of *Webster's International Dictionary*, not just venereal disease, which had been the original understanding.

This opened the clinics, as well as the doctors' offices, to women for birth control advice throughout the United States

PART II:
THE REFORMER

PART II THE REFORMER
15. Introduction to the Reformer

hirty days in the Queens County jail gave Sanger "a quiet time for reflection," a time to plan carefully how best to advance the cause of birth control.[1] Out of that quiet reflection was born the more adroit reformer, whose future strategies for advancing birth control would have the support of the middle and upper classes.[2]

For Sanger, now coming into her own sophisticated maturity and wit, was in the right place at the right time. Despite unrelenting opposition from the Roman Catholic hierarchy, from self-righteous Protestants, and from the most conservative elements of the governing and governed, American society at the beginning of the twentieth century was rejecting Victorian mores and its hypocritical attitudes toward sexuality and normal human expression. True, such sentiments as "A woman has the right to be the help-mate of man. That is all the right she has. That is enough," continued to be aired.[3] But the woman suffrage movement and the many progressive reforms of the first two decades of the twentieth century had worked a leavening and liberating influence.

Sanger's experience with *The Woman Rebel*, her contacts in England with the sophisticated Drysdales and the scholarly Havelock Ellis, and finally, her capacity to learn from experience and from others was to serve her well.[4] In the past, many in the radical community had supported the cause of birth control, but neither the radicals nor the newly involved upper classes nor the poor mothers who so desperately needed contraceptive information would take direct action and challenge the status quo. Even as she herself began to follow a less confrontational course, Sanger could never quite understand the conservative attitude of her supporters, who in all other ways appeared so zealous.

The disappointment of my life was the lack of action on the part of the women in New York, who, unlike the suffragists of England, sat with folded hands and stood aloof from the struggle for woman's freedom. Many of them had been interested enough to attend the trial, but there their interest ended. I really expected an active follow-up. I hoped to see those women who themselves had gained the knowledge of contraception, had benefited and developed thereby, to stand behind me, to re-open the Brownsville clinic, to undergo arrest, and if necessary go to jail. I expected a rise of indignation and protest such as the English women had voiced in going to jail and enduring days of hunger. Nothing of that kind happened. American women were not going to use direct action, nor were they going to put themselves on record in approving ideas at this controversial stage.[5]

Nor was Sanger convinced in 1917 that going through the courts would further the cause of birth control. From prison, she wrote to Ethel, who was home and still recuperating from her hunger strike and forced prison feedings:

> The whole law business makes me convinced how foolish one is to put any hopes in it. But we have given it a trial. It is true that the fashionable seem far removed from the cause and its necessity—but we can not doubt that *they* & and they alone dominate when they get an interest in a thing. So little can be done without them.[6]

If "The Fashionable" would not take direct action, they did take an interest. The protest rally organized by Gertrude Pinchot's Committee of 100 at Carnegie Hall had in one night drawn an audience of three thousand and netted $1,000. With the help of the radical community had come limited financial support and marginal public acceptance, but with the favor of The Fashionable came abundant financial support and a platform for public discussion. This then was the answer to the pressing problem of how best to advance the birth control movement. As Sanger put it,

> The answer was to make the club women, the women of wealth and intelligence, use their power and money and influence to obtain freedom and knowledge for the women of the poor. These laws must be changed. The women of leisure must listen. The women of wealth must give. The women of influence must protest. Together they must bring about a change of laws and convert public opinion to the belief that motherhood should be conscious and volitional. This, then, was the new plan I was to act upon.[7]

Acting on this plan also brought lifelong personal friendships. One of the most cherished was that with Juliet Rublee, wife of George Rublee, a Harvard lawyer and Wilson cabinet appointee on the Federal Trade Commission.[8] Juliet Rublee had money of her own. She believed whole-heartedly in birth control, in all that Sanger was doing, and during the twenties (before she lost a good part of her fortune in a moviemaking attempt), she often eased Sanger's financial struggles with generous gifts. Juliet and Margaret had similar values and similar spiritual beliefs, and they enjoyed many good times together.

But that was for the future. Sitting in prison in February 1917, Sanger reflected on the potential of these new contacts and laid out for herself the steps with which to proceed in her reform campaign to make contraception legal and available to American women. The steps, as she wrote in her 1931 *My Fight for Birth Control*, were four: "agitation, education, organization, and legislation."[9] The agitation of the rebel was—for the most part—behind her. Now she would become the mainstream reformer and pursue the steps of education, by publishing the *Birth Control Review*; of organization, by forming the American Birth Control League; and of legislation, by implementing the National Committee on Federal Legislation for Birth Control. But if these steps were easily laid out, the early years of initiating them were dispiriting. Sanger recalled those times:

> The years from the termination of my prison sentence in 1917 to 1921 were leaden years. Years of constant labor, financial worry, combating of opposition, besides battling with a now awakened tuberculosis, which had gained in ascendancy during my thirty days in the penitentiary.[10]

Years of constant labor indeed! Within those few early years Sanger founded the *Birth Control Review*; edited, wrote for, and kept the *Review* going in the face of the theft of all its records and funds; wrote *The Case for Birth Control, Woman and the New Race,* and *The Pivot of Civilization*; traveled twice to Europe (before the days of the Concorde); scoured postwar Germany for a contraceptive jelly rumored to be highly effective; responded to thousands of letters generated by an awakened public; made sometimes daily or twice daily lectures to small and large groups; attended innumerable meetings and conferences; engaged in public debates; dealt with an ongoing barrage of publicity, often negative, along with arrests and harassment of her workers by the police; and finally, organized for the cause the 1921 First American Birth Control Conference featuring speakers of international renown—all this interspersed with ongoing bouts of ill health and three operations.[11] All this without any dependable means of financial support, looking to lecture fees, *Review* subscriptions, and the variable largess of the club women whose favor she was currying as much for their political as for their financial support to cover the costs of office space, publicity expenses, and publishing of the *Review*.[12]

This nonstop activity, whose intensity can only be hinted at in this brief summary, continued throughout the two decades that led up to World War II. And such decades they were for Margaret Sanger. In 1922, she married Noah Slee, a self-made millionaire, who held a seat on the New York Stock Exchange and who devoted both his energies and a considerable amount of his fortune to the birth control movement. Moving now in thoroughly respectable circles, in 1923, Sanger founded the Clinical Research Bureau; in 1925 she organized the Sixth International Birth Control Conference, also in New York City; in 1927, the First World Population Conference in Geneva. In 1930, Sanger set up, in London, the Birth Control International Information Centre, a concrete step toward her dream of an international birth control organization. In the summer of 1930, the Seventh International Birth Control Conference, dedicated to the discussion of contraceptive techniques, was held in Zurich, funded by a loan that she personally guaranteed.

Meanwhile, in 1929 she had planted in Washington, D.C., the National Committee on Federal Legislation for Birth Control, designed to see through Congress legislation that made birth control legal. For seven years, she kept that effort rolling. And while that effort came to naught—timid congressmen, under the control of the Catholic Church and conservative constituents, could scarcely bring themselves to discuss birth control yet alone to pass its legislation—the One Package decision of 1936, which permitted physicians to send contraceptives through the U.S. mails, did make contraception *de facto*, if not *de jure*, available.[13]

Throughout the thirties, birth control was finding increasing acceptance, and Sanger's national fame, firmly in place since her first United States lecture tour of 1916, became firmly international. Her first trip to England in 1914 had been followed by many return trips. In 1922 she visited Japan on invitation, and from there, she went on a five-month mostly Eastern world tour, covering China, Korea, Singapore, Egypt, Ceylon, and Yemen. In 1934, she visited the Soviet Union. In 1935-36, she made a 10,000-mile tour of India, conferred with Gandhi in a highly publicized visit, and then continued on to China, Burma, Malay, Japan, Hawaii, Canada and the US West. Sanger was a ceaseless traveler, crisscrossing the world and the United States nonstop, lecturing, talking, advising, being interviewed—educating and promoting birth control—wherever she appeared, her very appearance invoking publicity of one sort or another for the movement, whether being banned from Rome, as she was in August 1932, or idolized and feted in Japan, as she was on all her visits there in the very face of the militarists.

Agitation, education, organization, legislation: The steps fell out as she had planned, with a little additional agitation interspersed. Under the tutelage of Ellis and the politic Drysdales, she had recognized that the agitation of *The Woman Rebel,* confrontation and lawbreaking, was not appropriate for the long term—or only occasionally appropriate. "I might have taken up a policy of safety, sanity, and conservatism—but would I have got a hearing?" Sanger asked.[14]

Along the way, she faced the unrelenting opposition of one of the richest and most powerful governmental bodies in the world: the rulers of the Roman Catholic Church. Wisely, Sanger never underestimated her opponents. "They would have burned us at the stake," she observed.[15] In dealing with the underhanded shenanigans of the Catholic Church hierarchy, Sanger did not hesitate to revert to what might be termed agitation. In 1921, when the church highhandedly ordered the New York Police Department to shut out the audience from the paid-for Town Hall—where the closing meeting of the First American Birth Control Conference was being held— and when in 1929 the New York Catholic diocese arranged for a raid on the Birth Control Clinical Research Bureau, the church got full payback. Sanger's response to its harassment was agitation turned so forcibly against it—lawsuits, investigations, and publicity—bringing the church such opprobrium and the cause of birth control such-abundant publicity from both the general public and the professional medical community that Sanger delightedly declared, "It was the best thing that could have happened."

For women all over the world, Sanger's two decades of reform were the best thing that could have happened to them. By forcing public attention on a matter that so engaged women, Sanger stimulated their activism, demand ing that women participate in the political arena. Sanger suggested a sisterhood, one that certainly encouraged for some a "Lady Bountiful" syndrome, but at the same time, one that required women to look beyond the home circle, to involve themselves and to develop volunteer and grass roots organizations, educating and preparing themselves and future generations of women for more aggressive political involvement. Contraception and by extension women's needs at the beginning of the twentieth century were considered a banal subject and beneath the dignity of the medical profession. At the goading of Sanger, contraception became a subject of serious medical consideration, eventually recognized as deserving government support for reaching marginalized populations of women.[16]

Most importantly, Sanger quashed nineteenth-century ideas and articulated the principles of self-worth that women today can accept as their right and due: that a woman has a right to the control of her own body, that a woman has a right to the use of contraception, a right to decide when and if she wants a child, and that she has a right to sexual pleasure. Through her ceaseless work, her self-promotion, and her one-pointed focus, Margaret Sanger created the platform for advertising and spreading that legacy. Today in the beginning of the twenty-first century, in support of these rights exist the Planned Parenthood "string of clinics," clinics open to all women at all income levels, modeled on those Sanger visited in Holland in 1915. Responsible health care for women, respect for women and for women's bodies live today as the legacy envisioned and spearheaded by Margaret Sanger as the Reformer.

PART II THE REFORMER
16. The *Birth Control Review*

S anger was just beginning her thirty-day jail sentence in Queens County Penitentiary when the first copy of the *Birth Control Review* appeared in February 1917. It had been prepared beforehand in the event of just such a contingency, and it cost fifteen cents a copy or a dollar a year. "It was," Sanger admitted, "not a very good magazine then."[1] But if the first number was one Sanger felt she had to apologize for, the news in that February issue was juicy, with poignant sketches by Bill Sanger and full coverage of the infamous treatment Ethel received when she was force-fed during her hunger strike.

Sanger considered the *Birth Control Review* "the spearhead in the educational stage" of her plan to advance the birth control movement, and from its inception, the *Review* was reaching audiences that Sanger could not reach personally, no matter how many lectures she gave, and reaching them repeatedly. Repeatedly, but for the first year not necessarily regularly. The *Review*, which had been advertised as a monthly publication, numbered only five issues in 1917 and only reached its promised number of the twelve, for which subscriptions had been sold, in August 1918, because of a strange dispute with the original manager of the *Review*, one Frederick Blossom.

Sanger had met the charming and enthusiastic Blossom in Detroit during her first national lecture tour in 1916. Blossom had loaned Sanger the money for startup of the *Birth Control Review*, and Sanger was happy to turn over to Blossom the organization details of magazine publication.[2] But for reasons known only to him, Blossom took the money designated to cover publication of the first year's twelve issues and put it all into publishing the first three issues. There was also a disagreement over policy (Sanger was a pacifist; Blossom an ardent Francophile), and about this time Blossom's

93

wealthy wife divorced him.[3] One morning Sanger and her secretary walked into what had been an office complete with records, furnishings, and furniture to find only a lone telephone sitting on a packing box.[4]

Sanger relates this history in the August 1918 *Review* on the occasion of publication of that promised twelfth issue, by which time, almost a year later, she was recovered from the devastation that Blossom had wrought.[5] In pursuing from Blossom a return of the office records and an accounting of journal funds, Sanger went for resolution to the Socialist Party, in which Blossom now claimed membership. The Socialists promptly took Blossom to their bosom and censured Sanger. Sanger was, after all, consorting with the enemy—receiving funds and moral support from the capitalists, from fashionable Manhattan socialites. The Socialist censure had unforeseen and, ultimately, for Sanger, fortunate consequences, for their rejection of Sanger ended once and for all Sanger's close dependence on leftist groups, this coming at a time when wartime jingoism and the subsequent Red Scare of 1919–1920 made such an association disastrous for a budding organization, certainly precluding any general public acceptance.

Abandonment by the Left was offset by Sanger's many newly developing friendships among The Fashionable, who brought with them solid financial backing for the *Review*. In 1918, Juliet Rublee headed the move to incorporate the New York Women's Publishing Company. The corporation took on the task of publishing the *Review*—or to put it more accurately— the task of funding the publishing of the *Review*. Although Sanger's financial worries were far from over, the formation of the New York Women's Publishing Company assured Sanger of a voice for her movement and financial support for the educational component of her plan.

With an article of hers appearing in almost every *Review* number during those first early "leaden" years, Sanger must have been fearfully busy, particularly when the writing was combined with her many other projects.[6] Without question, the *Review* served as an important forum for circulation of Sanger's ideas. "Dedicated to the Principle of Intelligent and Voluntary Motherhood," the *Review*, as noted, was able to present Sanger's version of the events of her trial, elaborate on Ethel Byrne's hunger strike and abuses by the prison authorities (though this was being thoroughly and happily covered by the general media), and keep supporters informed of any groundbreaking developments the media might miss.

In the *Review*, Sanger made sure that readers were regularly reminded of the ills that uninformed mothers bore. Letters from poor women burdened with poverty and illnesses, letters telling of sick and out-of-work husbands and malnourished children too numerous to be cared for came pouring into the office of the *Review*, and those letters depicting the most heartbreaking conditions were published.[7] Journalistic accounts of these mothers and searing fiction that had a real life basis were also featured. News of birth control leagues and the formation of new leagues (the number of leagues increased from 20 to 24 within the first two issues) was given. And regularly the *Review* ran articles on overpopulation, on the pressures and evils wrought by overpopulation, and on the contribution of overpopulation to war. The *Review* was the obvious place for advertising Sanger's several books as they were released during the twenties, for announcement of her self-promoting movie that was killed by the censors, for news on upcoming conferences and meetings—and news of new government insults.[8]

Even as wartime government repression intensified—reinforced by the Sedition Act of 1918 and the Espionage Act of 1917, threatening anyone criticizing the government with fines, imprisonment, or deportation— Sanger continued to make the *Birth Control Review* a forum for liberal ideas.[9] In the *Review*, she spoke out for Bill Haywood, protested the incarceration of Eugene Debs, the shutdown of *The Masses,* and ran antiwar cartoons.[10]

Sanger could proudly call readers' attention to emerging support for birth control by notables. From England came the good news that W. R. Inge, dean of St. Paul's, London, supported birth control; a strong article by him appeared in the January 1922 issue.[11] The bishop of Birmingham came out for birth control.[12] A two-page headline in twenty-four point type celebrated the endorsement of Dr. C. Killick Millard, listing all of his many affiliations: medical officer of health and chief administrative tuberculosis officer for Leicester, Medical superintendent of the Borough Hospital and Sanitorium, medical officer to the Municipal Infants' Milk Depot, vice chairman of the Leicester Health Society, and president of Leicester Literary and Philosophical Society.[13]

The *Review* had no shortage of other well-known contributors, and authors included such illustrious names as H. G. Wells, Havelock Ellis, C. V. Drysdale, Charlotte Perkins Gilman, Ellen Key, and Olive Schreiner, along with Sanger's personal associates, Walter Roberts, Anita Block, and Harold Hersey. The *Review* also had the financial advantage of regular full-page advertisements from Noah Slee's Three-in-One Oil Company.

The Manuscript

As noted, in her first autobiography, *My Fight for Birth Control*, Sanger had listed agitation as the first step of her plan for advancing the birth control movement. In her later *Autobiography*, she would carefully claim not agitation but "education" as the desirable first step.[14] But agitation and education often ran neck to neck in Sanger's promotional efforts. So it seems completely in character that Sanger, even while she, for the most part, with the publication of the *Review* and under the influence of the Drysdales had broken with the agitation approach identified with *The Women Rebel*—even so, it does not seem surprising that she would revert just a tiny bit and would include in the first number of her new journal a rebellious, feisty demand for direct action—an agitating call to break the law.

Shall We Break This Law?
Birth Control Review, February 1917

All our liberties are due to those who, when their conscience has compelled them, have broken the law of the land.—Dr. Clifford.

If some disease were found to be undermining the health and destroying the vitality of the women of the United States, I think it is safe to say that the manhood of the whole country would rise up and strive to abolish the plague.

And yet the men of this land are today shielding and fostering just such a disease—a disease which sends mothers to an early grave, condemns wives to ill-health and invalidism, causes children to be born feeble in mind and body, and crushes strong men under the weight of a burden they never asked to carry; a disease which eats into the very vitals of family life, tearing husband and wife asunder, crowding the divorce courts, depriving children of a mother's care, and robbing maternity of its keenest joys; a disease which brings in its wake poverty, unemployment, child labor, prostitution, war; a disease sprung from ignorance of the means of preventing conception, an ignorance enforced by a law so vicious, so arrogant, so inhuman that thousands of earnest men and women are today asking themselves: "Shall we obey this law?"

No law is too sacred to break! Throughout all the ages, the beacon lights of human progress have been lit by the law-breaker. Moses, the deliverer, was a law-breaker. Christ, the carpenter, was a law-breaker, and his early followers practiced their religion in defiance of the law of their time. Joan of Arc was a law-breaker. So, too, were George Washington and the heroes of the American Revolution and, in more recent times, John Brown of Ossawatomie, Henry D. Thoreau, William Lloyd Garrison, Wendell Phillips, Theodore Parker, and many more whose sturdy refusal to respect an inhuman law helped to emancipate a race and set free the chattel slaves of the Old South.

The law today is absolute and inexorable—it has even set itself above Justice, whose instrument it was intended to be.

In earliest times, there was no elaborate code of law; there was but a simple idea of justice. As the race moved forward, its conception of justice kept pace with the changing standards and customs of the times.

As society became more complex, a caste arose whose duty it was to administer justice. In the course of time, however, the law grew up out of their decisions and accumulated a stolid mass of outworn tradition, until today legality has become so encumbered with lifeless relics of the past that the courts no longer express living social standards and the ideal of Justice, but merely the dead weight of legal precedents and obsolete decisions, hoary with age.

The whole function of Justice has become petrified and encrusted with the barnacles of antiquated tradition. The people's will has been diverted into blind channels leading always further and further away from the fundamental principle *that the will of the people is the supreme law.*

Civilization is dynamic; our judicial system is static. The race has progressed, but the law has remained stationary—a senseless, stumbling block in the pathway of humanity, a self-perpetuating institution, dead to the vital needs of the people.

Humanity and justice have been displaced by a legal despotism, the chief concern of which is the protection of established interests.

Woman has always been the chief sufferer under this merciless machinery of the statutory law. Humbly she has borne the weight of man-made laws, surrendering to their tyranny even her right over her own body. For centuries she has been the helpless victim of excessive child-bearing. Meekly she has submitted to undesired motherhood.

Incoherently she has spoken in the past. Her protests have been in vain. Her supplications have fallen on the deaf ear of the administrator of law. Her petitions have lain unheeded under the cold eye of the legislator, caught in the network and quagmire of politics.

Against the State, against the Church, against the silence of the medical profession, against the whole machinery of dead institutions of the past, the woman of today arises.

She no longer pleads. She no longer implores. She no longer petitions. She is here to assert herself, to take back those rights that were formerly hers and hers alone.

If she must break the law to establish her right to voluntary motherhood, *then the law shall be broken.*

17. World War I

For months following 1916 as Germany was taking over Belgium and threatening Europe, she played a cat-and-mouse game with America, sinking American ships with efficient submarine attacks, then quickly apologizing, thereby allowing President Wilson to maintain his pledge of American neutrality. In those prewar years, even in the face of such insults and as Europe was being ravaged, America had little interest in going to war. Americans had elected Wilson president on his promise to keep them out of war, and Americans generally espoused pacifism, confirming their sentiments with large pacifist demonstrations. At the beginning of 1917, the major labor unions strongly opposed the war, and preparedness parades were met with strong opposition.[1]

But in January 1917, Germany resumed her all-out submarine attacks, and on April 2, 1917, two months after the first appearance of the *Birth Control Review*, the United States declared war on Germany. In the face of entrenched opposition from what seemed to be half the country, Wilson pushed through Congress draconian laws—including the Espionage and Sedition Acts of 1917 and 1918, respectively—that would tolerate no criticism whatsoever of the government, its actions, or its officials, The right to freedom of speech insofar as anti-government rhetoric was concerned had ended. A Committee on Public Information, in reality a committee for pro-government propaganda, was set up that whipped the United States into a state of ultrapatriotism and jingoism.

Suddenly, in a country much settled by German immigrants, with vital German-speaking communities and hundreds of German-language newspapers in circulation, the German language was outlawed and all things German refuted. German sauerkraut was renamed "Liberty Cabbage," and law-abiding citizens with German names were placed under house arrest, beaten, tarred and feathered, even lynched by paranoid police departments or spontaneously emergent vigilante committees. Labor strikes were blamed on German agents, and strikers, whatever their nationality, were branded as unpatriotic. In this political climate of repression, a demand for workers' rights fell into the category of antiwar rhetoric, while at the same time any remnant of progressive or radical activity vanished. On every side, the most extreme conservatism seized the day. Through severe restriction on civil liberties along with extraordinary volunteer activity, egged on by government propaganda, the United States became a formidable war machine, productive and efficient, bringing into Europe the fresh reserves that routed the Germans and ended World War I.[2] But the armistice did not restore civil liberties to Americans.

The armistice of November 11, 1918, was followed in March 1919 by the founding of Lenin's Third International Government in Moscow, which in turn incited communist uprisings in Europe and, in the United States, fear of a possible communist takeover. When the postwar American economy was shaken by a series of strikes, they were attributed to the Communists. Riding on the Red Scare paranoia, Attorney General Mitchell Palmer in January 1920 conducted his infamous Palmer Raids, rounding up in a single night six thousand "reds," who were then jailed and readied to be deported.[3] It was not a good time to be or to have been a radical.[4]

As the political climate of repression mounted, Sanger saw her former friends and associates victimized. Eugene Debs had been practically a folk hero to Americans, but when he spoke out against the war, he was sentenced to prison for ten years. Bill Haywood, though the evidence given at his trial showed no evidence of lawbreaking, was sentenced to twenty.[5] Elizabeth Gurley Flynn and Carlo Tresca were indicted and, though never incarcerated, kept under permanent surveillance. Sanger was also under surveillance, but was never arrested, possibly because she was associating more and more with the "right" people in uptown Manhattan, possibly because the government feared giving birth control more publicity in the event of an arrest.[6] Sanger had her own wartime plans, as Harold Hersey wrote, recalling a visit he made her in his new uniform, shortly after his enlistment.

> "I don't know what to say about your entrance into the army," she said quietly. "You are the first man in uniform to enter my house. I'm against all war, just as my father is—just as all my friends and associates are—but if I take a stand against it, become an active pacifist, the Birth Control movement will suffer. I cannot let this happen just as I have gotten order out of chaos. The other pioneers

have all made the same mistake: they have not concentrated on the one object to the exclusion of everything else. Their work was important, but their sacrifices were in vain. I am determined to bide my time, consolidate my forces, continue my studies, my lectures, my letters to the countless women who are writing me every week, and the publication of the *Birth Control Review*, until this madness is ended and one can think and work with the hope that something may be accomplished."[7]

Sanger did, indeed, bide her time. During the war, she did just as she said she would: delivered countless lectures, wrote countless letters, published the *Birth Control Review*, while enduring bouts of illness. As postwar America moved into an unsettled economy, with massive strikes and fears of communist takeovers occupying public attention, Sanger was also writing *Woman and the New Race*. It would be an antiwar book, not in an obvious, but in a very fundamental way.

Meanwhile, the *Birth Control Review* was twice censored, its mailing held up without explanation. In the September 1918 issue, a line in German, "Verboten! Verboten! Verboten!" on page ten may have been the cause—or the article titled "Birth Control: The Cure for War." In the August 1918 issue, a review of *Married Love* by Marie Stopes clearly provoked censorship.

The Manuscript

In the *Birth Control Review* of June 1917 appeared the frankly antiwar essay below—an essay that brings a seldom-heard woman's perspective on war. By printing it, Sanger may have been flirting with real danger. On the morning of June 15, 1917, the Espionage Act was signed. In the afternoon, Emma Goldman was arrested and jailed—she had been leading large anti-conscription (i.e., antidraft) demonstrations. Two years later, in December 1919 during the Red Scare, Goldman and her longtime pal, Alexander Berkman, were permanently deported.

"Woman and War"
Birth Control Review, June 1917

Realization of the world tragedy—war—has at last been forced upon the American people. Two years ago the fiendish internecine strife of the militarists of Europe seemed remote enough. Today our women of the working class find themselves facing an outrage unparalleled in the history of this republic. Their husbands, sons, and brothers are to be herded to the front as conscript fighters, in violation of every human instinct fostered in them by the great libertarians who founded this country.

America's participation in the war has been brought about by interested groups, not in response to the will of the majority. Not fifty per cent of the men could have been induced to vote "Yes" in a war referendum, not five per cent of the women. In Australia, a colony of the British Empire, where democracy was respected to the extent of submitting the question to a referendum, the votes of the women defeated conscription overwhelmingly.

Woman hates war. Her instincts are fundamentally creative, not destructive. But her sex-bondage has made her the dumb instrument of the monster she detests. For centuries she has populated the earth in ignorance and without restraint, in vast numbers and with staggering rapidity. She has become not the mother of a nobler race, but a mere breeding machine grinding out a humanity, which fills insane asylums, almshouses, and sweatshops, and provides cannon fodder that tyrants may rise to power on the sacrifice of her offspring.

Too long has she been called the gentler and weaker half of humankind; too long has she silently borne the brunt of unwilling motherhood; too long has she been the stepping-stone of oligarchies, kingdoms, and so-called democracies; too long have they thrived on her enslavement. Had she not been so submissive and inarticulate, the present war could not have been imposed upon the workers; for there would not have been the big battalions of superfluous humanity to be moved about like pawns on a chessboard.

The great horde of the unwanted has proved to be a spineless mass, which did not have the courage to control its own destiny. Had woman had knowledge of birth control and brought into the world only such offspring as she desired and was physically and spiritually prepared to receive, society would have been far too individualistic to tolerate wholesale massacre for the benefit of money kings. Under such an order, the child would have been considered a priceless gift to the community. Manhood would have been too valuable to be sacrificed on battlefields. Motherhood would have been revered, and the mother's voice raised to forbid the slaughter of her offspring would have been heeded.

But unfortunately the forces of oppression have cared nothing for the poignant grief of exploited motherhood. They have turned in callous indifference from her tears, while her flesh and blood have reddened every battlefield in history. There are statues in plenty to kings, statesmen, and generals who have driven her sons to the universal shambles of slaughter. But where are the statues to Motherhood?

In the present soul-trying crisis, the flower of European manhood has been sacrificed on the altar of Tyranny. The rulers of Europe are begging, imploring, crying to woman, using every subterfuge to induce her to breed again in the old-time submission to man-made laws. Soon the warlords of

America will be echoing the same plea. To all these entreaties the working woman must answer "No"! She must deny the right of the State or Kingdom hereafter to make her a victim of unwilling motherhood and the handmaiden of militarism.

Mothers of the working class, if your love for offspring, husband, sweetheart, or brother stirs within you as deeply as the love that fired the mothers of France and Spain who strove to halt unjust wars by throwing their bodies across the railroad tracks to prevent troop trains from leaving, you too will rouse yourselves to action. You will make it necessary for this democracy, which has set out to conscript your men for foreign warfare, to take them over the dead bodies of the protesting womanhood of the United States.

18. Rightful Causes

In the New York tenements, child labor had long been a scandal, but it had its proponents. It was praised as a cure for juvenile delinquency and female promiscuity, and it allowed mothers to remain home with their children. That the children were working long hours and confined physically and mentally to stultifying repetitious movement when they should have been in the fresh air, at exercise, at play, or in school was not a concern.

Work in the home served manufacturers well, for not only were the wages paid to home workers and children less, but the manufacturer was spared the costs of housing, heating, and lighting. School-age children and younger could easily perform the unskilled labor involved, and although the government might require certain conditions to be met, strict oversight was virtually impossible, not only of the legal operations, but of illegal ones that flourished on porches, in back rooms, or no doubt wherever there was room to sit or stand. Large, impoverished families would commandeer the back-breaking work of all to keep themselves afloat.

A description from 1914 gives an idea of the lives of some of these children.

> One investigator found, in a block off Hester Street, a room twelve by eight and five and a half feet high, in which nine persons slept and cooked and worked...in the light of grimy, vile-smelling rooms, pressing up to the window, or straining under the ghostly gas-jet, all the tired mothers and children of the tenements, stitching garments for a city and a nation.[1]

Sanger's concern for these children was not some passing fancy. In 1911, in one of her earliest articles for the *New York Call*, she had demanded an end to child labor.[2] In another article of the same year, she describes the pathetic child workers living in New York's East Side:

> One of the terrible sights which meets your gaze is the army of the pale-faced children which come into the streets at night to play. Accustomed to seeing the children, although ragged and filthy at least browned by the sun, playing about in the day time, your attention is attracted to these white and drawn faces, and you inquire about them. You are told that these little children, anywhere around 10 years of age, are products of the sweat shops. There they work all day, sometimes in cellars, picking over old rags, and sometimes in "shops" carrying huge bundles from place to place.[3]

Concern for children was relatively new to the American consciousness. When the U.S. census of 1900 revealed that almost 20 percent of America's children between the ages of ten and fourteen were child laborers, an aroused group was impelled to found in 1904 the National Child Labor Committee. In 1908, the committee hired photographer Lewis Hine to document the working conditions and wretched lives of these children. Hine's photos often show an unblinking child facing the camera directly, the portraits in their starkness the more poignant. The January 1920 issue of the *Birth Control Review*, a "Child Labor Number," included several of the committee-assigned photos as part of the article "The Child Slave and the Law."[4]

The Pivot of Civilization, published in 1922, devotes a chapter to child labor and reports on the living conditions of the children of migrant farm workers. Drawing on research of the National Child Labor Committee, Sanger describes

> a family of six living in a one-room shack with no windows....Little Charles, eight years of age, was left at home to take care of Dan, Annie, and Pete, whose ages were five years, four years, and three months, respectively. In addition, he cooked the noonday meal and brought it to his parents in the field. The filth and choking odors of the shack made it almost unbearable, yet the baby was sleeping in a heap of rags piled up in a corner.[5]

A study of child labor conditions in California's Imperial Valley is quoted: "Among the beets, children are 'thick as bees.' All kinds of children pick,... even those as young as three years! Five year old-children pick steadily all day." [6] A father says, "Please, lady, don't send them to school; let them pick a while longer. I ain't got my new auto paid for yet." One of the child laborers revealed the economic advantage—to the parents—in numerous progeny:

Us kids most always drag from forty to fifty pounds of cotton before we take it to be weighed. Three of us pick. I'm twelve years old and my bag is twelve feet long. I can drag nearly a hundred pounds. My sister is ten years old, and her bag is eight feet long. My little brother is seven and his bag is five feet long.[7]

In *Pivot*, Sanger nails the root cause of child labor: *"Uncontrolled breeding and child labor go hand in hand."*[8]

The great irrefutable fact that is ignored or neglected is that the American nation officially places a low value upon the lives of its children. The brutal truth is that *children are cheap*. When over-production in this field is curtailed by voluntary restriction, when the birth rate among the working classes takes a sharp decline, the value of children will rise. Then . . . will child labor vanish."[9]

Sanger continues with a quote from Havelock Ellis: "There have been no great peoples without the art of producing healthy and vigorous children. The matter becomes of peculiar importance in great industrial states, like England, the United States and Germany, because in such states, a tacit conspiracy tends . . . to subordinate national ends to individual ends, and practically to work for the deterioration of the race." Sanger concludes,

Under conditions prevailing in modern society, child labor [bespeaks] the *undervaluation of the child*. This undervaluation, this cheapening of child life, is to speak crudely but frankly the direct result of overproduction.[10]

The Manuscript

The Federal Child Labor Law to which Sanger refers in the "Editorial Comment" below is the Keating-Owen Act, passed by Congress in 1916, which attempted to regulate child labor under the aegis of federal control of interstate commerce. On June 3, 1918, with the *Hammer v. Dagenhart* decision, the Supreme Court declared the child labor law unconstitutional and an invasion of states' rights.[11] But Sanger points out what was generally admitted, that a law regulating only those companies involved in interstate commerce was an inadequate law, covering only 12 to 15 percent of the laboring children of America.

In considering another way to regulate child labor, Sanger asks why the federal government cannot tax the employers of child laborers—an idea being generally circulated—and six months later in December, with the support of President Wilson, Congress passed the Child Labor Tax Law. But less than four years later, on May 15, 1922, the tax law, too, would be declared unconstitutional. The other idea mentioned by Sanger and discussed generally was that of a Congressional amendment— that idea would also be broached by Franklin Delano Roosevelt in 1937, but it never would find a broad base of support.[12]

But all these ideas, says Sanger, are palliatives. Sanger argues for Birth Control as the ultimate answer and uses informed statistics to do so. At the same time, she has a realistic awareness of the desperation of impoverished families. Hunger does not stand up to mere humanitarian concerns. Her telling asides ("Indignation must be restrained these days when it is directed against any function of the Federal Government") and her justified sarcasm are well aimed.

Child Labor
Birth Control Review, July 1918

THE FEDERAL CHILD LABOR LAW has been declared unconstitutional and therefore void. This fact has been met by expressions of restrained indignation throughout the country. Indignation must be restrained these days when it is directed against any function of the Federal Government. But in this case even restrained indignation may be mistaken. The five learned justices of the Supreme Court, who rendered the majority opinion, may possibly have done a real service to the childhood of the nation by bringing this case once more before the people for study and discussion. For it was at best a weak and inadequate law with which to meet so great an evil as child labor. It did not meet this evil squarely with downright prohibition even within its limited sphere, but provided that no goods might be transported from one state to another if these goods were produced in a factory in which within thirty days of the removal of the goods, children under fourteen years of age had been employed or children between fourteen and sixteen years of age had been employed or permitted to work more than eight hours in any day, or more than six days in any week or after the hours of seven p.m. or before six a.m. In the "Survey" of June 8th it is stated that if fully enforced this law would have removed about 150,000 children from industry, but would still leave 1,850,000 children so employed. A patently inadequate remedy even if allowed to stand. The difficulty is that the Federal government is not in a position to deal properly with child labor, because laws of this sort interfere with home rule in the states. Nevertheless, there is a way to deal with national evils or with such matters as should be national in their character. It was not difficult to amend the federal Constitution in such a way that a federal income tax became possible. If Uncle Sam can go after the incomes of his people, why can't he go after those who make money from the toil of children? It should not be harder to pass an amendment to the Constitution that would permit national laws to be enacted so framed as to save the nation's children from the joyless houses of industry, save them not only from factories, but from mines and sweat shops and even from overwork in their own homes. Children are often stunted and dulled by long hours of farm work or by the care of younger sisters and brothers. Generous minded individuals and amiable societies have put years of work and pots of gold into child welfare legislation, yet child labor and child degradation, child starvation and child imbecility continue in giant proportions. If child labor is a bad thing, and there be but little doubt that it is, then we should demand an amendment to the Constitution permitting laws of this sort to be enacted.

In the meantime, the war has opened our eyes in still other ways to the appalling condition of our youth; the selective draft has shown physical, mental, and nervous afflictions due to neglect in childhood. Neglect caused by poverty produces ill-nourished children, stunted children, feeble-minded children. Ignorance and stupidity create too many children. An epidemic of effort to remedy and abolish these things by legislation has sprung into existence. Clinics and milk stations are being established, education for mothers provided, health examination enforced; labor laws, mothers' pensions, day nurseries all experimented with—the list is as long as your arm. Everyone is patriotically shouting "Save the babies." But when sober common sense suggests that this pest of ill-conditioned children could best be cured by a sane limitation of offspring by contraceptive methods, fear and ignorance manifest themselves, fear so strange and ignorance so appalling as to be positively dismaying. Those who work hardest to "save the babies" look with coldness upon the least suggestion of saving the mother from hideously frequent births.

Children must not work, but parents may not be helped to limit the number of their children to those they can care for in health and decency. It is not immoral nor illegal to bring helpless youngsters into the world to slave and rot and die; it is not immoral nor illegal to eke out the family income by the use of baby hands, but it is criminal to tell a woman how to protect her health and strength and that of her family by limiting the number of pregnancies. Civilized people cry out against child labor and are indignant when a clumsy, ineffective law is thrown upon the scrap heap, but think it quite all right to send Margaret Sanger to jail for telling a woman how to prevent conception when she already has several poor little candidates for the factories tugging at her skirts. If each family were limited to the number that could be reared in health and comfort, there would be no need for child labor laws, federal or otherwise; but desperately poor parents need the extra wages that their little tots can earn, and so they join bands with employers in opposing all legislation that would take these pennies away. Rich parents do not send their children to the factories or the mines; it is the poor parents whose little children need protection. It is a strange, illogical world that makes it a crime to teach the prevention of conception and encourages people to breed like rabbits and then makes no decent provision for the swarms of little tots that come tumbling into a sad world.

19. Motherhood

During the years Margaret Sanger was raising her children, the combined influence of Freud, Dewey, and Watson evolved unto a sort of no-discipline approach to child rearing. Permissiveness was the fashion.

> Hutchins Hapgood complained that he could not visit the homes of his married anarchist friends without being tormented by their "brats," who behaved "without correction or restraint....Many years after my experiences with the results of libertarian education among the anarchists," he wrote, "I found the same phenomena existing among the respectable and rich uptown people whose Modern School borrowed of the anarchist idea."[1]

For Margaret, influenced though she was by the ideas of the Ferrer Center's Modern School, permissiveness was not an option. But she did face the guilt that all working mothers face. In a newspaper interview, she talked about this.

> In my own case, my children were still very young when I left them in the care of their grandmother and went out nursing. I was a trained nurse before I married, and when I found that my family could spare me, I left the children in competent hands and went back to work.
>
> Of course young children need their mother a great deal. But children are by nature selfish and they will let you indulge them as much as you please. It isn't good for them, though. As a matter of fact, they should be taught by example that mother is not here

merely to be their attendant, but that she is a superior being, a personage as well. They have much more respect for her then. My children were very much interested in the influence I brought home from the outside world, especially the boys. It was unusual for a mother to tell her children about scientific things, and to let them read literature on science; so that the boys thought I was a much more wonderful mother than any mother of their friends.

But my little girl resented it when I went away. In the early days of the Birth Control movement she would say to me when I put her to bed: "Mother, must you go out to a lecture tonight?" And if I answered in the affirmative, she would vent her anger on lectures and cry: "I hate lectures...I hate them." I could easily have remedied her ills by promising not to go and going anyway when she was asleep. But I didn't see why I should lie to her even if she forgot about it the next morning.

But I confess, nevertheless, that when my little girl cried that way it always gave me a dull feeling until I got back home again. And yet can you see any earthly sense for a mother to stay at home merely to indulge her child?

That is what I had in mind when I said that children were selfish little beings. Whether they need their mother or not they want her to be near them all the time simply because they want her. To them that is reason enough.[2]

After Peggy died, work for Margaret was both a financial and an emotional necessity. Work saved her sanity.

So that when I renewed my battle it was not primarily to help other mothers as to save myself from "lonely sorrow." For my sons were now away at school.... Our marriage had died.[3]

For some time, Bill was not providing for the family, probably since shortly after the Sangers moved into New York City, so the responsibility was finally Margaret's. But good-paying jobs for women in the twenties were, to put it mildly, somewhat scarce. In the long run, Margaret's entrepreneurial endeavors offered the best financial security for her family, even while it meant she had no time for her family—a not uncommon dilemma for the single mother.

For several years I hung on to this dream of being with [my sons] constantly, but it was only a dream....Nor did I have all those hoped for years of watching the boys grow from one stage to another.[4]

Her situation was further complicated by the extraordinary demands of her "job," which not only demanded all her waking hours, but which kept her constantly traveling away from home. Like any working mother, she had to balance hours needed for work against those needed for child care.

> I had had to analyze the situation—either to keep them at home under the supervision of servants who might perhaps be incompetent, and to have no more than the pleasure of seeing them safely to bed, or else to sacrifice my maternal feelings and put them in country schools directed by capable masters where they could lead a healthy, regular life. Having come to this latter conclusion I sent them off fairly young, and thereafter could only visit them over weekends or on the rare occasions when I was speaking in the vicinity. If the desire to see them grew beyond control, I took the first train and received the shock of finding them thoroughly contented in the companionship they had made for themselves; after the initial excitement of greeting had passed away they ran off again to their games.[5]

But they did want to see their mother, however briefly. On November 17, 1918, Grant, at age ten, writes to his mother,

> Dear Mother, I received the marshmellows [sic]. Thank you very much. Mother, will you come down on Thanksgiving Day? Now you put down in your engagement book, "Nov. 28 Go down to see Grant." Ans. soon. Lots of love Grant.[6]

Stuart and Grant both went to Peddie Institute in New Jersey, where Margaret's brother, Bob, had had a football scholarship and then, thanks to stepfather Noah Slee, Stuart attended Yale and Grant, Princeton University. Stuart worked on Wall Street for a short time before returning to medical school and becoming a physician. Grant also became a physician, attending Cornell Medical School, as would Stuart after his Wall Street experience. Stuart married a nurse, Barbara Peabody, and had two daughters; Grant married a doctor, Edwina Campbell, and, much to the dismayed delight of Sanger, had five sons before a little girl came on the sixth try and fulfilled Grant's yearning for his lost sister, Peggy.

Stuart and Grant were devoted sons, and when Margaret was in the hospital for her gallbladder operation in early 1938, she wrote to Noah, "Grant and Stuart are both more anxious than I've ever known them to be, especially Stuart."[7] After the operation, Margaret went to Tucson, eventually moving there and building a house on the lot next door to Stuart, where he had settled with his family. Margaret visited Grant, who was living with his family in Mount Kisco, New York, whenever she was on the East Coast. With Margaret's penchant for travel, that was quite often.

Her sons long grown, Margaret sagely noted in later years in her *Autobiography*,

> Parenthood remains unquestionably the most serious of all human relationships, the most far-reaching in its power for good or for evil, and withal the most delicately complex.[8]

The Manuscript

Margaret Sanger took a realistic view of motherhood, and in this excerpt from an American Birth Control League pamphlet, she shares that realistic view, targeting sentimentalists, who wax ecstatic over newborn babies and the sacredness of motherhood, but who themselves live alone and celibate—much like the ecclesiastical priesthood of organized religions or the spinsters who advise abstinence to married mothers with tyrannical husbands.[9]

Sayings of Others on Birth Control[10]
Excerpt 1921

We hear a good deal of sentimentality about unfailing mother love. We are told that even these unwanted children have that to protect them in their hard lots. But how few of the poorer women have the time and the strength to let mother love develop and express itself? "…We forget that under the stress of caring for many children, under the strain of helping to earn bread for hungry mouths and clothing for bodies clothed in rags, the strongest mother love may turn bitter and cruel.

"Is anything more horrible, more hopeless than the cruelty of a mother worried and tired to distraction?…"

Which of us has not seen such cruelty, even in the streets? A case significant only because it is of frequent occurence, came to my attention a few months ago. A woman, evidently worn out by a day's work, was wheeling a child in a baby buggy in 14th St. Another child, about three years old, was trudging at her side, clinging heavily to her skirts….It cried monotonously as it walked. The mother, apparently in frantic haste to reach home, . . . suddenly felt the drag of the weary, crying child. She struck it, first across one side of its little face and then the other. The tiny thing, surprised by the sudden attack, fell face downward upon the sidewalk. The furious, nerve-wrecked mother, picked it up by the chin and struck it again and again on the back until a passer-by interfered. To a threat of arrest she retorted: "Oh, you shut up. This is my kid and I'll lick it when I want to."

20. Margaret Sanger as Feminist Author

Reviewing even superficially the events in Margaret Sanger's life of 1917 through 1921, it is clear why these years were among "the most strenuous" of Sanger's "already strenuous life."[1] By anyone's standards they were difficult. Throughout 1917 and 1918 over all hung the senseless violence of World War I to which three of her brothers had been called to duty. Government repression was jailing her friends; the ugly Blossom affair with its attacks and counterattacks dragged on. Bill Sanger refused to agree to a separation, money was a constant worry, Stuart had a lingering case of the mumps. As her own health deteriorated daily, her temperature lowered, her neck swollen from her diseased tubercular glands, memories assailed her of Lorenzo Portet, who had died, also from tuberculosis of the throat, in the summer of 1917 so unexpectedly.[2] In January 1919, Jessie Ashley, a friend since 1911, who had worked with Sanger on the Paterson strike and closely on the *Birth Control Review*, died of pneumonia at only fifty-seven years of age.

In her unheated office, Sanger struggled to put out the *Review*, prepared for her many speaking engagements, prespeaking nervousness compounded by her already fragile health; she was overwhelmed with a fatigue that practically immobilized her.[3] Rest offered no help; the weight fell off her. At one point, fearing that she was going to die, she returned old correspondence and wrote farewell letters.[4]

In February of 1919, ill and troubled and deeply depressed, she took Grant out of school and went to California, where she hoped to rest and recuperate while writing *Woman and the New Race,* the title settled on after consideration of "Voluntary Motherhood," "The Door to Woman's Freedom," and "The Modern Woman."[5]

In California, Margaret's depression only deepened, but Grant seemed to enjoy the trip, and she saw him becoming quite handsome. Her writing went slowly, but as she finished a chapter, she sent it for editing to Billy Williams, another of her many lovers and *Review* workers. Williams, a Socialist, had been a reporter in Kansas City before moving east to become involved in the radical scene. In the summer of 1918, he had stayed at Truro with Sanger's family, where he worked with Sanger on her notes for the proposed book, reveling in days that were "the happiest, the most inspiring that I have ever known."[6] When Sanger and Grant returned east from California in May, Margaret and Billy finished the editing together, and Margaret gave the manuscript to Juliet Rublee to read.

Juliet Rublee loved the book. It was the book of a visionary, but Juliet, too, was a visionary, and she, too, dreamed and understood visions. She wrote to Sanger,

> My darling child—
>
> I think the book is simply <u>wonderful</u>—I can hardly <u>wait</u> to have it published. I would hardly change a word—or take out a thought....There are so many people I want to send this book to, that I don't see how I can keep quiet until September! Can it not be advertised at once—as "Soon to appear—Margaret Sanger's Call to the World for the Freedom of Women." "A new theory—more basic than the League of Nations to stop all war." etc. etc. Some bully advertisements could be concocted—if you could get the right news paper men interested. If rightly advertised & you can keep the price down—I think it will sell by the hundred thousand.
>
> You see you are speaking for the <u>hearts</u> of women, all over the world—The book will help to free them—inside—to make them think for themselves, to give them courage to trust & to follow <u>their own</u> feelings, instead of accepting the stupid decrees of men & the church & a false tradition.[7]

Woman and the New Race expressed the feelings of Margaret's "heart" as well, and she referred to it as her "heart" book.[8] The assertion that Sanger was no longer concerned for the lower classes now that she had the support of The Fashionable is, in light of a reading of *Woman and the New Race*, absurd. Certainly, Sanger was no longer seeking to help working class women help themselves, as she had sought to do when publishing *The Woman Rebel*, but Sanger's express concern throughout *Woman* and the *New Race* is very much for exploited lower class women; indeed, concern for exploited womanhood drives the book

Published in August 1920, it did sell by the "hundred thousand," approximately 200,000. Fittingly, Havelock Ellis wrote the preface, urging the world to read it, and it received favorable reviews. Good sales (which may have occurred because buyers thought the book included specific information on contraception) brought much welcome income and yet more celebrity to Sanger.

The Manuscript
Juliet Rublee's enthusiasm for *Woman and the New Race* was more than justified. As she pointed out, women must recognize how "the stupid decrees of men & the church & a false tradition" have deliberately turned women into tools for the ends of patriarchal institutions.

> The early church taught that there were enough children on earth. It needed missionaries more than it needed babies....When the church became a political power rather than a strictly religious institution, it needed a high birth rate to provide laymen to support its increasingly expensive organization....It encouraged marriage under its own control....Shrewd in changing its general policy from celibacy to marriage, the Church was equally shrewd in perpetuating the doctrine of woman's subjection for its own interest.[9]

With marriage under its control, the church not only made the woman subject to her fertility, but it made her subject to her husband—or father or brother—along with subject to God and all the priests, more or less enforcing a sort of triple or quadruple jeopardy. Abundantly subjected, woman accepted her role as "that of an incubator and little more."[10] She was exhorted

> to bear as many children as possible...limiting her life's work to bringing forth and rearing children. These doctrines, together with the teaching that sex life is of itself unclean, formed the basis of morality as fixed by the Roman church.[11]

This morality has engendered for a select few, wealth and abundance; for the overpopulated masses, war and misery. Overpopulation with its evil twin progeny of war and poverty are all part and parcel of the ignorance and subjection of women. The Malthusians understood this, promoting birth control even as they argued against overpopulation. In 1919, the Neo-Malthusian League pointed out to the League of Nations that it had neglected to take into account *"the increase of population,* which is put forward as justification for *claiming increase of territory."* The Mathusians recommended to the League

> That each Nation desiring to enter into the League of Nations shall

pledge itself *so to restrict its birth rate* that its people shall be able to live in comfort *in their own dominions without need* for territorial expansion.[12]

In 1920, Sanger foresaw what the Malthusians had hoped to avert, as is sadly evident in the developing world in the twenty-first century.

The intelligence of a people is of slow evolutional development—it lags far behind the reproductive ability. It is far too slow to cope with conditions created by an increasing population, unless that increase is carefully regulated.[13]

If the large families that create overpopulation were of benefit to the mothers and children, there would be no complaint, but how are children to be cared for by and an ill and overworked mother? And what kind of an inheritance comes to the sixth- or tenth-born child of a sickly mother? Sanger shows what kind of an inheritance by correlating infant mortality with birth placement:

% of Deaths During First Year	% of Deaths During First Year
1st born children 23%	7th born children 31%
2nd born children 20%	8th born children 33%
3rd born children 21%	9th born children 36%
4th born children 23%	10th born children 41%
5th born children 26%	11th born children 51%
6th born children 29%	12th born children 60%

This does not conclude the case, however, for those who care to go farther into the subject will find that many of those [children] who live for a year die before they reach the age of five.[14]

On the basis of these statistics, Sanger grimly—and ironically—suggests, "The most merciful thing that the large family does to one of its infant members is to kill it"—a statement that is often quoted out of context to scoff at Sanger's humanity. [15]

In sharp contrast with these women who ignorantly bring forth large families and who thereby enslave themselves, we find a few women who have one, two or three children or no children at all. These women . . . live full-rounded lives.[16]

Not only do they live "full well-rounded lives," but they are far more likely to be wise and loving mothers. For the wise and loving mother is not a pair of breasts and a uterus. As we see from above, if a woman is to give birth to a healthy child, she must first have good health herself. The ideal mother will also have developed herself as a fulfilled and educated woman before she undertakes motherhood.

> We must permit womanhood its full development before we can expect of it efficient motherhood. If we are to make racial progress, this development of womanhood must precede motherhood in every individual woman. Then and then only can the mother cease to be an incubator and be a mother indeed.[17]

Though some of its issues are dated, such as the belief that the feeble-minded are especially prolific, that nursing a child after twelve months is injurious to both mother and child, and that the Comstock laws must be repealed, *Woman and the New Race* is a feminist manifesto as pertinent to the twenty-first century as when it appeared in 1920.[18] Even the abortion issue carries much the same freight as it did in 1920.

> When society holds up its hands in horror at the "crime" of abortion, it forgets at whose door the first and principal responsibility for this practice rests. Does anyone imagine that a woman would submit to abortion if not denied the knowledge of scientific, effective contraceptives?[19]

Since 1920, many women have taken Sanger's words seriously, and the possibility remains that many more will do so, that women will insist on the freedom to decide when and if they are to have children. The fulfillment of the feminine spirit and the contribution of that feminine spirit to motherhood, as well as to the arts, the sciences, church, and government is woman's true destiny. In practical terms, this can occur only if woman chooses consciously how many children, if any, she will care for. When woman asserts her control of her fertility, the new mother will be the loving mother, whose feminine spirit and wanted children will regenerate the race.

> Love is the greatest force of the universe; freed of its bonds of submission and unwanted progeny, it will formulate and compel of its own nature observance to standards of purity far beyond the highest conception of the average moralist. The feminine spirit, animated by joyous, triumphant love, will make its own high tenets of morality.[20]

Woman and the New Race 1920
Woman's Error and Her Debt, pp. 1-8
Chapter I

The most far-reaching social development of modern times is the revolt of woman against sex servitude. The most important force in the remaking of the world is a free motherhood. Beside this force, the elaborate international programmes of modern statesmen are weak and superficial. Diplomats may formulate leagues of nations and nations may pledge their utmost strength to maintain them, statesmen may dream of reconstructing the world out of alliances, hegemonies, and spheres of influence, but woman, continuing to produce explosive populations, will convert these pledges into the proverbial scraps of paper; or she may, by controlling birth, lift motherhood to the place of a voluntary, intelligent function, and remake the world. When the world is thus remade, it will exceed the dream of statesman, reformer and revolutionist.

Only in recent years has woman's position as the gentler and weaker half of the human family been emphatically and generally questioned. Men assumed that this was woman's place; woman herself accepted it. It seldom occurred to anyone to ask whether she would go on occupying it forever.

Upon the mere surface of woman's organized protests there were no indications that she was desirous of achieving a fundamental change in her position. She claimed the right of suffrage and legislative regulation of her working hours, and asked that her property rights be equal to those of the man. None of these demands, however, affected directly the most vital factors of her existence. Whether she won her point or failed to win it, she remained a dominated weakling in a society controlled by men.

Woman's acceptance of her inferior status was the more real because it was unconscious. She had chained herself to her place in society and the family through the maternal functions of her nature, and only chains thus strong could have bound her to her lot as a brood animal for the masculine civilizations of the world. In accepting her role as the "weaker and gentler half," she accepted that function. In turn, the acceptance of that function fixed the more firmly her rank as an inferior.

Caught in this "vicious circle," woman has, through her reproductive ability, founded and perpetuated the tyrannies of the Earth. Whether it was the tyranny of a monarchy, an oligarchy or a republic, the one indispensable factor of its existence was, as it is now, hordes of human beings—human beings so plentiful as to be cheap, and so cheap that ignorance was their natural lot. Upon the rock of an unenlightened submissive maternity have these been founded; upon the product of such a maternity have they flourished.

No despot ever flung forth his legions to die in foreign conquest, no privilege-ruled nation ever erupted across its borders to lock in death embrace with another, but behind them loomed the driving power of a population too large for its boundaries and its natural resources.

No period of low wages or of idleness with their want among the workers, no peonage or sweatshop, no child-labor factory ever came into being, save from the same source. Nor have famine and plague been as much "acts of God" as acts of too prolific mothers. They, also, as all students know, have their basic causes in over-population.

The creators of over-population are the women, who, while wringing their hands over each fresh horror, submit anew to their task of producing the multitudes who will bring about the *next* tragedy of civilization.

While unknowingly laying the foundations of tyrannies and providing the human tinder for racial conflagrations, woman was also unknowingly creating slums, filling asylums with insane and institutions with other defectives. She was replenishing the ranks of the prostitutes, furnishing grist for the criminal courts and inmates for prisons. Had she planned deliberately to achieve this tragic total of human waste and misery, she could hardly have done it more effectively.

Woman's passivity under the burden of her disastrous task was almost altogether that of ignorant resignation. She knew virtually nothing about her reproductive nature and less about the consequences of her excessive childbearing. It is true that, obeying the inner urge of their natures, *some* women revolted. They went even to the extreme of infanticide and abortion. Usually their revolts were not general enough. They fought as individuals, not as a mass. In the mass they sank back into blind and hopeless subjection. They went on breeding with staggering rapidity those numberless, undesired children who became the clogs and the destroyers of civilizations.

Today, however, woman is rising in fundamental revolt. Even her efforts at mere reform are, as we shall see later, steps in that direction. Underneath each of them is the feminine urge to complete freedom. Millions of women are asserting their right to voluntary motherhood. They are determined to decide for themselves whether they shall become mothers, under what conditions and when. This is the fundamental revolt referred to. It is for woman the key to the temple of liberty.

Even as birth control is the means by which woman attains basic freedom, so it is the means by which she must and will uproot the evil she has wrought through her submission. As she has unconsciously and ignorantly brought about social disaster, so must and will she consciously and intelligently *undo* that disaster and create a new and better order.

The task is hers. It cannot be avoided by excuses, nor can it be delegated. It is not enough for woman to point to the self-evident domination of man. Nor does it avail to plead the guilt of rulers and the exploiters of labor. It makes no difference that she does not formulate industrial systems nor that she is an instinctive believer in social justice. In her submission lies her error and her guilt. By her failure to withhold the multitudes of children who have made inevitable that most flagrant of our social evils, she incurred a debt to society. Regardless of her own wrongs, regardless of her lack of opportunity and regardless of all other considerations, *she* must pay that debt.

She must not think to pay this debt in any superficial way. She cannot pay it with palliatives—with child-labor laws, prohibition, regulation of prostitution and agitation against war. Political nostrums and social panaceas are but incidentally and superficially useful. They do not touch the source of the social disease.

War, famine, poverty, and oppression of the workers will continue while woman makes life cheap. They will cease only when she limits her reproductivity and human life is not longer a thing to be wasted.

Two chief obstacles hinder the discharge of this tremendous obligation. The first and the lesser is the legal barrier. Dark-Age laws would still deny to her the knowledge of her reproductive nature. Such knowledge is indispensable to intelligent motherhood and she must achieve it, despite absurd statutes and equally absurd moral canons.

The second and more serious barrier is her own ignorance of the extent and effect of her submission. Until she knows the evil her subjection has wrought to herself, to her progeny, and to the world at large, she cannot wipe out that evil.

To get rid of these obstacles is to invite attack from the forces of reaction which are so strongly entrenched in our present-day society. It means warfare in every phase of her life. Nevertheless, at whatever cost, she must emerge from her ignorance and assume her responsibility.

She can do this only when she has awakened to a knowledge of herself and of the consequences of her ignorance. The first step is birth control. Through birth control she will attain to voluntary motherhood. Having attained this, the basic freedom of her sex, she will cease to enslave herself and the mass of humanity. Then, through the understanding of the intuitive forward urge within her, she will not stop at patching up the world; she will remake it.

PART II THE REFORMER
21. Appeal to Science

In May of 1919, back from California with Grant, *Woman and the New Race* fairly completed, Sanger, once in New York, plunged into her strenuous life of touring and lecturing, editing the *Review,* and promoting birth control. Not quite a year later, in April 1920, Sanger was off to England for a lecture series and to Germany to track down a contraceptive jelly said by Ellis to be highly effective. Incorporated in the 1920 England trip was a less-than-leaden interlude touring Ireland with Havelock Ellis, an introduction to and a playful affair with H. G. Wells, and good (well, more than good) times with Hugh de Selincourt and his friends.[1]

Returning to New York in November 1920 for more U.S. lectures and work on the *Review,* Sanger remained until May 1921, then back to England and Europe she went, this time to round up speakers who would be a draw for the 1921 First American Birth Control Conference in November (she secures Harold Cox) and to attend a birth control conference in Amsterdam in early September. By mid-September, Sanger was again in New York, finalizing arrangements for her conference. Such ceaseless to-ing and fro-ing was to be the pattern of her entire life, until her extreme ill health confined her in her eighties to a nursing home in Tucson.[2]

Backtracking now in our narrative to the summer of 1921—prior to the First American Birth Control Conference in the fall—Sanger, as we have seen, was in Europe. And at the beginning of the summer of 1921, despite operations, rest, and various treatments, her health remained a problem. High in the Swiss Alps at the recommendation of yet another doctor, she had been sent, once more, to rest and regain her health in the mountain air. Her rest was only part time. *Woman and the New Race* had just been released in the fall of 1920, but Sanger was already working on a new book, *The Pivot of Civilization.* From Zermatt, Switzerland, she wrote in that summer of 1921 to Juliet Rublee.

> Pain all gone from neck, tissues softened & really I feel like my old self before you knew me. . . I never had greater confidence in the work [of Birth Control] than now. It is absolutely the only issue which is alive which is fundamental & which can save civilization from the wreck which charities & other weak & sentimental agencies have made of society. My new book is going well. I am calling it "The Pivot of Civilization."[3]

With *Pivot*, Sanger was making a frank "appeal to the scientist," eager to have birth control "pass through the crucible of science."[4] This was her "head" book, as she called it, and she was determined to present birth control as solidly and scientifically based.[5] For how else was the movement to be forwarded—how else was civilization to survive— if birth control was not to be accepted by the left-brain male scientists and male politicians governing the world?

> Unless sexual science is incorporated as an integral part of world-statesmanship and the pivotal importance of Birth Control is recognized in any program of reconstruction, all efforts to create a new world and a new civilization are foredoomed to failure.[6]

Pivot is extensively documented. Virtually every statement is reinforced and referenced to names of indisputable repute or academic substance or bureaucratic pedigree. Sanger argues logically for the superiority of birth control over other "isms," dispatches Marxism, improves on the Mathusians, and examines eugenics. She discusses the glandular system, education, child labor, and morality, but always returns to her premise that the answer to solving world problems, whatever they be, lies in recognizing the root cause of those problems, the power of the sexual drive and the necessity of birth control.

> Civilization, in any true sense of the word, is based upon the control and guidance of the great natural instinct of Sex. Mastery of this force is possible only through the instrument of Birth Control.[7]

Sanger challenges the status quo even further by insisting that birth control is to be practiced by the individual, the individual *woman*, to be exact, and that the practice must be voluntary. "Social regeneration, no less than individual regeneration, must come from within," she says.[8] This is, of course, the very antithesis of a solution ever offered by a hierarchical male-governed society, which historically imposes its order from without.

Since Augustine, most of the Western world has had a problem with sex, relegating it to something sinful, dirty, and yet, with everybody doing it, waging a losing battle. Particularly in America is the attitude toward sex counter to common sense and ageless wisdom. Such a hypocritical attitude informed the American public and was institutionalized by Anthony Comstock in the nineteenth and early twentieth century. That turn-of-the-century sensibility is precisely caught in this descriptive letter to Sanger from Agnes Smedley, one of Sanger's radical friends.

> You must realize that in America, children are taught that the sex act, or anything connected with sex, is a shameful, disgraceful thing, and every time the subject is broached a wave of horror or silence spreads over an audience. It is a shameful subject! The word "sex" itself is enough to throw "proper" people into a fit of stony silence, and the person who mentions it is an outcast for the rest of the evening. Now imagine what it means for a child, when her whole attitude toward life is formed in this period, to have the foundation laid in this manner. Then imagine a young woman with this attitude, suddenly married. Two minutes before, she is supposed to think the sex act is a degrading, debasing, shameful act; then she is married with a few words; and society tells her that now she may have sex relations every hour of the day if she wishes. Of course, an attitude formulated during the early years of her life, can not be changed in two minutes by the words of an official or a priest. There is a terrible conflict over this question; it is enough to disrupt the life of a nation. It develops hypocrisy at the *best*.[9]

Twenty-first century America is not the least bit hypocritical about sex, but regards it as the very acme and high pitch of experience. This may be an equally unbalanced attitude. Capitalism regards sex frankly as a commodity, completely debasing it for brainwashed couch potatoes, who see merely its physical dimension. But from its spirituality—or the universal energy that bases individual sexual energy—is derived its irrefutable force.[10] Sanger explains that force by drawing on her beloved Ellis, and Ellis's thoughts are much in line with Eastern philosophies, which have always recognized the validity and sacredness of sexual energy.[11]

Kundalini and tantic teachings from Asia have long taught that seven chakras— centers of energy—run along the spinal cord between the sacrum and the crown of the head. The research of Dr. Candace Pert, professor in Department of Physiology and Biophysics at Georgetown University Medical Center, Washington, D.C., has shown that at these chakra sites, identified so many centuries ago, are located nodal points of electrical and chemical activity, veritable "minibrains," which are interdependent and which receive, process, and distribute information from and to the rest of the body.[12]

The second chakra is identified with the raw power of the dual sexual energy, the energy of creativity, that allows individuals to open completely to one another and yet to retain their own selfhood. Individuals come to know their physical selfhood through activity with their bodies and by experiencing their sexuality. Responding to its power, individuals express the extent of their love (or their hate), but moving on these energy currents, the threat lurks always that the rational self might be lost within the uncontrollable. In America, a society that grew out of a puritanical Calvinist tradition from its earliest days, self-control has been valued above all else and sexual activity severely circumscribed. Ubiquitous media displays of titillating sex bestir the residue of centuries of repression and guilt and send the masses scurrying to the comfort of outside ecclesiastical dictates, to the scourge of prudish self-alienation, or to excesses and pornography.[13]

Caroline Myss, a widely known medical intuitive, is one of the many writers today who explains to the West the mysteries of Eastern thought and the power of sexual energy.

> Sexual eroticism is a form of physical and emotional liberation as well as of spiritual liberation. Why spiritual? Erotic pleasure is, by nature, "in the moment," an encounter in which we drop most of our physical boundaries in order to enjoy the full measure of human contact.[14]

Sanger recognized both the universal force and human dimensions of sexuality and, judging by her letters, felt herself liberated by engaging with her sexuality. On her visits to England, particularly through the twenties, as a vibrant, attractive—and now famous— woman, she was pursued by many, many men other than Noah Slee, men prominent like H. G. Wells and Havelock Ellis or charming and predatory like Hugh de Selincourt, the novelist manqué, with whom she corresponded throughout her life. In exploring the sensual and sexual freely and without shame, Sanger was following Havelock Ellis, who articulated what her soul believed to be true.[15]

> So far from being animal-like, the human impulses of sex are among the least animal-like acquisitions of man....The sexual activities of man and woman belong, not to that lower part of our nature which degrades us to the level of the "brute," but to the higher part which raises us toward all the finest activities and ideals we are capable of.[16]

Yet Ellis found that he could not live by all that he professed, and he was forced to confront the fact that sexual energy, if it is to be so integrated heathfully into our lives, must be handled with discipline and respect.[17] Sanger could never separate sex from romance and from what, to her, was its deeper meaning. She explained herself so well to Mabel Dodge, that Dodge wrote down their conversation at length, describing how her own being was awakened to a new reality, which before had always seemed to be a thing "forbidden." Sanger's words brought Dodge to see that we have a duty to allow the body to express the spirit of its love to the one to whom we are bound by love. Sanger, said Dodge,

> taught us the way to a heightening of pleasure and of prolonging it, and the delimiting of it to the sexual zones, the spreading out and sexualizing of the whole body until it should become sensitive and alive throughout, and complete. She made love into a serious undertaking—with the body so illumined and conscious that it would be able to interpret and express in all its parts the language of the spirit's pleasure.[18]

The freedom with which Sanger viewed her right to explore her sexuality was in keeping with the same independence of thought that galvanized her to publish *The Woman Rebel* and to urge workingwomen to speak and act in defiance of convention.[19] This independence was first affirmed and articulated for Sanger when she discovered the writings of Nietzsche. "In Liverpool, I went to hear a lecture on Nietzsche and was simply inspired & enthused," wrote Sanger in her "London Diary."[20] Nietzschean philosophy, which gloried in the courage to challenge the conventions of centuries and encouraged the individual to stick to one's convictions in the cause of a higher truth, confirmed for Sanger how right was the life path she was following, then in London and later, through the years. No wonder she was inspired by the lecture.

Writing to Hugh de Selincourt in 1921 are echoes of the Nietzschean courage Sanger embraced to realize her ideals.

> But oh Hugh dear, we in this new land have so much to learn. Here where one gives up home, a loving husband, children, reputation, friends, love money all the things most people live for, to work for an ideal.[21]

The Manuscript

The Pivot of Civilization explains Sanger's ideals in terms of early twentieth-century science. Together with *Woman and the New Race*, *Pivot* sets out the constructs that base Sanger's life work. When it was published in June of 1922, Sanger's critics quoted *Pivot* to prove that Sanger was destroying the nation's morals and defiling the purity of women, etc., etc. How many hard-core scientists *The Pivot of Civilization* appealed to will never be known.

The Pivot of Civilization[22]
Chapter VI
Neglected Factors of the World Problem, pp. 140-145

We can hope for no advance until we attain a new conception of sex, not as a merely propagative act, not merely as a biological necessity for the perpetuation of the race, but as a psychic and spiritual avenue of expression. It is the limited, inhibited conception of sex that vitiates so much of the thought and ideation of the Eugenists.

Like most of our social idealists, statesmen, politicians, and economists, some of the Eugenists suffer intellectually from a restricted and inhibited understanding of the function of sex. This limited understanding, this narrowness of vision, which gives rise to most of the misconceptions and condemnations of the doctrine of Birth Control, is responsible for the failure of politicians and legislators to enact practical statutes or to remove traditional obscenities from the law books. The most encouraging sign at present is the recognition by modern psychology of the central importance of the sexual instinct in human society, and the rapid spread of this new concept among the more enlightened sections of the civilized communities. The new conception of sex has been well stated by one to whom the debt of contemporary civilization is well-nigh immeasurable. "Sexual activity," Havelock Ellis has written, "is not merely a baldly propagative act, nor, when propagation is put aside, is it merely the relief of distended vessels. It is something more even than the foundation of great social institutions. It is the function by which all the finer activities of the organism, physical and psychic, may be developed and satisfied."[i] *(Editor's note: for clarity Sanger's original notes have been changed to roman numerals and will appear in this text as footnotes.)*

No less than seventy years ago, a profound but neglected thinker, George Drysdale, emphasized the necessity of a thorough understanding of man's sexual nature in approaching economic, political, and social problems. "Before we can undertake the calm and impartial investigation of any social problem, we must first of all free ourselves from all those sexual prejudices which are so vehement and violent and which so completely distort our vision of the external world. Society as a whole has yet to fight its way through an almost impenetrable forest of sexual taboos." Drysdale's words have lost none of their truth even today: "There are few things from which humanity has suffered more than the degraded and irreverent feelings of mystery and shame that have been attached to the genital and excretory organs. The former have been regarded, like their corresponding mental passions, as something of a lower and baser nature, tending to disgrace and carnalize man by their physical appetites. But we can not take a debasing view of any part of

---

[i] Medical Review of Reviews, Volume 26, p. 116.

our humanity without becoming degraded in our whole being."[ii]

Drysdale moreover clearly recognized the social crime of entrusting to sexual barbarians the duty of legislating and enforcing laws detrimental to the welfare of all future generations. "They trust blindly to authority for the rules they blindly lay down," he wrote, "perfectly unaware of the awful and complicated nature of the subject they are dealing with so confidently and of the horrible evils their unconsidered statements are attended with. They themselves break through the most fundamentally important laws daily in utter unconsciousness of the misery they are causing to their fellows...."

Psychologists today courageously emphasize the integral relationship of the expression of the sexual instinct with every phase of human activity. Until we recognize this central fact, we cannot understand the implications and the sinister significance of superficial attempts to apply rosewater remedies to social evils—by the enactment of restrictive and superficial legislation, by wholesale philanthropies and charities, by publicly burying our heads in the sands of sentimentality. Self-appointed censors, grossly immoral "moralists," make-shift legislators, all face a heavy responsibility for the miseries, disease, and social evils they perpetuate or intensify by enforcing the primitive taboos of aboriginal customs, traditions, and outworn laws, which at every step hinder the education of the people in the scientific knowledge of their sexual nature. Puritanic and academic taboo of sex in education and religion is as disastrous to human welfare as prostitution or the venereal scourges. "We are compelled squarely to face the distorting influences of biologically aborted reformers as well as the wastefulness of seducers," Dr. Edward A. Kempf [in arguing for state support of maternal and infant care clinics] recently declared. "Man arose from the ape and inherited his passions, which he can only refine but dare not attempt to castrate unless he would destroy the fountains of energy that maintain civilization and make life worth living and the world worth beautifying....We do not have a problem that is to be solved by making repressive laws and executing them. Nothing will be more disastrous. Society must make life worth the living and the refining for the individual by conditioning him to love and to seek the love-object in a manner that reflects a constructive effect upon this fellow-men and by giving him suitable opportunities. The virility of the automatic apparatus is destroyed by excessive gormandizing or hunger, by excessive wealth or poverty, by excessive work or idleness, by sexual abuse or intolerant prudishness. The noblest and most difficult art of all is the raising of human thoroughbreds."[iii]

[ii] The Elements of Ocial Science, London, 1854

[iii] Proceedings of the International Conference of Women Physicians, Volume VI, pp. 66-67, New York, 1920.

PART II THE REFORMER
22. The Town Hall Raid

Designated an historical site in 1978, Town Hall, on Forty-third Street in New York City, has been known since 1921 for its politically charged activity.[1] On its façade reads the inscription, "The Town Hall founded by The League for Political Education 1894-1920. Ye shall know the truth and the truth shall make you free." On the Web, Town Hall is referred to as belonging to "a nonconformist organization even in the beginning."

> Controversy surrounded the hall early on, mainly because it became a popular platform for free speech. Margaret Sanger, birth control advocate, was arrested and carried off the stage on February 12, 1921, for trying to speak on the subject.[2]

But the site has the date wrong and carefully ignores the circumstances of the arrest.

Recognizing the importance of a visible organization and the contribution of a well-publicized conference to that visibility, Sanger had put great effort into setting up in November 1921 the First American Birth Control Conference. To New York City came three hundred delegates, accredited scientists and prominent physicians and birth control supporters, from both sides of the Atlantic. Featured was Harold Cox, urbane, erudite, a speaker of international repute and former member of Parliament, editor of the venerable *Edinburgh Review*—a real coup as a draw.[3] Several days earlier, the American Birth Control League had been organized, and the conference was to be its send-off.

The three-day conference was to conclude on Sunday at the—then— new Town Hall, for which payment of rental and arrangements for the meeting had been made some weeks in advance. The meeting was to be an open forum on the question "Is Birth Control Moral?" Sanger had invited a number of eminent persons to this forum, including Archbishop Patrick Hayes of the New York diocese.

For two days the conference had gone well with good attendance; latecomers could not even squeeze into a medical meeting that discussed contraceptive techniques. On the final day, November 13, the day of the Town Hall meeting, Margaret's good friend Juliet Rublee, "the only woman [Margaret] ever knew who dared to wear bright greens, reds, yellows, all together," had given a dinner for Margaret and Harold Cox in "her small engaging dining room . . . as colorful as she herself."[4] Juliet must have seen how tired Margaret looked and remarked on it. Margaret was not only tired, she was uneasy. This was to be the high point of the conference; yet for some inexplicable reason, she found herself dreading the Town Hall meeting.

I shall never forget that night. Usually I had been able to visualize my audiences. But all day, try as I would to "tune in" to the evening's events, I could not do it. My dream the preceding night was a memorable one. I was carrying a small baby in my arms up a very steep hill. I came rather abruptly to a side hill which became a mountain side of rock and slippery shale, and I had nothing to hold on to to keep me from slipping. The baby kept crying, and I tried to comfort it, but I dared not use my right hand as it seemed to be held up like a balancing rod which kept us both from falling. The wretched dream kept me drowsy all day—always when I dreamed of babies there was some kind of troublesome news not far away. Another difficulty was that I could not think *through* what I was going to say at that meeting. My brain seemed numb; I felt a strange lack of the worrying anticipation one usually feels previous to a large meeting.

When the car crept along West Forty-Third Street to the Town Hall, we found the thoroughfare swarming with thousands of people. Finally arriving in front of Town Hall, we pushed our way to the door. Two policemen stood before us. The doors were closed, and as Mr. Cox and I attempted to enter we were barred by the arm of the officer.

"You can't get into this place tonight," he announced brusquely.

"Why not?" I asked.

"There ain't going to be no meeting," he replied.[5]

Indeed, there was to be no meeting that night, Town Hall paid for or not. When Sanger and Cox finally made it into the hall, they found chaos, policemen standing about seeming unsure what to do, the audience equally confused, equally unsure what to do. Climbing on to the stage, amid the commotion and the bedlam, Sanger tried to speak and was immediately stopped by Police Captain Thomas Donohue. Again and again she tried to speak, and each time she was stopped by the captain. But Sanger knew what she had to do.

> I knew that I had to keep on [trying to speak] until I was arrested in order that free speech might be made the issue....If the pulpit and press were denied you, you must take it to the dock.[6]

Finally, she, along with Mary Winsor, a former suffragist and a new member of the American Birth Control League National Council, were arrested.[7] Off the two women were marched to jail, Sanger furious—and hatless (that in itself almost a cause for arrest in 1921), followed by an equally angry mob of thousands (five thousand according to one newspaper), singing, booing, and jeering at the police, all the way across Broadway and up Eighth Avenue.[8]

The next morning, the case was immediately dismissed, but the commotion had made the newspapers—all the newspapers. Suddenly, the entire city of New York, and soon most of America, knew about the First American Birth Control Conference and the new American Birth Control League.

But there was no law against discussing birth control in regard to morality. What had happened? It soon came out that Police Captain Donohue had ordered the birth control conference locked out of Town Hall on orders. The orders had come through a call from a telephone operator—not exactly the voice of authority. Finally, the call was traced to Archbishop Patrick Hayes of the New York Archdiocese.

There followed an investigation of the police actions. During these proceedings, Juliet Rublee while on the witness stand acknowledged that she had read and disagreed with section 1142 of the penal code (the section that prohibits the dissemination of contraception information). Juliet was immediately arrested. Her arrest brought an investigation of the investigation, for Juliet Rublee's husband, Wilson presidential advisor and prominent attorney, and his well-placed friends were outraged.

The defendants were blocked at every turn by policeman and officials protecting themselves, while the prosecution turned the investigation into an investigation of the birth controllers along personal lines. Called on the stand by an attorney, Sanger faced this line of questioning:

"Do you know Carlo Tresca?"

"Yes."

"Do you know Alexander Berkman?"

"Yes."...

"Do you know Emma Goldman?" Here the attorney's voice rose in outrage, and he looked at [the] Judge as though to say, "There you have it."

"Yes," I reiterated, "but I also know Mrs. Andrew Carnegie and Mr. John D. Rockefeller, Jr. My social relations are with people of varying ideas and opinions...."

After hours of this cross-examination I was physically exhausted, as though I had been flung back and forth, beaten and pounded from the bottom of my feet to the top of my head. I almost looked at my arms to see whether they were black and blue, they ached so.[9]

The "investigations"—and the broad, balmy newspaper coverage—continued. The issue had plainly become one of freedom of speech, and the press, both newspapers and general magazines, were united in their outrage at the arrogance of Archbishop Hayes and the Catholic leadership—that they could so easily employ the New York Police Department for their own ends, that they dared so to abrogate civil law and stifle free speech. But ultimately, said Sanger,

It was all useless. The police went unreprimanded. Donohue was promoted when things had quieted down . . . In spite of the inconvenience, the humiliation of halls closed, covenants broken—exactly nothing had happened.[10]

But something had happened. Those who had known little or nothing about the birth control movement were suddenly very well informed. Untapped members of The Fashionable sector, the prominent, wealthy matrons who had the money and the influence to make so much happen, now became involved. Those who had been indifferent to Sanger and the birth control movement were now supporting her, especially the medical community from whom Sanger had long sought support. Furious voices were raised in defense of the rights of birth controllers to speak. And Sanger now had unarguable proof of unprincipled activities of the Catholic hierarchy, of its deliberate machinations to obstruct the birth control movement, of its willingness to break the law for its own purposes.[11] Her vociferous protests and what had been labeled her self-promoting antics were deemed fully justified. As Sanger wrote to the *New York Times,*

There is no objection to the Catholic Church inculcating the theories and doctrines in its own church and to its own people; but when they attempt to make these ideas legislative acts and force their opinions and code of morals upon the Protestant members of this country, then we do consider this an interference with the principles of this Democracy and we have a right to protest.[12]

A week later, on November 18, the interrupted Town Hall meeting was rescheduled and held in the Park Theatre, a much larger venue. Archbishop Hayes was invited; he did not attend.[13] The New York police did, this time to ensure order, for within fifteen minutes after a single door was opened, the Park Theatre was packed, filled to capacity with seventeen hundred people, while outside, people were climbing up fire escapes and peering in windows, trying to get or see in.[14] According to the newspaper *American*, under the headline "4,000 Attempt to Batter Way to Birth Talk,"

> For more than an hour last night Columbus Circle was the scene of chaos that at moments verged on actual rioting as 4,000 persons tried in vain to batter down the doors of the Park Theatre and gain entrance to the birth control meeting....Inspector Bolan and Captain Donohoe, with fifteen patrolmen, attempted to keep back the crowds and maintain order. In a few moments, however, they had been swallowed by the surging mob, which made repeated rushes for the entrances in spite of the patrolmen's nightsticks.[15]

Inside the Park Theatre, the meeting with Harold Cox and others proceeded as planned for the eager crowd, and Margaret Sanger delivered her address defending the morality of birth control to an enthusiastic audience.[16] A little more than fifteen years later, on January 15, 1937, Sanger was back in Town Hall on the same stage on which she had been arrested. This time, the prominent New York civic association, the Town Hall Club, bestowed on her its Town Hall Club Annual Award of Honor for "conspicuous contribution to the enlargement and enrichment of life." The AP photo of the event ran in all major and not-so-major papers, and coverage was national. Among the many letters and wires of congratulations, came one from Robert Latou Dickinson, the prominent gynecologist:

> Among foremost health measures originating or developing outside medicine like ether under Morton, microbe hunting under Pasteur, nursing under Nightingale, Margaret Sanger's world wide service holds high rank and is destined eventually to fullest medical recognition.[17]

The Manuscript

As Sanger says in *Woman and the New Race*, "Why is the question of morality always raised by the objector to birth control?"[18] Hence her choice of topic, which allowed her to deal directly with a charge common against birth control and to involve directly those who were making the charge.

Her speech, titled "The Morality of Birth Control," was delivered at the Park Theatre on November 18, 1921, five days after the Town Hall raid had been ordered by Archbishop Hayes and was revised to accommodate the circumstances of the raid.

The Morality of Birth Control, 1921
Address at Town Hall as Rescheduled[19]

The meeting tonight is a postponement of one which was to have taken place at the Town Hall last Sunday evening. It was to be a culmination of a three-day conference, two of which were held at the Hotel Plaza, in discussing the Birth Control subject in its various and manifold aspects.

The one issue upon which there seems to be most uncertainty and disagreement exists in the moral side of the subject of Birth Control. It seemed only natural for us to call together scientists, educators, members of the medical profession, and the theologians of all denominations to ask their opinion upon this uncertain and important phase of the controversy. Letters were sent to the most eminent men and women in the world. We asked in this letter the following questions:

1. Is over-population a menace to the peace of this world?
2. Would the legal dissemination of scientific Birth Control information through the medium of clinics by the medical profession be the most logical method of checking the problem of over-population?
3. Would knowledge of Birth Control change the moral attitude of men and women toward the marriage bond or lower the moral standards of the youth of the country?
4. Do you believe that knowledge which enables parents to limit the families will make for human happiness, and raise the moral, social and intellectual standards of population?

We sent such a letter not only to those who, we thought, might agree with us, but we sent it also to our known opponents. Most of these people answered. Every one who answered did so with sincerity and courtesy, with the exception of one group whose reply to this important question as demonstrated at the Town Hall last Sunday evening was a disgrace to liberty-loving people, and to all traditions we hold dear in the United States. [Applause.] I believed that the discussion of the moral issue was one which did not solely belong to theologians and to scientists, but belonged to the people. [Applause.] And because I believed that the people of this country may and can discuss this subject with dignity and with intelligence, I desired to bring them together and to discuss it in the open.

When one speaks of morals, one refers to human conduct. This implies action of many kinds, which in turn depends upon the mind and the brain. So that in speaking of morals, one must remember that there is direct connection between morality and brain development. Conduct is said to be action in pursuit of ends, and if this is so, then we must hold that irresponsibility and recklessness in our action is immoral, while responsibility and foresight put into action for the benefit of the individual and the race becomes in the highest sense the finest kind of morality.

We know that every advance that woman has made in the last half century has been made with opposition, all of which has been based upon the grounds of immorality. When women fought for higher education, it was said that this would cause her to become immoral and she would lose her place in the sanctity of the home. When women called for the franchise, it was said that this would lower her standard of morals, that it was not fit that she should meet with and mix with the members of the opposite sex, but we notice that there was no objection to her meeting with the same members of the opposite sex when she went to church. The church has ever opposed the progress of woman on the ground that her freedom would lead to immorality. We ask the church to have more confidence in women. We ask the opponents of this movement to reverse the methods of the church, which aims to keep women moral by keeping them in fear and in ignorance and to inculcate into them a higher and truer morality based upon knowledge. [Applause.] And ours is the morality of knowledge. If we cannot trust woman with the knowledge of her own body, then I claim that two thousand years of Christian teaching has proved to be a failure. [Applause.]

We stand on the principle that Birth Control should be available to every adult man and woman. We believe that every adult man and woman should be taught the responsibility and the right use of knowledge. We claim that woman should have the right over her own body and to say if she shall or if she shall not be a mother, as she sees fit. [Applause.] We further claim that the first right of a child is to be desired. [Applause.] While the second right is that it should be conceived in love, and the third, that it should have a heritage of sound health.

Upon these principles the Birth Control movement in America stands.

When it comes to discussing the methods of Birth Control, that is far more difficult. There are laws in this country, which forbid the imparting of practical information to the mothers of the land. We claim that every mother in this country, either sick or well, has the right to the best, the safest, the most scientific information. This information should be disseminated directly to the mothers through clinics by members of the medical profession, registered nurses, and registered midwives. [Applause.]

Our first step is to have the backing of the medical profession so that our laws may be changed, so that motherhood may be the function of dignity and choice, rather than one of ignorance and chance. [Applause.] Conscious control of offspring is now becoming the ideal and the custom in all civilized countries.

Those who oppose it claim that however desirable it may be on economic or social grounds, it may be abused and the morals of the youth of the country may be lowered. Such people should be reminded that there are two points to be considered. First, that such control is the inevitable advance in civilization. Every civilization involves an increasing forethought for others, even for those yet unborn. [Applause.] The reckless abandonment of the impulse of the moment and the careless regard for the consequences is not morality. [Applause.] The selfish gratification of temporary desire at the expense of suffering to lives that will come may seem very beautiful to some, but it is not our conception of civilization, nor is it our concept of morality. [Applause.]

In the second place, it is not only inevitable, but it is right to control the size of the family for by this control and adjustment we can raise the level and the standards of the human race. While Nature's way of reducing her numbers is controlled by disease, famine and war, primitive man has achieved the same results by infanticide, exposure of infants, the abandonment of children, and by abortion. But such ways of controlling population are no longer possible for us.

We have attained high standards of life, and along the lines of science must we conduct such control. We must begin farther back and control the beginnings of life. We must control conception. This is a better method; it is a more civilized method, for it involves not only greater forethought for others, but finally a higher sanction for the value of life itself.

Society is divided into three groups. [The first,] those intelligent and wealthy members of the upper classes who have obtained knowledge of Birth Control and exercise it in regulating the size of their families. They have already benefited by this knowledge and are today considered the most respectable and moral members of the community. They have only children when they desire, and all society points to them as types that should perpetuate their kind.

The second group is equally intelligent and responsible. They desire to control the size of their families, but are unable to obtain knowledge or to put such available knowledge into practice.

The third are those irresponsible and reckless ones having little regard for the consequence of their acts, or whose religious scruples prevent their exercising control over their numbers. Many of this group are diseased, feeble-minded, and are of the pauper element dependent entirely upon the normal and fit members of society for their support. There is no doubt in the minds of all thinking people that the procreation of this group should be stopped. [Applause.] For if they are not able to support and care for themselves, they should certainly not be allowed to bring offspring into this world for others to look after. [Applause.] We do not believe that filling the earth with misery, poverty, and disease is moral. And it is our desire and intention to carry on our crusade until the perpetuation of such conditions has ceased.

We desire to stop at its source the disease, poverty and feeble-mindedness and insanity which exist today, for these lower the standards of civilization and make for race deterioration. We know that the masses of people are growing wiser and are using their own minds to decide their individual conduct. The more people of this kind we have, the less immorality shall exist. For the more responsible people grow, the higher do they and shall they attain real morality. [Applause.]

PART II THE REFORMER
23. First Japan Trip

As she was slogging through the lengthy and time-consuming investigations of the Town Hall raid, lectures, conferences, and meetings interspersed back to back, Sanger was also preparing for her first trip to Japan. It was a hectic schedule that would become more so once she reached Japan.

Sanger had been invited in the summer of 1921 to visit Japan by *Kaizo*, a liberal group in Tokyo, publishers of a monthly magazine that reviewed politics, literature, and social theory. *Kaizo* had discovered Sanger after a Japanese journalist interviewed her in 1920 and had published articles of hers. Meanwhile, the *Birth Control Review* had published two articles by Agnes Smedley in June 1919 and February 1920 on Japan and its population problem.[1]

Writing in June 1919, Smedley noted that within the past sixty-five years, the population of Japan had doubled. In fact, the entire world was aware of this population explosion and the militaristic Japanese faction that was approving it. Not all in Japan, however, agreed with the militarists. By February 1920, a least a dozen Japanese men from the government and labor sectors had visited the office of the *Birth Control Review*, plied the staff with questions, requested literature, and returned again with more questions.

Their growing interest was urged by the Baroness Shidzue Ishimoto, whom Sanger had met, also in 1920, and who was to become "the Margaret Sanger" of Japan. The baroness' story was a remarkable one.[2]

When Baron Keikichi Ishimoto was 20 years younger, he told his pretty wife: "If the women of a nation stay on a low level, there is no progress in that nation as a whole. I am interested in what my friend said to me about the downfall of the Great Roman Empire, because my friend attributed it to the Roman women who stopped growing physically and intellectually. If the women of Japan remain on the same level as they are today and don't work to improve their intellect and their physique, there won't be any glory to the future of Japan!" . . .

A sheltered daughter of a Samurai family, Shidzue Ishimoto had left her two small boys in Tokyo to join her husband in New York, in 1919. The Baron was passionately interested in social problems. The young woman, who was accustomed to consulting her elders even about washing her hair, became a roomer with a Southern family in a flat on Broadway and 157th Street. She stayed away from Japanese friends. She learned both English and stenography in three months. And she met Margaret Sanger.[3]

It was to be a lifelong friendship. Inspired by Sanger, Shidzue Ishimoto returned to Japan, where she not only became one of the few Japanese women who dared to open a business in Japan in 1920, but she further challenged Japanese tradition by founding the Japanese birth control movement. It was probably not quite what the baron had in mind when he had shipped his wife off to America, but it was to be of great benefit to Japan and to Margaret Sanger.

When Sanger set out for Japan in 1922, the militarists were aggressively pushing their legislation outlawing Dangerous Thoughts, which Margaret Sanger had plenty of.

> Needless for me to say I had been surprised when I learned from the Consul General at San Francisco that the Japanese government had issued orders that my passport should not be vised and that I could not lecture on Birth Control in Japan. It is not easy to surprise anyone who has worked for long in the Birth Control movement. We get accustomed to the unexpected happening. In this case my surprise was real because I was led to believe by Japanese in the U.S.A. that there was a general interest in the Birth Control subject on the part of the younger members of the government.[4]

Sanger had not been led astray. Dangerous Thoughts or not, once in Japan, she was everywhere enthusiastically received. "My days and evenings are crowded with lecture and reception dates. Every evening, afternoon, dinner lunch, and morning taken until I leave Tokyo!"[5] In less than a month, she gave more than five hundred speeches and interviews.

Just as the opposition of the Roman Catholic hierarchy to Sanger's work had brought widespread publicity to birth control in the United States, so the obstacles set up by the Japanese government acted to whet interest in the forbidden. Interest in Sanger had been there before she had arrived; now it was widespread and growing.

As was her custom when visiting a new country, Sanger investigated the working conditions of women, walking through the mills, the silk factories, then the red light districts. For far too many centuries, Japanese women had been held down; now they were only gradually discovering feminism. Similarly, they were slow to organize their labor or halt child labor. In a silk-spinning mill in Najoya, Sanger saw

> seven hundred girls, some no more than ten years of age, swiftly twirling off the slender threads from cocoons and catching them on the spindles....imprisoned in rooms with all windows closed to keep them moist and hot. A quarter of their seven dollars a month wages had to go for board.[6]

But Japan was always to share a special place in her heart. The warm public acclaim, the personal friendship with Shidzue Ishimoto (later to be Shidzue Kato), the elegance that invested the most casual event, and the extended courtesies she appreciated and respected. Her son, Grant, who was with Sanger in Japan,

> learned the Japanese manners and became marvelously courteous. Practically every time he spoke to me he made the three bows, and unconsciously I soon found myself returning them with equal formality.[7]

The Japan trip was but a precursor to more extended travels. After Japan, the itinerary included Korea, China, Hong Kong, Singapore, Ceylon, Egypt, Peking, Shanghai, Cairo, Alexandria, the Adriatic Sea, Venice, Milan, Paris, and finally, London and the Fifth International Neo-Malthusian and Birth Control Conference.[8] (Sanger hoped to go to India as well, but her former radical connections made her unwelcome there.[9]) Throughout this trip, Sanger had been traveling not only with Grant (who said traveling with his mother was like being dragged at the tail of a typhoon), but also with Noah Slee, whose courtship surely must have been one of the most expensive of all time.[10] Nevertheless, for Sanger, it had been a working trip.

Lectures by her had been arranged everywhere; "a cablegram from Peking dated April 10th stated that she had addressed an enthusiastic audience of 2,000 at the National University of China."[11] Where she did not lecture, she was, nevertheless, met by an eager cadre of reporters for interviews, statements, and photos. News of her travels and her descriptions of conditions in the East were published regularly in the *Birth Control Review*, which also wrote of the "astounding amount of publicity" that Sanger was generating in both English and Chinese newspapers.[12]

Looking back on the trip, Sanger could boast that clinics had been established in Osaka, Kyoto, and Tokyo, Japan, and in Beijing and Shanghai, China.[13] Her vision for the international scope of birth control was being realized. As was her intention to marry for money. On September 18, 1922, in London, just before lunch, Noah Slee and Margaret Sanger went to the St. Giles registrar of marriages in Bloomsbury and were wed.[14]

The Manuscript

After attending the Fifth International Neo-Malthusian and Birth Control Conference in London July 11 to 14, Sanger was free to spend most of August in Switzerland with Juliet Rublee. They stayed in Mürren, close to the Jungfrau mountain, where at 11,400 feet sits the highest railroad station in the world, and where they had staggering views of the Schilthorn.[15] Sanger returned to London in September, and five days after having married Slee, sailed for New York, arriving in time to see Stuart and Grant begin their terms at Peddie Institute. In New York, she resumed board meetings with the American Birth Control League and kept her usual heavy lecture schedule.

Seeking to raise funds and to enlarge membership of the American Birth Control League, the Japan and Asia trip a topic of general interest, Sanger scheduled this lecture for October 30 at Carnegie Hall. Although it drew an audience of two thousand along with two police reporters, the lecture did not do well financially.[16] But it was an interesting evening for those attending. Below is the first half of the lecture.

Birth Control in China and Japan[17]
Speech at Carnegie Hall, New York, October 30, 1922

Your generous greeting delights me.... It gives me hope that we need no longer fight this battle alone. I want to believe that your being here tonight means that you share with me the vision of a new world, which may become, through the instrument of birth control, a beautiful reality.

In the first place, I want you to know that I did not go to the Far East as a self-appointed prophet to reform the habits of the yellow race. I have never tried to shout the message of Birth Control into unwilling ears. We have advocated this doctrine only to those who have expressed a willingness to bear interest in it. We do not believe in imposing upon anyone the principle or the practice of Birth Control. For a year previous to my departure, repeated invitations had come to me from Japan. On the part of Young Japan there has arisen a great desire to awaken their countrymen to the menace of overpopulation. A group of young Japanese intellectuals, called the Kaizo, or "Reconstruction," formulated the plan of inviting to Japan representatives of the most challenging ideas of our Western civilization. They invited Bertrand Russell to lecture on Reconstruction, Professor Einstein on the theory of Relativity, H.G. Wells on International Peace, and myself on Population and War. I was invited to follow Mr. Russell. You see, they put me in good company.

I agreed to visit Japan to deliver five addresses, under the auspices of the Kaizo group. With great joy I set forth last February to carry the message of birth control into the Orient. I booked passage on the *Taiyo Maru*, and escorted by my thirteen-year-old son, Grant, crossed the continent to San Francisco. Two days before my sailing, the Japanese Consul refused to visa my passport. With many apologies and great regret, he informed me that the Imperial Government had cabled directions that, if she applied for permission to visit Japan to lecture on Birth Control, Mrs. Sanger should be refused. Would I be permitted to enter as an individual, if I promised silence? The word came back—"No."

I was surprised, but not dismayed, for this official opposition was not new to me. As a matter of fact, the Imperial Japanese Government was only imitating the attitude of my own democratic government. And I knew, from past experience, that wherever this autocratic opposition to Birth Control is expressed by the official mind, there is always a tremendous popular interest not far away. I knew the new generation of Japan was interested and I resolved to overcome this obstacle, not merely for my own satisfaction, but for the international good of the movement.

Because I could not obtain that visa, the steamship company cancelled my booking. For a time, defeat stared me in the face. The voyage seemed impossible; I would have to turn back. But then I remembered that I had overcome greater obstacles than this one. My Irish blood was up. I would not take this autocratic "no" as the final answer.

Sometimes diplomacy is a better weapon than defiance. I decided to fight this battle behind the barricades of diplomacy. If the Imperial Japanese Government would not tolerate me, perhaps China would. There was no trouble in obtaining a Chinese visa. I returned to the office of the steamship company, secured passage for Shanghai, obtained the same stateroom on the *Taiyo Maru* I had previously booked and sailed from San Francisco on the day I had originally planned.

Aboard the *Taiyo*, I discovered, as fellow passengers, more than one hundred and fifty Japanese returning from the Washington Peace Conference, including the two delegates Admiral Baron Kato, now Prime Minister of Japan, and Mr. Hanihara, who at that time was vice-minister of

Foreign Affairs.[18] Besides these distinguished Japanese, there was another party of delegates, under the leadership of Mr. John Mott, on their way to Peking to attend the conference of the World Christian Student Federation. A meeting had been arranged for me in Honolulu, and although our boat arrived at one in the afternoon and sailed at five, I was able to speak to an audience, which filled the hall to its capacity. I was received with no less enthusiasm by the Japanese than by the American residents there. The Japanese press had even arranged a dinner for that evening, in the event the *Taiyo Maru* remained. This I could not accept, but during my few hours stay, the nucleus of a Hawaiian Birth Control League was organized.

The demonstration in Honolulu reacted upon my fellow passengers aboard the *Taiyo Maru*. During the next two weeks everyone aboard seemed to be discussing the pros and cons of Birth Control. They began to crowd into my cabin to ask questions. Finally, I was invited to address the Japanese delegation from the Peace Conference. This I did and Admiral Kato and Mr. Hanihara attended. The feelings of my own countrymen were hurt because they were not invited. So finally, I had to speak to the missionaries as well. Then the passengers of the second cabin besieged me with requests, and I spoke to them also.

After I had addressed the Japanese delegates, radio messages began to fly between our ship and Japan. In particular, Mr. Hanihara was especially kind. He sent a radio message to his government stating that, in his opinion, the subject of Birth Control, as he had heard it expounded, was in no way offensive to public morals. He recommended his government to lift the ban, to permit me to enter Japan and to allow the free discussion of this problem.

Meanwhile, as I later learned, discussion and protest were rising in Japan. Every newspaper was expressing its opinion on the exclusion of America's undesirable citizen. Not all of them thought that I should be admitted. But the great majority of them were of the opinion that the Home Office made a mistake in taking such drastic action, before I had at least made some remarks in Japan upon which an opinion could be passed.

Then I began to receive radio messages from Japan:

One reading: "Thousands disciples welcome you."

The next: "Possible both land Yokohama, welcome discourse."

The next day: "Possible land Yokohama, Impossible discourse."

Radio messages from all sorts of organizations asking me to lecture: a radio message from the medical association of Kyoto; a radio message from the "Cultural Society of Kobe"; a radio message from the New Women's Organization of Nagoya; a message from a commercial group in Tokyo; another from an industrial group of Yokohama; a greeting from the doctors of Nagoya; one, even, from the Young Men's Christian Association. And still

THE WOMAN REBEL

NO GODS NO MASTERS

VOL. I.   MAY, 1914.   NO. 3.

CANNIBALS

Compared with the diseased, perverted, hypocritical ghouls of American "civilization," cannibals strike you as simple, healthy people who live in an earthly Utopia. If they feed and fatten upon the charred flesh of human beings, cannibals at least do not hide behind the sickening smirk of the Church and the Y. M. C. A. They are open, frank, and straightforward in their search for food. They eat their victims outright. They do not use the charred skulls and skeletons of women and children as the foundation of institutions that will hide the cries and shrieks of the tortured, or attempt to kill the nauseating stench of their bloody breath by vomiting forth perfumed hypocricies of the Baptist Church—words of peace on earth and goodwill toward men.

Cannibals are not so cowardly that they must employ Maxim guns in the wholesale slaughter of men, women and children. They do not employ starving sneaks to burn the evidence of their nightmarish appetites, or fear themselves to look upon the disembowelled and dismembered corpses of the men, women and children who are sacrificed to promote great works of charity and philanthropy.

Cannibals, you see, are uncivilized, primitive folk, low in the scale of human intelligence. Their tastes are not so fastidious, so refined, so Christian, as those of our great American coal operators, who have subsidized the State of Colorado, and treat the President of the United States as an office boy—these leering, bloody hyenas of the human race who smear themselves with the stinking honey of Charity to attract those foul flies of religion who spread pollution throughout the land.

Have we workers been inoculated with this foul pollution of the spirit, this poison that is being spread by the Young Men's and Young Women's Christian Associations and by those churches which are subsidized by the murderous masters of America?

Certainly we have if we do not boycott the Baptist Church and its allies, those "Christian Associations," that are subsidized by the Rockefellers and other criminals in order to kill the spirit of the workers of America.

Certainly we have been if we remain silent or inactive in the campaign against the poison of the "religion" that is weakening and killing the spirit of the American workers.

Workingwomen! Keep away from the Y. W. C. A. as you would from a pesthouse. It is based upon the slavery and torture of the workers of America, upon the bodies of toilers who have been killed in the mines and factories, and upon the bodies of those who have protested against being so murdered—shot down by Maxim guns and burned up with Standard oil. These substantial buildings have been built by those Christians who riddled the bodies of women and children with bullets when they attempted to escape from a burning pit to a place of safety. It is they who are conferring favors upon you, in order to rob you of your freedom.

They want to inculcate in you the stupid spirit of submission to their mastery. They want to feed you upon the vapid innocuities of religion. They want to make you keep books with their God. They want to keep you in stupid ignorance of your own body, so that you, too, will some day be forced to breed children who can perform their horrible wholesale murders for them—who will shoot down all men and women and children who may dare question their mastery and their tyranny. They will force you to breed the cowards who murder those who are willing to die for freedom rather than to live in slavery.

But remember Ludlow! Remember the men and women and children who were sacrificed in order that John D. Rockefeller, Jr., might continue his noble career of charity and philanthropy as a supporter of the Christian faith.

Steer clear of those brothels of Spirit and morgues of Freedom!

BLOOD AND OIL

Huerta, the murderer of Madero and the minion of capital, has proven a failure. This is the main reason why Mexico, the great oil country, into which millions of dollars have been sunk by the investors of America and Europe, is now to be invaded and "pacified" by the workers of the United States.

Because, owing to the successes of the peons and of the social revolutionists, the title deeds of William R. Hearst are now so much waste paper; because the oil industry, the copper and other industries of Mexico are endangered, and because certain fusilades and cannonades did not take place in honor of "the flag"—whatever that may be—we and the Mexican people are now bidden to rush at each other like wild beasts and rip up each others' bellies.

And this startling order, issued in accordance with the supposed public opinion of the United States and of other civilized countries, is coolly repeated in every Liberal and advanced organ of the Press as well as by the leading prelates of the Catholic and other Christian Churches.

Because, moreover, in the last 104 years, the Mexican people have been enslaved, terrorized, brutalized, tortured, maimed and murdered under the iron rule of sixty-one successive dictators; because they have endured no less than 253 revolutions in that period of time, we are now bidden to take part in plundering and murdering this people, already distracted by continual war and revolution.

Those who have devised and prepared for these plunders and murders and who are instigating us to quarrel with Mexico are doing so only in the interests of Capital, on behalf of the Oil Octopus and for the legalized banditti who control the industries of Mexico. The insolence of these impostors has now reached its extremest development, for they form but an insignificant minority who live in luxury and idleness upon our labor.

Comrades, the deluded men now be-

"The doctor's here again and it ud better be a boy, 'cause there's no more room in our bed."

This poignant cartoon is also a realistic picture of a typical tenement in New York's Lower East Side in 1912, the year in which Margaret Sanger may have nursed Mrs. Sachs.

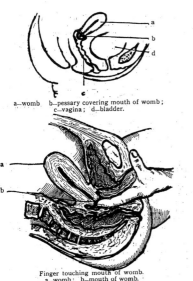

a—womb b—pessary covering mouth of womb;
c—vagina; d—bladder.

Finger touching mouth of womb.
a—womb ; b—mouth of womb.

douche until the following morning. Take part or
about a quart of an antiseptic douche BEFORE the
pessary is removed; after removing it continue the
douche and cleanse thoroughly.

Wash the pessary in clear cold water, dry well and
place away in the box. One should last two years,
if cared for.

Two pages and the cover of *Family Limitation*
(Fifth edition), 1916.

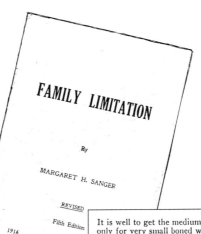

FAMILY LIMITATION

By

MARGARET H. SANGER

REVISED

Fifth Edition

1916

It is well to get the medium size, as the small ones are
only for very small boned women and easily get out of
place.

French Pessary—slightly different from the American.

In my estimation a well fitted pessary is the surest
method of absolutely preventing conception. I have
known hundreds of women who have used it for years
with the most satisfactory results. The trouble is
women are afraid of their own bodies, and are of
course ignorant of their physical construction. They
are silly in thinking the pessary can go up too far, or
that it could get lost, etc., etc., and therefore discard it.
It can not get into the womb, neither can it get lost.
The only thing it can do is to come out. And even
that will give warning by the discomfort of the bulky
feeling it causes, when it is out of place.

Follow the directions given with each box, and learn
to adjust it correctly; one can soon feel that it is on
right. After the pessary has been placed into the
vagina deeply, it can be fitted well over the neck of
the womb. One can feel it is fitted by pressing the
finger around the soft part of the pessary, which
should completely cover the mouth of the womb. If
it is properly adjusted there will be no discomfort, the
man will be unconscious that anything is used, and
no germ or semen can enter the womb.

If the woman should fall asleep directly after no
harm can happen, and it is not necessary to take a

"Your Honor, this woman gave birth to a naked child!"

Anthony Comstock, while much
feared, was also and rightly much
jeered. Cartoon by Robert Minor, *The
Masses*, September 1915.

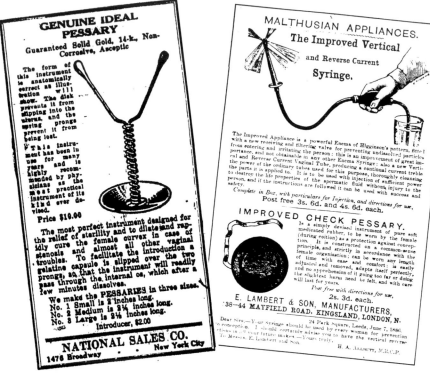

Early twentieth-century advertisements for feminine hygiene devices.

"Judge Returning Home After Sentencing a Birth Control Speaker to Six Months Is Met By His Two Children, Ages Three and Six" Cartoon by Cornelia Barnes, *Birth Control Review,* August 1918.

One of several sketches Bill Sanger contributed to the second issue of the *Birth Control Review,* March 1917.

Anti-war cartoon and article, *Birth Control Review*, April-May 1917.

Drawn by Chamberlain.

BREEDING MEN FOR BATTLE
Olive Schreiner

In supplying the men for the carnage of a battlefield, women have not merely lost actually more blood, and gone through a more acute anguish and weariness, in the months of bearing and in the final agony of child-birth, than has been experienced by the men who cover it, but, in the months of rearing that follow, the women of the race go through a long, patiently endured strain which no knapsacked soldier on his longest march has ever more than equalled; while, even in the matter of death, in all civilized societies, the probability that the average woman will die in child-birth is immeasurably greater than the probability that the average male will die in battle.

There is, perhaps, no woman, whether she have borne children or be merely potentially a child-bearer, who could look down upon a battlefield coverd with slain, but the thought would rise in her, "So many mothers' sons! So many young bodies brought into the world to lie there! So many months of weariness and pain while bones and muscles were shaped within! So many hours of anguish and struggle that breath might be! So many baby mouths drawing life at women's breasts—all this, that men might lie with glazed eyeballs, and swollen faces, and fixed, blue, unclosed mouths, and great limbs tossed—this, that an acre of ground might be manured with human flesh, that next year's grass or poppies or karoo bushes may spring up greener and redder, where they have lain, or that the sand of a plain may have the glint of white bones!"

And we cry, "Without an inexorable cause this must not be!" No woman who is a woman says of a human body, "It is nothing!"

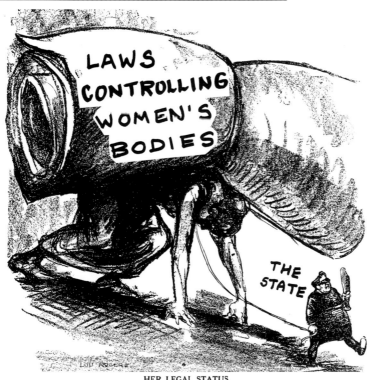

HER LEGAL STATUS

Cartoon from *Birth Control Review*, May 1919.

Cover of *Birth Control Review,*
November 1923.

A full-page ad for 3-in-One Oil
ran in each issue of *Birth Control
Review* after Noah Slee married
Margaret Sanger in 1921.

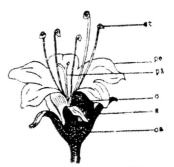

Illustration from *What Every Mother Should Know; or How Six Little Children Were Told the Truth*, 1916.

A complete flower: *st, stamen; pi, pistil; pe, petal; s, sepal; ca, calyx; c, corolla.*

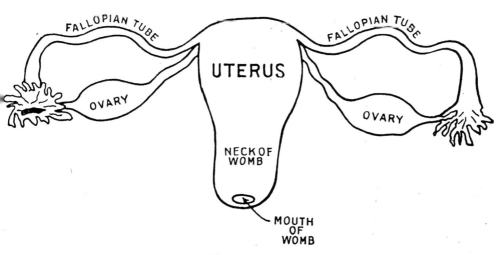

UTERUS TUBES AND OVARIES

Illustration from *What Every Boy and Girl Should Know*, 1927.

Cartoons from the thirties.

"Can I interest you in a book of recipes?"
"Not unless they're by Margaret Sanger."

Cartoon by Donald McKee, *Ballyhoo!* 1931.

"Hello, Birth Control League? Mrs. Sanger, please—"

"She *still* disagrees with Margaret Sanger"

I did not know whether I would be permitted to land. But it was some satisfaction, at any rate, to know that the opposition of the government had aroused the Japanese press and public to a discussion of Birth Control. For once people began seriously to discuss Birth Control, our battle is more than half won.

Such was the situation when we arrived at Yokohama harbor on the tenth of March. As the *Taiyo Maru* entered the bay, she was surrounded by a fleet of small craft. Government officials, health officials, representatives of the police department, and a mob of newspaper men and camera men flocked on board. I learned later that no less than seventy permits to board the *Taiyo Maru* had been issued to the representatives of the press. Then I had to submit to the severest test and strain of my journey.

First with a government official, an interpreter, and a stenographer I was closeted for an hour. At the end of that time, the official had committed himself to the effect that, providing the American Consulate General in Japan would make a formal and official request to permit me to land, the ban might be raised. Now, I had already, by radio, sent a message to the American Consul asking him, as an American citizen, to use his power in this direction, stating that I wished at any rate, to visit Japan, if not as a propagandist, at least as a private citizen. And so, after this conference, I hurried off another cable telling him I was awaiting his assistance. During this time, I was besieged by reporters and photographers. I waited for the reply of our American Consul. It did not come. Not only did the representative of my government refuse to make a formal request for my admittance, he did not even condescend to the courtesy of a reply to either of my messages. He did not explain the reasons for his indifference to the rights of an American citizen.

At seven-thirty that evening, due to great popular pressure and protest, it was as an individual that the Imperial Japanese Government opened its gates to me.

I must thank intelligent wide-awake young Japan, expressing itself in agitation and protest that showed the power of organized public opinion over official autocracy. Yet I could not help wondering, if the case had been reversed and I was seeking to enter this country, would there have been the same help, the same agitation and demand on the part of our citizens?

The final order was to undergo the inspection of the customs officials. They must have thought that I possessed some magic wand to depopulate Japan. After confiscating most of my books, I was allowed to go.

Just as I finished this inspection and was at last free, I was approached by several rickshaw men who came as representatives of the Rickshaw Men's Union to welcome me to Japan. One spoke a little English and courteously apologized for the unwarranted action of the Home Office. "You do

not mind," he said. "Sometime Japanese Government, he little autocratic."
I did not mind. I felt almost at home.

Addendum

The September *Birth Control Review* for 1922 announced in its News Notes
the passage of a new law by the Japanese Diet that allows women to form
and attend political associations....This "is highly favorable for the spread of
the Birth Control movement in Japan."[19]

But in his report to the 1925 Sixth International New-Malthusian and
Birth Control Conference, Isa Abe, sociologist at Tokyo University,
explained the great difficulties that the Japanese still faced in promoting
Birth Control in Japan:

> While we were free to discuss Birth Control from a theoretical
> standpoint, we are strictly forbidden to inform the public of practi-
> cal methods....[this] is considered by the government as injurious
> to the law of decency....A majority of [our statesmen] are still ruled
> by the jingoistic spirit and are naturally antagonistic to birth con-
> trol.[20]

24. The Eugenics Craze

The value of an historical narrative such as this lies in the opportunity it affords the reader to survey, from the distance of time, the forces—psychic, social, economic, political—driving a nation. Ideally, the reader may come to appreciate the mindset, to glimpse the construct of values that intermingled with the events and demands of the moment and shaped the posture of a people. Here, the reader is asked to consider briefly the milieu of America in 1900, a time before the horror of the Nazi camps, before the Nazis were even heard of, before the disabled had rights, a time when wealth as synonymous with goodness was the badge of entitlement, when racism was so embedded as to be invisible.

At this time, at the opening of the twentieth century, its marvels were beginning to appear with mind-boggling rapidity: "electric lights, trolleys, and machinery; phonographs, cinema, and radio; dyestuffs, fertilizers, and gasoline; anesthesia, medicines, and diagnostic X rays."[1] With these marvels came the effects, direct and indirect, of progress—the increasing mechanization of American farms and factories. Thus were forced out-of-work farmhands into the city, where they were crowded in with unemployed factory workers and underemployed artisans.

Concurrently, came tidal waves of immigrants, nearly a million a year for almost a decade, to build an army of cheap labor, worker unrest, and unspeakable poverty, teeming millions who collected in steaming tenements, compounding the poverty with the most dreadful of lifestyles in densely populated city blocks—such as those in New York's Lower East Side, where Margaret Sanger had nursed Mrs. Sachs.

Henry George, writing in *Progress and Poverty* in 1879—a veritable bible in the Higgins household when Margaret was growing up—suggested that the "progress" of industrialization was causing the increasing poverty. But America was enthralled with its progress and its economy driven by industrialization, and the scientists who had made this possible had become the high priests of any problem needing a solution. The chief problem in America, of course, were the people, the ill-bred, unemployed, uneducated, idle, shiftless, feeble-minded, promiscuous, diseased hordes of people. Now a new science offered an explanation for these people.

In England, Francis Galton had been applying statistics to hereditary patterns and developing what in 1883 he called eugenics. Eugenics was the science of improving the human race—"race betterment" would become the well-known term—and Galton's research showed that, along with physical characteristics, temperament and talents were inherited. Galton's science quickly found support. From Italy came the findings of Cesare Lombroso, a criminologist, who had identified a criminal type not only by his behavior, but also by his physical characteristics.[2] In 1877, Richard Dugdale published his study of seven generations of the Jukes family, which was interpreted to illustrate the power of hereditary to produce generations of unfit people.[3]

During the next two, almost three, decades, on both sides of the Atlantic, eugenics spread throughout the world, over western Europe and Scandinavia and, in the twenties, into South America and Japan. In 1912, the first International Eugenics Congress was held in London attracting 750 delegates; a second was held in 1921 and a third in 1932.[4] In Britain arose the Eugenics Education Society (later renamed the Eugenics Society), in America the American Eugenics Society with chapters in major cities, both groups engaging in educational campaigns with free lectures, lantern-slide presentations, and bundles of printed matter. In America, state fairs featured eugenic displays that explained Mendelian laws of heredity and offered eugenics contests, healthy baby contests and Fittest Families Contests: in Kansas, the fortunate family received for the latter the Governor's Fitter Family Trophy.[5] The American Eugenics Society reached out to the churches, distributed A Eugenics Catechism, and sponsored a Eugenics Sermon Contest that drew three hundred submissions.[6] Eugenics was the new religion, the religion with a scientific basis.

The absorption of eugenics into mainstream America was particularly assisted by—to quote a well-turned phrase—"the advantage of excellent patronage."[7] At a time when industry and the government had begun to turn to science and scientists for direction and advice, the wealthy and their foundations were eager to offer their patronage.[8]

Into this welcoming atmosphere swept a scientist with less expertise in his discipline than facility at self-promotion, Charles B. Davenport, who convinced no less than Mrs. E. H. Harriman, recent widow of the railroad magnate, and later the Carnegie Institution of Washington to endow and maintain his Eugenics Records Office at Cold Spring Harbor—handsomely.[9] In 1911, with the help of interns and assistants, Davenport began churning out the reams of data and training the hundreds of budding eugenicists, who would spread the eugenics gospel throughout America. Davenport's influence extended into Congress, when his right-hand man, Harry H. Laughlin, went to Washington on Davenport's laurels.[10] There, as the eminent scientist backed by the reams of data from the Eugenics Records Office, Laughlin convinced some congressmen of limited education on the importance of limiting immigration of the "inferior" European stock; hence, passage of the Reed-Johnson National Origins Act of 1924, which sharply limited immigration from southern and eastern Europe and barred all Asians.[11] Thus did eugenics spread to enjoy the embrace of mainstream acceptance, the usual result when any matter is supported by great sums of money and the reigning political nabobs.

Buoyed by governmental and professional approbation, eugenics was everywhere on the forefront of public discussion. Intelligent people talked of a "eugenic" marriage. Young people were warned of the dangers of a noneugenic union. Articles on eugenics appeared in newspapers and popular magazines; books on eugenics were bestsellers. Courses on eugenics were taught at almost every school, college, and university.[12]

There was Positive Eugenics, which sought betterment of the race through "eugenic" marriages, marriages that were made with those carrying desirable inheritable traits. Negative Eugenics promoted sterilization, saving the taxpayers thousands of dollars during the worrisome times of economic downturns and depression and relieving taxpayers from supporting future generations of diseased descendants, who could pass on through their defective germ plasma tendencies to shiftlessness, alcoholism, feeblemindedness, and insanity.

The advantages of sterilization were many, not only to the taxpayer, but to those sterilized, as Dr. Henry Clay Sharp, the Indiana prison physician who pushed through the first sterilization law in America in 1907, explained. Sterilization was not a punishment of those unfortunates, who through no fault of their own carried defective germ plasma. In such a case, sterilization saved the prisoner from himself and from his worse traits and allowed him to be released from prison and returned to his home and society.[13] Literature supplies explaining the benefits of sterilization were quickly exhausted.[14] By 1911, six American states had sterilization laws; by 1914, that number had reached twelve, and it would continue to grow. A poll taken by *Fortune* in 1937 showed that 63 percent of all Americans believed habitual criminals should undergo compulsory sterilization, 66 percent felt that mental defectives should be sterilized.[15]

Eugenics' recommendations for sterilization were supported by eugenics data that showed a frightening increase in the number of defectives. This was disturbing because defectives, the feeble-minded, were deemed to be especially prolific.[16] In seeking support for birth control, Sanger spoke often of the rising numbers of the feeble-minded and the insane and of the costs involved in their care, as in this typical piece from a *Birth Control Review* of 1918:

> The care of the insane cost the State of New York $8,320,000 last year. The total economic loss on the insane for the year is officially estimated at more than $35,000,000. The institutions for the insane in New York are overcrowded to the extent of nearly 6,000 persons. There are already 37,069 persons in public institutions for the mentally defective and it is to be presumed that if these hospitals were not now overcrowded there would be some thousands more. And the number of insane and feeble-minded is increasing.[17]

As the birth control movement gained momentum, Sanger sought every avenue whereby it might gain widespread general acceptance. She could scarcely ignore the apparent legitimacy of eugenics. Even in retrospect, eugenics was a move in the right direction. It asked the right questions: "Why are some persons shiftless? Promiscuous? Deformed? Sickly?" It gave rise to the scientific collection of data and to the birth of the science of statistics.[18] It demanded an objective examination of a problem to find its solution. At the same time, eugenics blithely ignored the mercenary side of capitalism and the protectionism offered by property-based law; it overlooked the advantages of being well born, of cliques, of social rank, of good nutrition, of trust funds, and inherited wealth. But these latter considerations were for the future. Under the laws of defective germ plasma and mainline eugenics during the early twentieth century, poverty and intelligence was as much a hereditary trait as blue eyes and short toes.

And so, on both sides of the Atlantic, scientists and statesmen were urging implementation of eugenics into national policy. In England, eugenics had the support of many of Sanger's friends: Dean Inge (the gloomy dean), George Bernard Shaw, H. G. Wells. Her mentor Havelock Ellis, though he believed that sterilization should always be voluntary, said that eugenics was the same as the woman question and argued that the woman who could control her fertility would naturally bring forth superior children and thus a betterment of the race. This, of course, was Sanger's argument.

Eugenics without Birth Control seems to us a house builded upon the sands. It is at the mercy of the rising stream of the unfit. It cannot stand against the furious winds of economic pressures which have buffeted into partial or total helplessness a tremendous proportion of the human race. Only upon a free, self-determining motherhood can rest any unshakable structure of racial betterment.[19]

Aside from desiring to be incorporated into their success, Sanger had any number of good reasons to accommodate the eugenicists. By aligning birth control with a middle-class popular movement supported by scientists, biologists, physicians, attorneys, government appointees, and the professional class in general, along with university and United States presidents (Theodore Roosevelt, Woodrow Wilson, Calvin Coolidge), Sanger was distancing herself and Birth Control from its radical associations of the past.

The Eugenicists spoke straightforwardly of sexual matters, a refreshing change. Their data was abundant and useful to her in arguing the need of birth control (as seen in the manuscript below). Many physicians and scientists who were Sanger's supporters were eugenicists, as were most of those on the American Birth Control League National Council and on the advisory board of the Clinical Research Bureau.

But it should be noted, these men on Sanger's boards were generally reform eugenicists, who condemned the poor science of Galton's mainline eugenics, which attributed all to heredity. Many of the reform eugenicists would eventually distance themselves from or exit the formal eugenics movement.[20] Sanger persisted in ignoring the growing reformist distinction. "The campaign for Birth Control is not merely of eugenic value, but is practically identical in ideal with the final aims of Eugenics," said Sanger.[21] Not so, said the mainline eugenicists. In methods and principles the movements were so far apart that it is not difficult to understand why mainline eugenicists really did not want anything to do with Margaret Sanger. When the eugenicists passed a resolution at the Sixth International Neo-Malthusian and Birth Control Conference in 1925, which stated

Persons whose progeny give promise of being of decided value to the community should be encouraged to bear as large families properly spaced as they feel they feasibly can.[22]

Sanger replied,

Surely it is not within the province of our program to offer gratuitous advice to intelligent adults who have achieved control and direction of their parental function as to the number of additional children they shall bring into the world. This is precisely the problem they must solve for themselves.[23]

In 1921, Sanger's prose had been less tortured:

If Eugenics is to exert any beneficial influence upon racial and human health it must resort to a full and complete acceptance of Birth Control....The fact remains that the path to a better human race lies through fewer and better children.[24]

Eugenics had its detractors, and in truth Margaret Sanger was one of them. As dearly as she wanted their endorsement and though she agreed with the prevailing argument of the time, believing "in the sterilization of the feeble-minded, the insane and the syphilitic" as an alternative to institutionalization, even here she disagreed that sterilization was an adequate remedy.[25] More importantly, Sanger suggested the real reason for the unfitness of the unfit.

Neither the mating of healthy couples nor the sterilization of certain recognized types of the unfit touches the great problem of unlimited reproduction of those whose housing, clothing, and food are all inadequate to physical and mental health. These measures do not touch those great masses, who through economic pressure populate the slums, and there produce in their helplessness other helpless, diseased and incompetent masses, who overwhelm all that eugenics can do among those whose economic condition is better.[26]

Underlying the "research" of the mainline eugenicists was their belief in a hierarchy. At the top of the hierarchy sat the Anglo-Saxon race, while lowest on the rung was the black race. Hierarchy implied rule by regulation and coercion. Sanger would have none of that. Sanger believed in the right of the individual to create a destiny. Idealistic? Certainly. But has the world ever made progress without the lodestar of an ideal? Again and again Sanger repeats what is practically her mantra: The woman herself must decide when and if she is to have children, how many, and under what circumstances. The child must be wanted.

First: we are convinced that racial regeneration, like individual regeneration, must come from within. That is, it must be autonomous, self-directive, and not imposed from without. In other words, every potential parent, and especially every potential mother, must be brought to an acute realization of the primary and central responsibility of bringing children into this world.

Secondly: Not until the parents of the world are thus given

control over their reproductive faculties will it ever be possible not alone to improve the quality of the generations of the future, but even to maintain civilization even at its present level. Only by self-control of this type, only by intelligent mastery of the procreative powers can the great mass of humanity be awakened to the great responsibility of parenthood.

Thirdly: We have come to the conclusion, based on wide-spread investigation and experience, that this education for parent-hood must be based upon the needs and demands of the people themselves. An idealistic code of sexual ethics, imposed from above, a set of rules devised by high-minded theorists who fail to take into account the living conditions and desires of the sub-merged masses, can never be of the slightest value in effecting any changes in the mores of the people. Such systems have in the past revealed their woeful inability to prevent the sexual and racial chaos into which the world has today drifted.

The almost universal demand for practical education in Birth Control is one of the most hopeful signs that the masses themselves today possess the divine spark of regeneration....The potential mother is to be shown that maternity need not be slavery but the most effective avenue toward self-development and self-realization.[27]

Sanger's dance with the eugenicists, her futile attempts to gain their support and her qualified support of sterilization, left a legacy of sentences that are separated from their context by her detractors. Meanwhile, volun-tary sterilization is one of the most popular chosen methods of contracep-tive by women in America and throughout the world, and in 2002 steriliza-tion was the world's most widespread form of birth control.[28]

Ultimately, the "science" of eugenics was recognized as bogus. Carnegie Institution withdrew its funding, and in 1939 Davenport's Eugenics Record Office at Cold Spring Harbor was shut down. In the wis-dom of retrospection and refined science methodologies, it was seen that eugenics was based on bad science, hearsay, reification, on secondhand reporting, the creative use of statistics, on nonsystematic records, on anec-dotal and subjective evidence masking prejudice and a false sense of indi-vidual worth, and that environmental and cultural factors were ignored. Once the world learned of the Nazi's use of eugenics, the very word became an anathema. Still, not until 1942 did the Supreme Court forbid the sterilization of criminals; sterilization of the mentally ill and the mentally retarded continued through the 1970s; and sterilization laws, though care-fully confined by federal laws, sat on the books of states as of 1995.[29]

If the word "eugenics" were popular today, there would be T-shirts, engraved mugs, and bumper stickers. In fact, eugenics is popular today and lives on in cloning, recombinant DNA, genetic screening programs and harvesting (read killing?) of embryos after preimplantation diagnosis. From the latter—a process whereby embryos are screened for certain genetics defects, the bad discarded and the good implanted—were born as of March 2002 some 700 children, along with little Adam Nash, who was chosen from several dozen embryos produced by in vitro fertilization and whose arrival was announced by the newspaper headline "Science helps parents design son."[30]

According to Professor Gregory Stock, head of the Program on Medicine, Technology and Society at the School of Medicine of the University of California, Los Angeles, genetic manipulations are inevitable. Finally, says he, "we will take control of human evolution bringing about the ultimate expression and realization of our humanity."[31] In 2003, despite a lifetime of world service, Sanger is slammed as a Eugenicist, with the word "Eugenicist" —sixty years later—carrying the Nazi taint, but in 2003, the effort to "better" the race is alive and well, no matter what that effort is called. And in 2003, the best hope for bettering the race yet lies with the child who is wanted.

The Manuscript

Sanger wrote this paper for presentation at the 1921 Eugenics Congress. The reader will notice that in 1921 the word "eugenist" was used and that there are a number of cuts—these do not affect the line of argument. In this paper, Sanger sets out many of the complaints that eventually discredited eugenics: the middle-class bias; the sexual bias, the coercive aspects; the denial of environment as a factor in development. Even as the mainline eugenics of Galton was enjoying its mainstream popularity, more thoughtful scientists, the reformists, were stressing that environment and nurture were equally important factors in the development of individual potential.

Further research was showing the limitations of the World War I draftee intelligence tests; intelligence was not so easily categorized as Robert M. Yerkes, the examiner in charge, had suggested.[32] The reformers were pointing out how great a role poverty could play in producing a degenerate. All persons, said reform eugenics, from all social and ethnic groups had a contribution to make to the genetic pool, and the population as a whole was enriched by the diversity within its source. With reform eugenics came a more rigorous science and eventually the demise of mainline eugenics. Sanger's paper moves in that direction.

Sanger recognizes the important contribution eugenics made to the scientific collection of data and statistical studies. Eugenics was, after all, the beginning of a science. Sanger gets in a nice jab at the not-so-nice lawmakers and suggests that warmakers are as much criminals as are those whom the authorities happen to incarcerate. She concludes, as she always does, with a demand for birth control as the basis of effective eugenics.

This paper became Chapter VIII, "Dangers of Cradle Competition" in *The Pivot of Civilization,* published in 1922. The manuscript itself is titled "The Limitations of Eugenics." Across the top of the first page of the manuscript, in what appears to be Sanger's handwriting, is written "Refused by Eugenics Congress 1921." The "limitations" pointed to by Sanger are no doubt why the Second Eugenics Congress refused her paper.

The Limitations of Eugenics[33]

Eugenics has been defined as "the study of agencies under social control that may improve or impair the racial qualities of future generations, either mentally or physically." . . . The term "Eugenics" was first used by Sir Francis Galton in his "Human Faculty" in 1884 and was subsequently developed into a scientific method and into an educational effort. Galton's ideal was the rational breeding of human beings. The aim of Eugenics, as defined by its founder, is to bring as many influences as can be reasonably employed to cause the useful classes of the community to contribute <u>more</u> than their proportion to the next generation. Eugenics thus concerns itself with all influences that improve the inborn qualities of a race, also with those that develop them to the utmost advantage. It was in short the attempt to bring reason and intelligence to bear upon <u>heredity</u>. But Galton, in spite of the immense value of this approach and his great stimulation of criticism, was completely unable to formulate a definite and practical working program. He hoped at length to introduce Eugenics "into the national conscience like a new religion." . . .

But the problem of human heredity is now seen to be infinitely more complex than imagined by Galton and his followers, and the optimistic hope of elevating Eugenics to the level of a religion is a futile one. Most of the Eugenists, including Professor Karl Pearson and his colleagues of the Eugenics Laboratory of the University of London and of the biometric laboratory in University College, have retained the age-old point of view of "Nature vs. Nurture," and have attempted to show the predominating influence of Heredity <u>as opposed to</u> Environment. This may be true; but demonstrated and repeated in investigation after investigation it nevertheless remains fruitless and unprofitable from the practical point of view.

Nevertheless, we should not minimize the great outstanding service of Eugenics for critical and diagnostic investigations. It demonstrates, not in terms of glittering generalization, but in statistical studies, of investigations reduced to measurement and number, that uncontrolled fertility is universally correlated with disease, poverty, overcrowding, and the transmission of heritable taints....Eugenists are right in pointing out. . . that medical surveys reveal the fact that two thirds of our manhood of military age are physically too unfit to shoulder a rifle;[34] that the feeble-minded, the syphilitic, the irresponsible, and the defective breed unhindered; that women are driven into factories and shops on day shift and night shift; that children, frail carriers of the torch of life, are put to work at an early age; that society at large is breeding an ever-increasing army of undersized, stunted, and dehumanized slaves; that the vicious circle of mental and physical defects, delinquency, and beggary is encouraged, by the unseeing and unthinking sentimentality of our age, to populate asylum, hospital, and prison.

All these things the Eugenist sees and points out with a courage and bravery entirely admirable. But when it comes to a constructive program of redemption, orthodox Eugenics can offer nothing more "constructive" than a renewed "cradle competition" between the "fit" and the "unfit." It sees that the most responsible and most intelligent members of society are the less fertile; that the feeble-minded are the most fertile....In a democracy like that of the United States every man and woman is permitted a vote in the government....

Equality of political power has thus been bestowed upon the lowest elements of our population. We must not be surprised, therefore, at the spectacle of political scandal and graft, of the notorious and so universally ridiculed low level of intelligence and the flagrant stupidity exhibited by our legislative bodies. The Congressional Record mirrors our political imbecility....

In passing, we should here recognize the difficulties presented by the idea of "fit" and "unfit." Who is to decide this question? The grosser, the more obvious, the undeniably feeble-minded should indeed not only be discouraged but prevented from propagating their kind. But among the writings of the representative Eugenists one cannot ignore the distinct middle-class bias that prevails. As that penetrating critic, F.W. Stella Browne, has said in another connection, "The Eugenics Education Society has among its numbers many most open-minded and truly progressive individuals; but the official policy it has pursued for years has been inspired by class-bias and sex-bias." The Society laments with increasing vehemence the multiplication of the less fortunate classes at a more rapid rate than the possessors of leisure and opportunity. (I do not think it relevant here to discuss whether the innate superiority of endowment in the governing class really is so overwhelming as to justify the Eugenics Education Society's peculiar use of the terms "fit" and "unfit.") Yet it has persistently refused to give any help toward extending the knowledge of contraceptives to the exploited classes. Similarly, through the *Eugenics Review*, the organ of the Society, frequently laments the "selfishness" of the refusal of maternity by healthy and educated women of the professional classes, I have yet to learn that it has made any official pronouncement on the English illegitimacy laws or any organized effort toward defending the unmarried mother.

This peculiarly Victorian conservatism may be inherited from the founder of Eugenics himself. Galton declared that the "Bohemian" element in the Anglo-Saxon race is destined to perish and "the sooner it goes, the happier for mankind." The trouble with any effort of trying to divide humanity into the "fit " and "unfit" is that we do not want, as H.G. Wells recently pointed out, to breed for uniformity, but for variety. "We want statesmen and poets and musicians and philosophers and strong men and delicate man and brave men. The qualities of one would be the weaknesses of the others." We want, most of all, genius.

Proscription of the Galtonian type would have condemned many of the great geniuses of the world who were not only "Bohemian," but actually and pathologically abnormal—Rousseau, Dostoevsky, Chopin, Poe, Schumann, Nietzsche, Comte, Guy de Maupassant—and how many others? But such considerations should not lead us into the error of concluding that such men were geniuses merely because they were pathological specimens and that the only way to produce genius is to breed disease and defect. It only emphasizes the dangers of external standards of "fit" and "unfit." Of the relation of Birth Control to genius I shall speak later, since the criticism is often made that this practice might prevent the birth of men of genius. I merely wish to emphasize here the limitations of the current standards of Eugenics.

These limitations are more strikingly shown in the type of so-called "eugenic" legislation passed or proposed by certain enthusiasts. Regulation, compulsion, and prohibitions enacted and effected by political bodies are the surest methods of driving the whole problem underground. As Havelock Ellis has pointed out, the absurdity and even hopelessness of effecting eugenic improvement by placing on the statute books prohibitions of certain classes of people to enter the legal bonds of matrimony reveals the weakness of those Eugenists who minimize or undervalue the importance of environment as a determining factor. They affirm that heredity is everything and environment nothing, yet forget that it is precisely those who are most universally subject to bad environment who procreate most copiously, most recklessly, and most disastrously. Such marriage laws are based for the most part on the infantile assumption that procreation is absolutely dependent upon the marriage ceremony, an assumption usually coupled with the complementary one that the only purpose of marriage is procreation. Yet it is a fact so obvious that it is hardly worth stating that the most fertile classes who indulge in the most dysgenic type of procreating—the feeble-minded—are almost totally unaffected by marriage laws and marriage ceremonies.

As for the sterilization of criminals, not merely must we know much more of heredity and genetics in general, but [we must] also acquire more certainty of the justice of our laws and the honesty of their administration before we can make rulings of fitness or unfitness merely upon the basis of a respect for law. On this point, the eminent William Bateson writes, "Criminals are often feeble-minded, but as regards those that are not, the fact that a man is for the purposes of Society classed as a criminal tells me little as to his value, still less as to the possible value of his offspring."[35] It is a fault inherent in criminal jurisprudence based on non-biological data that the law must take the nature of the offenses rather than that of the offenders as the basis of classification. A change in the right direction has begun, but the problem is difficult and progress will be very slow....

We all know of persons convicted perhaps even habitually, whom the world could ill spare. Therefore, I hesitate to proscribe the criminal. Proscription . . . is a weapon with a very nasty recoil. Might not some with equal cogency proscribe army contractors and their accomplices, the newspaper patriots? The crimes of the prison population are petty offenses by comparison, and the significance we attach to them is a survival of others days. Felonies may be great events locally, but they do not induce catastrophes. The proclivities of the warmakers are infinitely more dangerous than those of the aberrant beings whom from time to time the law may dub as criminals. Consistent and portentous selfishness, combined with dullness of imagination, are probably just as transmissible as want of self-control, though destitute of the amiable qualities not rarely associated with the genetic composition of persons of unstable mind....

Our debt to the science of Eugenics is great in that it directs our attention to the biological nature of humanity. Yet there is too great a tendency among the thinkers of this school to restrict their ideas of sex to its expression as a purely procreative function. Compulsory legislation, which would make the attempt inevitably futile to prohibit one of the most beneficent and necessary of human expressions or regulate it into the channels of preconceived philosophies, would reduce us to the unpleasant days predicted by the poet when

> Priests in black gowns will be walking their rounds
> And binding with briars our joys and desires.

Eugenics is chiefly valuable in its negative aspects. It has been "negative Eugenics" that has studied the histories of such families as the Jukes and the Kallikaks, which has pointed out the network of imbecility and feeble-mindedness that has been sedulously cultivated through all strata of society. On its so-called positive or "constructive" [arguments], it fails to arouse any permanent interest. "Constructive" Eugenics aims to arouse the enthusiasm or the interest of the majority of people in the welfare of the world fifteen or twenty generations in the future. On its negative side, it shows us that we are paying for and even submitting to the dictates of an ever increasing, unceasing spawning class of humans who never should have been born at all—that the wealth of individuals and of states are being diverted from the development and the progress of human expression and civilization.

While it is necessary to point out the importance of "heredity" as a determining factor in human life, it is fatal to elevate it to the position of an absolute....The Eugenist who overlooks the importance of environment as a determining factor in human life is as short-sighted as the [one] who neglects the biological nature of man. We cannot disentangle these two forces, except in theory....

The great principle of Birth Control, it may now be seen, offers the means whereby the individual may adapt himself to and control the forces of environment and heredity....Birth Control...must be recognized . . . as the only possible and practical method of human generation . . . as the very pivot of civilization.

25. Advice to the Married

W hen *Happiness in Marriage* was published in 1926, Sanger sent a copy to Agnes Smedley, then in Berlin, who had promised to review it for the press of India. Smedley felt that "the first part on courtship" was "strange" to her, but the last part was "very, very excellent." The last part of the book offers specific advice for attaining mutual orgasm, pointing out that the woman is less quickly aroused and her partner must pace himself. To Sanger, Smedley wrote,

> You have touched a problem that is more real than most people know: that of the rapidity of men in sex union. Few women will be frank enough to say that they are generally left in a most awful nervous tension, to lie awake in bitterness all night long, while a man slumbers peacefully. It is the cause of nervous trouble of many women. The cause of this in men you did not fully treat. I believe these are other than the selfish motives at work, although that is important, also, as you say.
>
> The other factors are 1) neurosis—actual psychic illness in men—and 2) their former relations with prostitutes. Many, many men get their sex start in life with prostitutes. A prostitute wants to get through the business as soon as possible. I've heard that they often say to a man: "Well, for Christ's sake, ain't you through yet!" In such a relationship a man need think only of himself—never of the woman. In brothels for soldiers—as on the Rhine after the War—each soldier was allotted 15 minutes with a prostitute and they stood in line before the brothels awaiting their turn.
>
> In this way, decent women get husbands of whose sex training has been gained from prostitutes. This training is as deadly as

syphilis. It is the revenge of the prostitute against the "respectable" women who consider themselves better. It destroys the woman's nervous system as syphilis destroys the body....There is no horror on earth to compare with the nervous tension in which millions of women are left after sex unions with men who boast of their knowledge & experience in sex.[1]

Sanger explains her own attitude toward marriage and implicitly toward the sexual relation in a letter written in 1953:

Marriages are very much like business contracts. It is a fifty-fifty giving and taking, and it is never good to have either the one or the other all one-sided. If a great love comes to one or the other, it is only fair to let it express itself as fully as possible....I am such a great believer in the Blake and Shelley ideas about love and friendship, which was that the more one feels the richness and fullness of love, the more it expands and gives health and healing and inspiration to all who come within its sphere. If one tries to shut it off it causes sickness, as well as neurosis and other mental and nervous disturbances in both parties.[2]

In *Happiness*, Sanger is a little more conservative in her discussion of love's ideals. She stresses the enjoyment a couple finds in sexual activity and that it should be mutual, noting that this enjoyment develops in time. In the first chapter are found no less than three references to "growth" and "roots" and how carefully nurtured happiness will "bear fruit."

Despite the idealistic but sensible opening, the specific advice on closing, and the good reviews, *Happiness in Marriage* did not sell well. Sanger's sexual information was offered in careful language at a time when such information was becoming more rather than less explicit, an ironic twist considering Sanger's very radical private lifestyle.

In 1930, Brentano's was able to sell the rights to *Happiness* to Blue Ribbon Books, which guaranteed "to sell over the next two years a minimum of fifteen thousand copies."[3] But by 1930 some pretty racy marriage manuals were available, and this writer found no evidence of any sale of fifteen thousand copies of *Happiness in Marriage*. Nevertheless, Sanger's advice in *Happiness* was sensible and sound and certainly never hurt any who followed it.

Happiness in Marriage
Chapter I: The First Step[4] (Excerpts)

"And so they married and lived happily ever afterwards." Such is the conventional ending of most love stories. In life, however, the real love story does not end with marriage. It begins with it. Happiness is not the inevitable consequence of marriage. Marriage does not necessarily create happiness. Too often it destroys it. If husband and wife are to live joyously together, they must create their own happiness....

Romance based on ignorance cannot bear healthy fruit. In the past, when men and women were victims of a huge conspiracy of silence concerning sex, experience was bought at a high cost. Young men were tacitly permitted to "sow their wild oats," venereal scourges resulted. Tragic and widespread and destructive as syphilis and gonorrhea are, spiritual destruction is even worse. Promiscuity, prostitution and disease destroy, sometimes forever, a clean and reverent attitude toward the physical sex relation. Premarital promiscuity has created in man an attitude of ruthless selfishness. More than any other single factor this has been destructive of mutual happiness in the lives of married people.

But women have, in the past, been too willing victims of this conspiracy of silence. Even today, with all our education, with all our organizations for social uplift, girls are brought up in absolute and fatal ignorance of the true meaning of the sexual function. To their normal, healthy curiosity the only answer has been that the sex instinct is in some mysterious way either a lewd, lascivious and unmentionable subject or too sacred and holy to mention....

For marriages built upon the shifting sands of fear, shame, and ignorance can never lead to happiness, yet if contracted with a frank recognition of the central importance of the beauty of sex in life, alike in its physiological, psychological and spiritual aspects, happiness becomes a glowing possibility. This is a buried treasure to be unearthed by true lovers. It may be imbedded in the rich soil of mutual respect and consideration. Carefully natured, it will strike deep roots in both lives, entwine and unite them together in ever-growing joy. It will grow, mature, bear fruit.

Few as they are, marriages of this type are nevertheless possible. To such unions we must look for guidance. Participants in happy relationships of this type are creators in the truest sense. Their intimate experience becomes a guide for all to follow. All the world loves such lovers. These are the creative artists pointing the way to spiritual awakening that is possible to all men and women of the next generation, affecting all generations to come. . . .

Sex expression is not merely a propagative function, nor the satisfaction of an animal appetite. It should not be considered merely as a necessary evil preliminary to the production of a family. Sex expression, rightly understood, is the consummation of love, its completion and its consecration. Sex expression is an art. To become artists in love, men and women must learn to master and control the instruments by which this art is expressed.

These instruments are not merely the so-called sex organs, isolated and unrelated to the body or personality. If marriage is to be fully consummated, the entire body and spirit as units must participate in the union.

Think long and deeply over the importance of this truth.... The body is not an enemy of the spirit. Our bodies are a visible expression of our inner selves. Every factor, every gesture, every organ and function of our bodies is given us for the expression of our impulses, thoughts and desires. More than any other bodily act, sex expression is a sacred gift which awakens men and women to the innate beauty of life. We must learn to use this gift instead of misusing it. We must learn how to master the instrument of bodily expression so that passion is transmuted into poetry, so that life itself becomes lyric. In his grotesque attitude and use of sex in life, the average man today is truly said to be like an orangoutang trying to play a violin. Discord instead of harmony has resulted.

Before reading the chapters that follow, cleanse your mind of prurience and shame. Never be ashamed of passion. If you are strongly sexed, you are richly endowed. You possess the greatest and most valuable inheritance a human being can enjoy. To be strongly sexed means that the life force can suffuse and radiate through body and soul. It means radiant energy and force in every field of endeavor. It means driving power, ambition, attainment, but on condition that this great dynamic power be mastered and directed, stored and controlled, instead of dissipated and misspent. Without passion, love would be a flaccid, lifeless thing. Passion is the driving power of life. It cannot be denied, destroyed, or thrust aside. It must and it will find expression in some way—in destruction if its power be denied or not directed to creative ends. While it is a cruel master, it is also a willing slave.

Men and women have been endowed with this dynamic energy which we name passion for the rounding out, the development, the fulfilling and the beautification of their natures. Those who deny it expression, who combat it, or who refuse to participate in it, cut themselves off from the zest and the poetry of life. They lead narrow, warped, one-sided lives. On the other hand, those who become the slaves of passion, or misuse it mainly through selfishness or in rebellion against the narrow traditions of the nineteenth and early twentieth centuries, also deprive themselves of greater development and attainment.

You men and women who stand at the threshold of maturity, learn to steer skillfully between the ascetic rocks and the sensual whirlpools. As George Meredith expresses it, "Onward to the creation of certain nobler races."

It is not enough to avoid the pitfalls of venereal disease, to trust to luck or blind instinct in the pursuit of happiness in marriage. It is not enough, great and invaluable as this gift is, to bring virility and passion to the nuptial bed. Clean bodies and minds you must bring, but romance, knowledge, poetry and art as well, and above all, keen anticipation and appreciation of the meaning of the most intimate and the most thrilling adventure life can offer you.

This is the first step towards happiness in marriage.

26. The First World Population Conference

Geneva, 1927

W ith the success of two international conferences behind her; secure financially through the good graces of Noah Slee; her two sons satisfactorily in college; the American Birth Control League apparently on track; the Clinical Research Bureau, open since 1923, under the secure direction of Dr. Hannah Stone; Sanger was free to devote her energies to what would prove to be an altruistic adventure.[1]

In the *The Pivot of Civilization*, Sanger had sought herself to put Birth Control on a scientific basis. Now she sought for birth control the backing of the scientists themselves. Her approach was politic: to assemble the most prestigious researchers in social science, demographics, economics, and biology, that they could consider scientifically the population increase and its possible threat to world peace and the world economy.[2] For not only was the world population growing explosively, but Germany, Japan, and Italy were demanding that their peoples propagate and sounding unsettling growls about lebensraum.

Yet no one seemed to want to discuss population growth, certainly not the League of Nations, whose purview it obviously was.[3] "The Economic Conference which I have just attended in Geneva failed to discuss the population question and it causes a great deal of comment and much criticism," noted Sanger in May 1927.[4] But by the time she wrote this, she already had in motion her plans to bring to the very doorstep of the League of Nations an awareness of the population problem.

It would seem that the population growth could not be sensibly discussed without, at some point, in some way, including a discussion of birth control. Nevertheless, only with the understanding that birth control would *not* be discussed would most of the eminent scientists, particularly the

European scientists, consider attending Sanger's First World Population Conference.[5]

It should be noted that this conference, which met from August 31 to September 3, 1927, in Geneva, Switzerland, was the first world conference ever to deal with the population issue, that it was organized almost single-handedly by Margaret Sanger, a woman, and that Sanger did so aware of the male prejudice she faced, aware also of the serious need for the population problem to be investigated, aware of the need for world education on this issue, hoping against hope that as these scientists investigated all aspects of this serious problem, that birth control might possibly be considered relevant thereto. In the latter regard, she was to be disappointed.

During the conference, the papers of two of the speakers "came perilously near mentioning the forbidden word Malthusianism, but as for birth control, it was edged about like a bomb which might explode any moment."[6]

This was scarcely a surprise. As the date of the conference had approached, newspapers were carrying such remarks as,

Sir Bernard Mallet, the president of the World's Population Conference, about to meet in Geneva, stated to me this morning that birth control or neo-Malthusianism forms no part of the programme of the conference.[7]

Or from an interview with Mrs. Sanger:

Mrs. Sanger, who has been helping with preparations for the Conference assured me that despite her presence here her pet subject has been definitely kept out from the conference, there being no place for it in scientific discussion.[8]

Obviously, birth control does have a place in a scientific discussion, and Sanger had done more than help, having spent the better part of two years organizing the conference, rounding up the two hundred delegates, scaring up funds, leaning heavily on Noah Slee's generosity, attending to the innumerable details, and paying her own expenses to boot.

The extent of prestige of the names she brought to her conference was impressive. The presidency of the conference had been accepted by Sir Bernard Mallet. Sir Bernard was former president of the Royal Statistical Society and a good friend of Sir Eric Drummond, current secretary-general of the League of Nations.[9] Among the many, many other famous attendees were Julian Huxley, John Maynard Keynes, and Dr. F. A. E. Crew (who had made hens crow and roosters lay eggs!).[10] These male names were all listed on the conference program. But that the names of the women who had worked so assiduously for the prior year, not only doing the grunt work for the conference but raising monies so that the delegates might travel and attend the conference—that their names should be deleted from the conference program was a bit difficult to swallow. As Sanger recalled the incident,

> The storm broke the Friday before our scheduled opening Tuesday August 31st. Proofs of the official program had just come to me for my approval. Sir Bernard came into my office and looked at them. "Well, we'll just cross these off," he said, drawing his pencil through my name and those of my assistants.
>
> "Why are you doing that?"
>
> "The names of the workers should not be included on scientific programs."
>
> "These people are different," I objected. "In their particular lines they are as much experts as the scientists."
>
> "It doesn't matter. They can't go on, Out of the question. It's not done."[11]

The entire female clerical staff struck in protest. Sir Eric Drummond explained to Sanger, "These distinguished scientists would be the laughing stock of all Europe if it were known that a woman had brought them together."[12] Sanger accepted the inevitable, spent a day coaxing her staff to return to work despite the insult, and in the service of her higher goal, was able to open the conference with all preparations in place.

The conference was covered by hundreds of newspapers and received glowing reviews.[13] Out of the conference came a new demographic organization; the International Union for the Scientific Study of Population, which lives on in 2003 with some two thousand members and on its website acknowledges that Margaret Sanger organized the First World Population Conference in 1927.[14] And by 1928, Dr. F. A. E. Crew had established a department on Contraceptive Research at the University of Edinburg.[15]

For entertainment, the delegates had been taken one night by boat to visit the chateau of Madame de Stael and, on another evening, to dinner and dancing at the fifteenth-century Chateau de Prangins of Katherine Dexter McCormick, the remarkable woman who three decades later would, with Sanger's encouragement, make development of The Pill possible. Not surprisingly, the gentlemen delegates did not hesitate to enjoy the gratuitous hospitality in the homes of two women.

Sanger summed the entire experience in letter on September 22, 1927, from Geneva to Hugh de Selincourt.

> [Noah] was such a darling all thr'u the conference & then at the end

he seemed to regret the work put into it, because he had not realized the b.c. was not to be in the front in it at all. The Scientists were
not very courageous I'll admit and the Catholic influence was
strongly felt.

Then some of those upon whom I had relied to stand by in the
time of war—failed & compromised—so it goes.

I am now working on the papers & editing the discussion for
the final volume & find it a great satisfaction to blue pencil the
opinions I don't like <u>Revenge</u>.[16]

Her revenge was slight enough. The scientific papers were dense and
difficult, and Sanger alone did all the editing, then published the proceedings. She insisted on being listed editor of the proceedings.[17]

It took another twenty-seven years before there was to be another
World Population Conference, another forty before a woman's conference—the 1994 Cairo conference, advertised as the first to be convened by
women in support of woman's rights—was held. Once again, Margaret
Sanger's courage and contribution remain unacknowledged.[18]

Editorial, *Birth Control Review*
June 1927

We are able to announce this month the preliminary plans for the
World Population Conference. We give also in our news columns a brief
account of the program of the International Economic Conference, held at
Geneva in May, under the auspices of the League of Nations. Our readers
may be disposed to wonder why the League, which can devote three weeks
conference to the World Economic situation, does not give equal attention
to the World Population situation. The answer is to be found in the official
program and the documents of the Economic Conference, which show that
the statesmen and scholars who direct the activities of the League of
Nations, do not realize that, even in the field of economics, population has
a very important bearing. They do not, or they will not, grasp the fact that
overpopulation underlies almost all the great international problems. But
though it was left out of the agenda, it seems impossible that the three
weeks conference did not bring out much discussion of overpopulation. If
this unbidden guest did force its way into the economic deliberations, it will
have prepared the minds of many representatives of the League to give a
fair hearing to the World Population conference, which three months later
is to sit on the doorstep of the League. One great step forward has been
taken this year, in the fact that scientists of all nations have taken the initiative in calling the first World Population Conference and in making Geneva,
the home of the League of Nations, the place of meeting. When the League

is awakened to the importance of the problem, it will find the material for its solution ready at hand in the proceedings of six Neo-Malthusian Conferences and of the World Population Conference of 1927.

Preliminary Notice[19]
The World Population Conference

The World Population Conference, first of its kind ever to be held, will meet in the Conservatoire at Geneva, Switzerland, on August 31, September 1, 2, 1927, under the auspices of leading scientists and scientific organizations of many countries. It will be, in effect, a conclave of many biological, sociological, and statistical authorities of the world, who have gone far in the study of the population problem, but who have never before assembled at a common meeting table to exchange their views and co-ordinate their knowledge.

Its Purpose and Possibilities

The nations of the world are keenly aware of their individual population problems; they are generally cognizant of the population problems of their near neighbors and all distant countries. It is known that the question of population growth holds possibilities of menace to the future of civilization, and yet the world population problem is one of the few great issues of today that have not been the subject of concerted international action.

One of the main purposes, therefore, of this Conference is to study the question from an international point of view. Such a conference must be strictly scientific, and accordingly eminent men and women in the fields of biology, economics, and sociology will be invited to participate. By this procedure it is hoped that some 100 or 150 leaders of scientific thought from various countries will be given an opportunity for mutual interchange of ideas and for the recognition of the common elements of the whole population question.

It is possible that from such a conference will come an international movement, which, through its findings, will help in the solution of other financial, economic, and health problems that are today the cause of grave concern.

Membership of the Conference is by invitation.
Application should be made to The Secretary,
The World Population Conference, 199, Piccadilly,
London, W.I.

PART II THE REFORMER
27. "Children Troop Down"

"Children troop down from heaven," intoned Archbishop Hayes in 1921, justifying the Town Hall raid and the entrenched opposition of the Roman Catholic leadership to birth control, "because God wills it. He alone has the right to stay their coming."[1] But once on this earthly plane, children have to be cared for—fed, clothed, housed, educated, loved with patience and understanding. Sanger understood this, as perhaps the celibate prelate did not.

Sanger answered Archbishop Hayes in the *New York Times*:

> I do not care to answer the Archbishop's theological statement concerning the will of the Almighty. His arguments are purely those based on assumption and he knows no more about the facts of the immortality of the soul than the rest of us human beings. What he believes concerning the soul after life is based upon theory and he has a perfect right to that belief; but we, who are trying to better humanity fundamentally, believe that a healthy, happy human race is more in keeping with the laws of God than disease, misery and poverty perpetuating itself generation after generation.[2]

In contrast to the miserable living conditions described in the letters below, Sanger envisioned another world for mothers, a world in which motherhood is voluntarily embraced by women educated to be mothers— a world in which families lived not in misery and want but in comfort and abundance. Such was the world that Margaret Sanger envisioned and such was the vision that drove her. But motherhood was anything but voluntarily embraced, as testified to by the million or so letters received by Sanger between 1921 and 1926 at the American Birth Control League offices.[3] A survey of 5,000 of the letters sent after 1920 showed that 80 percent of these mothers were wage earners on a $15 weekly salary, that 80 percent were mothers before the age of twenty, and they had, on an average, five children.[4] But many mothers had many more.

The misery of these women is captured in the succinct case histories of the Clinical Research Bureau:

1682,- Pt. 23 yrs. 3 chil. living, 1 died, 1 miscarr. 1st child at 17 yrs. Husb. Out of work 8 mos.

1604,- Pt. 35 yrs. 7 chil. living, 3 miscarr. 10 preg. in 12 yrs. All labors difficult or instrumental. Husband out of work 8 mos.

1517,- Pt. 27 yrs. 3 chil. living, 1 died, 3 miscarr. 7 preg. in 7 yrs. Husb out of work 4 mos. Pt. Large goitre-and cardiac case.

1315,- Pt. 23 yrs. 3 chil. living, 2 died, 3 miscarr. in 7 yrs. Husb. a sandwich man earns $15.00 a week. Probably lustic. 1st baby at 16.

1263,- Pt. 20 yrs. 3 chil. living, 3 miscarr. in 4 yrs. Husb. out of work over a yr. Pt. works in factory irreg. Earns $12.00 a week. 1st baby at 15 yrs.[5]

Letters printed in the *Birth Control Review* were more graphic.

I have been married eighteen years and during that time I have had ten miscarriages, seven living children and three dead. Have always been in poor health and at present am five months pregnant. Have been in bed the same length of time and will not be able to leave it until all is over. Now I have been to a number of doctors and all the information am able to get, is never to have any more children, as I can never stand it, or live through it, and also it would be a crime, but such advice has never helped me.—Letter No. 19 [6]

I am the mother of nineteen children, the baby only twenty months old. I am forty-three years old, and I had rather die than give birth to another child. The doctor does not give me any information. This letter may sound unbelievable, but the records will show that it is true. I have five boys and seven girls living; two daughters married, one has four children and the other has two. Both daughters have bad health. I need the information for them as well as for myself, so for my sake and for the sake of humanity, give me the proper information.—North Carolina[7]

I am the mother of nine children, and my health is poor, and I cannot give my children the mother's care they need, and I would love to know how to be sure of not having any more. I don't think it is God's will that I should bring them in the world and leave them to the mercies of I know not what. I think if you could give me this information which I crave you would be doing some good work with your knowledge. Please answer at once, for I am every day worried to death a little more.—Indiana[8]

I am very much in favor of birth control, as I speak for myself. I am the mother of nine children and if I could have prevented it without abortion, there would never have been so many. Two of my children were born in one year and two more only thirteen months between. No woman can stand that and do all her own work, and now I have to sew to help support them, as my husband is not able to do hard work and my baby is only 9 months. I sincerely hope for myself that you can send me information of some kind so I will not be come pregnant again, for I cannot ever stand to come through it again, as my health is not good and I am 42 years old and certainly think I have had my share of it. Hoping you will send me this information.—Letter No 9 [9]

Occasionally, comes some comic relief:

Dear Friend,

I have the honour most respectfully to apply for of your special and particulars catalogue.

I have married two women, so try your best and send me some of catalogue.

Try your best and send it to me very instantaneous.

Yours sincerely,
Matthew Brew[10]

Motherhood in Bondage

Sanger reprinted a selection of these letters in her book *Motherhood in Bondage,* which was published by Brentano's in 1928. Though highly praised for its important message, the book sold poorly. Sanger suggested to Brentano's that "with allowance made on the reduction of my own royalties, a little bit more [advertising] can be done."[11] But well advertised or not, the problems of indigent, multiparous women do not make for jolly reading.

Sanger persevered. As she explains in her reply to John Otis below, Sanger believed that these letters would be the most persuasive tool in deciding a government to support birth control. And she used the book for that purpose as she prepared to persuade Washington to change the Comstock laws through the lobbying of the National Committee on Federal Legislation for Birth Control. First, she sent out over five hundred letters to senators, representatives, federal appointees, government officials, authors, lawyers, university presidents, philanthropists, all the Episcopalian bishops, other ecclesiastics and clergymen, Supreme Court justices, news-papermen, state governors, captain of industry and financiers—anyone who might be prominent in the private or public sphere, including M. E. Forbes, president of the Pierce Arrow Motor Car Co.; H. D. Miles of Buffalo Foundry & Machine Co; and the war claims arbiter in Washington, D.C. She asked these important individuals if they would like a complimentary copy of *Motherhood in Bondage*.[12] Mr. John Otis of San Francisco, California, want-ed a copy and offered to pay for it, to which Sanger replied on January 19, 1929,

> May I say that I hope you will read [*Motherhood in Bondage*] and will not feel that you must pay for it, as that special author's edition cannot be sold. It is my agreement with the publisher that there will be no charge for these copies.
>
> My only object in sending this book to important people is that more men and women will know something of the need of Birth Control. In my estimation there is no document that reveals the need of it so poignantly as the letters in this book and I am won-dering if it will help us in our campaign in the future.
>
> We hope to go to Washington to have the law amended. As the federal law stands now, it is a violation of Section 211 of the Penal Code to refer the mothers who have written me either to a physi-cian or clinic for contraceptive advice. I do not believe that the law ever intended that such interpretation be put upon it. There are twenty-two clinics throughout the United States where such instruction is legally given, yet it is a crime and a punishment of five years in prison for anyone to tell a mother to go to any of these clin-ics. Is it not absurd?
>
> Trusting that you may have an opportunity to pass around the book to anyone who may wish to read it, I am
>
> > Sincerely yours,
> > Director.[13]

Most were happy to have a copy and wrote Sanger of their appreciation, sharing with her their horror of the situation of these women. Still, *Motherhood* copies remained unsold. Sanger asked the ever generous Noah

Slee in November of 1929 if he would buy at forty-five cents a copy the remaining 3,241 copies from Brentano's, who had sold none during all of 1929.[14] Meanwhile, Sanger had sent out the many hundreds of complimentary copies of *Motherhood*.[15] No immediate change in the tide of public opinion was seen as a result of mailing these free copies, but they must have contributed to the gradual and general acceptance of birth control that was building during the thirties.

To the modern reader, abounding in contraceptive information in the twenty-first century, the attitude and extent of the ignorance in earlier decades may seem scarcely plausible. But the affluence of the twenties had a limited reach in America. Rural and farming communities, lumber, mill, and factory areas, the ghettos and slums of the cities, where education was limited and poverty brutal kept women equally brutalized and ignorant. The letters in *Motherhood* came from such women. It should not have been so.

PART II THE REFORMER
28. The Raid on the Clinical Research Bureau

The outstanding achievement of this Clinic has been to remove the whole question of Birth Control from the field of hot and angry theoretical controversy to the calm quiet of scientific research, and to enlist the cooperation of competent scientists and physicians in amassing a wealth of incontrovertible evidence supporting the feasibility and the desirability of contraceptive practice.

> —Margaret Sanger, Address of Welcome,
> Conference on Contraceptive Research and
> Clinical Practice, New York City, December 29, 1936[1]

In June 1933, the Birth Control Clinical Research Bureau issued a progress report:

> Since its establishment in 1923, the Bureau has instructed over 36,000 women, and advised many thousands more in other branches of its service. Thousands of doctors from all over the world have received their first instruction in contraceptive techniques at the Bureau.... The Bureau now occupies one of the fine, old houses... for which New York is famed. The staff at present consists of 9 women physicians, 7 nurses, 1 trained social worker, 2 clerical workers and 1 nursery attendant. The clinic is open daily from 9 a.m. to 5 p.m., and one evening a week from 6:00 p.m. to 9:00 p.m. Patients are an equal proportion of Protestant, Catholic, and Jewish. Patients pay as they can; private donations support 50 percent of costs. If already the patient is pregnant, the Clinic cannot perform abortions.
>
> The case history cards of the BCCRB carry without doubt the

173

most complete information available in America today regarding the economic, social, and marital background of over 36,000 patients who have applied for advice at the Bureau. A Statistical Analysis of the first 10,000 of these cases has been completed [and the Clinic has investigated the] types and relative efficacy of various contraceptives methods now in use.[2]

Ten years earlier, Margaret Sanger had quietly opened the Clinical Research Bureau in January with startup funds from good friend Clinton Chance, a wealthy manufacturer of Birmingham, England, and for some time, she ran the bureau just as quietly.[3] Although legal under the 1918 Crane decision as long as a licensed physician was giving contraceptive advice for "the prevention or cure of disease," the operation of a birth control clinic in New York was still a bit dicey—as the raid in 1929 after six years of peaceful activity would show.[4] After recovering from a false start with a director whose record keeping was found inadequate, two years later Sanger had the marvelous good fortune to bring in Hannah Stone, who rightly became known as the "Madonna of the Clinic."[5]

Sanger had met Hannah Mayer Stone at the First American Birth Control Conference in 1921, and she was a member of the Clinical Research Bureau's medical advisory committee, when in 1925 Sanger offered her directorship of the bureau. Stone, who had excellent credentials and was on the pediatrics staff of Woman's Lying-In Hospital, accepted the directorship. Dr. Stone was then immediately asked to resign from her position with Woman's Lying-In Hospital, birth control having such an unsavory reputation. During the next sixteen years, Hannah Stone, working without pay, was known for her sensitive care of patients and for her excellence as administrator and clinician. Her thorough research became the basis for several important studies by other medical scientists. Said Sanger of Stone, "It was she who . . . was most responsible for the introduction of the knowledge of contraceptive techniques to the medical profession."[6]

Hannah Stone instructed hundreds of physicians in the techniques of contraception, increasing acceptance of birth control within the medical profession. Hers was one of the first studies on contraception to be published in a medical journal, and her work proved to the medical community not only the safety and extent of reliability of diaphragm and jelly as contraceptives, but that neither caused sterility, a common belief of the day.[7] She also helped to devise an effective jelly formula that was affordable.[8] With her husband, Dr. Abraham Stone, a urologist, the Stones pioneered marriage counseling and offered their services in that area at the Bureau.

Hannah Stone died of a heart attack at the age of forty-eight, tragically young, in July of 1941. At her death, she left detailed records on 100,000 patients whom she had seen personally. Her contribution to the birth control movement through her teaching and research had been incalculable, and in Stone's death Sanger lost one of her most important workers. Hannah was succeeded as director by her husband, who became as well a bulwark in Sanger's birth control movement.

The raid on the bureau in 1929 was totally unexpected.

Shortly after the attendant in charge of the waiting room at the Clinical Research Bureau had told a visiting physician that the days of police raids on legitimate Birth Control activities were over, the police patrol drew up to the door, two police women and half a dozen uniformed policemen entered. They drove out the fifteen patients waiting to be called—forcing some first to give their names and addresses—seized materials and case records and arrested five of the workers.[9]

Hannah Stone was one of those arrested.[10] Charges were quickly dismissed, but once again the police had acted "on orders," just as they had during the 1921 Town Hall Raid, and once again no one would acknowledge who had given the orders. Again, those who had opposed birth control rushed to defend it, only this time, the medical community, outraged and furious at the arrogant appropriation of private medical records by police, actively involved themselves and issued a strong public statement:

We view with grave concern any action on the part of the authorities which contravenes the inviolability of the confidential relations which always have and should obtain between physicians and their patients.[11]

Those opposed to birth control were—once again—bested in the publicity game, for after newspaper coverage of the raid brought the bureau so much attention, the bureau calendars were filled three weeks in advance and the bureau had to stay open two additional evenings a week.[12] At the subsequent trial, the birth control defendants were discharged for lack of evidence, and the Crane decision was confidently reaffirmed.[13] A little detective work indicted the Roman Catholic hierarchy as the instigator of the raid, which came because talk by the many Catholic women who had benefited from clinic services reached a much-annoyed Catholic hierarchy. As Sanger explained it,

Approximately fifty percent of our cases were being sent by social workers on the lower East and West Sides, a conglomerate of all peoples and classes, including Irish, Italians, and other Catholics. So many had benefited and told their neighbors that others also were asking of their agencies how to get to our clinic. Catholic social workers, at a monthly meeting with officials of the Church, had sought guidance in replying to parishioners, and the ecclesiastics had been shocked to find that a clinic existed. Catholic police-women had been summoned,[14]

and the raid shortly followed. The publicity surrounding the raid not only bolstered the image of birth control, but a look at its clientele disproved the charge that Sanger was catering only to middle and upper class women.[15] On opening the Clinical Research Bureau, Sanger always had in mind that it would serve in a number of ways: by proving the effectiveness of birth control with hard statistical evidence; by exploring and developing innovative contraceptive techniques; by educating the medical profession; by providing referrals; but above all, by offering affordable contraceptive information to women.[16] All of this the bureau accomplished and more, but in so doing, it always was run under a deficit; women who could not pay were never turned away, and Sanger was fortunate in having a generous husband to whom she could turn when she could not raise sufficient funds to cover the deficit from the Rockefeller or other foundations or her society sources.

Since her first studies in Holland in 1915, Sanger had envisioned in America "a string of clinics" of the caliber that Hannah Stone fostered at the Bureau. Sanger's Clinical Research Bureau, in great part because of the work of Hannah Stone, became the template for birth control clinics all over America. Although Catholic opposition remained dedicated and government support negligible or negative, more and more birth control clinics appeared—by 1938 more than three hundred in the United States—and these in turn, became the string of clinics that were eventually to operate under Planned Parenthood Federation of America—Sanger's vision of a "glorious string of clinics" becoming a glorious reality.[17]

The Manuscript
In accepting this manuscript for publication, the *New Republic* wrote Sanger that they "were delighted" with her article and asked if she had any changes.[18] Sanger changed the "Anna K. McNamara" name to Mary Sullivan, saying,

> I didn't want Mrs McNamara's name here because it didn't seem necessary. She was under Mrs. Sullivan's orders, I suppose.

McNamara, a Catholic, had been the original decoy. Under Sullivan's orders (Sullivan was also Catholic), McNamara had come to the bureau ostensibly to be fitted for a contraceptive and learned at the trial, much to her surprise, that she had a number of serious physical problems. After the trial, and after the police admitted they had overstepped themselves, McNamara returned to the clinic, this time for medical attention. Sullivan was temporarily demoted, but soon returned to full rank.[19]

In our readings as printed here, McNamara's name remains as Sanger wrote in her original manuscript.

The Birth Control Raid[20]
The New Republic, May 1, 1929

"This is my party!" shouted Policewoman Anna K. McNamara in the midst of her personally conducted raid on the Birth Control Clinical Research Bureau last week. Subsequent developments have demonstrated that this boast was as premature as it was untruthful. Policewoman McNamara's little raiding party, carried out with a vigor that swept aside as unnecessary common courtesy and ordinary good manners, has proved to be of vital interest to every thinking member of this community. And the end is not yet in sight.

As I write these indignant words, comes the announcement that Chief Magistrate William McAdee now admits that the police, in seizing the case histories of our patients, had exceeded the scope of the search warrant he had issued authorizing this raid.

After you have spent some fifteen years slowly and with infinite pains and patience working for the right to test the value of contraceptive practice in a scientific and hygienic – and lawful – manner, without interfering with the habits or the morals of those who disagree with you, it is indeed difficult to submit with equanimity to such indignities as were gratuitously thrust upon us at the clinic a week ago. Compensations there have been, of course – mainly in the enlightened attitude of such dailies as the *New York Herald Tribune*, and the generous offers of aid from distinguished physicians. But even these compensations have scarcely counter balanced the evidence of the sinister secret power of our enemies. As in the incident of the breaking up of the Birth Control meeting in Town Hall, in 1921, the raid on the Birth Control Research Bureau gives us a glimpse of the animus that directs the action of the police. Our hypocritical antagonists have not the courage to fight us squarely and frankly in the open, but must adopt the cowardly subterfuge of utilizing the minor and crassly ignorant members of the police force in their futile efforts to annihilate a social agency, which had already been given a clean bill of health by the Health Department of the municipality, by the State Board of Characteries, and by the Academy of Medicine. Our Research Bureau has been functioning since 1923, operating within the law, and cooperating with recognized charitable institutions.

Policewoman McNamara's "party" was a distinct and deplorable failure, from whatever point of view it is analyzed. A failure, first of all, because it has exposed the complete lack of intelligence in those who conducted it, and [second] the woeful lack of coordination in the functioning of the department itself. It is not enough for [Police Commissioner] Grover Whalen or District Attorney Banton to disclaim all foreknowledge of the raid. Modest as may be the headquarters of the Research Bureau, its significance is of inestimable importance in the community. To permit the minor members of the police force, or prejudiced assistants in the Office of the District Attorney, to pass judgment upon its fate—in my opinion—denotes either a complete lack of coordination of powers or carelessness in directing them.

Certainly no official of the city government, cognizant of awakened public opinion concerning contraception and aware of the searching criticism to which the Police Department of New York City is now subjected, would ever have chosen the present moment as one psychologically suited to inaugurate a brutal and wholesale raid upon a modest social agency, which was functioning quietly and successfully in an obscure side street, minding its own business, and hoping that its powerful ecclesiastical neighbors would mind theirs. At a time when the criminal elements of the city— the racketeers, the gangsters, the gunmen, and the hijackers—are time after time displaying their cleverness in outwitting the Police Department, at a time when it would seem to an innocent bystander [that] all the intelligence, all the skill, and all the brawn of the force should be mobilized and focused upon crime control, [the police] can, apparently, think up nothing better to do than to stage a raiding party which brings upon them the unqualified condemnation of the press and the intelligent public.[21] Even in the carrying out of this raid, they are not equipped with sufficient intelligence to understand the limits of their boasted authority. Therefore, I say, there is no evidence of intelligent foresight in the planning and the carrying out of Policewoman McNamara's little party.

Already it is proving a boomerang. Ambitious to accuse and convict the physicians who conduct the Clinical Research Bureau of lawbreaking, the raiders themselves have broken the law, since exceeding the authority of the warrant is in itself a misdemeanor. I mention again the compensations of the thrill of satisfaction we have in the offers of distinguished doctors to testify in our behalf, of the letters to the press, and the courageous outspoken editorials. But, even these cannot obliterate the memory of Police[w]oman Anna K. McNamara standing in the clinic and shouting vigorously and victoriously, "This is my party!" I would rather forget that here was a woman, betraying women who were devoting their lives to succor and to save their fellow-women. By trickery and lying and hypocrisy, this woman sought and obtained her miserable "evidence" and now without pity for the poverty-stricken patients who had come there for relief, Policewoman Anna K. McNamara commanded the doctors and nurses into the awaiting patrol wagons. Yes! I cannot forget that. I can not laugh that off. But perhaps it is too much to expect of a police officer any perception of ethical standards.

Whatever the outcome of this raiding party, I hereby call upon the citizens of New York to find out for themselves how and where it originated and why it was carried out. I ask them to recall the breaking up by the police of the Birth Control meeting in Town Hall, with the subsequent revelation that this illegal action was instigated by Roman Catholic ecclesiastic authorities. We are paying and paying heavily for the support of a great police force. It is our right and our duty to insist that it shall function in an efficient, legal, and socially effective manner. Policewoman Anna K. McNamara's "party" exposes it as operating in the uncoordinated, misdirected, and unbalanced manner, which in an individual would indicate insanity.

PART II THE REFORMER
29. National Committee on Federal Legislation for Birth Control

S anger was understandably excited when she learned in November of
1931 that she had been named "outstanding woman in the metropolitan area" of New York by the American Woman's Association (AWA).[1]
She was, moreover, to be awarded their First Annual Gold Medal at a testimonial dinner for her "vision, integrity, valor." She wrote to Mrs. Adelaide
Archibald, an old family friend,

> November 23, 1931. Dearest Addie, Grand news, I get a medal! I
> think it's gold. Mr. Slee says it won't be, that it is probably bronze
> covered with gold. I think that inasmuch as Ann Morgan, sister of J.
> P. your banker, is head of the American Woman's Association who
> is awarding me this prize, that it must be gold. Don't they say that
> John D. & J. P. have hoarded all the gold in the world since the war?
> Thereby ends the tale of a medal![2]

Her excitement was justified. Although the medal turned out to be
bronze, the testimonial dinner on April 20, 1932, was a glittering event.[3]
Sanger was praised as "the greatest biological revolutionary the world has
ever known."[4] Professor John Dewey, Hendrik Willem Van Loon, and Karl
Reiland, rector of St. George's Episcopal Church, paid tribute. "A glittering
audience of notables in science, philanthropy, and society listened and
applauded," wrote the *New York Herald Tribune*.[5]

With the November announcement, twenty-two leading newspapers
carried a large three-column spread with picture and the full Margaret
Sanger story, while innumerable other papers covered the news with shorter columns. Naturally, the Catholic church inveighed against it. Monsignor
Belford in the *Brooklyn Eagle* deplored the award, calling it "disgusting," say-

ing "birth control breaks down the barriers of decency and morality."[6] The *Catholic Review* in Baltimore railed at the Catholic women who were living in the AWA clubhouse, appalled that they were not protesting vehemently and moving out of the club residence.[7] And Eleanor Roosevelt, a member of the AWA and one of the speakers at the November dinner at which Sanger was announced as awardee, was roundly criticized by the Catholic press.

Other newspapers credited Sanger with "changing the entire social structure of the world."[8] And throughout the thirties Sanger was engaged in doing just that, now as president of the National Committee on Federal Legislation for Birth Control.

Sanger had continued as editor of the *Birth Control Review*, or at least was so designated on the masthead, until 1929. Her frequent trips and long stays in Europe, her heavy schedule of lectures at home and abroad, the many hours of effort required to organize conferences, particularly the 1927 World Population Conference in Geneva, surely left little time for long hours of editing. While Sanger was away organizing the Geneva conference, the *Review* had been turned over to Mrs. F. Robertson-Jones, who was given free hand in the running of affairs in the absence of Sanger.

Mrs. Robertson-Jones had her own ideas of how a campaign for birth control should be run. Inevitably, these ideas conflicted with those of Sanger, who was not about to kowtow to an upstart. After a certain amount of infighting, Sanger resigned from the American Birth Control League and left her editorship of the *Review*.[9]

Sanger retained control of the Birth Control Clinical Research Bureau, which was in the excellent hands of Dr. Hannah Stone, leaving Sanger free to turn her attention to new challenges, in this case, to national legislation. In August 1929 Sanger announced formation of the National Committee on Federal Legislation on Birth Control. Intensely and minutely organized, the National Committee drew on the support of birth controllers in every town and city of America.[10] By 1932, when Sanger received her AWA medal, the Federal Legislation Committee was deep in the throes of its struggle with Congress. And struggle it was. As usual, Sanger took every opportunity to publicize birth control activities, and so, on receipt of the medal at the testimonial dinner, she launched into a description of the work of the National Committee.

The National Committee was working to rewrite the Comstock laws with the passage of a "doctors' bill," which gave physicians the right to give contraceptive advice and to use the mails to do so. But the first step in passing any legislation is to find a sponsoring congressman. Responses of the congressmen to the women of the National Committee were less than sanguine. Said Senator Ellison D. Smith, "It jars me. It is revolting to interfere in people's personal affairs." A committed worker complained, "I almost felt he was about to call the guard and have me arrested."

The congressmen's rejoinders were variations on discouragement: "We have not the right to deny the joy of life to millions." . . . "Every nigger knows about birth control." . . . "Did not believe there would be any virtue among women if such a law were passed." . . . "I will not discuss this subject with a woman." . . . "I'm not ready to teach our children to become whores yet." . . . "Birth Control is murder."[11] In addition, congressmen candidly or inadvertently acknowledged the strong Catholic lobby that made their particular support impossible.

While Sanger's hope for congressmen Henry Hatfield and Frank Hancock, the current sponsors, was strong, as it was with every sponsor every year, these men scored no more success than did their predecessors or followers.[12] From 1930 to 1936, with every session of Congress, Sanger's doctors' bill was either tabled, held up, recalled, or died. But four hearings in the Senate and two in the House did offer Sanger public education and publicity opportunities.

In June of 1936, when Sanger dissolved the National Committee on Federal Legislation, no bill had been passed, no Comstock law rescinded. Yet seven years of unrelenting effort had accomplished much. Despite the determined, aggressive offense of the Catholic hierarchy and the recalcitrance of diehard conservatives, public climate had changed, certainly in part attributable to the unrelenting, organized assault by the National Committee on public opinion. By the end of 1935, for example, "Fieldworkers were completing the collection of a million signatures in three hundred cities in thirty five states."[13]

Seven years of lobbying, of being regularly in the news had brought to the birth controllers' side numerous organizations with their political clout. More than a thousand clubs—civic, political, religious, and social—including the National Council of Jewish Women, General Federation of Women's Clubs, the Y.W.C.A., local Junior Leagues—in all representing between twelve and thirteen million individuals—had given their endorsement.[14] In 1936, birth control was favored by 63 percent of the American public; by 1939, that figure had risen to 79 percent of American women.[15] And in 1936 the One Package decision had been handed down.

That decision was a long time coming. It had its genesis in 1932, when the U.S. government confiscated a package of contraceptives sent to Sanger from Japan. Sanger discussed this with her attorney, Morris Ernst, and he advised Sanger to request that a similar package be sent to Dr. Hannah Stone at the Clinical Research Bureau. When the U.S. postal authorities confiscated Stone's package, Ernst filed suit, declaring Stone's right to a medical exemption. *United States v. One Package Containing 120 more or less, Rubber Pessaries to Prevent Conception* wound its way through the courts over the years. When Judge Grover Moscowitz ruled that physicians were permitted to use the U.S. mails to receive contraceptives, the government appealed, but lost its appeal in the spring of 1936.[16]

Just as the Crane Decision of 1918 had partially knocked the teeth out of the Comstock laws by allowing physicians to discuss contraception "to cure or prevent disease," similarly the One Package decision of 1936 now permitted doctors to send contraception information and materials through U.S. mails and common carriers. This One Package decision, in effect, nullified the remaining Comstock prohibitions. In June 1937, the Committee on Contraception of the American Medical Association informed its convention that physicians were legally entitled to give contraceptive advice, in person or through the mail. On learning of endorsement of the AMA, "In my excitement I actually fell downstairs," wrote Sanger. "Here was the culmination of unremitting labor ever since my return from Europe in 1915, the gratification of a dream come true."[17]

Sanger's National Committee, no longer deemed necessary, was disbanded. But the One Package decision was not the "dream come true." Shortly thereafter, the state of Massachusetts closed down all birth control clinics, and in Connecticut contraception remained illegal. Not until 1965, with the *Griswold v. Connecticut* decision of the Supreme Court, was the right of privacy within the marital bedroom seen as a constitutional right, making contraception legal for married couples. Contraception by the unmarried only became legal in 1972 with *Eisenstadt v. Baird*.[18] The federal Comstock laws were rewritten by Congress and contraceptive information and contraceptive devices finally removed from the obscene list in 1970.

AWA Clubhouse Testimonial Dinner Address[19]
New York City, April 20, 1932

You must all know that my heart is too full to express adequately my gratitude in words. Sitting here listening to all these touching and beautiful tributes, I asked myself, "Is it really true? Am I awake or is it all a pleasant dream?" For after nearly twenty years of indictment, suppressions, courts, jails, patrol wagons and police raids, it is simply wonderful. [Laughter and applause.] It is wonderful to receive something besides a warrant. [Laughter.]...

I wonder if I can take this opportunity to tell you something of the work that we have been doing in Washington. When I think of Washington in the past five months that I spent there, I feel that we have gone into the Congressional trenches, so to speak. Our little group of workers, valiant, intrepid, have been a sort of shock troop in trying to get our bill introduced in Congress.

When we arrived there last December, the very air seemed surcharged with all the important, pressing problems of the day. The mind of each Senator and each Representative seemed like a busy telephone switchboard. It was difficult to plug in anywhere because every wire was busy. It was busy with questions such as war debts, reparations, moratoriums, unemployment relief, tariffs, as well as war in Manchuria, peace conferences and disarmament, prohibition, budgets and finally bonuses. Now, what chance had we to plug in with a question like birth control in that hectic atmosphere? As a matter of fact, the very mention of birth control to the hectic, worried, troubled Congressmen was very much like announcing a messenger from Mars, except that I think that would have been more interesting and not quite so remote.

"Busy;" "Busy in conference;" "Busy in committee meetings;" Busy on the telephone;" "No time to see you;" "No time to talk about this subject, come back later;" "Come back tomorrow;" "Come back next week;" "Come back after your bill has been introduced," – anything to get rid of you, anything to get you out of the way.

Always we came back promptly and on the hour. Some days our workers called upon thirty to forty Congressmen with the result of seeing perhaps one or two of them. In fact, we considered two interviews a good day's work. Up to date, we have seen and talked to and we think partially converted, more than 200 Congressmen and over 50 Senators. [Applause.]

We found that the great difficulty was misunderstanding. We further found that the great majority of these men were both badly informed and misinformed. Of course, we found that the younger men, some of the newer ones, knew something of the pros and cons of birth control. One could easily know that by the size of their own families. But, when it came to asking for a law to allow others to have the same privileges that they had had, the subject became a serious one that had to have their due consideration.

Nevertheless, we found that the main thing that hung over them all like a pall was fear – fear of prejudice, fear of cloakroom joshing, I hesitate to say "kidding." [Laughter.] But more than all was fear of our opponents. Our opponents are skilled in the art as well as the science of tactics. We find that they move to block our every move and plan before we have scarcely known it ourselves. They move in block and group activity. Our supporters, as you know, give us casual and individual support, but the opposition moves en masse and there is no use in our trying to compete with them in those tactics.

So we had to outmaneuver them in another way. We met them in the tactics of psychology. Theirs is the weapon of fear; ours, the inspiring instrument of courage. Finally, we inspired one Congressman to have the courage to introduce our bill [Applause.], congressman Frank Hancock, of Winston-Salem, North Carolina! [Applause.]

I have here a telegram from a Senator who says:

Please extend my regrets to those responsible for inviting me to the banquet in your honor, in my inability to attend as much as I would like to.

He goes on and says something about the question of birth control, its humaneness and justification, and then he says, "I will introduce it." [Applause.]

This is Senator Hatfield of West Virginia. [Applause.]

We have had our eye on Senator Hatfield for a long time. [Laughter.] He has shoulders as broad as this table and a jaw equally as strong. We feel that in getting him to take an interest in this cause, he will put his back into it. Also, he will put his teeth into it, and I am sure he will never let go until it is won. [Applause.]

Now all this, friends, means that we have had our bill introduced in the House; it is about to be introduced in the Senate. This lovely meeting, this distinguished committee, this award, all mean that we are on our way to victory. Who can compute the tremendous suffering saved the human race when this bill shall be passed? For I firmly believe that when the fear of pregnancy is eliminated from the lives of women, heaven will be millions of miles nearer this earth. I believe that much of the social, economic and crime chaos that exists in the world today extends directly back to the reckless breeding of our forebears. As a result, we see countless men and women here today whose lives are enmeshed and entangled by the prejudice and the ignorance of the past. We must disentangle their lives. We must release them from ignorance and fear. We must free them from tyrannical laws. We must direct our own efforts and our own energies into settling questions that we know so well and in order to enlarge and explore the sphere of the unknown, the sphere of real life. We know that in every village, hamlet and town in this country women are living troubled and tortured lives through fear; many of them come appealing to us for help, but out of our reach millions are helplessly inarticulate, like doomed souls crushed beneath the weight of a cruelly prolific nature. It is these women we are dedicated to free.

This medal, this award, shall be the pledge to bind us together and to spur us on to the continuation of our fight for the liberation of womankind. Thank you!

[The audience arose and applauded.]

PART II THE REFORMER
30. A New Deal for Babies

With accession to office in 1932, President Franklin D. Roosevelt became the architect of the New Deal. During the First Hundred Days, he called for a bank holiday and began the reconstruction of the American government with Keynesian or "pump priming" economics. Roosevelt's National Recovery Act gave to a consortium of businesses the power to set rules and regulations for the American economy, with the intent of giving to individual Americans a new deal to replace the devastation wrought by the years of the Depression.

Sanger saw birth control as the ultimate new deal for mothers and babies. Her efforts to see birth control supported by the government during the Roosevelt years were stymied again and again by the powerful influence of the Roman Catholic hierarchy on the Roosevelt administration. The stance of the Catholic Church was reinforced by the controversial nature of birth control itself, which left even its potential defenders nervous and compounded the difficulty of federal approval.

The distribution of contraceptives to needy mothers would seem to have been an obvious advantage to all concerned, relieving the government of supporting so many children (half of the children born during the Depression years were born to families on relief according to Sanger) and relieving mothers from the economic burden and health hazards of child bearing. But contraception education and supplies were for the most part limited to activities by the Farm Security Administration in the migrant camps in non-Catholic California. Without a committed champion who had the inside clout of a General William Draper, birth control had little chance to be accepted as a governmental responsibility. Only with Roosevelt's election to a third term would circumstances and the helping hand of Eleanor

Roosevelt combine to create an opening for minimal inclusion of birth control into government services.

The Manuscript
This article for the popular *American Weekly* is an excellent example of the many articles Sanger wrote to support her ongoing campaign for mainstream acceptance of birth control. Here riding on the topicality of FDR's much-discussed New Deal, Margaret Sanger suggests a New Deal from the standpoint of mothers and babies.

America Needs a Code for Babies[1]
American Weekly, May 27, 1934

The National Recovery Act has codes for nearly every other field of production. Why not a code for babies?

I can see the National Association of American Babies with chubby hands signing a solemn agreement with President Roosevelt, which shall be the standard of fair competition in the field and of improved relations with parents and the public.

In Article I, the Code for Babies would state, as a definition, that the business of babies is to grow up, physically and mentally, into healthy, useful citizens, and that parents and other adults, as executives in charge of the babies' businesses will be respectfully requested to shoulder full responsibilities for success under the New Deal for that business.

As a first protest against this unfair competition for food, clothing, shelter, and other necessities the National Association of American Babies would probably adopt a clause something like this:

God bless our brothers and God bless our sisters; they are awfully nice—most of them. But we don't need any more right away.

The exact allowance per couple cannot be determined by Congress. It is not a proper subject for legislation. It would be very wrong, for example, for the law-makers in Washington to decree that no couple would be permitted to have more than one child every five years of their married life, and that the birth of twins would be considered as having exhausted the quota for a decade, and that the penalty for violation, whether innocent or not, would be a minimum of five years in a Federal penitentiary.

On the other hand, it seems to me equally wrong for Congress to stipulate that couples cannot space their children so that they will come at times when the parents are best able to care for them. Yet that is exactly the sort of interference with private conduct exercised by the musty Federal laws that forbid the use of the mails and common carriers for conveying contraceptives or information about their use.

While the babies are clamoring for a code of their own, I can hear them piping: Give our mammas a Happy New Deal!

The N.R.A. says to husbands: "You need not work more than 40 hours a week." This is the decree of the "blanket code." But to the wives the law says in effect: "As for you, if you wish to enjoy married life, you must go on bearing as many children as possible; and you must work night and day taking care of them, whether your husband has a job or not."

The irony is that all husbands will in time secure jobs, with working days becoming shorter and shorter. All over the land advisory councils are spending a lot of money and thought in planning leisure-time activities for employees whose hours have been cut. I wonder if the councils will recommend that one desirable leisure-time activity for fathers is taking care of the babies while the overworked mothers enjoy a few hard-earned leisure-time activities?

Mothers may be slaves, but the duties of motherhood are not yet considered employment under any N.R.A. definition. It is not feasible, some one may argue, to limit the hours of mothers in taking care of their babies, because the babies cannot, like a factory, be locked up at night and over the weekend. However, there is a clause in the President's Reemployment Agreement which provides that "time and one third shall be paid highly skilled workers on continuous processes" when they are compelled to work overtime in order to keep a plant going.

I wish that this provision might be applied to overworked mothers. I wish, in the friendliest way, that it were obligatory for the husbands to pay their wives real wages for bearing and taking care of their children, with "time and one third" for all hours in excess of 40 a week, and in any case where the husband seeks in vain for opportunity to earn enough to carry out this contract, I wish that it were obligatory for city, county, state, or nation to pay wages, time and overtime, to wives employed in motherhood.

Just imagine how promptly and how universally birth control would be approved by the tax-payers if such a burden were thrust upon them!

"We want fewer new brothers and sisters!" cry the 6,000,000 babies for whose food and clothing and shelter their parents cannot pay. But if these babies could broadcast their protest through every radio station in the land, the fact would still remain that right now the babies already on the way number about one and a half million; and of these it is pathetically probable that several hundred thousand will be added to the masses of those who cannot live except through the support of public relief funds.

Obviously, contraception cannot do anything to control the births of children already conceived. Poverty, starvation, disease, death in infancy, await an appallingly large percentage of them. These will become the victims of nature's method of population control.

Of the children born into American homes during the new year the percentage of the unwanted is hard to estimate. But no statement in mathematical terms is necessary. From what we see and hear about us we all know how numerous are these tragedies of unwanted births. Unwilling mothers and unwanted children are the grim sacrifices to the willfulness of nature, which habitually, wherever uncontrolled by human intelligence, is lavish in fertility and correspondingly active in early destruction of its creatures.

When children make a mistake, they are easily forgiven if they can truthfully say to their parents, "I didn't mean it!" But if parents who have just added an unwanted child to the world say ever so truthfully, "We didn't mean it!," they can hardly expect forgiveness from anyone, and least of all from the unwanted children.

Where are the unwanted children? They may happen in the best of families. But if all the parents of unwanted children were classified according to grades of intelligence or education, it would surely be found that the great majority of them are in the lower grades. If they were classified according to economic condition, the great majority of them would be among the poorer classes. Thus, the unwanted children get a bad start in life, and a large percentage of them will never live to be one year old. Furthermore, the mothers who die in giving birth to unwanted children are proportionately greater in number than [in] the other cases of maternal mortality.

According to the reports of experts made at the famous White House Conference on Child Health and Protection, there were in 1930 more than 10,000,000 handicapped children in the United States. This total included those improperly nourished, tubercles, those with weak or damaged hearts, crippled, blind, deaf, those with defective speech, mentally retarded, delinquent, and dependent.

I do not know just how many of these 10,000,000 were unwanted children, nor would I imply that all unwanted children fail to grow up into health and strength and useful citizenship. But I see the pathetic majority brought as it were, to a vast banquet of life and I hear them pleading, "Nobody invited us; we didn't choose to come; so we were compelled to come, brought here in the dark. There is no way to get back; so we insist on a place at the table, even if it means a second sitting."

It is a pity that the babies cannot be consulted before they come into the world. The next best thing would be to have a Code Authority for Babies draw up some demands in behalf of the children of the future. Perspective parents would have to give satisfactory answers to the following questions:

1. Have you any disease or weakness, physical or mental, that you might transmit to offspring?
2. Is there any special danger that the woman will die in childbirth? or will permanently impair her health by bearing the child?

3. Is it likely that you can meet the cost of feeding, clothing, sheltering, and rearing the child?
4. Have you at least the minimum of physical, mental, and moral qualities which a child deserves of its parents?...

This is the day of social planning. We have come to believe in planning the production and distribution of goods. We plan the government of city, state, and nation. We plan jobs, and we plan vacations. We plan almost everything, big and little, except families. Now let us do some hard thinking about how to plan families. Let us listen to the National Association of American babies!

31. India and World Tour for Birth Control, 1935–36

S anger had long wanted to visit India, where the need for birth control was obvious, so when invited to speak at the All-India Woman's Conference convening December 28, 1935, to January 2, 1936, she accepted with alacrity.[1] The National Committee on Federal Legislation for Birth Control was well staffed and could function without her, and Sanger had in mind that the international press generated by this trip might impress Congress and inspire it to take birth control more seriously. Sanger set up a three-month tour of India under the auspices of the London International Information Centre, sending Edith How-Martyn, executive secretary of the Centre, on ahead by almost a year to make advance preparations.

At home, Sanger also made preparations, reading books such as *Eastern Philosophy for Western Minds* by Hamish McLaurin, taking lengthy notes, filling the versos pages of her India diary with details of the customs and culture of India, leaving the recto pages for daily diary entries. Sanger packed up gynaeplaques (take-apart models of the female reproductive organs), two educational films, contraceptives, contraceptive literature, and Anna Jane Phillips, a young journalist, who would be writing a steady stream of publicity releases and news stories throughout the tour and who turned out to be "a perfect companion" for travel.[2]

Never one to keep her trips short or simple, Sanger first spent a week in London, where she met Jawaharal Nehru, successor to Gandhi and an avid birth control supporter, and Paul Brunton, who invited her to meet the Sage of Arunachala living near Madras. Once on board for the twelve-day trip to India, Sanger immediately noticed

> several Indian men & women on board. They keep to themselves & are utterly ignored by the English passengers. It must be a source of

191

resentment to see these people by the thousands going to rule them in their own land & yet be ignored by them as tho they were inferiors or servants....I can see nevertheless that the English can never know the Indians so long as they keep control over them. They fully & firmly believe they are inferior & one and & all have warned me not to depend on their promises. They will promise anything they say but do nothing. They criticize their habits & integrity.[3]

Sanger and Anna Jane debarked at Bombay, where the welcome was warm and enthusiastic—as it was to be throughout all of India. Leaving ship, Sanger found herself so bedecked with flowers, that she must have looked "more like a bridesmaid than a propagandist."[4]

Bombay Nov 25. The voyage of 12 days is over. Bombay came in sight about noon....I laughed at the first glimpse of man power to see 50 native Indians lift the gangplank & sixty lifted a smaller one hundreds of coolies came for the luggage but it was such a scramble and confusion. I was taken off . . . gave the keys to Herbert who in turn gave them to cooks who cleared them & six hours later the bags were all here in my large & spacious room.[5]

Once in India, Sanger and Anna Jane were assisted by Joseph, their bearer and manservant, truly valuable during their travels, for he spoke Hindustani, Tamil, Bengali, and English. Joseph was much needed, as was Anna Jane, for this was a politic working trip meant to educate India and the world about birth control, that it was not only needed but wanted. At the planning stage of the India tour, Sanger had made herself plain: "I am not going to India in order to persuade everybody to have a small family. I want rather to convince them of the desirability—for themselves and posterity—of having families of the right size and right quality."[6] Sanger was determined to cover as much ground, to get out as much publicity and education advantage from this trip as humanly possible. Sanger and Edith How-Martyn, who was also part of the India tour, never traveled together. In this way, more ground was covered by the birth controllers, and Sanger was not tainted with the tar of India antagonism to the British, paramount at the time with India demanding its independence from Britain. Sanger covered ten thousand miles, How-Martyn sixty-five hundred and the total meetings between them numbered a hundred and five, thirty-two of which were medical meetings. Wherever they visited, they left behind birth control clinics.

As always, although staying in the finest homes and spending time with government officials and wealthy patrons, Sanger insisted on going into the city of the people, into the areas where poverty was rampant and birth control most needed. She wrote of her first impression of Bombay.

> We walked back to the hotel from dinner about 11:30 & saw men & boys stretched out on the sidewalk asleep. This is their home. The only belongings they own is the mat on which they sleep....Alas![7]

On November 28, Sanger was taken by a young Indian woman to the "Chails" slums. Mrs. Khandralta volunteered her time as a social worker and had established her own small crude settlement.

> There...100 children are taught songs & co operative play. Two language groups in separate rooms but boys & girls are together in each group. They are given clean gowns & washed every day. They come at 12 AM & stay to 4. No toys & no equipment. It takes courage to hope for something in the lives of such children especially when you see where they live. Corrugated slab of zinc or iron is put up as roof & sides (3) no doors or windows curtains hung up to keep people from the streets out.
>
> There was one place for water & toilet in the block. Simply holes dark & creepy foul & smelly....Infant welfare works may be a humane gesture, but when it is carried out without giving parents advice on limiting the size of the family it actually works as a hardship on all concerned & deceives the community & undermines the morale of those concerned – the parents.
>
> Increased medical care, the spread of hygiene, sanitation & preventative medicine will tend to result in the increase of a disproportionately weaker race than were nature allowed to take her course. This does not mean that care & attention should not be bestowed on the weakly & immature children, but it does mean that knowledge & practice of birth control must precede charity & humanitarian efforts to realize & make permanent a civilization (healthy).
>
> ...There is far too much needless suffering & misery around us to continue to look at it as natural and inevitable. To deal with it needs a rational view point & method in accord with common sense & intelligence.[8]

Sanger's activity in Bombay set the pace for the rest of the tour.

> I sat and talked with many influential people in Bombay. I lunched at Government House with the Governor and his wife. I spoke to a meeting of young volunteer social workers....I showed two techni-

cal films on contraception to a meeting of fifty doctors at the K.E.M. Hospital. I broadcast a fifteen minutes talk from the Bombay Station on "What Birth Control Can Do for India," and this was heard as far afield as Colombo, Caylon;Delhi, and Nagpur.[9]

From Bombay, Sanger, with Anna Jane and Joseph, went to Wardha and then to Bolpur, beyond Calcutta, to meet Dr. Rabindranath Tagore, the great poet, who (unlike Gandhi) understood "the needs of women and the disadvantages and suffering they have to endure."[10] Leaving Tagore, the party went to Calcutta, where "It is stated authoritatively that over 200,000 people . . . sleep on the ground as they are too poor to live in homes."[11]

In her newsletter, Sanger outlined her itinerary:

In two days I am leaving Calcutta to visit Darjeeling, Benares, Allahabad, Delhi, Agra and Baroda and then I shall return to Bombay on December 20 and take an aeroplane on to [Trivandrum, capital of] Travancore to attend the All-India Women's Conference....Distances are so great in India and night journeys in the trains so tiring and time so precious that where possible I shall travel by plane.[12]

Indeed, India is very big, and the train rides were very long.

Our train went to Madras. Twenty-two hour journey had to change at 3 am Arrived Sat Jan 25 tired....went to Connors Hotel. Slept & kept in bed all day. Sunday very very tired. The first time I'm really all in!! The thought of a train journey makes me weep. Another long 26 hours to Calcutta.[13]

Briefly without scheduled lectures, Sanger was able to see Siliguri and stay in Kalimpong, lying in the shadow of Mt. Everest near the "mighty snowy barrier of Kinchenjunga," Near Kalimpong,

Women on the road were wearing Scotch plaid shawls which were out of place entirely. Later I learned that Dr. Graham, a Scotch missionary, came here forty years ago & established the place. His wife started the home industries & taught the natives how to knit, sew & weave....There are 300 lovely children here with black & white faces all speaking English with a Scotch brogue.[14]

At Darjeeling, Sanger bought Darjeeling tea and, for Grant, the skin of a tiger shot in a recent hunt. Later, at the end of the trip in Honolulu, the tea and the tiger skin wrapped in moth balls would be packed together, leaving Sanger in Arizona with many, many boxes of Darjeeling-Moth Ball tea—

not quite what she had planned. Back in Calcutta, Sanger ran into a swami, who, briefly returned to India from the States, remembered himself to her and drove her to her train in his Rolls-Royce. Benares she found dirty, the Ganges she thought clean. At Allahabad, she visited Ranjit Sitaram Pandit, sister of Nehru, who sponsored a meeting with six hundred students.

Sanger saw the Taj Mahal at Agra and was a state guest at Baroda, where she met the Gaekwar and his wife. At the All-India Women's Conference, she was unable to accommodate Her Highness of Trivandrum. On her way to Madras, she was mistakenly left with all of Anna Jane's luggage along with her own when Anna Jane went to Ceylon. Adyar, the former home of Annie Besant, was no more than an hour from Madras, so Sanger, always interested in spiritual practices, saw the home of the deceased theosophist. Next, Sanger went to sit at the feet of the Sage of Arunachala.

Paul Brunton, author of *The Search in Secret India*, whom she had met in London, was investigating the authenticity of the fakirs and holy men of India. The one holy man for whom he had great regard was the Sage of Arunachala, the Maharshi of Tiruvannamalai (1870-1950).[15] As recorded in her diary, Sanger went in good faith and with an open mind to the ashram of the Maharshi. Her original diary comments were nonjudgmental, but on reflection, Sanger found herself less impressed with the Maharshi than with Brunton. When she recounted that experience later in her *Autobiography*, she wrote,

> I regretted that I did not feel the Maharshi's power. His utter indifference—sitting all day in a semi-trance, engaging in no activity—seemed to me a waste. Nevertheless, I was most grateful to Paul Brunton for the experience, and understood the Indians better thereafter.[16]

She added Calcutta on the Malabar Coast to her itinerary, then went to Mysore, where she cured Joseph of a cough with Vitamin A and D tablets. In Bangalore, she was again a state guest, this time of the Dewan of Mysore, Sir Mirza Ismail. Hyderabad was pleasant and social. And then suddenly the India trip was over, and she was in Hong Kong, where the temperature was brutally cold, especially cold after the heat of India. On to Rangoon and Singapore and Honolulu, No doubt Margaret Sanger would still be traveling today as this is being read had she not been taken ill in Hong Kong. Never one to be stopped by illnesses of any sort, although many of her Shanghai engagements had to be cancelled, Sanger was determined to speak in Honolulu.

On reaching Hawaii, under the care of an exceptionally solicitous manager, Sanger was restricted to bed and rest when not actually required to speak, for she was by this time ill and completely exhausted.

In Washington, the Committee on Federal Legislation was continuing its offensive. Senators and representatives introduced variations of the doctors' bill, which continued to die or be overlooked. But if Washington remained indifferent, India welcomed Sanger. There was no question that there her work was needed and wanted. As she later wrote,

> If, however, at any time I should feel tired and wonder whether this campaign in India is worth while, I should only have to walk for five minutes through the side streets of Bombay or Calcutta, or else take a stroll into any small town or village and look at the teeming masses of poverty-stricken, starved, emaciated men, women, and children to be spurred on to even more grim determination that Birth Control is an immediate and necessary practice of world-wide importance. In Bombay, I visited the chawls, that is tenement houses inhabited by the poorest people, where two or three families are living in one small room and children and adults alike look pitiably miserable and undernourished. We asked the women, squatting before their squalid huts how many children they had living and how many dead. Then we asked how many more they wanted, and all except one said, "Please God, no more."[17]

The Manuscript

While on her tour of India, Sanger sent home a series of newsletters to her intimate friends. This is one of the series.

News from MARGARET SANGER

Letter No. 3 – For Mrs. Sanger's Intimate Friends and Family

Mandura, South India

January 2, 1936

Hello Everybody:

Here I am in a railway station en route for Madras!!! I left Trivandrum last night at 9.30 being promised I was on a fast express to Madras. For some reason, we are all dumped out here at 10.40 this morning, and must now wait for the 7.40 train to take us to Madras.

As Anna Jane worked so hard at the Conference, I decided she needed a little let down, so she remained at Trivandrum to see the younger girls and women, who all loved her, and whom she wanted to know better, girls of fine families and influential in Indian life. So I left her and insisted on the Bearer remaining with her, thinking I'd not need anyone until I got to Madras, where Edith and Herbert are waiting.[18] So when I was "ejected" here, I laughed at the absurdity of taking all the luggage of the party with me, and to have no bearer to help or watch over it!

Well, the Conference was well attended by Catholics!!! All the red tape and influence of the Royal House and ingenuity of a small active group were put into play to defeat the Birth Control resolution! Her Highness had two Sessions with me to side track the resolution!!!

She begged me to use my voice and influence to persuade the Conference to exert all energies on the removal of "brothels," etc., etc. I replied that the Conference had passed a resolution against "traffic in women" and that this subject was already covered by others who knew more about this traffic than I did. Nevertheless, she pleaded with me to swing the interest of the women into other lines!!! As State guest it was awkward, but it was as impossible to do it as to change the color of my eyes! I dashed back to the Conference, as my last interview with the Maharani was 9 a.m., and the Conference Session with the birth control resolution began at 9, so I got back in time to enter the discussion and to speak last before the vote was taken.

I opened by saying I would have had more respect for the sincerity of the opposition's interest of the Moral aspect of the subject (they based their opposition on the moral issue) had they brought forth a resolution or urged the conference to take action to wipe out the brothel system, etc., etc. So I threw out that bit for Her Highness and went straight ahead on the attack.

Everyone realized the difficulty, as Her Highness of Trivandrum was not only acting President and presiding at every Session but this one, but the Social hostess of the Royal House is a Miss Watts, an ardent Roman Catholic, who has great influence with Her Highness, who in turn dominates the Maharaja – her son – who is in power and rules in this Matriarchal State! It's all full of intrigue underneath, but it was a lot of fun to me, to see the inside machinery going round. Anyway, the resolution was carried by 84 to 25!! The Catholics resigned at once, including Miss Watts! Such poor sports. Unless they can dominate the game, they won't play!

The amusing part of the Session was that all those who spoke were "Miss" this or "Miss" that! They spoke with great fervour about the passions of men in and out of marriage. One of the women pointed out that, so far, it was the unmarried women present who seemed to know so much about these passions that it shocked some of them to hear their views. This sent the audience into roars of laughter, and then each woman who spoke emphasized the brothers and the family relationship in excuse for knowing so much about men. But their case was weakened, because most of them were foreigners or Eurasians. No important Indian woman spoke against the resolution, and I doubt if any one of the opponents at all was wholly Indian.

The men of the press were turned out at the request of Her Highness, and the women did not like it at all. They were, however, present at the Opening Session, when I presented our Greetings. It was received with tremendous applause, and all agreed that it was the most "electric" message of the Conference and had the best reception given to it. Of course, I had it re-done on a larger parchment, about the size of the usual diploma. It was nicely done and looked like a real greeting and will be kept on record and framed.

I was given an evening for a meeting before the resolution. But as to the meetings, I had just about the finest the evening after. The Youth Movement – 1,000 men – young, of course, sat on the ground in the open air before the Y.M.C.A. and drank in every word. I spoke without as much as a sound, throughout an hour and a half address. It is the men who are deeply alive to this question.

Doctors came from all over the south of India, men and women too, asking me to come to their towns or cities and help them to get things started. I gave demonstrations in my room, in the dressing room, in the car, in the ante-rooms of the Conference, and in the toilet!! I was followed and besieged to tell them what to do and how to help others. Finally, on the train last night, a young woman had a compartment next to mine. She knocked on my door and asked to come in. She had been to the Conference with her six month's old baby, whom she nursed. She is 27 years old, and has four children, has had five abortions and one stillbirth. Her husband had sent her to the conference to see me, and the poor darling had no chance even to get near me, so when it was announced at the afternoon session that I was leaving that night, she promptly decided to take the same train and got her bed next to me!!! I was simply amazed at the tenacity and gentleness of this little thing, almost a child in her attitude, and yet determined to do something to prevent having more children.

The Bombay Corporation passed a resolution that has been before them for three years to ask a Special Medical Committee to report on the question of Birth Control and the Municipality.

Also, Edith wired me that the Medical Conference at Nagpur had endorsed the Birth Control resolution.

I am to show the films and speak before the first All-India Conference of Gynecologists and Obstetricians tomorrow afternoon and address a Public Meeting by the Y.M.C.A. on January 6th and heaven knows how many more.

I have already had thirty-three meetings and have established about thirty centres or places where birth control information is to be given; Maternity Wards and Hospitals and other centres where gynecologists are in charge and are enthusiastic about the gynaeplaque, of which I have had fifty shipped here from U.S.A., besides large batches of jellies and pessaries and condoms of a different quality and formulas and a powder that foams.

I am trying to get the big rubber company at Trivandrum to make rubber sponges and pessaries. You would be surprised to know that the men and women, too, prefer to use the diaphragm pessary, and the Doctors want to introduce it here cheap.

I have carried and shipped Maurice's leaflet all over India, and as the Catholic Truth Society got hold of several copies, they raised a scene by saying we were spreading information among young people etc., etc. I then got up another leaflet on "Questions and Answers" and that is going the rounds as Education....

I have a very fine medical man who speaks English, Tamil and Hindi, who is a fine public speaker and will give up his private practice for one year, if we can give him 100 rupees a month and travel expenses (which will be little). This would mean $40 a month, and I am going to try him out at Mysore and Hyderbad. He can give a special demonstration to the men, after I give the regular address. He did this at the Youth Meeting at Trivandrum, and it was a great joy to find him well versed in knowledge of the technique. This man was trained in Madras Medical college and lived with Dr. and Mrs. Cousins for five years and knows and speaks English well.

The interest here is beyond expectation. At the bank today at Madura, when I went to cash an American express cheque, one of the men at the desk came up to Dr. Sundaram and asked if I could come and speak at the Y.M.C.A. tonight. It's like that everywhere. Interest is keen, and I hope it won't lag and die down. That is why it would be wonderfully helpful if we could keep someone here on the job. $40 a month is only $480 a year, less than 100 pounds. Expenses would be about the same, but $1,000 could do an enormous amount of good this year, following up this interest by a medical person.

Edith and I are seeing the important people connected with the Government and Medical Colleges in Madras. I go from here to Mysore and then to Hyderbad and expect to attend the population conference at Lucknow on January 27th and 28th and then I go to the Conference of the International Council of Women in Calcutta.

I sail from Calcutta on February 2nd for Rangoon, and then homeward bound.

Cordial greetings to friends in America and England.

MARGARET SANGER.

PART II THE REFORMER
32. M. S. Meets Gandhi

As soon as Sanger knew that she would be visiting India, she had written Mahatma Gandhi, saying that she would like to pay him her respects. Aware of the publicity potential of such a meeting and desirous as well of the support that birth control could gain from his endorsement, she was delighted, on reaching Bombay, to receive his reply.

Do by all means come, whenever you can & you shall stay with me if you won't mind what must appear to you to be our extreme simplicity.[1]

When she arrived at Wardha on December 2, 1935, she and Anna Jane "were put in a small horse-cart with backs to the driver & came jogging down to see Gandhi." Later she learned the horse cart was called a "tonga."

We went directly to his place & met him tho this is his day of silence. He rose to greet me smiling from ear to ear. I put down my bag and gloves and flowers and magazine in order to take both his hands. He has an unusual light that shines in his face; that shines through the flesh; that circles around his head and neck like a mist with white sails of a ship coming through. It lasted only a few seconds, but it is there. When I looked again it was only the shiney appearance of his flesh that I saw but always the smile and a hospitable welcome.[2]

Sanger was then taken to the guesthouse,

A four-partitioned house with rough hews, white plastered walls half way to the roof. The upper half open for air.... It is all spotless and clean—rough stone floors....all very simple but clean and peaceful. The bath room is a large stone floor room in the same building but not adjoining; one has to go outside and around to get to it.[3]

At eleven A.M., Sanger was brought a bowl of porridge and milk.

I asked no questions about milk being boiled or anything as to its being goats' or cows' milk. I just ate all of it I could swallow. It was sweetened with either honey or brown sugar and was very nice. I happened not to be hungry at all but down it went just the same.[4]

At her first company meal, she noted that all took off their shoes before entering, guests including servants sat on the floor, and a large rubber plant leaf served as table, napkin, and plate.

Food was passed by a woman servant and put on the leaf. One cut-up wet vegetable hot, one curry dry vegetable, rice cooked in milk like a gruel in a small silver or brass bowl. Another small bowl of milk soup. Then three different kinds of flap jacks, two hot and buttered, one dry and hard made of rye, beside a crisp wafer used for curry. Fruit salad mixed with tomatoes and bananas and oranges. All kinds of spiced ingredients on the leaf to help yourself. We all sat cross-legged and ate with fingers. One spoon for the soup. No one else used spoons except Anna Jane and Self. After tiffin [a light midday meal] another washing of hands and upstairs to sit and discuss topics.

At three o'clock, I go to see the industries....There are several industries going in their infancy. The cotton is planted and seeded by a jenny hand machine, then rolled and spun on hand-made looms. The hand-made paper industry also is making strides. The linseed oil is made from seeds and pounded by hand to a pulp and then pounded in huge stone jars and pressed as a white bullock goes round and round to press the oil into a jar underneath. The pulp is made into flap-jacks or cereal. The water mill is also operated by two bullocks and water from the huge deep well is drawn up and emptied into irrigation pipes.[5]

The next day, Sanger had two appointments with Gandhi, and both were disappointing. She came away convinced that

his personal experience at the time of his father's death was so shocking and self-blamed that he can never accept sex as anything good, clean or wholesome.[6]

In fact, Gandhi had made a great concession to Sanger during their conversations by saying that possibly the rhythm method might be permissible, but even while acknowledging that India was overpopulated [India hit the one billion mark in late 1999], Gandhi would not agree that birth control was *not* a sin, and much to Sanger's disappointment, Gandhi would endorse only abstinence as birth control for India's overburdened mothers.[7]

Although Gandhi was generally revered, not all of India agreed with his point of view. A typical response was printed in the *Bombay Chronicle*.

> Prof. Kadha Kamal Mukherjee considered that the remedy of continence was a remedy for the Gods, and not for the masses who were steeped in ignorance and poverty. To preach to them the principles of Brahmacharya was as absurd and preposterous as asking China to adopt non-resistance in the face of present Japanese aggression.[8]

The Manuscript

If Sanger could not use Gandhi's endorsement, she could publicize the face that she had had a meeting with him, which indeed generated worldwide coverage for Sanger and the birth control movement. Articles such as the one below were published in *Asia Magazine* and *The Illustrated Weekly of India,* among others.

What He Told Me at Wardha[9]
January 19, 1936

Mr. M.K. Gandhi says he knows women!

When I talked with him at Wardha a few days after my arrival in India he said, "I have known tens of thousands of women in India. I know their experiences and their aspirations. I have discussed it with some of my educated sisters, but I have questioned their authority to speak on behalf of their unsophisticated sisters because they have never mixed with them. The educated ones have never felt one with them. They have regarded me as half a woman because I have completely identified myself with them. I feel I speak with some confidence because I have worked with and talked with and studied many women."

This is an amazing boast to come from any man to claim that he knows women!

Mr. Gandhi's Advice

And after reading Mr. Gandhi's autobiography and after having had two long conversations, 24 hours apart, with him, I must challenge his statement because I do not believe he has the faintest glimmering of either the "experiences and aspirations" or the inner workings of a woman's mind, heart, or being.

There are two major points upon which I base my challenge. First, Mr. Gandhi advises the women of India to "resist" or in extreme cases, to "leave" their husbands in order to control the size of their families rather than resort to birth control methods. Second, he does not recognize that sex expression between men and women can be based on love and not lust.

Our conversation began on my part with an appeal to him to help find a solution for the masses who are the burden bearers of poverty, misery and large families. Continence for unmarried men and women is not an impossibility but it was to the married woman that Mr. Gandhi's advice to "resist" was directed.

"Strangely Illogical"

Mr. Gandhi is strangely illogical in his demand that women "resist" their husbands to avoid frequent pregnancies. A woman might resist 364 days of the year and give it on the three hundred and sixty-fifth only to become pregnant. If this practice of resisting the husband every day in the year but one continued, the woman could have a child every year during her child-bearing period.

But let us look at the state of affairs which would result in the homes of India if Mr. Gandhi's advice were followed. Picture for yourself a young, loving couple in the fullness of maturity, with health, vigour and vitality. Perhaps they already have two, three or four children and realize fully that if they were to have more it would rob the children already born of their birth-right of health, proper care and an adequate start in life. Or perhaps another child would jeopardize the mother's life.

Try to imagine the irritations, disputes, and thwarted longings that Mr. Gandhi's advice would bring into the home. There could be no loving glances, no tender goodnight kisses, no gentle words of endearment lest such attentions, such natural expressions of affection might excite the sexual emotions.

Nothing but frowns, refusals, dark glances, and frigid repulses could come from the wife or the young loving mother in order to keep from a pregnancy she did not desire. The husband would hardly dare look tenderly at the woman he loved, fearful of his own powers of self-control.

Advice Not Followed

If, as he says, Mr. Gandhi has been "dinning" this advice into the ears of Indian women "all his life," it is quite certain such advice has not been followed. The census figures for 1934 are proof of that. They show that the population of India increased by 34 million in 10 years.

I contend that if he knew women as he claims he knows them, he would not have given nor would give advice of this character, which can never be carried out as a general scheme and never will be carried out as long as love of man for woman and woman for man exists in the human heart.

Mr. Gandhi assumes in giving such advice that women are not amorous and do not express their love sexually. This again proves how little he knows women and how far away he is from knowing their "experiences and aspirations."

I may not be so familiar with Indian women as Mr. Gandhi claims to be, for I have not known "tens of thousands" of them. But I do know women of the Western countries. In the past 20 years in which I have dedicated my life to the service of the women of the world, I have had private talks with intimate confessions from thousands of women of all nations, all religions, and all classes.

They have told me of their troubles and their heartaches. I have shared their sorrows and their joys, as well as their hopes and longings. And I believe firmly that the heart of the Indian woman is not different from the heart of the American, Chinese, Italian, or European woman where love is concerned. And, Mr. Gandhi himself concedes that the "women will not resist their husbands."

Does anyone think a husband could or would remain devoted very long if his emotions and instincts were continually denied expression by the wife he loves? I predict that, if such advice were followed, it would be a calamity in Indian homes! It would create an atmosphere of dissension, and even brutality in the home. Marriage would become a question of legal rape and laws would soon be enacted to deal with the rebellious, resistant wife, greatly to her disadvantage.

Broken Homes
Then consider the economic implications of this advice. A husband thwarted, driven to desperation by the constant repulses of his wife, would ultimately refuse her support and the shelter of his home. Doubtless, public opinion would support him.

Probably, if Mr. Gandhi's advice were followed to any great extent, the men of the land would band together to make laws, such as we have in many states in America, giving legal sanction to their refusal to support wives who refuse to live with them in natural union.

What would the women of India do if they found themselves turned from their husband's doors? The majority of them have had no training to enable them to earn a living for themselves in the competitive world of today.

From an early age they have built their entire lives about their husbands and their homes. They have depended upon their husbands for their support. And still more important, what woman would be so unnatural as to want to see the home she has built up through the years by thoughtful, loving care wracked by discord and discontent?

Yet a mother may realize that her own life and health and the health and training of the children she already has must be sacrificed if she has more children to claim her strength, her time, or perhaps, her life.

What is she to do? Resist her husband as Mr. Gandhi advocates? Bring dissension into her happy home? Or use the simple birth control methods which science has brought forward as the answer to her problem?

A Calamity

The second thing that proves Mr. Gandhi does not know women is his general attitude towards sex union. I asked, "Mr. Gandhi, do you not see a great difference between sex love and sex lust?" He answered, "Yes," but his words of explanation showed he does not understand.

Mr. Gandhi cannot conceive of this force being transmitted from lust into beauty. He cannot believe that women know this to be true and have in their own lives and relationships with men transmuted this force into one of the most stimulating, beautifying, spiritual acts of human experience.

Mr. Gandhi cannot understand this. He is too inhibited by his own emotions to accept this fact, but were it not true, marriage would indeed have become a vulgar, debasing institution and would long ago have collapsed.

I would not feel free to mention this point were it given in confidence, but Mr. Gandhi has already expressed it in his autobiography and with unusual frankness and candour discussed his own experience.

Fear as Restraint

Mr. Gandhi has an appalling fear that licentiousness and over-indulgence will occur unless there is a fear of pregnancy to restrain the Man. Has he ever thought that the same fear can occur during the nine months of a woman's pregnancy? Does he think of that condition in the lives of married people who know that for reasons of sterility or barrenness, pregnancy cannot result? I said to him, "But, Mr. Gandhi, there are thousands, millions, who regard your word as that of a saint. How can you ask them, who are not so strong nor wise as you, to follow your advice when you yourself acknowledge that it has taken you years to overcome and control the force that nature implanted in your being?"

Mr. Gandhi merely smiled.

PART II THE REFORMER
33. Fortunate Support: The Clinical Trials of Clarence Gamble

W hile Margaret Sanger was preaching the cause and educating the world on the importance of birth control, nationally through the National Committee on Federal Legislation and internationally through international conferences and constant international travel, the "glorious chain of clinics" needed to make birth control practical was in the making.[1] No formal agreement was ever set up between Margaret Sanger and Dr. Clarence J. Gamble, but as it fell out, the work of the highly visible Sanger was to be perfectly complemented by the publicity-shy one-man band that was Gamble.

Gamble was his own man, and he could afford to be. An heir to the Ivory Soap Proctor & Gamble fortune, Gamble found his wealth a cross of sorts. When he received his first million dollars at twenty-one years of age in 1915, he went into a period of agonized reflection. But being a man of great common sense, he then decided to enjoy his wealth and to put it to good use.[2] As conscientious as he was wealthy, he had chosen medicine as a career, rather than astronomy, which had great fascination for him, because he believed he could contribute more to the world weal as a physician. In the same frame of mind, he devoted himself to the establishment of birth control clinics as the best use of his wealth.[3]

Gamble became active in the birth control movement when he was beginning his career at the University of Pennsylvania. In 1929, close friend Dr. Stuart Mudd and his wife, Emily, organized the Southeastern Pennsylvania Birth Control League and then, with others, set up a Maternal Health Clinic in Philadelphia.[4] But the gynecologists and obstetricians involved wanted to know which birth control jellies were the most effective. Gamble, researching and teaching at that time at the University, was asked to investigate.

It was the beginning of a formal involvement with what had apparently been a private interest—his personal desire to space his five children (which he and wife Sarah did) and his personal friendship with Robert Latou Dickinson, the prominent New York gynecologist and founder of the National Committee on Maternal Health.[5] Thenceforth over the years, Gamble worked for birth control with many birth control organizations, holding various titles and positions, always managing to make practical Sanger's vision of possibilities and always conscious of the larger picture.[6] Ultimately, it was he who urged and coaxed Sanger into merging what had become Mrs. F. Robertson-Jones's American Birth Control League with Sanger's Clinical Research Bureau to create the Birth Control Federation of America—ironically enough, for Gamble, like Sanger, was not a lover of organizations.[7]

As Sanger wrote Gamble in 1953, her attitude expressive of that which had always guided her and referring to William Vogt, then president of the Planned Parenthood Federation of America,

> It is very flattering of you to say that I am a money raiser, but if so I have no intention whatsoever of bending the knee and bowing the head to Mr. Vogt or to anyone else in this activity. I am going to follow your example, my dear Clarence, and pursue ideas that originate with me....This asking permission or informing the [Planned Parenthood Federation] is much out of order of my line, and in my character.[8]

In late 1929, in opening a birth control clinic in his hometown of Cincinnati, Gamble developed his own modus operandi.[9] It was, first of all, clear to him that money spent on contraception was a great financial savings to taxpayers: Half of all children born during most of the Depression years were born to those on relief. And contraception was an equal blessing to overburdened mothers who already had too many children. He also saw that organizations supported by outside sources expected perennial support. But Gamble believed in self-sufficiency. His idea was to provide seed money and then require that the newly founded clinics immediately become self-supporting.

And so Gamble began his great work of seeding the clinics that Sanger desired. "I look forward to seeing, not twice that number, but *ten times* that number at the close of this year," said Sanger in reference to the 320 clinics existing in 1937. "We must also reach and help thousands of women who are unfamiliar with or isolated from clinics, by sending nurses into their homes to teach them."[10]

Which is pretty much what Gamble did. Gamble had a genius for finding women who were tireless workers, women of maturity, educated but streetwise, with engaging personalities, who as fieldworkers would go into a new town and drum up interest in establishing a birth control clinic or who, as visiting nurses, would teach women in their homes about birth control. To the communities, the fieldworkers offered seed money from Gamble for a clinic. After—usually—a year of support, the center was to become self sufficient, and most of the time, it did. In this way, Gamble established what must have been hundreds, if not thousands, of clinics that exist to this day throughout the United States and the world.

Elsie Wulkop was one of Gamble's first fieldworkers. She found her new employer focused, enthusiastic, and a stickler for detail. Writing her in one of his lengthy, detail-filled letters, he added, "I suppose you think I spend most of my waking hours thinking of things for you to do. Perhaps this letter will confirm your suspicions."[11] When Miss Wulkop arrived in Detroit in the first month of 1930, all of Michigan had one birth control clinic. On October 6, 1936, Gamble wrote, "I have followed with interest the process whereby the seven or eight clinics organized by Miss Wulkop in Michigan have multiplied themselves to the present twenty-five."[12] In 1939, the now established Michigan Maternal Health League reported twenty-eight birth control committees and twenty-two birth control clinics. Of the 15,000 women served, half had been on relief, 40 percent were Roman Catholic.[13]

Gamble sent Lena Gilliam into Berea, Kentucky, where she visited mothers with birth control information and supplies to addresses such as "A mile and a half beyond the letterbox Black Lick Road." "One mile up Jack Branch." "One quarter of a mile in a log house above the school across the creek."[14]

Gamble never minded asking too much of his workers or himself and was always on the prowl for new opportunities to promote birth control. When the federal government in 1936 withdrew for the second time, under Roman Catholic pressure, birth control funds for Puerto Rico, threatening destruction of the islandwide clinic infrastructure, Gamble asked the American Birth Control League—three times—if they would step in to save birth control services for the Puerto Ricans. The League demurred. Gamble promptly put his fieldworker, Spanish-speaking Phillis Page, on the next boat to Puerto Rico, and within two weeks, seventeen clinics were in place.[15] Years later, Gamble would discover that this prompt action in 1936 was to assist immeasurably the development of The Pill in the fifties.

The American Birth Control League (and other birth control organizations coming into the field), struggling to establish themselves as trustworthy, politic, and credible, were loathe to confront and could not countenance this aggressive, get-it-done approach. Moving ahead with or without prior organizational approval, Gamble, who had the funds and the determination and the big picture in mind, would accomplish the deed and acquaint his colleagues of the *fait accompli* in the most courteous and detailed letters.[16]

His life, as well as his conversation, was devoted to birth control. Dr Yoshio Koya, the remarkable doyen of birth control in Japan, was amused by Gamble's one-pointed focus. When Koya showed Gamble a magnificent view of Mount Fuji, Gamble talked about family planning. When Koya pointed out the stunning flower gardens, Gamble changed the subject to contraceptives.[17] Gamble's oldest daughter tells a similar story. Whenever her Uncle Cecil, Clarence's older brother, would invite Clarence and Sarah to dinner, Cecil would call up Clarence and tell him there was to be no talk of birth control at the dinner. Presumably, Clarence sat silent throughout the evening.

The Manuscript

On December 29 and 30, 1936, Sanger's Clinical Research Bureau held a conference at the Hotel Roosevelt in New York City to discuss present day research on contraception. The conference received good press, and the *New York Post* blazed the headline (December 30, 1936), "Contraceptives Don't Cause Sterility, Survey Shows. Study of 2,500 Women Explodes Theory, Birth Control Session Hears."[18] Sanger had kept the newspapers busy that fall, for early in November, she learned she was to receive the newsworthy Town Hall Award. She had been constantly on the go; much of the fall had been taken up with lectures and travel, and on the seventeenth of December, she had the nuisance job of moving to 14 East Sixtieth Street.

Sanger's letters reflect her busy life and pick up on the equally busy involvement of Gamble with administrative details. In 1937 as president of the Pennsylvania Birth Control Federation, Gamble was always on the lookout for more efficient and economical administrative measures. On December 9 he had written suggesting that the various birth control clinics join a "printed material exchange," thereby saving printing costs. Gamble was extremely innovative, full of ideas, and never hesitated, as he himself acknowledged, to send on his ideas. As he wrote to Mrs. F. Robertson-Jones, "As you may have discovered . . . I enjoy pronouncing opinions, so may I give you my thoughts?"[19]

Gamble was as eager as Sanger for endorsements of birth control from leading national organizations. Back on January 18, 1932, Sanger had addressed more than seven hundred Junior Leaguers of New York City and found an enthusiastic response. The Junior League of the City of New York City then went on record as favoring birth control legislation and passed a resolution. The Association of Junior Leagues of America, whose offices were located at the Waldorf-Astoria, would have none of this, and Sanger received a very plain-spoken letter from President Eleanor Pratt explaining that Junior Leagues did not make endorsements. Meanwhile, a number of Philadelphia Junior League members formed a "Committee for Freedom" and circulated petitions that were to be presented to the association board on April 26, its last meeting before the Junior League annual conference in Chicago. Gamble, typical of his go-ahead style that kept the bureaucrats on edge, was busy locating mailing lists with Junior League names and addresses.[20] He then financed a mass mailing to all thirty thousand Junior Leaguers, which included a three-page letter, a postcard, a petition, and a small twelve-page pamphlet urging Junior Leaguers to sign the "Freedom" petitions and endorse birth control.[21] Individual Junior Leagues, though not the association, finally did give their endorsements.

When Gamble was not busy with local matters involving the Pennsylvania federation, he was busy spreading the good news of birth control beyond the borders of the state of Pennsylvania, seeding clinics in the South and saving the clinics of Puerto Rico. On May 14, 1936, Gamble, who was a member of the American Birth Control board and one of its five vice presidents, was the object of a disciplinary resolution passed by the ABCL board. A year later, on March 4, 1937, a second resolution reaffirming the first, came with a letter from Mrs. Allison Pierce Moore, chairman of the ABCL board, pointing out that

> Certain activities financed by you in Kentucky, Florida, Puerto Rico, and North Carolina have not been cleared with the Board of Directors of the American Birth Control League. If knowledge has come to us of such projects it has been after they were initiated rather than before.... This has embarrassed the board. [22]

When Gamble received this letter, he sat down and wrote a nine-page single-spaced letter to every board member, explaining exactly what he had done, why he had done it, and how satisfactory had been the results. Mrs. Moore, expecting a reply directed only to her, was outfoxed. At the board meeting, she merely said something about the executive committee not having a report on the matter, and that was more or less the end of the disciplinary resolution.[23] Gamble, unfortunately for Mrs. Moore, was not concerned about embarrassing the board. He was concerned that women should have Birth Control clinics.

Gamble and the Pennsylvania Birth Control Federation arranged a two-week Pennsylvania tour for Sanger at the end of March 1937 that included Easton, Bethlehem, Reading, Allentown, Chester, Hatboro, Wilkes-Barre, and Philadelphia. With lots of newspaper coverage preceding her—Sanger had a year ago returned from her highly publicized India and world tour—Sanger spoke to audiences of seven and eight hundred and more. By the end of the Pennsylvania tour, she was "more tired" than she had been in a long time.

Letters from Margaret Sanger to Clarence J. Gamble[24]

January 8, 1937

Dr. Clarence J. Gamble,
537 Allen Lane
Philadelphia, Pa.

Dear Dr. Gamble:

Your letter of December 24th was received but I delayed replying to it until I could think through my schedule and know more definitely my own plans after the conference was out of the way.

I am glad to send you word that I will be able to give the last two weeks in March to the Pennsylvania Birth Control Federation and to speak before any groups, public or private, which will help in strengthening your State clinics or in raising money for their support.

While I will be happy to contribute my time and to make no charges for my lectures, it will be a strain on my resources to pay for railroad fare or hotel bills, so if your organization can look after my traveling expenses and arrange for hospitality during the time I am to speak, that is all that will be necessary.

I am sending a copy of this letter to Mrs. Mudd who wrote me a most gracious letter a few days ago.[25]

I look forward with great interest to testing out this experiment. I assume that the object of these meetings will be to: (a) arouse public interest in the local clinics; (b) to encourage attendance at the clinic; (c) to raise funds for the support of the clinic.

Publicity, of course, must be considered and if there is any plan that you have in mind, or any special condition in a locality which should be given consideration, I will be glad to adjust my talk accordingly, if my attention is brought to these facts at the time.

In our conversation there was a suggestion on your part that Miss Rose would assist in promoting this campaign. Would you be good enough to write me just what you visualized and what you would wish Miss Rose to do. We are not certain that anyone, no matter how able she may be in my work here, would be able to accomplish similar results in a strange locality where local conditions may be better understood and better handled by someone on the spot. We are very willing, however, to meet your suggestions with due consideration.

Thank you for your memorandum containing six suggestions covering the lecture.[26] These can easily be embodied and I am very glad to have them.

Again assuring you of our cooperation in every possible way, I am

Cordially yours,

Director

MS:RG

January 23, 1937

Dr. Clarence J. Gamble
537 Allen Lane
Philadelphia, Pa.

Dear Dr. Gamble:

Your letter of December 9th has had to wait until I could get a breathing spell. I consider the suggestion contained therein an excellent idea for coordination—just what is needed for inspiration and help and starting good ideas on the way.

We will be glad to cooperate on this, and I am passing the correspondence along to Dr. Stone for his attention.[27]

I do not know whether we will have enough funds to get out another copy of the *National Birth Control News* – but if we do we shall also carry in it a reference to this idea.

Cordially yours,

Director

MS:RG

April 13, 1937

Dr. Clarence J. Gamble
537 Allen Lane
Philadelphia, Pa.

Dear Dr. Gamble,

By this time Mrs. Hart has doubtless reported to you on the conversation at the luncheon at the Waldorf Astoria yesterday.[28]

The situation seems to be one of policy rather than of issue. Mrs. Harvey is all for Birth Control, having identified her contact with me in the early days in Albany when she was reporter who gave our cause a good boost, but now feels that she must safeguard the position of the Junior League so as not to cause dissension and discord in their ranks.[29]

I tried to show her that the Junior League, like other organizations, was building up strong fine structures in harmony while the hubris of their being an organization at all dies a slow lingering death.

We tried to poopoo the idea that they must have a hush-hush policy of controversy, but I can quite understand that if a change of policy is brought down it must not come from outsiders but from their own ranks.

I do not know what will come of it, but I am not hopeful of an invitation.

Thank you for making it possible for me to meet Mrs. Harvey and Mrs. Hart. I liked them both immensely and enjoyed hearing some of the inside problems that the executives have to solve.

I understand that you come out a victor at the Board of Di[r]ectors meeting of the American Birth Control League. Congratulations. I trust that you will continue to press forward on getting out of that organization those who are not equipped with vision or selflessness sufficient to make the League anything more than a "pink tea social centre" for pleasant conversation or gossip.

Now that the Pennsylvania trip is over, I am more tired than I have been in a long time. While it was strenuous, it was very pleasant and I think if this tour had not been at the end of the se[a]son, it would have gone much easier. It takes a good deal of energy to lift up an inert audience and stir their brain cells sufficiently to make them receptive for an idea.

Most of the meetings were very good. The only ones that did not come up to expectations were the one at Boston and at the Labor Lyceum at Philadelphia. However, Boston had about 500 present in a 1000 capacity hall but as they were the real factory workers, it wasn't bad.

The one group that I believe really needs help and to whom you might offer a social worker, is the group at Bethlehem. They are in quarters on the third floor and need some assistance. I think if Mrs. Page went there and looked over the situation, you might be willing to give them a social worker for three months instead of Scranton.[30] They pay their doctor $6 a session – which is too high – and he only takes 3-4-5 patients during the two hour session. This slows down their work. I would suggest another doctor and a social worker to check up on the few cases they have had. They are a very nice group.

In fact, all of the Birth Control people throughout the State are just about the finest group that you can meet anywhere. I think we are to be congratulated that we drew to the movement people so intelligent, sympathetic, selfless and usually charming.

Again, I cannot say too much of how grateful I am to know Mrs. Page and to have had her with me during these few days. I congratulate you on your ability to "pick them right." Everyone in Scranton was charmed with her and I think there should be a fine future for a woman of her caliber.

Having accepted hospitality, expenses were greatly decreased and the other minor expenses are so small that I am glad to make that contribution to the Federation. I owe Mrs. Page $3 for tipping and Mrs. Love spent a good deal in buying gas and oil and touring me from place to place.[31] If these items could be taken care of, I would appreciate it very much. I shall be writing Mrs. Kitzmiller and will give her a report and will send you a copy.[32]

Again my congratulations on your victory at the American Birth Control League board and thank you again for suggesting my very wonderful tour, which brought me in contact with the various centres, to say nothing of the delightful people who were my hosts and hostesses.

Most cordially yours,

Director

S:R:B

PART III:
THE CONSERVATIVE RADICAL

34. Introduction to the Conservative Radical

S anger's India and World Tour for Birth Control had been planned to include much of China and a stay in Japan, but illness in Hong Kong cut short her time in China and forced her to skip Japan entirely. No sooner did Sanger arrive home—in the spring of 1936—than she immediately planned another trip to Asia. The Chinese Medical Association had invited her to return to China, and she very much wanted to see Japan. Sanger armed Dorothy Brush with letters of introduction for advance preparations, much as she had Edith How-Martyn for the India and world tour, and in the fall of 1937, accompanied by Florence Rose, her devoted secretary, and Dorothy Brush, Sanger set out.

She arrived in Tokyo to great acclaim and to dedicate the first modern birth control clinic of Japan, the labor of two decades by Shidzue Ishimoto. Four months later, the new clinic was shut down by the Japanese government and Ishimoto arrested for Dangerous Thoughts. Not just a painful broken arm, the result of a fall on the ship, but a world now at war signaled by the Japanese invasion of China forced Sanger to return to America's shores—after little more than a week in Japan and China still unconquered by birth control.[1] But it took World War II to keep her in America.

At home, there were some compensations. In requesting sponsors and an advisory committee for the Western States Birth Control Conference on Public Health and Population to be held in Los Angeles, California, in December 1937, Sanger received many letters of acceptance, all positive in tone: "We will be happy to serve," "You may count on me to lend every assistance possible," "I shall be honored," "I shall be glad to feel that I am making some humble contribution to the great work to which you have given such wise and devoted effort." One noticeable refusal came from Judge George McDill of Los Angeles, to which Sanger replied:

Dear Judge McDill:

I have received your letter of October 13th, regarding your request that your name not be used as a sponsor for our WEST-ERN STATES BIRTH CONTROL CONFERENCE ON PUBLIC HEALTH AND POPULATION to be held in December. This is to advise you that we will comply with your request and understand your position. However, we are hoping that it will be possible for you to attend our Conference. We are very happy to have Mrs. McDill as one of our Sponsors.[2]

Since shortly after the autumn of 1934, when she had driven Stuart to Arizona to help his chronic sinus condition, Margaret had been spending some of the winter in Tucson and summers in Willowlake.[3] Now confined stateside, Sanger agreed to a long overdue gall bladder operation in November 1937 and to a stay in Tucson with Noah for the long convalescence necessary. (But by the end of Januyary she was giving a speech at the Biltmore Hotel in Los Angeles—so much for the long convalescence.) In Tucson, in deference to Noah, she was known as Mrs. Slee, and Tucson, which she came to love dearly, was to be her home—when she was home—for the remainder of her life.[4]

The Tucson relocation was encouraged by the merger of Sanger's Clinical Research Bureau with the Mrs. F. Robertson-Jones's American Birth Control League. The two organizations, both in debt, were duplicating efforts. Sanger, recognizing this, probably a bit tired of the infighting, acquiesced to the merger, and in 1939, at her own request, became honorary chairman of the new Birth Control Federation of America, which, it had been decided, was to be run by males. Once in Tucson, Sanger was removed by physical distance and confined by male indifference to a nonposition in the birth control movement of America. She gave attention to the Tucson Mother's Health Clinic, which she had set up on her first visit with Stuart in 1934.[5] She involved herself in painting, took lessons, specialized in small landscapes, and became a member of the Tucson Watercolor Guild, even holding a showing.

As the war clouds loomed and World War II took center stage on both private and public venues, birth control and women's concerns became a non-issue. Instead came the call for more babies. Accordingly, in 1942, the Birth Control Federation of America became the Planned Parenthood Federation of America and promoted child spacing, selling for ten cents a copy a topical pamphlet "The Soldier Takes a Wife," urging family planning on the soldier's family, opening with,

It isn't much of a military secret that mating usually is followed—

by reproduction.....Getting married and having a family is like a military campaign. It takes forethought, preparation and a certain amount of strategy....Take "Flash" Edwards, for instance—he was a great guy at jungle warfare. He knocked out a machine gun nest no one would take a chance on and he used the same tactics in marriage....Planning—that was for sissies....Then there was good old "Steady" Steve. He was on the Escort Carrier Merrimac. A better gunner's mate never lived.[6]

During the war, Sanger was just another anxious mother: Stuart was in the army on the Western Front, Grant in the navy on a carrier in the Philippine battle. Sanger, always an avowed pacifist, despaired of the takeover by the fascists worldwide and their categorizing women as baby-making machines, and she abhorred the atrocities being committed by the Nazis. In 1933, she wrote to Edith How-Martyn,

This sudden antagonism in Germany against the Jews & the vitriolic hatred of them is spreading underground here & is far more dangerous than the aggressive policy of the Japanese in Manchuria.[7]

Sanger joined the American Council Against Nazi Propaganda and in the play of world war events saw all her apprehensions and warnings against overpopulation becoming realized.[8] Waiting out the war, she worked her way through endless government forms and complex bureaucratic demands to rescue at least twenty European refugees from Nazi reprisals and bring them safely to the States.[9] She sent care packages to her friends in England and endured the seasons of change and the deaths of Havelock Ellis in 1939, Hannah Stone in 1941, Noah in 1943. H. G. Wells would die in 1946. In 1945, celebrating Christmas in Tucson with her sons returned from war and their families—Stuart with Barbara, his wife, and their two little girls; Grant, married to Edwina, with their two boys—Sanger declared it "the happiest Christmas I ever thought possible to enjoy."[10]

In these later years, she could have slipped into comfortable Tucson retirement.[11] She built a beautiful modern house, with an art studio on the top floor, next to that of Stuart, where her two granddaughters were daily and welcome visitors. She entertained lavishly; her granddaughters had the opportunity to meet Eleanor Roosevelt; Lakshmi Pandit, sister of Jawaharlal Nehru; Sumiko Kato, stepdaughter of remarried Shidzue Ishimoto Kato; John D. Rockefeller Jr. and his wife; Frank Lloyd Wright; Lady Dhanvanthi Rama Rau; and many other famous personages.[12] But Sanger had far-more reaching concerns than nonstop entertaining, and if conservative males on the national scene did not want Sanger demanding that women have control of their fertility, Sanger had her "plans for a planet."[13] In this, she had the quiet support of Clarence Gamble, who was continuing to conduct field trials in his search for a simple, safe, inexpensive contraceptive and who, with the end of the war, had begun seeding start-up clinics internationally. Gamble was to finish his life devoted to the same two causes to which Sanger was to be devoted for the remainder of her years: the development of a simple, safe, inexpensive contraceptive and the organization of birth control availability all over the planet. The result of the first was The Pill; of the second, the International Planned Parenthood Federation. Both of these causes Sanger recognized as increasingly important to counter the post-war population explosion that was fostering impoverishment of millions, straining the earth's resources, and would ultimately lead to increased world disturbances.

Throughout the last two decades of her life, in the face of constant illnesses, Sanger traveled the world continually, again and again in defiance of doctors' orders, promoting birth control and warning against overpopulation. As the wife and then the widow of the capitalist Noah Slee, Margaret Sanger Slee was indeed "The Conservative Radical," moving in the most conservative, upper-class circles, but continuing, until her heart literally gave out, the radical stance and nonstop activity with which she had begun her life's work at the beginning of the twentieth century.

35. The Negro Project

In November 1939, with the infighting of the birth controllers settled by the formation of the Birth Control Federation of America, Sanger immediately put under its umbrella her Negro Project, with plans to make contraception available to black communities.[1] Just as Sanger when sailing on the *Viceroy of India* deplored the superior attitude of the British toward the Indian citizens, when in Peking that of the Americans toward the Chinese, and on the Japanese liners that of the whites toward the Orientals, equally she deplored the racism that permeated American culture.[2] Margaret Sanger believed that every woman should have the right to control her fertility, that every mother should be able to decide for herself how many children she could care for, and that in this way a better life was ensured for the entire family. It did not even occur to her to categorize a mother as black, white, yellow, or other.

Despite the assertion by some blacks that birth control was a tool to exterminate the black race, as early as 1918, the Women's Political Association of Harlem expressed the interest of the black community in birth control, and 1923 their leaders invited Sanger to come to Harlem and speak.[3] On December 7, 1932, Sanger was again invited to Harlem, where she lectured at the Abyssinian Baptist Church.[4] Over the years Sanger enjoyed the support of W.E.B. DuBois, Mary McLeod Bethune, and the Reverend Adam Clayton Powell Jr., pastor of the Abyssinian Baptist Church; the NAACP; the National Association of Colored Graduate Nurses; National Negro Youth Administration; the Urban League, and the National Council of Negro Women.

From its inception, the *Birth Control Review* carried articles and stories sensitive to American racism and expressing the black point of view. The September 1919 issue of the *Review* was dedicated to the "Negro Question" and included articles such as "The New Emancipation" and "The Negroes' Need for Birth Control, as Seen by Themselves," along with Angelina W. Grimke's "The Closing Door," a two-part story exploring racism in the September and October 1919 issues.

Sanger had her first opportunity to speak to an audience of blacks and whites together in November of 1919, when William Oscar Saunders, the liberal editor of a progressive weekly in North Carolina, invited Sanger to Elizabeth City, a shipping town of cotton and hosiery mills. Thirty-seven percent of its population was black. In North Carolina, no laws forbade North Carolinians from discussing contraception, and at her afternoon lecture in Elizabeth City, Sanger had an attendance of about eight hundred. After the lecture, in response to demand, Sanger discussed birth control with about two hundred women in a women-only meeting. That evening, at the request of their committee, Sanger spoke at a local black church, the next morning at a black normal school, and in the afternoon, still within the black community, on methods of birth control to a women-only meeting.[5]

Reporting on her North Carolina trip in the *Birth Control Review*, Sanger wrote,

> Never have I met with more sympathy, more serious attention more complete understanding than in my addresses to the white and black people of this Southern mill town.... These audiences were a striking demonstration of birth control's universal message of freedom and betterment.[6]

In the North, Sanger's first organized effort to assist the blacks specifically resulted in the Harlem Clinic, opened in 1930 by the Birth Control Clinical Research Bureau. At the time of the opening of the Harlem Clinic, the need was clear: "In 1929 out of a thousand births there were 101 deaths among Negro children as compared with 56 among white children."[7] The Harlem Clinic was endorsed, again, by many important black community leaders including W.E.B. DuBois and Mary McLeod Bethune and the local black paper, the *Amsterdam News*, but in four years of operation, half of the patients visiting the clinic were white. Although a black physician and a black social worker were hired, the white origins of the clinic and the lingering sentiments of Marcus Garvey—who demanded more, not fewer, babies from black women—had their influence.

Nor is there any denying the racism of some of the white women working at the Harlem clinic, a matter that Sanger immediately and forcefully addressed. For instance, when Antoinette Field, a nurse at the Harlem Clinic turned in a report claiming that the colored patients "failed to keep to definite time for appointments" because of "irresponsibility and laziness," she received a sharp rejoinder from Sanger:

Dear Miss Field:
Never, never in your report state what you do not know. The word "laziness"' is out of date. On what do you base such but your own notion. Try to make reports accurate based on knowledge.

Miss Field was shortly let go.[8] But a chief obstacle to acceptance of the Harlem Clinic was the lack of an inexpensive and dependable contraceptive. The New York Clinical Research Bureau, because it had found diaphragm and jelly to be the safest contraceptive, prescribed it exclusively. But research showed a strong correlation between continued use of the diaphragm and income level. For women on low income without private bathroom, the diaphragm and jelly was too expensive and difficult to use. Eighty-three percent of the Harlem clinic users were on public or private relief. The Harlem Clinic closed in 1937, never having been fully used by the black community.[9]

Yet experience with the Harlem Clinic had its uses, for it refuted the myth of black promiscuity that circulated and made clear that black women were as open to contraception as were white. But for both white and black women, the problem of a simple, safe, inexpensive contraceptive remained.

Clarence Gamble was throughout his life concerned with this problem; he funded a number of Sanger's projects and many of his own along this line. His clinical trials in North Carolina of foam and sponge contraceptives and the fieldwork of Hazel Moore in Virginia in the late thirties demonstrated the interest of black women in contraception.[10] And when Sanger toured the South in the fall of 1938, she saw for herself the neglect of government services that the black community suffered. Concerned that blacks were not being properly served and conscious of the oppression and disadvantage that they lived under, Sanger knew that "birth control knowledge brought to this [Negro] group is the most direct, constructive aid that can be given them to improve their immediate situation."[11] With this in mind, Sanger began the Negro Project.

Working with Florence Rose, her loyal secretary, tireless worker, and zealous birth control advocate; and Mary Reinhardt, soon to be Mary Reinhardt Lasker, the women sought funding from Albert Lasker, recently retired from advertising and beginning his medical philanthropic career.[12] Sanger requested of Lasker funds to train a "modern minister, colored, and an up and doing modern colored medical man" at the New York clinic, who would then tour and educate black communities in the South. Sanger well understood the justified resentment of the blacks to white teachings and preachings and the necessity for black individuals to be the educators of their own community. Her earlier experiences in Harlem, her interactions with many black leaders, and her common sense had made this very clear to her, and in setting up the Negro Project, she stated,

I do not believe that this project should be directed or run by white medical men. The Federation should direct it with the guidance and assistance of the colored group.[13]

If black leaders devoted a year to educating their people, then, Sanger pointed out birth control clinics could be established as a result of demand, and black communities would have contraception available to them. In reiterating the need for blacks themselves to be involved in their birth control education, Sanger wrote, in a letter whose last sentence has been much misquoted,

> It seems to me from my experience...that while the colored Negroes have great respect for white doctors they can get closer to their own members....If we can train the Negro doctor at the Clinic he can go among them with enthusiasm and with knowledge, which, I believe, will have far reaching results among the colored people....The minister's work is also important, and he should also be trained, perhaps by the Federation as to our ideals and the goal that we hope to reach. We do not want word to go out that we want to exterminate the Negro population and the minister is the man who can straighten out that idea if it ever occurs to any of their more rebellious members.[14]

From such a statement taken out of context, writers Angela Davis and Dinesh D'Souza, among others, have spread the lie that Sanger was a racist and by implication that contraception and birth control lead to race suicide.[15] This is an unfortunate insinuation, insulting to black women—and all women—who may not want more children than they can care for, and showing as well ignorance of the relationship between birthrate and infant mortality.[16]

Lasker did fund Sanger's Negro Project, but unfortunately, once funded, it was taken over by white bureaucrats who had no interest in allowing the black community to educate themselves. No black doctors were hired, and understandably black women were not about to go to white doctors to be fitted for a diaphragm. The Negro Project lapsed into a few demonstration clinics that toured parts of the South. There, progress was stymied by both white racist bureaucrats and an unsuitable contraceptive method—the diaphragm and jelly—which was simply not practical at a time when many in the South were without indoor plumbing and running water.[17]

With Sanger off in Arizona, the Negro Project was placed under the renamed Planned Parenthood of America's newly created Special Projects Department, where Florence Rose doggedly kept it going. At the 1942 annual meeting, the meeting at which the Planned Parenthood name change was announced, Florence Rose arranged for Dorothy Boulding Ferebee, an outstanding black physician, to give a paper, "Planned Parenthood as a Public Health Measure for the Negro Race." Ferebee listed the arguments being brought against birth control within black communities: 1) Birth control encourages race suicide; 2) The men object; 3) Birth control is confused with abortion; 4) Birth control is considered immoral.

Ferebee's presentation made little impact. In the face of federation indifference, Florence Rose, with her indefatigable zeal, pushed on, mounting exhibits, arranging local and national press coverage, and flooding every black organization existent in America with birth control literature. The bureaucrats caught up with Rose, however, and when she was forced out of the federation as a Sanger sympathizer, the Negro Project was out as well.

But life has its mysterious ways. The Laskers were good personal friends of F.D.R. and Eleanor Roosevelt. With the accession of F.D.R. to a third term, Eleanor felt free to come out—quietly— for birth control, in great part because of her concern for American blacks, aware as she, like Sanger, was of the benefits birth control could give the black community.[18] Coincidentally, in 1941, came the need to ensure that women working in the World War II factories would not become pregnant. And so in the name of the war effort and with the strength of F.D.R.'s third-term hold on office and despite the stranglehold of the Catholic Church on the Roosevelt administration, birth control moved quietly, without any publicity, at last, finally, into a federal government program where it had long belonged.

In May 1942, the U.S. Public Health Service supported "child spacing for women in war industries, under medical supervision," an area judged of federal concern, offering a program that was free, nominally at least, from the constraints of racism, a move that then opened the way for other family planning offerings in government.[19]

Fast forward to 2003: In the United States, as federal funding is consistently slashed, women of all colors are denied access to abortion, to contraception, and under the banner of the Abstinence Program, to honest sex education.[20]

Throughout all of these years of infighting, Margaret Sanger had her own very personal involvement with a black woman, Daisy Mitchell, her longtime employee, who was for forty years maid, cook, and caretaker.[21] Daisy called Margaret "My Madam," and always approached Margaret with sweetness and charm. With others, the sweetness was somewhat less. In fact, she was known to be "mean as a snake," especially when she later worked for Grant and his wife, Edwina. "This is ma kitchen. Get outta here," was her standard greeting. Stuart on his occasional visits would shake his head and giggle.[22]

Noah Slee found Daisy difficult. After dinner and dishes, Daisy would come into the living room, sit in a corner, and listen while conversation went on. Finally, Noah would say, "What are you doing in here, Daisy?" "Gettin' an education. Jes' getting' an education," was her reply. But the best Daisy story came with an Italian dinner that Noah and Margaret were giving. A jug of Italian wine had been set out for the dinner. When Margaret asked Daisy to bring the wine, Daisy said she didn't "know nuthin' 'bout no wine." "Of course you do. I put it right on the bottom shelf in the main cupboard," responded Margaret. After a few minutes, Daisy came back with a wine jug that was empty. Margaret, dumfounded, said, "Daisy, what happened to the wine?" To which Daisy replied, "Evaporation. Pure evaporation, ma'am."[23]

When her working days were over, the Sanger family found a retirement home for Daisy where she was comfortable, paying for her care there until she died. Daisy was buried in Fishkill next to Margaret Sanger at the implicit request of both.

The civil rights movement of the sixties remembered Sanger's stubborn defiance. Her willingness to step forward in the name of rights for the dispossessed put her in jail for thirty days and brought other arrests, but by defying prejudice with nonviolence and an insistent disregard for inhumane laws, she created a template for challenging the status quo. In 1966, on acceptance of the Planned Parenthood Federation of America Margaret Sanger Award, the Reverend Martin Luther King, Jr. expressed his appreciation for the award and for the work of Sanger.[24]

> There is a striking kinship between our movement and Margaret Sanger's early efforts....Our sure beginning in the struggle for equality by nonviolent direct action may not have been so resolute without the tradition established by Margaret Sanger.[25]

The Manuscript

Within the context of the above history, the message of this letter by Sanger is beautifully clear. D. Kenneth Rose had been with John Price Jones, the company that had mediated the merger of the Clinical Research Bureau and Robertson-Jones' American Birth Control League. Rose then became national director of the new Birth Control Federation of America.[26] He was part of the all-male leadership that would now head the birth control movement, who believed that only with male leadership could birth control become generally accepted, since the organizations on which birth control depended were run by men. It was, after all, men who were the heads of "Federal and State legislatures, hospital boards, public health boards, etc." government, business, and finance.[27] It was one point of view. Considering the advances one woman had made over two decades despite the men in high places and despite the opposition of men in church and federal governments, Margaret Sanger had not done so badly.

The End of the Negro Project: A Letter from Margaret Sanger to Ken Rose[28]

F.R. Return to MS please [Handwritten notation]

2318 East Elm Street
February 8, 1945

Dear Ken:

Yours of January 25th regarding the negro programme has been received. Please be assured that my notes on the back of the printed programme were not intended to be "a blast," but simply an intimation of the impression made by a lack of any mention of negro work on the programme. It was especially impressive to me, for I as one was mainly responsible for arousing interest in the negro programme, obtaining the first twenty thousand dollars from Mr. Lasker. After that, and knowing that the end of his contribution had come for that particular project, I got Mrs. Fuld and D[oris] D[uke] to continue their already keen interest.[29] So, dear Ken, if you call my slight criticism a blast, then I only regret I did not go "all out" in what I really feel in disappointment on that. I realize, of course, that the project would be taken up and discussed somewhere during the annual meeting, but the fact that the plans and programmes for negro education are discussed during the work shop session is symbolic of the treatment the negro work has been granted from the beginning, three years ago. You have often complained to me that the negro problem was kept isolated and made a side issue from the Federation's general work by Florence Rose. You rightly protested, and I agreed with you, that it should not be hidden in a corner, but should be part of the whole general National Education Plan of the Federation. But quite recently I have especially watched the reports of the Federation and noticed that nowhere for the past year in field reports or elsewhere has any notice or report been printed on negro activities.

I have spoken on at least two occasions to Mrs. Trent and suggested that her reports carry some mention of negro activities in the States that her report covered, and she promised and agreed that it was a good idea and it should be done, but such good appeasing resolutions and promises have, like many other things, gone with the wind.[30] I do not know just what your aim is in trying to keep up the loyalties and interest and enthusiasm of former members of both the [American Birth Control] League and the [Clinical Research] Bureau, but certainly confining discussions and plans and programmes to the employees and to workshop sessions puts a tremendous limit on enthusiasm and interest and those other old-timers who have not been consulted. Personally, I find that I have lost enthusiasm for your negro project, though I am deeply interested in the whole racial question and in the progress and freedom of the negroes in this country. Pearl Buck in her East and West organization, where I contribute a wee $5.00 a year, pays me the compliment of asking my opinion on issues of national and international importance before these questions are taken up in the policy committees. There are so many splendid movements going on of national importance today and many that I am deeply interested in, that it is very hard to hold one's self down to activities that have been in the past when a new world is being made all around us. At one time little Florence Rose did her best to keep me informed by sending me her negro reports, but for the last year she has not done this nor has she discussed any phase of her activities within the Federation with me any more than Mrs. Trent, Miss Delp or Mrs. McKennon.[31] Consequently, I am adverse to having my name on any committee that is supposed to know what is going on. It is only my own natural integrity and honesty that the public supporters have respected in the past, as they found that we were never playing a game, but that we did carry out our promises to them, and kept them fully informed. I appreciate and agree with you that being so far away, especially during the winter months, is a handicap, and only when some one person has sought my interest and through him or her that I could regularly communicate, could this distance not be a handicap, but you as Director of the Federation have no right to be tied down to the past, or to past personalities, no matter how highly they may regard their own experience. You have had my full cooperation on the majority of ideas and activities that you have wanted to put through, but your short experience of the Movement, plus your being tied to one spot cannot give you the vision nor the background to become the one single person in the movement to dictate how others more experienced must think, or curtail their activities, unless such are cleared through you.

I am one hundred per cent behind Dr. Gamble's and Dr. Dickinson's protest regarding this curtailment of Field or State support, because I realize how not wanting to go over your head, I have gradually withdrawn my own interest, enthusiasm, and activities from this State and from the Tucson Birth Control work as well, for by the time I get to dictate a letter to you on what I should like to do plus getting a group together here, and getting them to decide on activities, I find they resent the idea of having to wait for Mr. Rose or any other person in far-off New York to tell them what they shall do in this locality, so I am free to confess that after one or two attempts this got me down so I decided to take up the more interesting work of painting the mountains.[32]

Now as to yours of January 25th, I do sincerely appreciate your wanting to keep me informed, and a weekly letter is, of course, the ideal means of doing this. But I know too well what the pressure on you is, and far too great for you to take up this obligation, and personally I do not think it is worth the effort now. It is a little late to get me all hot and bothered over Federation activities, and I am glad to say that I feel that you have such a splendid support and such excellent personalities around you that you can well go straight ahead.

I was always anxious and desirous that you send out a news letter personally signed by you to old friends and to large contributors at least once a month. I made a habit of doing this for many years, and I was always able to return to the "big shots" for a renewal of their contribution with practically never a refusal. Even the largest of them were pleased and complimented that they had not only been informed as to good results, but of conflicts and doubts as well.

Mr. Packard, Miss Paschal, Mrs. Field and dozens of others used to say that they knew more of what was going on in the Movement through the reports from the Bureau than anywhere else, and we made it our business to see that they were informed and it worked out.[33] If little Miss Rose is too naïve to think that the present set-up in the P.P.F. cares to know what M.S. or other contributors thought or wanted, it just shows how unfitted she is for her present job. She never belonged to the Spartans with routine and drill, but more did she belong to the Athenians who were guided by a spirit of cooperation and usefulness, and as such her accomplishments are eternal in the hearts of her coworkers at least. But she is now guided by you as Director, and if she does not fit into the Spartan spirit, you have every right to let her go.

I want to thank you again for the telegram you sent me regarding the United States Supreme Court's decision on Connecticut. The local morning paper carried the statement of the Court the next day. I hope the telegram that I sent to you to be read at the dinner was adequate, for I did not want to just repeat what I gathered was to be the theme of the dinner speakers.

I think, dear Ken, that my reply to Mrs. Meli's letter is final, for there is no real reason to make an exception of me.[34] If at a later period I could come to meetings regularly, perhaps I shall then be invited to come back on the Board, but you shall need all the Field help that you can lay your hands on now for the duration, and as such you have my best wishes and loyal spiritual support.

Most cordially,

MS

Mr. D. Kenneth Rose
501 Madison Avenue
New York, N.Y.

MSS/B

A Second Manuscript
Sanger never hesitated to speak out against racism, as this letter to Gray Bus Lines in defense of Daisy shows.

June 19, 1938
Gray Bus Lines of New York
254 West 61st Street
New York City

Attention General Manager:

Dear Sir:

I wish to enter a complaint and make a vigorous protest against the treatment accorded a colored woman in my employ who came from Tucson, Arizona, to Philadelphia, Pennsylvania, several weeks ago on your bus. Her name is Mrs. Daisy Mitchell. She has been in my family for over fifteen years. She bought a ticket at Tucson, Arizona, to Philadelphia.

She was refused food at the various stations where your bus stopped because she was colored. Fortunately, she had a little food with her, but not enough to last her the entire way. Various passengers on the line helped obtain a sandwich or a cup of coffee for her. But she was refused food at various stops through the state of Kansas. In fact, it was in Madison, Ohio, that she was able to get some food. This was the only place where it was possible for her to have something to eat. Even a cup of coffee was refused her through Kansas and at Wheeling, West Virginia.

When she arrived in Philadelphia, she was ill. It seems to me the most inconsiderate procedure for any organization to accept the responsibility of transporting a client to a certain destination and not make arrangements for the various necessities of the journey. Perhaps you can explain this to me to my satisfaction. I certainly am anxious to know how you could allow this discrimination or at least why you do not provide against it if it exists in certain states.

Sincerely yours,

National Chairman

NS/SL

36. Entertaining and Chicken Curry

A long with the tapestries and objects d'art collected on her foreign travels, Sanger also picked up recipes. These she trained her cooks to use, and the results were served at Sanger's "fabulous" Tucson parties, to use Margaret Sanger Lampe's word in the Foreword that opens this volume.

> Her parties in Tucson were fabulous. If she was serving a Japanese dinner, all the guests removed their shoes and donned socks as they entered her home, drank sake, and sat on the floor for dinner. If the menu called for an Indian curry, you can be sure it was hot.

Sanger loved to entertain. She was masterful at it, for often her parties, teas, or dinners culminated in a donation to whatever project she was fundraising for at the moment. But she also just enjoyed people; not all her entertaining had a subtext. Sanger describes one of her Tucson parties, probably the same party referred to above, in a letter written in May 1953 to Dr. Shinichi Mihara:

> You will be amused to learn that I was requested...to give a Suki Yaki dinner....I had lots of fun making up the enclosed menu; would you be good enough to pass one of these on to Mr. Honda, just to give him a laugh at what we consider a Japanese dinner! May I also tell you that we had a very hard time getting Sake, but I had a friend bring some over from Los Angeles. All the guests had to remove their shoes coming into the house; I had the moist napkins and Japanese baskets passed around and everyone had to sit on the floor, on cushions. I had difficulty in getting Japanese records for

music but we got by with "Madame Butterfly" and Gilbert and Sullivan's "Mikado"- so a good time was had by all.[1]

Sanger was also known for loving chicken salad sandwiches and Champagne. Noah even set up a trust fund allotting Sanger $160 a month for her permanent supply of Champagne.[2] Later, when she was installed in the retirement home in Tucson, friends often brought her chicken salad sandwiches and Champagne for an impromptu party in her room.

But when Sanger was the hostess, one of the dishes she most often served was chicken curry, and what follows is her approach for developing and the ingredients of her own recipe for chicken curry.

The Manuscript
June 8, 1939

Mrs. J. N. H. Slee,
Willowlake,
Fishkill, NY

Dear Mrs. Slee,

Thank you very much for your order, which is going forward today as requested. In your calculation you overlooked the cost of the bottle of Vita Vege Salt. However, this being such a small amount we are sending the salt anyway and carrying over a small balance of 47¢, which you can settle with your next purchase.

I am glad to enclose two recipes for Curry, which I hope you will find useful. If you run across any interesting recipes I would appreciate very much if you would reciprocate.

Very truly yours

Beauveau Borie 3rd.

BB3rd/M

June 15, 1939

Dear Mr. Borie –

Enclosed find my receipt for Curry –

I am trying out the proportions of turmeric, cardamom & (coriander) & fennel in curry. Each give a distinctive flavor but I've never been able to find out exactly how much is used.

Will be glad to send you word as I make discovery. One thing is impor-

tant, one should be generous with curry powder to make it good –
Thank you for recipes.

Sincerely,

Ms. Slee

Margaret Sanger's Chicken Curry Recipe[3]

One cup olive oil in iron pan, heat until it smokes. Add large cup sliced onions and two cloves garlic. Cook until golden brown but not crisp or burned (take little scraps out). When brown and soft add one medium can tomatoes. Allow to heat and simmer until fairly thick. To this add one or two cups chicken broth, 1/4 cup Madras or Bombay curry (John Wagner or Cross and Blackwell). Make thin paste of curry with broth and add to onions and tomatoes in pan. Add 1/2 teaspoonful ginger, 1 teaspoonful salt. Chile powder if wanted hot. Let all cook <u>slowly</u>, simmer not boil for 1/2 hour. When sauce tastes smooth, not raw – add chicken, which has been boiled and bones removed.

Do not cook but place all into deep bowl, cover and allow chicken to stand in this curry sauce over three hours – overnight is preferable.

When ready to serve, heat, add more salt if necessary, half a lemon and a teaspoon Worcestershire sauce. Now is the time to flavor the curry dish. Serve with boiled rice, coconut, chopped peanuts, chutney, and bananas. A delicious curry dinner served with salad. When some is left over, make hash.

I buy a four-pound roasting chicken and boil with two pounds of chuck veal for the above.

37. Marriage and J. Noah H. Slee

T he women of the world owe a paean of praise to J. Noah H. Slee for his contribution to birth control. His unstinting support of Margaret Sanger's personal life and professional cause allowed her small and large indulgences that made her life rich and efficient, gave her breathing space, and thus assisted beyond reckoning the growth of the birth control movement.

The introduction of Slee to Sanger was timely, both for herself and for her burgeoning movement. Shortly before the First American Birth Control Conference convened in New York City in 1921, a meeting of the advisory council of the newly organized American Birth Control League, whose incorporation was to be announced at the conference, was held at Juliet Rublee's lovely home. Sanger writes that she "experienced a moment of triumphant pride" as she gazed at this "brilliant gathering" of men and women, all with distinguished and famous names, all working to forward the cause of birth control. It was on this warm occasion that Juliet introduced Margaret to a newcomer to the group, Noah Slee, the Three-in-One Oil Company millionaire, sixty years old, a "staid pillar of finance."[1] Margaret describes that meeting at length in an unpublished memoir.

> He was a tall, gray-haired man, with clearly cut, strongly chiseled features. His figure still retained the vigor of youth. He was a man of the type usually described by novelists as in "the full plentitude of his power." His expression, I decided, was one of benign irony. And his frankness was so complete that it completely disarmed me.
>
> "But you cannot be *The* Margaret Sanger!" he exclaimed after we were introduced.

"And why not?" I challenged him.

"You don't look like much of a fighter or a lawbreaker. I expected to meet one of those foreign agitators who are trying to upset the apple-cart. That's what some of the newspapers say."

"I am impervious to slander," I retorted. "I am a better patriot than those who denounce me as bent on the destruction of this country. My father fought in the Civil War. Three of my brothers fought in the Great War....I come of a fighting family; but there are all sorts of battles to fight, and many ways of expressing one's patriotism."

My new friend—for instinctively we were friends at once—agreed. A self-made man himself, a man who from the humblest beginnings had built up a great business international in scope, he expressed admiration for my courage in overcoming obstacles. Behind his gruff manner, the disarming frankness, I sensed a profound understanding and sympathy.

He insisted on driving me home in his car. I hesitated; I tried to think of excuses. I could not bear the thought of having this man discover my lonely refuge nor be humiliated by letting him escort me into that dilapidated old house into that overcrowded, almost poverty-stricken street.

But he insisted. And as he left he asked if he might call. I gave up in despair. The interior was better than the exterior of the house, but it was bad enough. Nevertheless, I had to admit to myself that this new friendship thrilled me deeply—more than anything had in years.

If I had had any hope that my friend would maintain a polite silence when he came to call concerning the quarters in which I made my home, they were bound to be crushed the moment he entered.

"No wonder your health is poor!" he exclaimed. "It's unsafe for a woman to live in such a place. Such a neighborhood!"

After years of abuse and denunciation as a menace to American society, battling with the police and having been hustled off to the police station in a patrol wagon, it was delightful to be treated as a clinging vine, to be considered as a poor lone woman craving protection and love. For deep down in my heart such was the simple fact—and this man, no longer young, had sensed this truth at our first meeting.[2]

By Christmas of 1921, Sanger was writing Hugh de Selincourt from 18 Gramercy Park, scarcely an unhealthy or unsafe neighborhood, in an apartment adjoining that of Noah Slee. Before settling at Gramercy Park, Sanger had lived at 246 West Fourteenth Street in the same building as Ethel, north of Greenwich Village, not far from Manhattan's meat-packing district.[3] But Sanger had more to say about Noah Slee in her memoir.

> Outwardly he seemed conventional. He was a "pillar of the church." According to all the traditions of his class, as a highly successful business man, no one could have guessed that he would be attracted to a woman who had so shocked the complacency of the prurient.... Instinctively I knew that he would propose marriage; but I knew that it would not be possible. Having worked for years to develop my cause, I could not throw it aside, even for the security of marriage. I had dedicated my life to this movement.
>
> Nevertheless, when he suggested marriage, I was taken by surprise. I hesitated, "I cannot give up my work," I answered finally. "I have made too many sacrifices, given up too much for it. It means everything to me. . . I must go on with it."
>
> "But marriage need not interfere," he persisted with understanding patience. "I have my work too, I shan't give it up because I marry."
>
> "You can't realize how little time it leaves me, how far it takes me from New York," I explained. "[This winter] I have been invited by a young group of liberals in Japan to visit the Orient. From there I go to lecture in the universities of Shanghai and Pekin [sic]...to Korea and India...and then next summer to the fifth international conference in London. Do you want to marry me and spend your honeymoon in a railroad station kissing me goodbye?"[4]

Slee not only went on with his courtship despite the possibility that he would spend much of their marriage kissing Margaret goodbye—which certainly did come to pass—but he pursued Margaret ever more vigorously. When Margaret departed on the *Taiyo Maru* for her first trip to Japan, Noah Slee was aboard ship. Noah was with Margaret—and Grant—as they traveled to Shanghai and Peking and Korea and Egypt, with her in Italy, and finally, four months later, with her in London. Throughout the trip he must have proved himself indispensable. Sanger was several times ill during the tour and, occupied as she was at every port with lecturing, interviews, charming the press and her hosts, she had more than her share of business matters to attend to.[5]

Details were Noah's strong point. Even at his wealthiest, he always kept a pocketbook of his daily expenses, down to the nickel carfare. On this extended world tour, he handled the luggage, the planning of routes, booking of hotels and travel. He was every inch the masterful English squire, whose very presence sent clerks to scuttering and bureaucrats to acquiesce. He pressed his suit with vigor, and, wrote Sanger,[6]

> He met every feeble objection I tried to voice; I confess that my objections became feebler and feebler. Not only was I to go on [with] my work, but he would help me with it, in every way possible.[7]

And help he did. Far beyond the generous provisions for Sanger's personal life and the office conveniences mentioned in the letter below, J. Noah H. Slee gave liberally and munificently to the Clinical Research Bureau, to workers in the cause, to Margaret's various birth control projects, and to Margaret's family and friends. He became treasurer of both the American Birth Control League and the Clinical Research Bureau. He paid off the *Review* deficit, contributed generously to the League, bought Dr. Stone an examination table and other equipment. Slee made possible the 1927 First World Population Conference in Geneva; purchased the New York brownstone as an office for the Clinical Research Bureau; gave Havelock Ellis a house, a secretary, and a yearly stipend for his old age; enabled Margaret to put one of her brothers into business and a niece through college; provided for Margaret's father in his late years; saw Stuart through Yale and Grant through Princeton.

One of his most valuable gifts to the birth control movement was to make possible the lecture tours of Dr. James F. Cooper.[8] Cooper's experience as a medical missionary in China had convinced him of the necessity for birth control. As a former instructor at the medical school of Boston University and author of *Technique of Contraception*, Cooper's lectures were listened to with respect by the medical profession, by doctors and nurses as well as social workers and businessmen. Within two years, beginning in 1925, Cooper gave more than seven hundred lectures, covering every state in America but Vermont, educating physicians and building a national network of several thousand professional practitioners.[9]

To these physicians, Sanger could then refer the distressed writers of the many letters she was receiving and be assured that these women would receive sound birth control advice. This nationwide group of physicians who were dispensing contraceptives contributed greatly to the mounting acceptance of birth control in America, for, as we have seen, the resistance of the medical profession at the organizational level continued until the 1936 One Package decision finally convinced the American Medical Association to endorse birth control in 1937.[10]

Noah Slee's largess was bountiful, yet in all he was scrupulous in separating Margaret and himself from kickback or profit-making propositions. Noah did take the risk of smuggling diaphragms through Montreal into the States using his Three-in-One containers, an act that could have brought serious government charges. And it was a fairly sizeable smuggling operation: Pessaries (diaphragms) were then being consumed at the rate of five hundred to a thousand a week.[11] Even though Slee's operation was supplemented by socialites returning from Europe, pessaries strapped around their waists, as the birth control clinic began to attract more clients, and as more physicians across America, in response to Dr. Cooper's field work, began to offer Birth Control, the demand for pessaries grew correspondingly, outstripping the smugglers' supply. The need was for locally manufactured product.

At this point, Noah loaned Herbert Simonds, a friend of Margaret's, start-up funds for the Holland-Rantos contraceptive company. For both Noah and Margaret, this could have become an enormously profitable involvement, but other than accepting repayment of the original loan, neither Noah nor Margaret benefited. The Holland-Rantos output increased the pessaries supply, aiding the work of both Cooper and Sanger, and for this the generosity of Noah Slee was responsible.

Sanger had once written to her sister, Ethel, that maybe she would go out west, find a widower with money, and settle down.[12] With Slee, she found the money, but she certainly did not settle down, and she took her time accepting Slee's offer. In June 1921, Juliet Rublee received Sanger's letter from London, where she was enjoying herself immensely with Hugh de Selincourt and Havelock Ellis and meeting H.G. Wells.

> Don't you worry your blessed dear head a minute about me & Mr S—darling girl—He has not money enough to pay the price—He could not inspire me to love—So as I wrote you before—it would be for love or money enough to put the b.c. movement on the map. He has not the means to do either. But besides that and all joking aside dearest, I am not inclined to marriage. Freedom is too lovely & I want to enjoy it for a time.[13]

At the same time, Sanger recognized

> that the cooperation of a man whose business experience had been gained in building up for thirty years a well known business, with such backing and interest as he could give, would help enormously in extending the work [of Birth Control] and expanding it along the lines I had mapped out on an international scale.[14]

In January 1922, prior to taking off for Japan in late February—with

Noah, though she did not know that at the time—she wrote to Hugh de Selincourt,

> Two very fine men have been thrust my way. One a millionaire and sixty—terribly American typical type of respectable business man, church going widower—generous, happy, thinks I'm "<u>sensible</u>" likes me for that stupid quality. He could with his wealth make life very comfortable & insure the financial success of my cause—Shall I accept him?[15]

Havelock Ellis, to whom she also confided her dilemma, hoped that Sanger would "think a long, long time about it first."[16] As Sanger later admitted, she made it "terribly hard" for Noah.[17] But when in September of 1922, Sanger married Slee, she kept her freedom, too. As she writes below, a prenuptial agreement was drawn up, allowing Sanger to keep a separate apartment. After Noah had built Sanger as a wedding present the house of their, or perhaps her, dreams in Fishkill, New York, Sanger had her own separate office on the property.

Willowlake was a magnificent mansion built of stone quarried from the hills nearby, sitting on a hundred acres of rolling hills and woods, the mansion itself rising almost straight from the banks of a little mountain lake surrounded by willow trees, and so naming the estate itself. With bridle paths (the couple rode horseback many mornings) and spacious grounds, rose garden, guest bedrooms, it was ideal for entertaining family and friends. Stuart and Grant brought their friends from college. Noah's grandchildren came for the summer, and a special nursemaid was hired to care for them. Space was there as well for meetings with professionals and receptions for dignitaries.

James Noah Henry Slee was the grandson of an Episcopalian minister, born in Capetown, South Africa in 1860. After his father died, in 1873 his mother brought Noah and his brother to Baltimore. Noah was twelve at the time. Noah Slee began working in a bicycle shop at just about the time America became completely enraptured with bicycles. Slee developed a formula for an oil compound that was most efficient on bicycle gears. Out of this grew his Three-in-One Oil Company, which he made highly profitable by streamlining production and cutting back on the number of employees his factory required.

When Sanger met Slee, he belonged to the exclusive Union League Club. For many years he was superintendent of Sunday School at the St. George's Episcopal Church on Stuyvesant Square in New York City (on learning this, Sanger is reported to have said she almost fainted), and he was always close friends with the Karl Reiland, pastor of St. George's.[18] Slee had three grown children and was enduring his longtime, loveless marriage, though Sanger reports in *My Fight for Birth Control* and to Juliet (above) that Slee was a "widower" with three grown children.[19]

Slee was immediately smitten and, while not a widower, he quickly became a suitor—and divorced. Marriage to Sanger followed shortly after Slee's divorce became final (Sanger had been divorced from Bill since October 1921), but the newspapers did not pick up the Slee-Sanger marriage until almost two years later—a coup that delighted Sanger.

And not unreasonably so. For immediately after the media announcement, Sanger was deluged with letters requesting help, money, aid, contributions for anything and everything, from people she had never met and never before heard of.

When the newspapers descended on her after discovery of the marriage, Sanger, living by then in her luxurious home at 39 Fifth Avenue, declared that since her marriage, she had been able to devote herself more than ever to her work and that her husband had been of much aid to her, never interfering with what she did. He has his business and she has hers was her explanation of the secret of their happiness.[20] The newspapers were kept very busy after the discovery. Under the headline "Old Loves Best and Second Marriages are Happiest Says Mrs. Sanger," she was quoted as saying, "An older man has experience back of him. A young man has only book ideals to guide him. He suffers disillusionment when he gets another person within four walls and sees that she isn't behaving according to any of the rules."[21]

Certainly the Sanger-Slee marriage was unconventional. As we see in the letter below, Sanger had very clear ideas how her second marriage should be conducted. She was unquestionably unfaithful at times. Noah was extremely difficult in his later years in Tucson; the "sadist," Sanger calls him briefly in her diary. Yet Sanger was ever grateful to Noah. As she acknowledged to Clarence Gamble, "It was so different when my husband was living and could write out a check from month to month for anything that was needed, and for a period of twenty years thousands upon thousands were needed to keep the Margaret Sanger Bureau going."[22]

Noah Slee was "all bark and no bite," said Sanger.

> He revealed the qualities of character that all truly great men— leaders in business, strong personalities—possess: accuracy, promptness, reliability, ability to take full responsibility and to drive things through, interest in detail, quick intuition, unerring judgment of character—all these, plus kindliness and the heart of a child! Success had come to reward hard work.
>
> On the other side there is his conservatism—at that time, I had not yet awakened to the sterling merits of true conservatism. JNH

was typically American in his conception of life, his religious affiliations, his set attitude toward all "liberal" movements. But fundamentally he was a spiritual radical and a revolutionist in common sense. A sense of humor, a wicked desire to tease, and a common love of human achievements and endeavor attracted me strongly to him.[23]

The genial host, Slee was known for his puns: "Why ain't we got no chillen, Mandy? You just a goose." Replies Mandy, "I may be a goose but you ain't no propaganda," And Slee would ask why was *night* like the letter *p?* Because it puts *Slee* to *sleep*.[24] Above all, Noah Slee adored Margaret Sanger. Said Noah, "Before I met Margaret, nothing important had ever happened to me. She was, and always will be, the greatest adventure of my life."[25]

In late 1941 Noah had a fall in Willowlake, then another. Margaret saw him much changed and curtailed her travel. In the spring of 1943, back at Willowlake, Noah fell again, and a slight stroke followed. He wanted to be in the sunshine of Tucson. There he spent the last months of his life, Margaret with him constantly, summoned by buzzer attached to his wheelchair, attending to his every need. Noah Slee died peacefully in sight of the Tucson hills on June 21, 1943. His ashes were buried at Willowlake. In her will, Sanger left instructions that she was to be buried next to Noah. "He was," recalled Barbara Peabody Sanger, Stuart's wife, "a very, very nice man."[26]

The Manuscript

Lawrence Lader, who had been published in *The New Yorker* and *Esquire*, spent two difficult years on his biography of Sanger, staying for periods with her in Tucson, interviewing her, and going through her papers at Smith College and the Library of Congress. *The Margaret Sanger Story and the Fight for Birth Control* was published in 1955. It updated Sanger's autobiographies, but did not offer any new material and could not be assessed as objective. Said Dorothy Brush, it covered Sanger in "clouds of gush."[27] Sanger wrote this letter to Lader when he requested information on Noah Slee for his book.

A Letter from Margaret Sanger describing Noah Slee[28]

March 29,1954
Mr. Lawrence Lader
5 E. End Ave., NYC

Dear Larry,

Just finished a dictation (buzzing with indignation to someone in the P.P.F. at 5:01). I'm willing to "soothe" the heart by writing to you about J.N.H.S. . . .

First—yes, we were married in London—month, year? I'd have to look up certificate. Yes, he decided to take the same boat to Japan. He did not intend to go further and had been invited by American friends of his, Mr. Frazier of Yokohoma, to visit him. But after Japan I was invited to go to Pekin, . . .

So J.N. and Grant, who was with me, came along to China and from there to Malaya, to Egypt, and England to the Conference....

J.N. was along on that trip with Grant. I took Grant out of his school (Peddie at Highstown, N.J.) because I could not have an ocean separate us again after Peggy's call (never out of my mind) "Mother, are you coming back?" After the trip and the conference in London we were married at Justice of the Peace, or some such legal place with the regular three days bans. We went to Paris and then to U.S.A. I did not want an announcement of our marriage, as there was much work to do, Conferences to organize. The families, his and mine, knew of our marriage. I was not certain that two people so very different in background, could make a success of marriage, unless things were organized and handled in a different way than the average. So we decided to have separate apartments nearby, but not connecting. We would invite each other to dine as we could arrange it. Neither had a key to the other's apartment and always a phone call asking if it was convenient to call.

I knew my friends were not the conventional, conservative kind that he liked. He liked and respected success, accomplishment, wealth. I liked the same, but my horizon took in those trying for the same results. The younger generation, artists, writers, poets, musicians, and suffrage and peace advocates, International Friends of Freedom for India. Naturally, I would not inflict this group on my conservative husband. I kept the name of M.S. because it was easier, my children's name, and the name I signed to articles and reviews and books. He agreed to this and often later in our marriage years at a reception, where we were introduced as Mr. and Mrs. Slee, he would turn to the person and say, "That woman is my wife, but she is 'The Margaret Sanger.'" Proudly he would say that over and over again through the years.

Our marriage did much for me. His habits of punctuality, paying bills promptly, carrying out his promises to the letter, these were qualities ingrained in me also, but bills and hours were often not so easy to arrange. My catching of trains seemed a great source of distress to him. I figured as closely as possible, distance and time in a taxi. Usually correct, but also to find a husband at the gate to the G[rand] C[entral] train mopping a perspired forehead, furious and angry to have: been kept waiting with just enough time for the gate to close and "all aboard" shouted, as we hopped on the nearest car as it moved on to its destination. Then we smiled as we found seats and all was forgiven.

There were times when J.N. felt very sorry for himself. One winter in particular when we kept "Willowlake" open, the lovely 16th-century English-type house he had given me for a wedding present (I designed and built it out of fieldstone on the place), I spent most of the weekdays in Washington, D.C. working on the Federal bill, Section 211, trying to get it revised to exempt members of the medical profession in the use of the U.S. mails and Common Carriers. That day was the end for us. We lost, owing to Sen. Pat McCarran's vote.[29] I felt depressed as I came back from the "Hill" to the office. I decided to get away as I was exhausted, mentally and harassed by workers and friends who kept asking "What next?" I called up Willowlake and told [my] husband that we had lost the fight and did he not want to take me down to Bermuda for a week or just on a cruise—whoow! What a blast came over the phone, "Wasting your life in that d_____ B.C." The doctors don't want it, no one seems to care, no one wants that d____ law changed but you and a lot of "nuts" who seem to cling to you. I, who remain here alone in this big house, with only servants as companions day after day. I could be sick. I could die in the night. Who would care," and on and on with no possibility of a word from me. So I gently hung up the receiver, announced to my staff that they were to clear up and pack up, called the railroad to get a reservation to N.Y. Called N.Y. office to get me reservation to Nassau on the boat leaving that very afternoon. Secretary to be on the dock with some money for me. She was not to whisper to a soul that I was going any where. So I arrived and found a last cabin on the boat sailing for Nassau. I was dead to the world and heartsick that I had to do this to J. N., but he had to learn to respect my feelings, as well as his own. So— about a few minutes after I felt the boat set sail and away from the docks, the door opened, and who should walk in, trembling with laughter, but Hazel Moore, the pal and co-worker I had left in tears on the Hill because McCarran had voted us down. What a surprise! She had returned to the office to find a mysterious atmosphere and in her special way guessed I had gone to N.Y. and perhaps to Willowlake. She had friends in Nassau and had decided to call up and see if she could get a berth that day. On her way to the dock, she ran into the secretary who had come with cash for me, and then she knew I was there. There was only one upper berth, and that in my cabin. So back again together we decided not to talk about the Hill, the bill, and the defeat. Nothing of these hard weeks of walking marble halls, being avoided, and pushed aside by our precious senators. Morning, afternoon, and nights were we, several of us on the Hill, seeking promises of Senators to help us change the law. Now we were here to relax and rest and play....

Now, as to husband, who kept scolding into the telephone, as he had not heard my very gentle hang up—finally, he asked a question, and no answer. So he called the office only to be told I had gone to N.Y. So he thinking it was to Bermuda I wished to go, called up and reserved a nice cabin for Mr. and Mrs. Slee to leave the next day. As I did not call up and did not come by train as he expected me to do, he worried, but got himself ready to go to Bermuda. He was expecting to either hear from me, or if I was really angry, to surprise me by being on the same boat!! Alas, he did not find me on the boat or in Bermuda. So he made the usual boat friends but did not enjoy the trip and flew back to New York, only to have my office know nothing of where I was.

J.N. took the train at G[rand] Central for Beacon, had the chauffeur meet him at the station, but hesitated to ask if "Madame" was at home. But the chauffeur asked if I was to come on a later train. So there he was alone again, with no idea where I was and if I was ever to return. He knew he had been rude on the phone, but never in all his experience before with women had rudeness not paid—! Here was a very different person to deal with. He put a bottle of French yellow Clicquot Champagne on the ice, started a fire in the fireplace, took out his pipe, ordered a good dinner and decided to wait and think.[30] My week in Nassau ended. I, too, was jittery but rebellious. I was going to let the Brute suffer and pine and worry. As I knew he would. I realized how spoiled he was. What a rough exterior, but a great gentle heart. He admired women who struck out on their own. Though in his heart he had not the faintest idea that any female: could make good without a man's guidance, his experience, his money, and his help (sometimes his love). (More of this about Mrs ____ coffee shop, and many women he set up in business.)

It was finally with an emotional urge, but determined to take no nonsense, that I took the train two hours later than he did for Beacon. I did not phone for the chauffeur to meet me. I took a taxi and told the driver to wait. I decided to pack up and leave if one word of complaint or one shout or blast greeted me at the door. The door was unlocked—unusual—for J.N. locked everything. I opened the door to see the handsomest man I ever saw in a velvet smoking jacket, smoking a pipe by the blazing fire, the police dog at his feet. He looked up—"Hello, darling, did you have a good time in Bermuda?" We rushed into each other's arms and laughed and partly cried. I dismissed the taxi, or rather J.N. did with aside (damn extravagant when there are three cars on the place). The final note of that event was, why should we quarrel when we care so much about each other? I replied, "J. Noah, you are English, oh so English, in fact you are British, while I am Irish, pure to the backbone, not a drop of blood but Irish for centuries. For three hundred years the English and Irish have fought, so we just have inherited the routine. It's of no importance really, but be careful not to step on the toes of the Irish when there's a redhead about."

His business experience gave him a keenness as an executive. He liked order and discipline. In his own Three-in-One factory he reorganized the entire works by replacing man labor with machinery several years before any other manufacturer dared to do such a thing. Three hundred men were replaced by machinery and only thirty men were necessary to treble the output of the oil, at one third the cost.

When it was necessary for me to get to my office early, say 8:30 a.m., he was at a loss to understand why. I was not getting a salary, never getting a penny for all the hours and hours of work. I walked to the office and back to the apartment, a proper procedure for exercise, of which he strongly approved. But why so early to the office? leaving him to breakfast alone. His curiosity led him to visit the office at 104 5th Ave. and found us at work opening the morning mail, at least 1,000 letters in the eight o'clock delivery. That was an inspiring sight to his executive eyes. He reorganized the office, had a letter opener, stamps of dates, contents, departments, etc., finally ordered a whole new supply of noiseless typewriters and discarded the old ones. The whole office was enlarged and a specialist for filing engaged. I lost track of the many new gadgets he ordered. Soon efficiency was dominating the whole place and the master executive looked in every day to supervise his handiwork.

PART III THE CONSERVATIVE RADICAL
38. The Birth of the Pill

With the end of World War II, Sanger was able to resume her work, but now her focus was international, as she forced through sheer grit the birth of what would become the International Planned Parenthood Federation. Equally pressing, if there were to be international success, was the need for that simple, safe contraceptive. In 1953, in the November that followed what would be remembered as the historic June 8 Shrewsbury meeting with Katherine McCormick and Gregory Pincus, Margaret Sanger responded to Dr. Kan Majima, organizer of the Japan Birth Control Center, who was investigating rubber plants to supply inexpensive raw material for contraceptive devices. Wrote Sanger,

> I am not so optimistic that the rubber plant, or rubber diaphragm will ever be the ideal solution to family planning. We need a simple pill, or capsule, or cup of tea to immunize the ovum temporarily for month by month, or longer as desired.[1]

Contraception and the desire to immunize the ovum with something as simple as a cup of tea is as old as the history of mankind and something that Sanger had yearned for since her nursing days in the Lower East Side. Anthropologists have established that within many traditional societies, women took teas or herbs that prevented pregnancy.[2] In the days of the Roman empire, women employed the herb silphium, a species of giant fennel growing only in a thirty-mile band on the dry mountainsides facing the Mediterranean Sea. Overuse quickly made the plant extinct—which says something about one civilization's attitude towards contraception.[3] And probably no scientist cares to believe the story of a twentieth-century American woman who had been eating the ground-up seeds of Queen

Anne's lace for some ten years but became pregnant when she went on a trip without her seeds.[4]

Interestingly enough, only with the rise of male-oriented science has contraception become a problem, for only with the rise of Western science and its male technology has come an unprecedented population explosion that menaces the planet. Despite the "sacrifice" of millions and billions of mice, rats, rabbits, guinea pigs, and goodness knows what other animals and years and years of pure research, a safe, inexpensive contraceptive suitable for all women in all cultures is still not available—with what is available in America too often resolutely withheld.[5]

Clarence Gamble, in seeking an inexpensive, simple contraceptive, faced ridicule and determined opposition from both men and women. When he conducted salt trials, he infuriated Dr. Helen Wright, who was supported by Lady Rama Rau.[6] Wright and Rama Rau asserted that anything less than the diaphragm and jelly was an insult to Indian women by white male chauvinists (this in a country of six thousand women to one doctor where the birthrate was soaring).[7] In all fairness, medical examinations during field trials in America often revealed gynecological problems that needed treatment and which otherwise would not have been known. But can one really distinguish between egotistical defense of intellectual territory and objective scientific discourse? And would not relief from pregnancy automatically ensure a woman some relief from any physical illness? In the 1990s, women in undeveloped countries were dying in childbirth on an average of 500 per 100,000, while in the developed countries the rate was approximately 25 per 100,000.[8]

In 1920, Sanger journeyed to Germany to scout for a jelly; in 1934, to Russia for a rumored speramatoxin.[9] In 1939, she investigated herbs from Fiji, and at about the same time, Gamble was talking to Hoffman LaRoche Company about an African root and to Johnson & Johnson about herbs from Ecuador.[10] Later, hearing that rats were left sterile after eating the common field pea of India, Gamble supported a study of by Dr. S. N. Sanyal, who developed a contraceptive pill, unfortunately ineffective, using the oil of the pea.[11] In 1930, Sanger convened an international conference dedicated to contraception techniques; the Seventh International Birth Control Conference in Zurich devoted five days to the latest developments in contraceptives. Subsequent studies of contraception use showed that all methods were better than nothing, different methods were preferable for different people, but none offered the potential that Sanger and Gamble dreamed of, until the possibility of The Pill.

In this scientific age to science we must turn. Katherine Dexter McCormick was a product of her age even as she defied many of its norms.

Katherine McCormick was beautiful, brilliant, and independent of mind. She graduated from Massachusetts Institute of Technology with a major in biology, the second woman to do so, in 1904. That same year, in what was a fairy-tale romance, she married Stanley Katherine, whose wealth far exceeded hers, he the heir to the International Harvester Company fortune. But the fairy tale almost immediately became a nightmare. Within two years, it was clear that Stanley was a schizophrenic with little hope of cure.

Determined, nevertheless, to cure Stanley, McCormick set up and channeled vast sums into her Neuroendocrine Research Foundation run by Roy C. Hoskins, an endocrinologist in the Department of Physiology of Harvard Medical School. Through Hoskins, McCormick would one day meet Gregory Pincus.

Retaining the clothes and fashion of her halcyon days of romance with Stanley, Katherine devoted her married years, her energy, and her money—such as she had, for Stanley's money was still controlled by the McCormick family—into the woman suffrage movement, becoming vice president and treasurer of the National American Woman's Suffrage Association, helping Carrie Chapman Catt found the League of Women Voters, and serving as its first vice president. It was probably in 1917 that McCormick met Margaret Sanger. Beginning in 1918, she and Sanger maintained a correspondence, sometimes intermittent, McCormick helping Sanger in small ways, including opening the Chateau de Prangins, which is located near Geneva (where she and Stanley had been married), to the three hundred delegates of the 1927 First World Population Conference; underwriting the 1948 Cheltenham conference; contributing to the 1928 startup of the Clinical Research Bureau, and incidentally smuggling diaphragms into the Clinical Research Bureau from Europe. After Stanley's death in 1947 and after she wrested control of her husband's estate from his family and satisfied the 85 percent tax take of the United States Department of Internal Revenue, McCormick was ready to turn to matters that interested her.

Contraception interested her. Unwilling to bear a child who might inherit the insanity of Stanley, revolted at the sight of filthy, overcrowded slums created by multiparous women, McCormick agreed wholeheartedly with Sanger on the need for a cheap, safe contraceptive.[12] Sanger had written prophetically to McCormick in 1950 that "the world and almost all our civilization . . . is going to depend" on a cheap, safe contraceptive.[13] At the Stockholm conference in 1953, two months after the Shrewsbury meeting, Sanger would reiterate this need:

> I firmly believe that one of the first and most important efforts of this [Stockholm] conference, and for all of us when we get back to our homes and work, is to put all our energies into research for a

simple cheap contraceptive, one which will perhaps immunize temporarily against pregnancy.[14]

Since 1917, the many individuals who would make possible The Pill had unknowingly been building a network. During the years that McCormick had been supporting the adrenal cortex research of Roy C. Hoskins on schizophrenia, Hoskins was conducting his clinical trials at the Worcester Hospital with the assistance of Hudson Hoagland. Thus, McCormick became acquainted with Hoagland, who in partnership with Gregory Pincus, ran the Worcester Foundation for Experimental Biology in Shrewsbury. Meanwhile, in 1950, Sanger had met Gregory Pincus through Abraham Stone, who had taken over as director of the Clinical Research Bureau on the death of Hannah Stone. Sanger had heard of Pincus's steroid research and in 1951 questioned him about the possibility of developing an oral contraceptive.

Pincus then went to Planned Parenthood for a grant to explore this possibility. With this grant, which was funded unknown to McCormick by her donations, Pincus fed rabbits progesterone and suppressed ovulation in 90 percent of them.[15] When Sanger told McCormick of Pincus's success, McCormick already knew of Pincus through Hoagland. When Sanger received a letter from McCormick about her desire to see a reliable contraceptive developed, Sanger had a concrete suggestion.

Subsequently, Pincus's research reached the point where clinical trials were necessary. Pincus first involved John Rock, the eminent gynecologist and obstetrician retiring from nearby Harvard. Pincus had known Rock since the thirties, when Rock, who was recognized for his success with infertility, had requested help from Pincus on ovum implantation.[16] But the clinical trials that Rock could arrange in Massachusetts were limited, and once The Pill was ready for more extensive trials, the question was, in McCormick's words, where to find "a cage of ovulating females."[17]

Cut back to 1936, when, as the reader may recall, Clarence Gamble, after a second abrupt withdrawal of United States government support, had sent a worker into Puerto Rico to rescue its system of birth control clinics from folding. Gamble's timely rescue had impelled Puerto Rico in 1937 to make birth control legal in this very Catholic territory. Not quite two decades later, when Pincus was seeking his cage of ovulating females, there, thanks to Clarence Gamble, was Puerto Rico, close by, not only rife with ovulating women who wanted contraceptives, but legal for birth controllers. Pincus, who had contacts at the University of Puerto Rico Medical School, was able to organize there a small clinical trial.[18] Gamble, learning of the need for additional trials, then used his contacts to arrange extended clinical trials in Humacao. When the final set of clinical trial figures on The

Pill were gathered in 1959, over one fourth of the numbers came through Gamble's contact in Humacao.[19]

Pincus, a talented scientist forced out of academia for all the various reasons that academia does such things, had devoted his scientific life to research on conception and had a dubious reputation for having produced "fatherless rabbits."[20] In Catholic Massachusetts, where it was against the law to advise contraception and certainly to do research on the matter, Pincus was doing just that. Sanger was amazed at the indifference of Planned Parenthood to the potential of Pincus's work, and on June 8, 1953, she and Pincus and Katherine McCormick met in Shrewsbury in that historic meeting at which McCormick immediately promised Pincus $10,000 with more to follow.[21] Over the years, another two million dollars followed, and another million on her death in 1967.

Without question, The Pill, once initially bankrolled, was promoted into commercial success by the salesmanship and showmanship, the executive and administrative skills of Gregory Pincus, the scientist and the entrepreneur, who along with his own scientific expertise had the skill and the perception to use wisely propitious events and the timely discoveries of other scientists.[22]

But first and foremost, The Pill was the result of women working for women. When Sanger made her first trip to India, referring to the demand for contraceptives, she wrote in her diary,

> It had been predicted that only Eurasians and the lower classes would listen to me on birth control, but the question turned out to be not Shall it be given but What to give.[23]

Two years after The Pill was released in 1960, it was being used by 1.2 million women.[24] In the developed countries, The Pill found its greatest success, in 1965 being taken by 70 percent of the women of Great Britain.[25] Its popularity of the sixties was undercut for a time by questions of The Pill's safety, and as the IUD and other alternatives became available, The Pill never regained the same widespread usage.[26] Today The Pill, with a much-reduced estrogen content, is the preferred contraceptive for American women in their twenties and continues to be used predominately in the developed countries of the world. According to UN figures for 2002, the Pill constitutes 8 percent of contraceptive use worldwide.[27]

In the less developed countries, where Sanger and McCormick had most hoped it would help, The Pill ran into cultural and social roadblocks, along with a distrust of Western science and Western imperialist motives. Despite the persuasive efforts of Pincus in promoting The Pill and the financial gifts of McCormick that subsidized its free distribution, both India and China, countries with committed and aggressive population policies, said no to The Pill. The government of Japan only allowed it in the 1990s after Viagra was permitted and angry feminists stampeded at the double standard.[28]

The Pill did not become the universal panacea exactly as envisioned by Sanger and McCormick, but its benefits and effects more than justified their efforts. Its appearance broke down unspoken barriers. The discussion it generated required a more frank discussion of sexual matters throughout the world, this in turn leading to increased contraceptive use by women, and the research required for The Pill has led and continues to open the way to new contraceptive methods, including the morning-after pill, implants, and long-lasting injections.[29]

The development of a simple contraceptive for women did not take years of research, did not take committees and studies and polls examining the attitudes of women or the possible response of environmental factors to undecided factors or the ratio of demographics to infant mortality, etc., etc. As Pincus himself declared, "I invented The Pill at the request of a woman."[30] All it took to make a cheap, oral contraceptive available was two determined women, both of whom wanted to see it done, one of whom, fortunately, had a lot of cash.

The Manuscript

Katherine McCormick, said Sanger's first grandchild, was the only person to whom she ever saw her grandmother defer. A tad of that deference is seen in Sanger's letters to McCormick, which mirror the combination of friendship and agreement of purpose they shared. McCormick's generosity in making her Santa Barbara guest home available to Sanger during the brutally hot months of the Tucson summer was much appreciated by Sanger. Sanger reciprocated with gifts of papayas, health tips, and her devoted friendship.

Letters from Margaret Sanger to Mrs. Stanley (Katherine) McCormick[31] March 3 to October 12, 1953

March 3, 1953

Mrs. Stanley McCormick
1600 Santa Barbara Street
Santa Barbara, California

Dear Mrs. McCormick:

You doubtless have had the report of the meeting of the Research Committee from Mr. Henshaw of the Planned Parenthood Federation in

New York.[32] I was glad to see that the larger percentage of their income has been allocated for research projects. I also noted that Mr. Pincus is given a small amount from their fund and I wish that Mr. Henshaw and Mr. Vogt could go up to see what Dr. Pincus is doing.[33] That personal contact makes such a difference in opinions and faith of a project.

Mr. Rollins has written me that you were good enough to suggest that I might have your guesthouse from April the first to June the first. That is most generous and thoughtful of you, my dear Mrs. McCormick, but the fact that I am feeling very much better than I have felt for the past four years gave me the courage to do more in the way of public speaking than I had planned to do. Consequently, I am going to be out of Tucson for a good part of April and May. I am leaving the end of this month for Columbus, Ohio, for their twentieth anniversary and spending several days there. Then in April, I go to Cleveland and Washington and New York, at different meetings, and so, if my health continues as it has, I shall be doing these things and not be continuously confined to the heat of Tucson, although I shall have to return and probably be here part of the time in between dates.

The question of Stockholm is, of course, one that would take me there about the first of August and while I have had to make reservations, I am not entirely certain that I will go. They're a very self-sufficient group in Stockholm and aside from the possibility of meeting some of the committee of the Nobel group, I will not be needed as I was needed in Bombay. If I go to Stockholm, I will not stay long and as I mentioned in an earlier letter, I would like to come over to Santa Barbara after my return from Stockholm and if your guest house is unoccupied. I would love to stay there for a little while as Tucson remains very hot through September and on until November. These are my plans as far as "man proposes." I do thank you and greatly appreciate your kind offer. I love Santa Barbara, I love your house, and had I not already promised to do these meetings I would certainly accept your kind offer and be there early in April.

Trusting you are well and again my thankful affection,

Most cordially,

Margaret Sanger

65 Sierra Vista Drive
Tucson, Arizona

March 27, 1953

Mrs. Stanley McCormick
1600 Santa Barbara Street
Santa Barbara, California

Dear Mrs. McCormick:

Ever since your letter of the 15th came, I've been meaning to reply. It just happens that a young man, Lawrence Lader, is here with a contract from Doubleday, publishers, to write my biography. This has taken every second that I could spare; consequently, letters have piled up. I hope you will understand.

First let me say that I'm terribly pleased that you heard the Chicago Round Table broadcast. Yes, it was in Bombay; it was Lady Rama Rau, Mr. Vogt, Dr. Blacker, and myself and it seems to me there was one other Indian scientist at the board.[34] There was another given for the Northwestern University, in Tokyo, but I don't know when that was broadcast. I am more than delighted that you like the reports from Japan and India. Many people have written, expressing their appreciation that they were remembered.

You are quite right in feeling as you do about research. I am trying to whip up some interest, hoping that I might get Doris Duke to give the necessary amount each year to the Pincus project, and now that you have been kind enough to ask that I come to see you in Boston, which I should adore to do and which I will do when convenient for you. In June, perhaps, we could go to see Dr. Pincus. I don't like to go to anyone to ask for support of a project unless I am fairly familiar with its principles at least and also I like to be enthusiastic about it. I know that you felt that work he and his co-workers were doing was constructive and good and from what I understand, he can put his project through within a few years if he had the means to enlarge his staff. Perhaps you could tell me a little more about your impressions of the Pincus project which would enable me to go over to Bel Air and see Doris Duke before I get away and she, also leaves for Europe during the summer as a rule. I have been impatient of the slow motion that surrounds these scientists who could work faster if they had the assistance which would make the project go faster.

Not long ago a friend in Honolulu sent me a box of papayas that were the most delectable fruit that I've ever had on this side of the Pacific. Knowing how much you like papaya juice, I have ordered a few of these to be sent to you, with my compliments, as you may like to know where these can be had in Hawaii and received in the best of condition. . . .

The possibility of your going to Stockholm is most thrilling and if you could not take the trip this year, why not carefully consider going with us to

Japan in 1954?[35] I enclose a copy of a letter from Dr. Gamble's son that will give you some idea of the interest and the possibility of such a conference.

I miss being your neighbor in your little guest house when I have much to tell you and it will be a great delight to come to Boston to see you and to catch up on all of the present and past events, including a few plans for the future.

Most cordially yours,

Margaret Sanger

October 5, 1953

Mrs. Stanley McCormick
1600 Santa Barbara St.
Santa Barbara, California

Dear Mrs. McCormick,

I am back in Tucson again and after so many months living in suitcases, I am more than happy to get into my own surroundings. I did not stay long in the East after my arrival on the Mauritania.[36]

Lady Rama Rau will be in Tucson October 25th. They have given her a very difficult tour, with no regard whatsoever to geography. But she is strong and healthy, and I think can take it. I do hope that you will be in Santa Barbara when she is there, but from your letter of September 28th, I gather that you will leave October 11th for Boston. If I am feeling well enough I may go with her to Los Angeles and then to Santa Barbara. The Indians were so gracious and helpful to me when I was there, always escorting me to the next place, hither and yon.

They asked me to introduce her at the University Auditorium, but I decided that was a little too much pressure for me at this time, so I suggested that the President of the University do so instead. I will give a small reception for her after the meeting and then turn her over to the committee to take her to El Paso. Mrs. Watumull, who is now in Honolulu, will return to Los Angeles to greet her and to help with her stay there.

I cannot tell you how much your letter delights me to know that the papaya has been so helpful. Indeed I read some of your letter to my Doctor son Stuart, who has had a special course in gastro-intestinal disturbances and was most delighted and interested to learn of the effects of papaya in your case. Of course, the Watumulls will be more than delighted, as Mr. Watumull, who also has some such disturbances, practically lives on papaya. He knows exactly where to get it and in what condition to get it, so that it will be perfect on its arrival. I never knew anyone to be so appreciative of so little as you are. Mr. and Mrs. Watumull came two or three times to your guesthouse and suggested very often that they send you pineapple or some of the strange fruits from Honolulu. I did not encourage that suggestion until after you introduced me to that famous and delectable papaya juice drink, and then I knew that papaya was the answer, and I am indeed so pleased and happy that it was just the thing for you.

Now as to the Dr. Pincus Research. There were rumors in New York that all of the four tests going on, including the Pincus and Rock work, did not have money enough to cover them through January 1954.

I did not verify this with Mr. Henshaw, but you will know directly since you are in touch with Dr. Pincus, what the situation is. I went to see the Secretary of the Commonwealth Fund before I left for Stockholm, but all the executives were away on holiday and would not be back until October. I did not see them again, but I think there is one place where money might be obtained for research of the kind we are interested in. I only wish that the Federation would allow Mr. Henshaw to meet people and to put forth the situation where money is needed for research, for there is some strange feeling that he is not equipped to do this.

Did you by any chance receive a copy of the Bombay Proceedings?[38] If not, I shall be happy to send a copy to you. Many of the orders were held up in the post office, but I have plenty of copies on hand now and will be more than happy to send a copy to you with my compliments.

Always my affectionate regards,

Margaret Sanger

October 12, 1953

Mrs. Stanley McCormick
393 Commonwealth Avenue
Boston, Mass.

Dear Mrs. McCormick,

How wonderful of you to offer your guesthouse to Lady Rama Rau and to me. And also the wonderful luxury of your car and chauffeur to take us from Los Angeles to Santa Barbara. I know it will be a wonderful thing for Lady Rama Rau to drive and to have the comfort of your guesthouse, and it will be for me too. I am sending word to her agency in New York that you have generously offered this, so that there will be no confusion as to her taking the train, or whatever her lecture agency has planned.

Under separate cover I am sending to you a copy of the Proceedings. I am sending it to Santa Barbara instead of to Boston, as you may have more time to look through it on your return than you will have in your busy days in Boston.

I hope you will see Dr. Pincus, and do let me know what you find. His work, it seems to me, is the nearest to reality and it would be a shocking and devastating happening to the future of the work if he should not be able to bring it to a final conclusion.

It is wonderful of you to let us have your guesthouse. I am looking forward to it with great pleasure.

Most affectionately,

Margaret Sanger

PART III THE CONSERVATIVE RADICAL
39. Rules for a Life

The June 1953 meeting with McCormick and Pincus had been preceded by Sanger's usual breakneck travel schedule. Her health always an issue now,[1] Sanger never let it stand in her way, spending the summer of 1952 in McCormick's guest cottage in Santa Barbara, as she organized the 1952 Bombay conference for November, Bombay her final destination after stops at Honolulu, Japan (two weeks), Bangkok, Singapore, Ceylon, and Paris. During the winter of 1953 in Tucson, between trips to New York and Honolulu, Sanger was staying in close touch with McCormick. In Tucson, Sanger was helping her houseguest, Tamikki Ohmori, Shidzue Ishimoto Kato's stepdaughter, improve her English; and responding to questions by Lawrence Lader, who was writing Sanger's biography. By spring of '53, Sanger was ready to return to the East Coast, to see Grant in Mount Kisco (or at his summer place in Fisher's Island) and Juliet in Cornish, the Simonds in Stephney, and—Gregory Pincus and Katherine McCormick in Shrewsbury on June 8.[2]

On August 4, 1953 Sanger sailed from New York to attend the Fourth International Planned Parenthood Federation conference being held that month in Sweden. She was on board the SS *Stockholm* in the company of Harriet Pilpel, an attorney who began her practice as an associate to Morris Ernst, attorney on the One Package case. Pilpel dedicated her practice to reproductive rights and became Planned Parenthood's regular lawyer. In Sanger's company, Pilpel was another awed spectator of the fantastic fanfare that greeted Margaret on her arrival in Sweden and one of the audience who approvingly heard Sanger speak at the closing dinner of the Stockholm International Planned Parenthood conference.[3]

Pilpel could have heard that speech again, when it was aired on May 18,

1954. During the fifties, Edward R. Murrow, the popular radio newscaster, presented a Monday night series entitled "This I Believe." The series featured statements by "thinking useful people in all walks of life" who were asked to speak on the governing principles of their lives, and Margaret Sanger's thoughts were included. She was in good company; the following Monday, the statement of Dr. Charles W. Mayo, surgeon of the Mayo Clinic, was given.

The Manuscript

Sanger told her granddaughter always to work for something bigger than yourself. In Sanger's case, the bigger something was to make things better for women, and so Sanger's statement reflects that desire. As Sanger herself acknowledged, her desire and her work gave her own life great richness.

This I Believe[4]
May 18, 1954

This I believe, first of all: that all our basic convictions must be tested and transmuted in the crucible of experience—and sometimes the more bitter the experience, the more valid the purified belief.

As a child, one of a large family, I learned that the thing I did best was the thing I liked to do. This realization of doing and getting results was what I have later called an awakening consciousness.

There is an old Indian proverb which has inspired me in the work of my adult life. "Build thou beyond thyself, but first be sure that thou, thyself, be strong and healthy in body and mind." Yes, to build, to work, to plan to do something not for yourself, not for your own benefit, but "beyond thyself"—and when this idea permeates the mind, you begin to think in terms of a future. I began to think of a world beyond myself when I first took an interest in nursing the sick.

As a nurse I was in contact with the ill and the infirm. I knew something about the health and disease of bodies, but for a long time I was baffled at the tremendous personal problems of life, of marriage, of living, and of just being. Here indeed was a challenge to "build beyond thyself." But where was I to begin? I found the answer at every door. I began to believe there was something I could do toward increasing an understanding of these basic human problems. To build beyond myself I must first tap all inner resources of stamina, of courage, or resolution within myself. I was prepared to face opposition, even ridicule, denunciation. But I had also to prepare myself, in defense of these unpopular beliefs; I had to prepare myself to face courts and even prison. But I resolved to stand up, alone if necessary, against all the entrenched forces which opposed me.

I started my battle some forty years ago. The women and mothers whom I wanted to help also wanted to help me. They, too, wanted to build beyond the self, in creating healthy children and bringing them up in life to be happy and useful citizens. I believed it was my duty to place motherhood on a higher level than enslavement and accident. I was convinced we must care about people; we must reach out to help them in their despair.

For these beliefs I was denounced, arrested, I was in and out of police courts and higher courts, and indictments hung over my life for several years. But nothing could alter my beliefs. Because I saw these as truths, I stubbornly stuck to my convictions.

No matter what it may cost in health, in misunderstanding, in sacrifice, something had to be done, and I felt that I was called by the force of circumstances to do it. Because of my philosophy and my work, my life has been enriched and full. My interests have expanded from local conditions and needs to a world horizon, where peace on earth may be achieved when children are wanted before they are conceived. A new consciousness will take place; a new race will be born to bring peace on earth. This belief has withstood the crucible of my life's joyous struggle. It remains my basic belief today.

This I believe—at the end as at the beginning of my long crusade for the future of the human race.

PART III THE CONSERVATIVE RADICAL
40. Mainstream Acceptance

During Sanger's lifetime, the two nations whose governments officially supported birth control were India and Japan. Japan was the country especially dear to Sanger, for always she was welcomed enthusiastically whenever she set foot on its soil. The Japanese ties were made the more meaningful by Sanger's lifelong friendship with Shidzue Ishimoto Kato.

During World War II, thrust into jail for Dangerous Thoughts, her birth control activities forbidden, Shidzue divorced Baron Ishimoto and married Senator Kato Kanju; at the age of forty-eight she gave birth to their daughter, Taki. When the right of Japanese women to vote and hold office came in 1945, Shidzue Kato ran for office and after 1946, like her husband, she was a senator. She was active in the Japanese parliament for twenty years, working always for the rights of Japanese women, and it was she who brought Japan to accept, as the norm, the two-child family.

In 1954, on Sanger's second visit to Japan after World War II—she came also in 1952— Kato saw that Sanger was presented to the Emperor Hirohito and that she was invited to speak to the Japanese Diet (Senate). As the first foreigner to be so invited and, for a woman, it came as an extraordinary compliment to Sanger from that male-dominated society. During Sanger's 1954 trip, the Japanese birth control movement that Shidzue Kato had nurtured in Japan since 1920 culminated in the formation of the Family Planning Federation of Japan. Immediately, the Japanese Federation took on the job of hosting in Tokyo in the following year the Fifth International Conference of the International Planned Parenthood Federation; Sanger, as president of the IPPF, was heavily involved in the preparations.

The Tokyo conference of 1955 was a high point in Sanger's life and brought out the best of Japanese hospitality. The receptions, entertainment, and tours arranged for the IPPF delegates were exceptional events by any standards. At the conference itself, her good friend, Clarence Gamble, was awarded the splendid Margaret Sanger trophy, and Gregory Pincus, to the excitement of all, announced publicly the coming of The Pill.[1]

Returned to the States, the tributes of Japan and the success of the Tokyo conference did not fortify Sanger against the need for recognition that had been such a steady companion and a tonic for most of her working life. Away from Japan, Sanger faced somewhat less approval of her person (in America, for the most part, she might have been living in Colonial days with a scarlet letter on her breast). Many in her movement considered her ideas passé: Sanger was still talking about "defectives." At the Stockholm International Conference, she had said "Our institutions are full of people who are mental defectives, morons, unhealthy diseased people"[2]—rhetoric out of the twenties and thirties, when the United States, in the midst of the Depression, was convinced that a population of "feeble-minded," their care straining the already overburdened tax base, was fast growing. In 1950, with the word "sterilization" carrying the Nazi taint, as it would for so long after, Sanger had proposed a government bonus for any couple who, knowing themselves "defective," would accept voluntary sterilization.[3]

And just as John D. Rockefeller III and the Population Council would ignore her lifetime of practical experience in clinical application, limiting themselves to degree-carrying male scientists, so others at home preferred to ignore her. Sanger was, after all, only a practical nurse. The Murrow show and a *Readers' Digest* article were not the daily lectures and interviews and steady public appearances that had occupied so much of her life.

At the same time, during the late fifties and sixties when Sanger was personally receiving less attention—and before the American government decided to ignore the overpopulation issue—birth control was being noticed and overpopulation becoming a matter of public concern. As we see below, in 1956, Sanger even had her article published in that barometer of American general acceptance, the *Readers' Digest*.

Publicity of her causes roused then, as it does today, attacks on her personally. In 1957, when first asked to appear on the Mike Wallace show "to hear your views on the necessity of birth control," Sanger was warned that Wallace conducted the show "in a manner to entrap the interviewee" and she declined.[4] Wallace pursued Sanger until she accepted, then suddenly withdrew his invitation, frankly acknowledging and naming the two Roman Catholic priests who told him if "you put that Sanger woman on, we can't support you in the future."[5] Wallace never said why he changed his mind when he reinvited Sanger,[6] but it is not too difficult to guess why Sanger foolishly accepted. Accustomed to being in the public eye and relishing the prospect of a national television appearance, Sanger flew to New York. Once on the air, Mike Wallace had little interest in the necessity of birth control. Instead, he began a snide personal attack so patently prejudiced, it brought a letter from a Mike Wallace fan. Mrs. Helen Gorelick wrote,

> I was very disappointed and annoyed at the line of questioning. For one thing I felt there was too much time devoted to the Catholic view on the subject of Birth Control.[7]

With so much to say about her "views on the necessity of Birth Control," so many accomplishments to be discussed—the increased number of birth control clinics, the possibility of The Pill, the formation of the International Planned Parenthood Federation, the millions of women whose lives were saved or improved by being able to space their children—the interview was a disgrace to Wallace and an embarrassment to Sanger, made all the more disturbing because she did not realize how cruelly she was being used. Looking beyond the pettiness and discourtesy involved, the attempt by Wallace to show an old, ill woman as an immoral hedonist illustrated graphically how great is the underlying fear by the ruling class in general and by the hierarchy of male-governed religions in particular of a woman who dares to take control of her sexuality and who dares to encourage all women to do the same.

But if Wallace had failed in courtesy and Sanger in dignity, she enjoyed both on her many visits to Japan. On her last visit, the last of her seven trips, she traveled with her two Tucson granddaughters, Margaret and Nancy Sanger, who were most impressed at the extent of the celebrity their grandmother enjoyed away from her home country.

In Japan, Sanger received, as she had from nowhere else in the world, public affection and honor. The gratitude of Japan was made concrete in 1965, one year before her death, when the Japanese government bestowed upon Sanger one of Japan's greatest honors, the Third Class of the Order of the Precious Crown. Sanger felt so tied to Japan that in her appreciation, she wrote on a paper scrap, obviously meant as part of her will,

> In case of my death – I want to be cremated....The heart to go to Japan to be buried in Tokyo – any place the Govt or Health and Welfare Minister, together with Senator Shidzue Kato wish to have it buried, as it is or in ashes – This in gratitude to the Japanese people & Govt—The only country in the world who have officially recognized me & the BC work.[8]

If the physical heart never went to Japan—which turned out to be impossible because of involved laws and regulations—Sanger's overarching spirit did, reaching out to embrace and thank a country that so cared for her.[9]

The Manuscript

At the end of World War II, the baby boom came to Japan, as it had to the rest of the world. But in Japan, contraceptives were scarce, and Japanese women, who were beginning to experience their sense of independence, were forced to turn to abortion, legal in Japan, as a means of birth control. So high was the abortion rate, that Shidzue Kato invited Sanger to come to Japan to promote birth control over abortion.

But in 1949, Japan was still under allied military occupation with General Douglas MacArthur as its supreme commander. For whatever his reasons, MacArthur decided that a visit by Margaret Sanger was not in Japan's best interests, and though negotiations dragged on for months and the invitation was clearly one extended by Japan itself, MacArthur refused to allow Sanger to enter Japan.[10] Only in 1952, after MacArthur had been fired for insubordination and allied occupying forces had left Japan, and, only after a lengthy wait for a visa (Sanger in 1952 still being regarded as a suspicious radical by the FBI) was Sanger able to accept Kato's invitation. Her visit in 1952 did much to encourage the people's demand for government support of contraception, eventually reducing the rate of abortion.

Asia Discovers Birth Control [11]
Reader's Digest, May 1956

When, in 1922, I lectured in Japan as a guest of the Kaizo publishing house, the Imperial Government forbade me to advocate birth control publicly. To do so was a violation of the Dangerous Thoughts Law. But 32 years later, in 1954, I was invited to address the Upper House Welfare Committee on efficient methods of combating overpopulation, and last year the Fifth Conference of the International Planned Parenthood Federation was held in Tokyo. As president of the Federation, I was presented to the Emperor as a benefactor of humanity!

These personal experiences show how Japan has faced up to the challenge of overpopulation. And there is encouraging evidence of similar concern in the rest of Asia, where more than half of the human race is crowded upon about one sixth of its land area and the yearly increase is about 34 million. Dr. E. Stuart Kirby of Hong Kong University, an authority on the demography of the Eastern Hemisphere, has said, "The P-bomb (population bomb) is a greater threat to the world than is the A-bomb or the H-bomb."

In 1922 the population of Japan was estimated at 61 million. By 1945, despite the war, it had grown to 72 million, and today it is estimated at 89 million. So desperate had the population problem become by 1948 that a Eugenic Protection Law was enacted, permitting the termination of any pregnancy [that] could "seriously injure the health of the mother [due] to physical or economic conditions." As a result, the Ministry of Health and Welfare estimates that there are now over one million abortions a year—about one induced abortion for every live birth.

I have always condemned abortion as dangerous and inhuman. But what better method could I offer to curb population, Japanese officials asked me in 1954. I replied that Japan could train its 20,000 midwives to instruct married couples in practical and hygienic methods of contraception; for this service they should receive the same compensation as they do to deliver an infant. With this group as the nucleus for a policy of sex education, I pointed out, Japan in a generation or two might lead the world in creating a fit population based upon parenthood by choice and not by chance.

Apparently this advice was not without influence. Shortly thereafter, the advisory council on population problems of the Ministry of Health and Welfare made a series of recommendations to the government. Among other things it proposed that the official health services provide birth control facilities; that medical schools include family planning in their curriculum; that doctors called upon to induce an abortion be required to give the woman information about birth control for the future; and that national wage and taxation policies should avoid "encouraging large families."

Gradually but surely the abhorrent abortion policy will thus be replaced by hygienic contraceptive techniques. The trend will meet with little opposition, since almost no Japanese religious groups are opposed to birth control.

In China and India the situation is also acute. China's population of some 600 million exceeds that of Europe (including European Russia), Africa, Australia, and a large section of the Western Hemisphere put together. Though not officially proclaimed, the importance of birth control is recognized even today in Communist China. Instructions on contraceptive methods are today being published in the Communist press.

India, whose population grows by five million annually, has assumed a position of world leadership in the movement for planned parenthood. Its five-year plan of 1951 included provisions for the reduction of the rate of population growth through contraception. Under the plan, family limitation has now become an integral part of the government health services, with eight million dollars currently allocated to the work. More than 165 clinics or family planning centers have already been started, in addition to several hundred centers under army auspices. The Health Minister, Raj Kumari Amarit Kaur, is supporting family planning work wholeheartedly, and has agreed to supply contraceptives free to the poor.

India is also engaged in ambitious efforts to increase food production to meet the needs of its growing population. But there as elsewhere such efforts will be doomed to failure unless there is population control.

Already one half of the inhabitants of our planet subsist on a woefully inadequate diet. To ensure bare adequacy, available foodstuffs would have to be increased 25 per cent. Recently, a population expert asserted that "efforts to increase the production of food cannot alone suffice to achieve any steady or rapid rise in nutrition levels. A firm control of the number of births is indisputably necessary."

It seems unbelievable that in an age when we have harnessed the atom we still have not perfected a simple method for the control of human fertility. But research now under way in many parts of the world will surely result in important discoveries. These may provide the means not only of curbing the quantity of the world's population but of changing its quality to give an upward and onward lift to human dignity and freedom.

It may be that the East, which has most to gain from such a development, will lead the way.

41. The International Planned Parenthood Federation

T he two days of February 14 and 15, 1959, were surely two of the most wonderful days of Margaret Sanger's life, two days in which she received open, wholehearted acknowledgement of her life's work. Much against the advice of physicians, family, and friends, Sanger insisted on attending the Sixth International Conference on Planned Parenthood convening February 12 to 15 in New Delhi. It was well worth her effort.

There, after she officially retired as president, she heard herself pronounced founder and president emeritus of the International Planned Parenthood Federation. During the conference, she was further elated to hear the government of India support birth control with hard cash: Prime Minister Nehru announced a pledge of ten million dollars in public health monies for family planning in India—a long-sought pledge. Then, in "an historical event in my life and joyous," amid the cheers of 750 delegates from twenty-eight nations, Sanger was warmly and publicly greeted by Nehru, who personally escorted her to the podium, hundreds of flashbulbs and cameramen recording the occasion.[1] It was the climax of a lifetime of dedication and the recognition she deserved.[2] The photos and story were run in newspapers all over the world.

The next day, February 15, Gregory Pincus dedicated his report on completed field trials of The Pill to Sanger. While celebrating this event, so much her doing, she was presented with "Our Margaret Sanger," a two-volume collection of rich, loving reminiscences, contributions from eighty-two longtime friends and workers, which is, to this day, a treasure trove of Margaret Sanger lore.[3]

The previous decade had included for Sanger much hard work made the more arduous by indifference from the field and her own erratic mental and physical stamina. In the summer of 1949, Sanger had had her first heart attack, and from that point on, she was increasingly fragile. Many close to her were critically ill—her sister Ethel had had a heart attack, Edith How-Martyn a stroke—and, in the case of Hugh de Selincourt, were dying.[4] For a time, Sanger became drug dependent, owing to a prescription of Demerol by Stuart, who much to his great distress learned later that he had been misinformed on use of the drug. And alone too much, Margaret turned to drinking heavily.[5]

Meanwhile, since the days of *The Woman Rebel,* Sanger and the Malthusian League had been talking about overpopulation and its consequences, and now the fifties, goosed by Hugh Moore's *The Population Bomb* pamphlet, were just beginning to think overpopulation might be an issue of urgency.[6] The sixties was sure of it. The International Union for Scientific Study of Population, which had emerged from Sanger's 1927 Geneva Population Conference, pointed out specifically how and why the oncoming population explosion would be a problem for the world. The United Nations, which should have been able to act on the problem, was prevented from doing so by a coalition of the Communist bloc, Muslim extremists, and the Roman Catholic Church.

Sanger saw that action would have to come from the private sphere. It had, after all, been Sanger, a woman without a Rockefeller fortune, who virtually alone, with much of the funding coming from Noah Slee (Slee lost much of his money during the Depression and prior to that, even though a millionaire, was never in the Rockefeller league), had organized and pulled off in 1927 in Geneva the First World Population Conference. It was Sanger who had set up the Birth Control Information Centre in London, forerunner to the IPPF, from—amazingly—leftover Geneva funds and who raised additional funds to enable the center to continue under How-Martyn for the next seven years. Sanger it was whose personal loan made possible the Zurich Seventh International Birth Control Conference in 1930.[7]

And it was Sanger who after attending Ottesen-Jensen's family planning conference in Stockholm in 1946 went immediately to London to begin organization of a follow-up conference, pledging five thousand dollars from the anticipated sale of her Tucson house to cover startup expenses, and, once in New York, coaxed additional monies from John D. Rockfeller III, thus ensuring that the International Congress on Population and World Resources was held in Cheltenham, England, in 1948.[8]

At the Cheltenham conference, Sanger proposed formation of an International Committee on Planned Parenthood (ICPP). She proposed it, and again, she raised most of the monies, donating her Lasker prize, to support it.[9] The ICPP was a provisional organization, headquartered in London, involving representative groups from England, the Netherlands, and Sweden, and Planned Parenthood Federation of America and Margaret Sanger Research Bureau from America.[10] Eventually, the ICPP worked with some twenty countries throughout the world, disseminating information, testing contraceptives, and assisting in family planning clinics.[11]

Working through the ICPP, Sanger took the better part of a year to organize the 1952 Third International Conference on Planned Parenthood in Bombay, India, first bringing in names of international repute that would entice worldwide attendance, then setting up the program, organizing delegates, inveigling sponsors, delegating volunteer responsibilities, securing travel grants.[12] At the Bombay conference, the ICPP officially became the International Planned Parenthood Federation (IPPF), with India, Hong Kong, Singapore, and West Germany joining the original four ICPP members to become the founders and with Japan named an associate member. By 1961, the IPPF had thirty-two members.[13]

Sanger attended and contributed to and worked to fund all three conferences that followed: the 1953 Fourth Conference in Stockholm, Sweden; the 1955 Fifth Conference in Tokyo, Japan; and the sixth in 1959 in New Delhi, where she formally stepped down to deserved accolades.

Said Dorothy Brush, whose Brush Foundation in Cleveland, Ohio, was a major funder of Sanger's projects, recalling the Bombay and the later conferences, "It would be impossible to define Mrs. Sanger's work in this period. Almost single-handedly, she created this conference, and those that followed, out of nothing but willpower. She was unyielding, relentless, and egotistical in a way that was something to behold."[14]

Speaking at the 1953 Stockholm conference, Sanger had described the same old opposition with the same old fighting spirit.

And just before I left the States this year, I was told that the Proceedings of the Bombay Conference had been held up in Washington. Three hundred copies of the Report of the Proceedings, containing the papers of scientists and other distinguished men and women, who had attended that Conference...but there were some papers on contraception and its techniques. We'll have a wonderful fight when we get back to free those books."[15]

At the 1955 Tokyo meeting, with delegates from fifteen countries. Sanger warned,

During the last 300 years global population has shot from five hundred million to two billion five-hundred million....In spite of our great technical progress, at least two thirds of the world's people at the present time cannot obtain enough calories to maintain normal standards of health and efficiency.[16]

The Tokyo delegates, they at least sensitive to the evils attendant on cataclysmic population growth, passed a formal resolution recommending that the World Health Organization encourage family spacing and education for responsible parenthood.[17]

While the conferences convened and reconvened throughout the fifties, Clarence Gamble was working internationally, distributing contraceptives and seeding birth control clinics all over the world, giving practical visibility to Sanger's political toil.[18] Since 1933, he had been sending birth control information and contraceptives to Christian missionaries in the Far East and after 1949 small sums, which grew steadily larger, to projects in Japan.[19] On September 28, 1953, Gamble wrote to the International Planned Parenthood Federation in London,

> Let me tell you briefly of our work. In Lahore...the Family Planning Association of Pakistan was formed....In Colombo, enthused by Mrs. Sanger's recent visit, the Family Planning Association of Ceylon [was formed]....In Thailand, again building on Mrs. Sanger's recent inspiration, a strong nucleus of a group was formed....In Singapore...the establishment of that active Association of contraceptive groups.[20]

The next day, Gamble wrote another letter to London, which hinted at the extent of his reach:

> My son, Richard, and I are planning to return early in 1954 to Asia to continue the birth control work begun there last winter....It is our plan to visit Pakistan, Ceylon, Burma, Thailand, Singapore, Indonesia, Hong Kong, Taiwan, and Japan....In India it will be important to visit the places where simple contraceptive methods are being tested.[21]

An inexpensive contraceptive method that appeared in 1961 was the IUD, the Lippes loop.[22] Gamble immediately began sending these abroad. By the end of 1963, Gamble was sending IUDs to, and receiving reports from, doctors in twenty countries; by 1965 he was supplying 340 doctors in sixty-nine countries. [23] The well-funded Population Council was distributing loops in only three countries. When Gamble died, 504 doctors in seventy-five countries were receiving loops.[24] His visible legacy, the complement of Sanger's vision, lives to this day throughout the world wherever women know about and use birth control.

But in 1966, the IPPF wanted further testing of the loops. Struggling to assert itself, it was embarrassed by Gamble. He was considered impossible to work with; he would not wait for organizational approval.[25] In like fashion, Sanger was regarded as impossible. Sanger was regarded as old and out of touch, with outmoded ideas. She insisted on being informed about what was going on, and then, like Gamble, she went ahead and did things without consulting anyone. When Sanger appealed to the John D. Rockefeller III for travel grants to the 1955 Tokyo conference, he allowed $22,000 as a gesture of kindly goodwill.[26]

During the fifties, John D. Rockefeller III had become concerned about overpopulation, but brother Nelson Rockefeller was running for office, and the Rockefellers did not want to lose the political support of the Catholic hierarchy for Nelson's election. In 1952, Rockefeller III convened at Williamsburg, Virginia, a group of distinguished academics and scientists, white prestigious males, who saw the importance of founding an avowedly scientific organization for research into the population issue.

Bill Vogt, then with Planned Parenthood and the one member with practical experience, suggested that possibly research and scholarship were not the entire answer to the population problem. His doubts were ignored, and the rest of the convocation then dedicated their Population Council to research "at a high level of competence and public esteem." Within three years, the Population Council spent more than $500,000 on research, studies, investigations, and piles of paper.[27] Probably, no one missed the $22,000 given to Margaret Sanger, a woman who wanted merely to help women.[28]

In 2003, the International Planned Parenthood Federation surely fulfills Margaret Sanger's vision of an organization of international scope. Six regional offices unite the federation, linking family planning associations in more than 180 countries. Worldwide, the federation works to provide sexual health care and family planning, always respectful of individual culture, women's rights, and local mores. The Web site for the IPPF is elaborate, extensive, complicated, and cutting edge. Nowhere is Margaret Sanger's name mentioned.[29]

The Manuscript

At the Third International Conference in Bombay, India, in 1952, Sanger spoke on the humanity of family planning, as birth control was now termed. It was a subject dear to her heart, one she had spoken on all her life.

She spoke of the necessity of breaking down prejudice over sterilization, a term that since the Nazis has been viewed with repulsion. Could she have seen that sterilization would become the preferred method of birth control in the twenty-first century? She spoke against abortion as a means of birth control and against war as a way of life. Her message was much the

Young Margaret Higgins, age 16,
December 1899.

William (Bill) Sanger.

Stuart, Peggy, and Grant Sanger, Paris 1913.

Publicity photo taken
after the death of Peggy,
of Margaret Sanger with
Stuart and Grant, 1916.

Juliet Rublee, circa 1920.

Shidzue Ishimoto Kato, circa 1930.

Margaret Sanger in the U.S. Senate, May 19, 1932.

Pearl Buck, Margaret Sanger, Katherine Houghton Hepburn at a dinner, February 1935.

Mahatma Gandhi with Margaret Sanger at Gandhi's ashram, Wardha, India, December 1935.

Margaret Sanger in the '30s.

Margaret Sanger with Stuart's daughters, Nancy and Margaret Sanger, Tucson, Arizona, 1945.

Margaret Sanger receiving honorary LL.D. at Smith College, Northampton, Massachusetts, 1949

J. Noah H. Slee, 1942.

Dr. Clarence James Gamble, circa 1959.

Margaret Sanger with relatives of Shidzue Ishimoto Kato, Tokyo, Japan, 1951.

Margaret Sanger in the '50s.

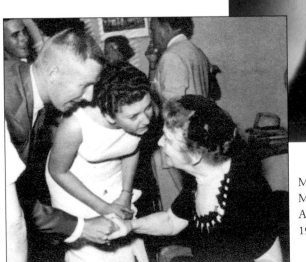

Margaret Sanger Lampe, her friend, and Margaret Sanger at Family Planning Association gathering, Hong Kong, June 2 1959.

Jawaharlal Nehru and Margaret Sanger, International Conference on Planned Parenthood, New Delhi, India, 1959.

same as it had been all her life, just as meaningful, just as reasonable, just as difficult to implement.

The Humanity of Family Planning
Address, Third International Conference on Planned Parenthood
Bombay, India, November 25, 1952[30]

We have seen during the past decade, that those for and those against birth control or the control of the size of the family live in different mental climates. We must realize psychologically that ignorance attracts ignorance, faith attracts faith, intelligence attracts intelligence. We know, too, from experience, that no reasonable discussion is possible with minds still focused in the dark ages, where scientific advances are ignored. We cannot wait for these minds to evolve as they eventually do but we must go ahead with all the courage and understanding we possess to overcome their prejudices in the interests of life, liberty, and the pursuit of happiness.

My first visit to India was from November 1935 to March 1936. I came at the invitation of the All-India Women's Conference, requesting me to address their Congress in Travancore. Arrangements had been made for me to visit your great leader and, to many, the world's greatest living Saint—Mahatma Gandhi—at Wardha. I spent three days there as a guest of the Mahatma's. Needless to say these three days *were not ever* to be forgotten *or* paralleled in human experience. I could spend all the time allotted to me this evening relating our conversation—enough for me to say that neither of us convinced the other that we were wrong. Gandhi's conclusions, however, were interesting and had already been given publicity. He said that India was then (in 1935) overpopulated—"It was this condition of overpopulation that enslaved her"—that four children should be the limit born to a couple—after that, *separation or continence.* I am not going into the birth and death rates of that period. The leaders of India are aware of a population problem and will doubtless attempt in every way to solve it.

Every one who thinks will realize that people must and should be fed. When too many people occupy the land and use up its resources faster than they can be replaced, these problems begin—and often increase at a faster rate than the solution to solve them. This is the condition in many countries today and all the "ifs" and "buts" do not solve the immediate problem of feeding, clothing, and sheltering the vast populations constantly increasing all over the world.

The vast essential problem of almost all nations today, including political problems, could be greatly alleviated by the national encouragement and practice of birth control. Nearly every country is overtaxed to pay for enormous armament. The cry for babies is the cry for armament, the cry for war. There is also the tremendous expense of care of defective mentalities and the army of delinquents. There is also the problem of poverty, of child labor, of unemployment, of crime and enormous maintenance of prisons, and asylums; the standards of public education with the demands of more and more from the tax-payer; demands to support charities, community chests, Red Cross, all of these mount year by year in nearly every country in the world. Everyone who has studied the advance of science and of technical progress is aware that machinery in all industrial pursuits can take the place of manpower, that more can be produced with less hours and fewer men, so that there is not the need of vast populations for industry as in former years.

As population increases in any given territory, it encroaches upon all natural resources—forests, grasslands, soil fertility, levels and water sheds. The increasing population threatens not only the food, clothing and shelter of the present living people, but the living standards of the present population lower as naturally as the night follows the day. Cultural, educational and scientific advances remain in the background or are relegated to the past.

Sir George Sansome in a recent B.B.C. broadcast said that he was alarmed by the magnitude of the problems of population throughout Japan and India where he had recently traveled.[31] He said, "The Japanese, the first in Asia to use modern technology for the increase of their resources, have not solved it. Their population has grown faster than the means for its support and their economic situation gives cause for anxiety."

While it is right to extend all possible means of science to cultivate land as a means of food supply, it is also right to use intelligence and apply it to the individual family and its responsibility of adding numbers to the already overcrowded land. Family limitation is the intelligent approach to problems of housing, of marriage, of education, of medical care, of high taxes as Governments take over the philanthropic attitude toward people too poor to provide for themselves and of the problem of War or Peace.

In World War II, over twenty-one million young men were killed in battle; fifteen to twenty million women, children and old people killed in air raids; thirty million wounded, mutilated, or incapacitated for work; forty-five million people evacuated, deported or interned; thirty million homes reduced to ashes; one hundred and fifty million people left without shelter, prey to famine and disease. Up to 1946, the Second World War cost three times as much as the First. This money could have provided a $30,000 house, $12,000 worth of furniture and $6,000 cash present to every family in the United States, Canada, Australia, Britain, France, Germany, Ireland, the Soviet Union, and Belgium. In addition, every town of over 200,000 inhabitants could have been given a cash donation of $75,000,000 for libraries, $75,000,000 for schools, $75,000,000 for hospitals. These are the actual sordid facts of war.

We must break down prejudices against sterilization—we might enlighten and educate our people as to its harmlessness.

Abortions break down the health of the mother without preventing renewed pregnancy at an early date. Abortions are the very worst way to prevent increase in the population. Let us make an end to all this suffering, waste, enfeeblement and despair.

Anyone who has a free mind and the welfare of the nation at heart will recognize that one single principle should stand *first* and *foremost in the solving* of these problems, which is birth control. This subject concerns every one of us in its most intimate aspects, while in its more remote consequences it affects the very life of every man, woman and child of the nation, as well as the future of the race.

The first object in population control is to achieve cultural progress rather than military advance.

Second—research institutions to be established by scientists classifying basic factors in eliminating harmful dysgenic births in the nation.

Third—cooperation in educating the population to consider the cultural qualities of offspring and efface the egotistic desire to perpetuate the self in offspring.

Basic principles of the Planned Parenthood movement will help to achieve these results, as follows:

1. Any adult having a transmissible or hereditary disease should not have children. Marriage may be contemplated, but only if the person submits willingly to sterilization as a safeguard against propagating offspring carrying such diseases.
2. Women afflicted with temporary diseases, where cure is retarded because of pregnancy, should practise contraception until cured. Tuberculosis, heart disease, kidney disease, goiter, and other ailments not transmissible, put a definite strain on a woman's health when conception has taken place.
3. No more children when parents, though showing no affliction themselves, have given birth to offspring with mental and nervous disease— morons, cleft palate, Mongolian idiots. Somewhere in the heredity there is the cause of these conditions.
4. Spacing of children in a family where husband and wife are in good health should be from two to three years. If the family is planned for four children, the first two could be a year or 18 months apart. Then a spacing of two years before another pregnancy is contemplated. Two more children 18 months apart bring both groups together with fair spacing, to consider the mother's health, the father's earning capacity, and the standards of living the parents are ambitious to maintain.

5. Early marriage can be helpful to young people with the postponement of parenthood. Twenty-two years is a good age for a woman to bear her first child. Children born of young mothers in the teen ages are more frequently neglected. Infant mortality is highest where mothers are under twenty-two years of age.

6. Economic conditions should be seriously considered. Certainly the father whose wage-earning power can properly feed, house and educate three, even four children, should not have eight, ten or twelve children. Records for delinquency of children in poor, large families fill the courts, jails and penitentiaries.

7. Parenthood should be considered a privilege, not a right. It should be considered an assignment, and those about to, or desiring to be parents should be examined physically and mentally as to their responsibility and knowledge of the care of infants. There should be compulsory education by the State for parents to be able to cope with problem children and the changes occurring yearly in childhood and puberty.

In voicing the above principles it is well to realize that responsibilities are twofold. First, the individual couple, who have the intelligence, insight and wisdom to plan the number of children desired who can be cared for, can be considered the cultural group in every country. Second, there is the responsibility of our officials in public health and social welfare. It should be their duty to the State, to the public and to our future civilization to see that those who do not have the individual initiative and intelligence to plan and control the size of their families should be assisted, guided and directed in every way to eliminate the undesirable offspring, who usually contribute nothing to our civilization but use up the energy and resources of the world.

42. Overpopulation and the Draper Report

Those who deride overpopulation as a "myth" fall into the earth-is-flat category. This is not the place for a treatise on deforestation, global warming, for facing the prospect of an America with an additional two hundred million people by midcentury, or for noting that the Yellow River Channel in China, which waters a fifth of China's wheat and a seventh of its corn, had 226 dry days in 1997.[1]

Let us merely say that during the twentieth century the population of our planet quadrupled. Which would have been fine if the infrastructure could have absorbed the new millions, if they had had waiting for them jobs and education and water and good food and creature comforts. But this did not happen.

In Latin America, at the end of the 1990s, eleven million more lived in poverty than at the beginning of the decade.[2] The Philippines, with the third highest fertility rate in the world, more than doubled their population from slightly more than thirty-six million in 1970 to approximately eighty million in 2002.[3] In 2003, 40 percent of the Filipinos live their entire lives in temporary shelters, almost a third have no access to sanitation, while 70 percent of those who live in rural areas own no land.[4] As the world population grows—and grows—the rich are getting richer, the poor more poor, and for all, the supply of fresh water and options are dwindling.[5]

More alarming than the increase in hard numbers is the composition of those numbers. The nonspacing of children and the lowered rate of child mortality has unbalanced population makeup, particularly in the developing world where more than four fifths of the world live and where the population increase has been most rapid. Thus, the group under the age of twenty-five is disproportionate to its society and the infrastructure unable to expand sufficiently to offer education and opportunity to young people at a time when they are their most energetic and idealistic, and young men, in particular, their most bellicose.[6]

Such large numbers of young, aggressive males are of particular concern. Their group has been referred to as "rogue males" because males between the ages of fifteen to twenty-nine are historically identified as those responsible for civil uprisings and revolutions.[7] Yet more disturbing is the fact that the numbers of this already disproportionate group of young males have been augmented by prebirth technology and the abortion of female fetuses. In China, for instance, where the male child is preferred, in the year 2002, there were 116.9 males for every 100 females, with that figure reaching as high as 135 males in some provinces, against the norm of 105 to 107 male births to 100 female.[8]

Unemployed and underemployed rouge males, living primarily in the developing world where options are already limited, own the potential to brew an incendiary mix of unrest that threatens their own and other nations, heightening the potential for internecine conflict over turf and limited resources and making themselves available for national acts of aggression against outsiders.

This aspect of world population growth had yet not shown its face in 1958, when then-President Eisenhower wrote General William H. Draper, asking him to leave the private sector for renewed government service. Draper was being asked to chair a panel, the President's Committee to Study the United States Military Assistance Programmes, and the panel was to evaluate the effectiveness of United States aid and advise on its best use to ensure American security.

General Draper had an impeccable reputation. During his career, he had served under generals George C. Marshall, Lucius Clay, Dwight Eisenhower, and Douglas MacArthur with distinction. As Special Representative of the President of the United States in Europe, responsible for efficient operation of the Atlantic Alliance during 1952 and 1953, Draper received praise and plaudits for a job well done.[9] The nine other individuals comprising his committee were men with impressive government experience.[10]

In the summer of 1959, Eisenhower received the completed Draper Report. The committee had had no trouble identifying future threats to American security nor suggesting prompt remedies. American foreign aid was meant to improve the lot of the individual, but American economic aid was being undercut by runaway population growth. Despite the infusion of American dollars, world poverty was increasing and living standards decreasing. There could be no greater threat to American security or world peace than hungry, dissatisfied populations, and on that basis, the Draper Report recommended that the United States "through its aid program give help to population programs of foreign governments, on their request."[11] This recommendation—as Margaret Sanger mentions below and as Draper noted—was immediately attacked by the Roman Catholic bishops.[12]

Eisenhower promptly decided population control was a religious issue and none of America's business. Although Eisenhower did not act on the recommendations of the Report, those who felt that population control was America's business found in the Draper Report a strong moral support for their position, and population control programs were developed in the State Department and in the Agency for International Development.

Four years later, in 1963, Eisenhower reversed himself, stating, "The population explosion is the world's most critical problem" and accepted the position, along with ex-president Harry S. Truman, as honorary Co-Chair of the Planned Parenthood Fundraising Campaign. Meanwhile in these four years 369,873,000 people had been added to the planet—the equivalent of 1,850 large cities.[13] Those falling into the lowest one fifth of the world's income group in those cities, most of whom would be women and children, were partaking of the 1.4 percent of the world's income.

The Manuscript

Six years before her death in 1966, the *New York Times* published this letter from Margaret Sanger, who, as she had all her life, was protesting the short-sighted policies of a government that refused to acknowledge the importance of birth control, the dignity of women, and the dangers of overpopulation.

Speaking in the year of her death, Martin Luther King might have been speaking for Sanger, when he stated, "Unlike the plagues of the dark ages or contemporary diseases we do not yet understand, the modern plague of overpopulation is soluble by means we have discovered and with resources we possess. What is lacking is not the sufficient knowledge of the solution, but the universal consciousness of the gravity of the problem and the education of the billions of people who are its victims."[14]

Letter to the *New York Times*[15]
January 3, 1960

To the Editor of the *New York Times*:

Birth control, family planning, and population limitation are most important in any effort to bring real peace in the world. Less population will bring less war. Fewer people means more peace. Population planning through Government health and welfare departments will both improve the health, welfare, and happiness of children, mothers, and families and provide the essential foundations for world peace.

Leaders of Asian nations which I visited this year have learned this lesson. They are acting on this belief. Government officials, as well as voluntary agencies, scientists, teachers, and preachers are responding to the message about birth control which I took to them twenty-five years ago. Prime Minister Nehru of India and Premier Kishi of Japan are in the forefront of this leadership toward peace through birth control.[16]

Expenditures by India

India alone has budgeted and appropriated for this program the amount in rupees equal to 10,000,000 United States dollars in the present five-year plan. No fewer than six times, the Indian Government officials have indicated and suggested to our country that aid from us in this program would be most welcome.

Our United States was struggling along behind, finally coming to realize that population planning must be part of our Government policy. The Draper Report recommended to President Eisenhower that the United States as a matter of Government foreign policy should help other nations which request such aid.

Then a few dozen Roman Catholic Cardinals, Archbishops, and Bishops gathered and proclaimed an edict to the effect that the United States Government cannot give such recommended aid.

President Eisenhower embarked on his world-wide junket, announced to promote peace. Before he departed, he crippled his entire project by stating that birth control is "simply none of the Government's business." He says it is a religious matter. How the President came to hold such an opinion is open to analysis and study.

The President's short comments about birth control do not state the problem fairly and are far short of being well-informed about the path toward world peace today. The fact is that Government health departments are active in such population programs which the President denies to them. They are giving funds, spreading advice, and conducting research to wipe out epidemic and other killing diseases.

In so acting without attending to the population-balancing factor of birth control, our Government is increasing the population pressures against peace and bringing ever closer the population "explosion" and World War III.

Effective Balance

Clear-headed thinkers of impartial scientific outlook have realized that such Government policies of increasing population by reducing the death rate must be balanced sensibly by practices reducing the birth rate.

A majority of the people in the United States hope that our country and our Government will give emergency aid to the countries in need who ask our assistance, including birth control information, family planning advice, and population research assistance. Only a minority oppose this plan for world peace. The short-sightedness of the Roman Catholic hierarchy in this country shows in their bold assault upon the Draper committee's report about a medical and welfare project for the well-being of the entire world.

Most Roman Catholic Church members do not fight the program of birth control. The records show that those members use this path to planned, wanted happy children and better families, as well as world peace, just as much as do Protestants, Jews, and persons of no religion. They, of course, use in some cases the official Roman Catholic Pope-approved method of (unreliable) "safe-period" or so-called "rhythm." But, in addition, they quite frequently use the same, better methods that other family planners use, labeled by the Pope, "artificial means" of birth control.

This dogmatic attitude about their special religious belief as controlling their personal and official conduct through life is all right for Roman Catholics in the United States, but their edicts and bulls should not be allowed to stifle the basic American freedom of people who are not adherents to the Roman faith.

Today, our United States Government needs to listen to the voice of a majority of its voters. We believe the majority want proper medical care and aid to be given the sick, undernourished, troubled people—children, mothers, and families everywhere in the world. Birth control and contraceptive practices are a medically recognized part of current ethical healing.

The majority of this nation sincerely hope the President will revise his statement upon the basis of more information than he had at hand when he announced this unfortunate position for our Government.

Margaret Sanger
Tucson, Ariz.
December 28, 1959

PART III THE CONSERVATIVE RADICAL
Finis and Epilogue

In the end, she grew forgetful. Servants and hangers-on began stealing from her, and people used her. In 1961, Margaret became bedridden, and in 1962 Stuart arranged for care in a private nursing home in Tucson. These were difficult days in the nursing home, difficult for Margaret, difficult for her nurses. She went through any number of nurses. They left in tears or, finding Margaret impossible, just left. Stuart—or if Stuart was out of town, his medical partner—stopped by regularly to go through the mail and hire new nurses.

The body was worn out, and the mind was tired. Certainly body and mind had been enjoyed and explored and pushed to the utmost. But if the body was tired and the mind befuddled, the spirit lingered. How she hung on to life! Such tenacity, there in the nursing home, no longer working for something "bigger than yourself." Such a life—a life that sparkled with energy and light. Now, cut off from the richness of her life—the travel, the heart-to-heart talks with Juliet, the sweet love of Bill Sanger, the children, the lovers, the sights, the rush of the confrontation, the satisfaction of acclaim, vacations in Europe with the generous Noah Slee—no wonder she did not want to let go.

But finally she did, sleeping quietly, around noon, on September 6, 1966, eight days before her eighty-seventh birthday.[1] "H.G. Wells said I was the greatest woman in the world," she had written to her granddaughter Anne on a last visit. And so she was. Margaret Sanger, a woman who had envisioned change for half of the world's population, was surely the greatest woman in the world.

★ ★ ★

And what of Margaret Sanger's legacy?

Throughout her life, Margaret Sanger waged a lonely and unacknowledged battle against conservative forces that would permanently subjugate women. The force most fiercely conservative in the West was and is that of the Vatican, and the extent to which the Roman Catholic hierarchy would attempt to impose their views on the United States non-Catholic population came to general public notice as early as 1921 with the Town Hall raid. The steady assault by the Roman Catholic hierarchy on a woman's right to control her fertility and on Margaret Sanger as the figurehead for that right has never lessened.

Within a decade after the death of Margaret Sanger, the Roman Catholic hierarchy intensified their assault on Margaret Sanger the individual and on the democratic processes of the United States. The passage of *Roe v. Wade* was met by deep pockets, the dedicated determination to pass a Constitutional amendment that outlaws abortion, and a new rhetoric, in which the need for freely available contraception and the dangers of overpopulation have been deliberately subsumed by the Vatican and its New Right subsidiaries into a sentimental and vicious debate over abortion. Through an ongoing public education effort, an unaware and sentimental public has been adroitly manipulated, the rights of the mother and the symbiotic status of the unborn child ignored, and the developing fetus, even as a collection of undifferentiated cells, has become a TV-perfect "baby"—this tactic to be recognized for what it is: a prelude to enforced motherhood.[2] In this deliberate campaign of disinformation, Sanger is branded "the abortionist" to conform to the new depths to which that word has been consigned—despite her writings that repeatedly decry abortion—and coupled with Hitler and the enforced sterilization of Eugenics on the web and by a compliant press, which claims that it is practicing religious tolerance.

The Draper Report in 1959, the Report of the Rockefeller Commission in 1972, and the National Security Study Memorandum 200 in 1974 all proposed positive steps for American leadership to take in regard to population and family planning nationally and internationally, steps that would have worked to ensure women the right to control their fertility and to minimize the population explosion. However, the position set out by the Vatican in the *Humanae Vitae* of 1968, which is alterably opposed to contraception and abortion, increasingly permeates United States government policy.

Had the recommendations of the 1972 Rockefeller Report and the 1974 National Security Study Memorandum 200 been fully implemented, world population might well stand at five billion in 2003 rather than an actual 6.2 billion, and the unspeakable poverty that marks much of South America, the Philippines, along with the Sub-Saharan Africa and the Middle East where Muslim fundamentalists hold values and power similar to that of the Vatican, would not exist.

In 2003, United States Government policy ignores the need for a population program for the American people, even as United States population is predicted to increase by more than 200,000,000 by 2050, raising United States population levels by more than fifty percent. Concurrently, federal spending on contraceptive services has fallen by sixty-five percent since 1980, while the United States has one of the highest rates of unintended and teen pregnancies among Western nations.[3] In our hungry and already overcrowded world, a world in which renewable as well as non-renewable resources are being severely strained, a world in which the population of the planet could double by 2050, the suffering borne by the women who are giving birth and attempting to care for these teeming millions is seldom discussed.[4]

As Margaret Sanger insists, the decision to bear a child is a woman's decision. The travail may be lessened with modern Western medicine, but the outcome of a pregnancy is never certain—for mother or child—and in the developing world even less so. How dare an arrogant state or pietistic religionists interfere with a woman's right to her life?

And again we ask, what of Margaret Sanger's legacy?

In 2003, sixty-two percent of the world's married women use birth control.[5] In the face of dire population statistics that predict virtual destruction of our planet through overbreeding, all over the world, at the beginning of the twenty-first century, women appear to be responding to some intuitive demand of the feminine spirit. As Edward O. Wilson has pointed out, there is a quirk in the maternal instinct that women, even those who have not attained economic and social betterment—heretofore considered necessary before women would limit their fertility—are now choosing to have smaller families.[6] India, it is now believed will, by 2100, see six hundred million fewer births than earlier predicted.[7] Whether six hundred million fewer will deter the onward rush to self-destruction that accompanies cataclysmic population growth is unknown. In this widow's mite must we place our hope. The feminine spirit, which demands that woman take control of their lives, holds the key to survival of our planet and struggles on.

In closing, the final words must be those of Margaret Sanger:

> Women are too much inclined to following the footsteps of men, to try to think as men think, to try to solve the general problems of life, as men solve them. If after attaining that freedom, women accept conditions in the spheres of government, industry, art, morals and religion as they find them, they will be but taking a leaf out of man's book. The woman is not needed to do man's work.

She is not needed to think man's thoughts. She need not fear that the masculine mind, almost universally dominant, will fail to take care of its own. Her mission is not to enhance the masculine spirit, but to express the feminine; hers is not to preserve a man-made world, but to create a human world by the infusion of the feminine element into all of its activities.

Woman must not accept; she must challenge. She must not be awed by that which has been built up around her; she must reverence that within her which struggles for expression. Her eyes must be less upon what is and more clearly upon what should be. She must listen only with a frankly questioning attitude to the dogmatized opinions of manmade society. When she chooses her new, free course of action, it must be in the light of her own opinion—of her own intuition. Only so can she give play to the feminine spirit. Only thus can she free her mate from the bondage which he has wrought for himself when he wrought hers. Only thus can she restore to him that of which he robbed himself in restricting her. Only thus can she remake the world.

The world is, indeed, hers to remake. It is hers to build and to recreate. Even as she has permitted the suppression of her own feminine element and the consequent impoverishment of industry, art, letters, science, morals, religions, and social intercourse, so it is hers to enrich all these.

Woman must have her freedom—the fundamental freedom of choosing whether or not she shall be a mother and how many children she will have. Regardless of what man's attitude may be, that problem is hers—and before it can be his, it is hers alone.

She goes through the vale of death alone, each time a babe is born. As it is the right neither of man nor the state to coerce her into this ordeal, so it is her right to decide whether she will endure it. That right to decide imposes upon her the duty of clearing the way to knowledge by which she may make and carry out the decision.

Birth control is woman's problem. The quicker she accepts it as hers and hers alone, the quicker will society respect motherhood. The quicker, too, will the world be made a fit place for her children to live.

—Margaret Sanger, Chapter VIII:
"Birth Control—A Parents' Problem or Woman's?"
Woman and the New Race, 1920, pp. 98-100.

Appendix A
Pertinent Biographies

Leonard D. Abbott (1879-1953), British-born literary editor, liberal journalist, socialist, later an anarchist and pacifist, a free speech advocate, who became, president of the Free Speech League. Abbott loyally supported both Bill and Margaret Sanger during their trials with advice and by securing funds to help cover legal and living expenses, sending sums as well overseas to Margaret.

Maude Adams (1872-1953), much loved American actress, known for her kindness and generosity in life and backstage, was the original Peter Pan for whom Sir James M. Barrie wrote the part in the play of the same name as well as Lady Babbie in Barrie's *The Little Minister* and Maggie in *What Every Woman Knows*. Her most successful plays were produced by Charles Frohman, who paired her with John Drew. Shortly after Frohman's death, Adams announced her retirement, though at that time, in 1918, she was still one of the theatre's most popular stars.

William Archer (1856-1924), well-known British drama critic, who recognized and promoted the genius of Henrik Ibsen.

Elizabeth Arden (1878-1966) was born Florence Nightingale Graham in Canada and appropriately became a nurse. In 1910 she moved to New York City, where she found a chemist to help her devise the first beauty cream. She then became Elizabeth Arden, operator of the first beauty salon and founder of a new industry and a major corporation, one still highly profitable in 2003. Extremely innovative, she made cosmetics socially acceptable at a time when only actresses wore cosmetics for stage. During World War II, she developed a Montezuma Red lipstick to match exactly the red trim on the uniforms of enlisted women.

Jessie Ashley (1861-1919), "with Boston accent and horn-rimmed glasses" (p. 71), the first woman lawyer in New York City, was a feminist and IWW member. Her wealthy father was President of the New York School of Law, but she provided pro bono support for the radicals. One of the organizers of the National Birth Control League, the Paterson Pageant, and part of the Committee of 100, Ashley worked closely with Margaret Sanger on the Paterson strike and the *Birth Control Review*. In the summer of 1913, when she and Bill Haywood were lovers, she brought Haywood to recuperate in Provincetown, where he suggested to Sanger that she visit France to learn about birth control.

Aurelius Augustine (354-430) also known as St. Augustine of Hippo, where he was bishop, author of *Confessions* (400) and *City of God* (412-427), whose twisted reasoning regarding sexual intercourse as evil and a newborn baby as born in sin has been accepted as superior logic by centuries of men and used by the Roman Catholic church as the basis for their condemnation of contraception and abortion.

George Wesley Bellows (1882-1925), American painter and lithographer, pupil of Robert Henri. Bellows' bold style belongs to the Social Realism movement. His most famous painting "Firpo and Demsy," hangs in the Museum of Modern Art, New York.

Arnold Bennett (1867-1931), English novelist known for *The Old Wives Tale* (1908) and playwright of *Milestones* (1912), Bennett was also recognized as a discerning critic and play reviewer.

Victor L. Berger (1860-1929), represented Wisconsin as the lone Socialist in the House of Representatives for six terms and with Eugene Debs organized the Socialist Party of America. In Wisconsin, as the Socialists gained in power, Berger among them, they turned Wisconsin into a state noted for its outstandingly honest and effective government. During the Red Scare that swept America from 1919 to 1920, Berger was indicted for sedition, a charge he successfully challenged and which was overturned by the Supreme Court in 1920.

Alexander Berkman (1870-1936), Russian-born lover and "pal" of Emma Goldman, "the gentle anarchist" (p. 71), "blond, blue-eyed, slightly built, with thinnish hair and sensitive, mobile face and hands," who served fourteen years of a twenty-year jail sentence for attempting the assassination of Henry Frick. "He was a thoughtful ascetic, believing sincerely that the quickest way to focus attention on social outrages was to commit some dramatic act, however violent or antipathetic it might be to his nature—and then suffer the consequences. He was not at all embittered by his sojourn in jail and had a great sense of humor"(p. 72). He wrote *Prison Memoirs of an Anarchist* (1906). With Goldman, Berkman opened the New York Ferrer Center and the Modern School in 1911 and 1912, respectively.

Mary McLeod Bethune (1875-1955), was the daughter of a former slave. She became a teacher, then founder of the Daytona Normal and Industrial Institute for Negro Girls, of which she was president for forty years. Her school became the Bethune-Cookman College. Bethune integrated the Red Cross, opened a hospital for blacks, and was the first black woman to serve as head of a federal agency.

Annie Besant (1847-1933), Birth Control advocate, social reformer, and Theosophist. In 1877, she and Charles Bradlaugh—(1833-1891), "the brilliant rationalist and freethinker (p. 127)—were tried for publishing a Birth Control pamphlet. In winning their case in 1877, contraceptives were removed forever in England from the obscene category. After she became as Theosophist, Besant left her native England to live in India, where she worked for India's independence and became president of the Theosophical Society and an important writer of their teachings.

Anita C. Block, "a grand person, a Bernard graduate, and editor of the woman's page of the Call" (p. 76), was an ardent Socialist and on the board of National Birth Control League. Later, she was associated with the Theatre Guild.

John Brown (1800-1859), violent anti-slavery fighter, at Pottawatomie he ordered five-pro-slavery men to be shot. An unbalanced visionary, on October 16, 1859, he led the attack on the federal arsenal at Harper's Ferry and was executed for insurrection.

Stella Browne (1882-1955), a believer in free sex and birth control, wrote on labor and Socialist issues for the Neo-Malthusian Society. Sanger referred to Brown as the "intrepid rebel feminist" (p. 101), recognized her as a discerning social critic, and quotes her in *The Pivot of Civilization*: "The official policy [the Eugenics Society] has pursued for years has been inspired by class-bias and sex bias" (p. 181).

Pearl Buck (1892-1973), 1938 Nobel prize winner for literature, novelist whose Chinese experience gave her the material for the Pulitzer Prize winning novel *The Good Earth* (1931), her East-West Foundation worked for the betterment of Chinese-American relations and promoted adoption of Asian children by non-Asians.

Dorothy Brush (1894-1968) (her second marriage to Alexander Dick ended in divorce, and she is usually referred to as Dorothy Brush), "had the old-fashioned head of a daguerreotype, but was thoroughly modern in her verve and gay personality and her quick agility of mind" (p. 417). She was from Cleveland, Ohio, and she and her husband Charles Brush had "from the beginning one of the best organized and conducted state leagues." In 1928, Charles and their little son died within the same week. Dorothy, who had met Sanger in the late 1920s, came East to New York and devoted the rest of her life to birth control. Through the Brush Foundation of her husband's family of the Brush Electric Company, she funded many Sanger projects, including the *Committee for International Planned Parenthood Newsletter*, which she also edited. Brush traveled frequently with Sanger and was a valuable assistant in Sanger's later and ill years. A Smith College alumna, Brush arranged for Sanger's personal papers to be archived at the Sophia Smith Archives at Smith College, though Sanger did continue to leave some of her papers at the Library of Congress, where she had first begun to deposit them. Brush also arranged for Smith in 1949 to award Sanger an honorary LL.D. degree.

William Jennings Bryan (1860-1925), twice a Democratic presidential candidate, the great stump-orator, best remembered for his "Cross of Gold" speech, was a conservative, who opposed the teaching of evolution in Tennessee in the Scopes Monkey trial, and a humanitarian, who favored the free coinage of silver, Bryan was also a pacifist, who resigned from his position as Wilson's Secretary of State when Wilson refused to tolerate the German submarine attacks.

Ethel Higgins Byrne (1893-1955), younger sister of Margaret, went on a hunger strike when imprisoned in 1917 for opening the first Birth Control clinic in Brownsville with Margaret.

Andrew Carnegie (1835-1918), Scots-born multimillionaire, who made his fortune through the largest iron and steel works in America and set out his philosophy of life in *The Gospel of Wealth*. A wise philanthropist, he endowed public libraries throughout America and Britain and universities in America and Scotland.

Edward Carpenter (1844-1949), British writer, homosexual, and Fabian socialist, "full of wit, fun, and humor" (p. 130). He examined free love and sexuality of all mixtures in *Love's Coming-of-Age* (1869) and believed in mutuality of the sex relation. Carpenter assured Sanger that birth control belonged to the future.

Carrie Chapman Catt (1859-1947), American suffragist leader. As President from 1900 to 1920, of the National American Women's Suffrage Association, Catt led the women's suffrage movement to its victory with ratification in 1920, then became president of the League of Women Voters and, after 1924, devoted herself to pacifism and world peace.

Anthony Comstock (1844-1915), author of the infamous Comstock laws passed by Congress in 1873, which made all contraception information and devices "obscene" and the use, sale, or mail transport thereof, even by licensed physicians, punishable by law.

Harold Cox (1859-1936), economist, brilliant conservative member of Parliament (1906-1909), "one of the finest orators of his generation" (p. 272), was a strong Birth Control advocate. In 1912, he became editor of the influential *Edinburgh Review* (founded in 1802) and remained editor until its demise in 1929.

Eugene V. Debs (1855-1926), began his life a labor leader and in the latter part of his life worked through political action to advance workers' rights, demanding their right to organize, to strike, and to job security. Debs insisted that American capitalism should be replaced with a cooperative Socialist system, and with Haywood and Mother Jones founded the IWW, but Debs was opposed to violence. On June 16, 1918, he gave an antiwar speech and was sentenced to ten years in prison, a sentence that was commuted in 1921 by Harding. Debs fought child labor and strongly supported birth control and women's rights. He ran five times on the Socialist ticket for U.S. president.

Mary Ware Dennett (1872-1947), along with Jessie Ashley, Lincoln Steffens, and others, founded the National Birth Control League in March 1915 while Sanger was in Europe. As its executive secretary, she and the League became strongly identified with one another. Dennett had little love for Sanger's ambitions and less for Sanger's tactics, initially refusing the help of the NBCL to Sanger when she returned in the fall of 1915 to face trial. Though Dennett got on the bandwagon at the Brevoort dinner, she ultimately founded her own short lived Voluntary Parenthood League, which sought to make birth control legal through legislative reform.

Hugh de Selincourt (1878-1959), sexually adroit lover, cricket critic, and novelist, with whom Sanger would correspond throughout her life.

John Dewey (1859-1952), influential American philosopher and educational theorist, who followed Williams James in promoting pragmatism and the importance of ideas and judgments in solving problems. He held positions at Johns Hopkins, Michigan, Chicago, and Columbia universities and published *The School and Society* (1899), *Experience and Nature* (1925), *Experience and Education* (1938).

Appendix A

Robert Latou Dickinson (1861-1950), eminent gynecologist and avid supporter of birth control at a time when the medical community regarded sex as unsavory and women's health as beneath their notice, he was the founder of the National Committee of Maternal Health and worked closely with Clarence Gamble and finally with Sanger.

Mabel Dodge (1879-1962), Beginning January 1913, heiress Mabel Dodge held regular "Evenings" at her sumptuous apartment at 23 Fifth Avenue in New York, where gathered all of the Greenwich Village radical set—John Reed, Haywood, Goldman, Margaret and Bill Sanger, Lincoln Steffens, to name only a few—until she ran off to Europe with John Reed after the performance of the Paterson Pageant. When Mabel returned to the States, she eventually moved to Santa Fe and married a native American, Tony Luhan (Lujan), and became involved in Native American arts and issues.

General William Draper (1894-1974), a major in World War I, was an investment banker between the wars. During World War II, Draper worked under Generals George Marshall supervising German industry and Lucius Clay as economic advisor. Draper headed an economic mission to Japan and served as U.S. Special Representative in Europe for Presidents Truman and Eisenhower. He was with Mexican Power and Light, when in 1958 he was asked to chair Eisenhower's Committee to Study the U.S. Economic and Military Assistance Program. For this he authored the Draper Report, which emphasized the need for action on the world population crisis. The remainder of Draper's life was devoted to working with overpopulation issues as chairman of the Population Crisis Committee in 1966 and Vice Chairman of International Planned Parenthood Federation.

Alice Vickery Drysdale (1849-1929), after a tremendous struggle became the first woman doctor in England. She and her husband, **Dr. Charles Robert Drysdale** (1829-1907) with his brother George Drysdale, author of *The Elements of Social Science* (1854), in 1861 founded the Malthusian League, the first organization in the world to advocate birth control.

C.V. Drysdale (1874-1961), the son of Charles Robert Drysdale and Alice Vickery, was "in his ebullience not at all British, but his pleasant warm, and courteous personality was British at its best." C.V. Drysdale was carrying on the work of his father with his wife, **Bessie Drysdale** (1871-1950), a suffragette, who dispensed "charming hospitality" (p, 129).

W.E.B. DuBois (1868-1963), American black writer and editor, professor of economics and history at Atlanta University (1897-1910), cofounder in 1909 of the National Association for the Advancement of Colored People, editor of its magazine, *Crisis* (1909-1934), wrote extensively on slavery and racism and advocated radical black action.

Dr. Binnie Dunlop (1874-1946), a physician, "dark, Scotch, thin, and dapper, intellectually enthusiastic, although not emotionally so" (p. 129), a member of the Malthusian League and good friend to all the Drysdales, wrote on birth control in relation to social and economic issues.

Doris Duke (1912-1993), "Million Dollar Baby," heiress of the American Tobacco Company fortune, parlayed her $30 million inheritance into $750 million at her death. The Duke Charitable Foundation supported many important charities and works, including Duke University and often Sanger's Birth Control proposals.

Will Durant (1885-1981), the gentle philosopher and historian, taught at the Ferrer Day School and spent his life working on the extraordinary multivolume *The Story of Civilization*.

Crystal Eastman (1881-1928), sister of Max, a Greenwich Village radical, lawyer, feminist, Socialist, and strong-minded activist, drafted New York state's first worker's compensation law, which became a model for other states, founded a number of anti-war organizations, including what is today the Women's International League for Peace and Freedom, contributed to averting war with Mexico, fought racism, and with Roger Baldwin established what became the American Civil Liberties Union. Eastman established conscientious objection to war as a legal option. Eastman also contributed to the *Birth Control Review*.

Max Eastman (1883-1969), brother of Crystal, belonged to the Greenwich Village radical intellectual circle and editor of *The Masses* (1913-17), the controversial magazine that championed all radical causes. Max was a communist until he became disillusioned, which he wrote of *Stalin's Russia* (1940).

Havelock Ellis (1859-1939), an English physician, was literary editor of the excellent Mermaid series of literary works until he turned to the study of sexuality and authored the seven-volume *Studies in the Psychology of Sex* (1897-1928). The very first volume was promptly banned in Britain. Ellis wrote objectively and seriously on sexual matters, including homosexuality. At the same time, he accorded to sex a romantic and spiritual energy.

Morris Ernst (1882-1976), attorney who contributed to the protection of civil liberties, particularly in the areas of freedom of speech, press, and assembly and of reproductive rights. In a series of well-known cases, Ernst was successful in removing government censorship of a sex education pamphlet by Mary Dennett (1929), of *Married Love* by Marie Stopes (1931), of *The Well of Loneliness* by Radclyff Hall, and of *Ulysses* by James Joyce. As attorney for Margaret Sanger, he argued against police closure of and the raid on the Clinical Research Bureau, and he was responsible for the *One Package* decision, which overturned the government ban on the importation of contraceptive devices. Two suits brought in Connecticut against their ban on contraceptive devices were unsuccessful, but his cases did lay the groundwork for the 1965 Supreme Court decision *Griswold v. Connecticut*, which established a constitutional right of privacy. For almost thirty years, Ernst was co-general counsel and on the Board of Directors of the American Civil Liberties Union. At the same time he was a close friend of J. Edgar Hoover and supported the actions of the House Un-American Activities Committee, believing in the rights of both the people and the government for having information. He abhorred segregation and the monopoly control of big business. Ernst wrote or coauthored over twenty books on censorship, privacy, and other matters.

Francisco Ferrer (1859-1909), founder of the Escuela Moderna (Modern School), schools in Spain that he established throughout Spain to offset the stultifying education being instilled by the Catholic church and to educate the Spanish people in modern ways. Ferrer was accused of plotting to assassinate the Spanish king and shot.

Sigmund Freud (1856-1939), Austrian neurologist and founder of psychoanalysis, whose groundbreaking work identified the id, ego, and superego and the workings of the unconscious but who could not recognize the slanted patriarchal underpinnings of his work.

Elizabeth Gurley Flynn (1890-1964), a worker for the Socialists, a labor organizer for Industrial Workers of the World (IWW), and later an active Communist, persistently advocated women's rights and was a founding member of the American Civil Liberties Union. She was known as "silver-tongued," for from her youngest days she was a powerful orator, and she used her talent throughout her life in the service of the workers. She lived with Carlo Tresca.

Henry Clay Frick (1849-1919), American industrialist, a millionaire at 30, chairman of Andrew Carnegie's steel company, used two hundred hired Pinkerton guards and the Pennsylvania National Guard to break a strike at the Carnegie Steel Plant in Homestead, Pennsylvania (1892). Frick recovered from Berkman's attempt on his life, became director of J. Pierpont Morgan's United States Steel (1901), and built up the distinguished Frick Collection of Fine Art, now a museum at One East 70th Street, New York City.

Charles Frohman (1860-1915), was a leading Broadway producer. With his brothers he organized complete road companies of Broadway hits, thus changing the nature of provincial theatre. With three other leading producers, Frohman created the Theatrical Syndicate, or Trust, which soon controlled all the important theatres in America and which charged exorbitant fees. He cultivated and made stars of many, including Ethel Barrymore, Maude Adams, and Billie Burke, and enhanced the stardom of John Drew. He brought to the American stage the works of Oscar Wilde, Sir James Barrie, Arthur Wing Pinero, Somerset Maugham, and Georges Feydeau. He presented American works abroad that had not been produced in the States, thereby promoting international respect for American playwrights. At the height of his career, he was drowned on May 7 with the sinking of the Lusitania.

Sir Francis Galton (1822-1911), English scientist, cousin of Charles Darwin, founder of Genetics, whose investigations of meterology were the basis of modern weather maps, also devised the system of fingerprint identification and did valuable research on color blindness and mental imagery.

Clarence Gamble (1894-1966), founder of Pathfinder Fund, spent much of his life and fortune searching for a simple, inexpensive contraceptive.

Mahatma Gandhi (1869-1948), leader of the movement of independence for India from Great Britain, which was accompanied by civil disobedience, hunger strikes and prolonged negotiation. Gandhi was assassinated by a Hindu fanatic.

William Lloyd Garrison (1805-1879), avid abolitionist, founder of *The Liberator* and the American Anti-slavery Society (1831), later crusaded for women's suffrage and American Indians.

Marcus Garvey (1887-1940), Jamaican-born and Harlem-based black leader, whose strikingly bright military attire and attention-getting rhetoric made influential in the '20s. Garvey founded the Universal Negro Improvement Association and promoted success for the Negro, preaching the importance of wealth and using Carnegie's *The Gospel of Wealth* as an inspirational model.

Henry George (1839-1897), an American economist, known for *Progress and Poverty* (1877-1879), in which he advocated, as a cure for poverty, a single tax levied on land exclusive of improvements. George was lost with the sinking of the Lusitania.

Charlotte Perkins Gilman (1860-1935), American feminist and writer, known for her powerful short story "The Yellow Wallpaper." She was a member of Heterodoxy, which originally turned down Sanger's request for support, but Gilman was later a staunch supporter of Sanger.

Emma Goldman (1869-1940), Goldman with Berkman, both ardent Anarchists, founded the Ferrer Association and the Modern School, where Stuart Sanger was a pupil. Goldman, "short, stocky, even stout, a true Russian peasant type, her figure indicated strength of body and strength of character" (p. 72), was a riveting orator, and tireless worker, editor of her outspoken journal, *Mother Earth*, and supported all radical causes, including birth control.

J.J. Goldstein (1886-1967), born in Canada, was the lawyer for Sanger in the Brownsville case. Goldstein, influenced by Lillian Wald, began his career as an aide to Al Smith, became majority leader of the New York State Assembly, and after practicing as an attorney, became a distinguished judge and family law theorist.

Angelina Grimké (1805-1879), American feminist, writer, and social reformer, with her sister, Sarah, fought against slavery through their writings and as speakers on the American Anti-Slavery Society circuit, the first women to do so. The sisters also fought for women's emancipation.

Hutchins Hapgood (1869-1944), a Village radical and writer whom Margaret and Bill knew well, made his name with *The Spirit of the Ghetto* (1910). "Hutch" worked for the *Globe*, more radical than the *Call*, and "stood by Goldman and Haywood although he had much more to lose economically and socially than the out-and-out reds" (p. 74).

E.H. Harriman (1848-1909), the railroad magnate, bought his first railroad in 1881 and eventually took over the Union Pacific and made his quite ample fortune thereby.

Archbishop Patrick Hayes (1867-1938), the very conservative archbishop of New York, founder of Catholic Charities (1920), which coordinates the many welfare agencies in the New York archdiocese. In 1924, Hayes was made a cardinal.

William ("Big" Bill) D. Haywood (1869-1928), "His great voice boomed; his speech was crude and so were his manners...but I soon found out that for gentleness and sympathy he had not his equal"(p. 71). Haywood was a founder of the Industrial Workers of the World, believed that the IWW union should include all workers of all races, that unions should be established by industry rather than by craft, and that the wage system should be abolished. The IWW grew from 200 in 1905 to 100,000 members by 1917 because of this argument and on the basis of its demand for an eight-hour day, forty-hour week. Decentralization of the IWW was both its allure and its downfall, for dues and moneys were not properly administered. The IWW was destroyed by the United States government under the Espionage Act of World War I, and Haywood skipped bail and fled to Russia, where he died.

Robert Henri (1865-1929), American painter, leader of the Ashcan School of Art, taught that art should be popular and democratic.

Harold Brainerd Hersey (1894-1956), poet, writer, and first biographer of Sanger. His biography was never published because Sanger discouraged it at about the same time that the publisher went under. Highly laudatory, Hersey's page proof volume is in the Manuscript Room of the New York Public Library and is the only biography of Sanger which draws on Sanger's early contemporaries for sources.

Lewis Hine (1874-1940), seminal figure in American photography, took poignant photographs that made graphic why social reforms were needed. His remarkable exhibition of the Empire State Building (1930) stressed the contribution of the workers.

Edith How-Martyn (1875-1954), staunch British suffragette—"the zealous ardor of this small and slight person had landed her in jail" (p. 170)—and she began working for birth control. She and Sanger had a warm relationship, and How-Martyn assisted Sanger in organizing the 1927 Geneva World Population Conference (1927), was director of the Birth Control International Information Centre in London (1930-1940), and prepared for and traveled on the India and World Tour (1935-36). How-Martyn was an impressive lobbyist in her own right, for under her urging, in 1934 the British Parliament passed a bill that required contraception to be included in government sponsored public health programs.

Sir Julian Huxley (1897-1975) English biologist/zoologist and philosopher, brother of Aldous, "a brilliant, young, enthusiastic scientist, alive and having a mind that not only took things in, but gave them out."(p. 379). Huxley taught in the United States and Great Britain and extended his biology discipline to understanding political and social problems. He formulated a theory of "evolutionary humanism" and questioned eugenic assumptions that ethnic and character traits were inherited. His writings include the *Science of Life* (with H.G. Wells, 1931), *Evolutionary Ethics* (1943), and *Towards a New Humanism* (1957).

Henrik Ibsen (1828-1906), innovative Norwegian dramatist, known for realistic plays that examined social issues that Victorians did not believe should be examined. *The Doll House* (1879) and *Hedda Gabler* (1890) are strong feminist statements.

Dean William R. Inge (1860-1954), "the Gloomy Dean, so-called because of his pessimistic sermons, dean of St. Paul's Cathedral (1911-1934), approved of birth control but not of divorce or socialism. Sanger found the Dean "not gloomy at all; he was full of mischief. In his late fifties, tall, thin as an exclamation point, quite deaf, he reminded me of a Dickens character" (pp. 377-378).

Robert Ingersoll (1833-1899), was an attorney, an orator, and an agnostic, who dared to question Christian beliefs in his speeches and writings, such as *Why I Am an Agnostic* (1896). He was an early supporter of birth control, and Sanger reprinted some of his output in the *Birth Control Review*.

Oliver M. Johnson was "the faithful secretary, who had worked for many years with the Drysdales" (p. 129). He left a cache of papers documenting the activities of the Malthusian League.

Shidzue Ishimoto Kato (1897-2001) was "the Margaret Sanger" of Japan.

Helen Keller (1880-1968), left deaf and dumb at nineteenth months by illness, overcame her disabilities through persistence and the help of her teacher, Anne Sullivan, to become a distinguished lecturer and writer.

Ellen Key (1849-1926), Swedish feminist and writer, whose work appeared in the *Birth Control Review*, recognized the distinctly different energies of the male and the female and wrote about child welfare, love, and marriage. Key much admired by Margaret Sanger.

John Maynard Keynes (1883-1946), British economist, "had become famous almost overnight as the result of his book, *The Economic Consequences of the Peace* (1919). He was tall and well-built, with clear, cold, blue eyes, a fine shapely head, brow, and face, a brilliant bearing and brilliant intellect....Because he gave each question of yours so much consideration, he seemed constantly perplexed" (pp. 354-355). Keynes believed that full employment could be created and his views on a planned economy influenced Franklin Delano Roosevelt. He was instrumental in establishing the International Monetary Fund. With his ballerina wife, Lydia Lopokova, he founded the Vic Wells Ballet.

Lawrence Lader wrote *The Margaret Sanger Story and the Fight for Birth Control* (1955), *Politics, Power, and the Church: The Catholic Crisis and its Challenge to American Pluralism* (1987) and *A Private Matter: RU-486 and the*

Abortion Crisis (1995). He founded the National Abortion Rights Action League and received the Feminist of the Year Award from Feminist Majority Foundation.

Ramsey McDonald (1866-1937), was active in British government, often through the opposition, for all his life, and was the first British Labour Prime Minister. He often leaned to a pacifist point of view, which naturally appealed to Sanger.

Enrico Malatesta (1853-1932), an Italian anarchist, preached "direct action," believing people needed to emancipate themselves. To prove the sincerity of his anarchist beliefs, he gave away his inherited wealth. Often imprisoned, he became a legend in his own time, for his small stature allowed him easy escape. When he settled in London in 1900, he advocated peaceful opposition to authority.

Thomas Malthus (1766-1834), in his *Essay on the Principle of Population* (1798) warned Britain that unless the birth rate was checked, population would exceed means of subsistence. He urged abstinence and late marriage to slow population growth and was much persecuted for his views.

Karl Marx (1818-1883), German political and economic theorist, a critic of capitalism, which he said exploits the working class and alienates man. Ironically Marx wrote the Communist Manifesto and *Das Kapital* (1867), while working in the British Museum.

George Meredith (1828-1909), English novelist, whose works consider the relations between the sexes and the perfection of man through natural selection in *The Egoist* (1879) and *The Amazing Marriage* (1895).

Kathryn McCormick (1875-1967), funded development of The Pill.

Hazel Moore (1894-1948), Sanger wrote, "Hazel Moore, who later died in China, was one of the most unusual women I have ever known, gay, laughing, musical, singing, persistent, never giving up, indefatigable. She attended Conferences of Rabbis, Episcopalian Bishops, Trade Unions, Methodists, every religious group except the Roman Catholics. Always she came away with an affirmative vote by the majority" (p. 417).

J.P. Morgan (1837-1913), financier, art collector, and philanthropist, owned the most powerful private banking house in America, was instrumental in developing the American railroads, and forestalled the panic of 1901.

Gilbert Murray (1866-1957), critic, pacifist, and British classical scholar, known for his translations of Greek classical dramas.

Jawaharlal Nehru (1889-1964), Indian lawyer, and statesman, follower of Gandhi, leader of the socialists, first prime minister and minister of external affairs when India gained independence in 1947. During the Cold War, Nehru committed India to a policy of industrialization and followed a policy of non-alignment and neutrality.

Friedrich Nietzche (1844-1900), German philosopher, poet, repudiated Christian liberal ethics and venerated the will to power that allowed the individual to create and impose his own law unto himself. He celebrated the Übermensch, a concept that was taken up in a perverted form by the Nazis. His writings influenced the development of existentialism.

Eugene O'Neill (1888-1953), prolific playwright and 1936 Nobel prize winner, best known for soulful dramas of heavy introspective intensity, such as *Desire Under the Elms* and *Long Day's Journey into Night*.

Elise Ottesen-Jensen (1886-1973), was born Elise Ottesen in Norway and in 1915 married Albert Jensen. Ottesen-Jensen was a socialist, a journalist, and became well-known as a Scandinavian lecturer, who spoke and worked actively for women's rights and birth control. With World War II over, Ottesen-Jensen was the first to revitalize the Birth Control movement internationally by organizing, in 1946, an international family planning conference in Stockholm, Sweden. Margaret Sanger attended the conference.

Vijaya Lakshmi Pandit (1900-1990), sister of Jawaherlal Nehru, fought for Indian independence and was jailed three times by the British. With independence, she held many government posts, including Minister for local self-government and public health and ambassador to Soviet Union. She led the Indian delegation to the United Nations and was President of the United Nations General Assembly.

Emmeline Pankhurst (1857-1928), was a militant English suffragist, often imprisoned and forcibly fed during her frequent hunger strikes. She founded the Women's Franchise League and, in 1903 with her daughter, the Women's Political and Social Union. Later, she joined the Conservative Party.

Theodore Parker (1810-1860), New England Unitarian clergyman and ardent abolitionist.

Wendell Phillips (1811-1884), American abolitionist, chief orator of Garrison's Anti-Slavery Society, who later championed the causes of temperance, women, and the rights of Native Americans.

Gertrude Pinchot (1872-1939), wife of Amos Pinchot, who helped organize the short-lived Progressive Party and sister-in-law to Gifford Pinchot, who was instrumental in creating our national parks system under President Theodore Roosevelt and later governor of Pennsylvania. "Aristocratic of bearing, autocratic by position, she was one to command and be obeyed, and was easily a leading personality in the philanthropic smart set of New York" (p. 230). Gertrude Pinchot was a suffragist, a National Birth Control League member, supported Sanger's children while she was in Europe, paid fines, supported the *Birth Control Review*, funded the translation of *Family Limitation* into Polish and Lithuanian, and organized the Committee of 100. She continued her support of birth control with involvement in Dickinson's Committee on Maternal Health.

Lorenzo Portet (1870-1917), Spanish anarchist and friend and heir of Francisco Ferrer. Portet became famous in 1909 after organizing a massive protest when Ferrer was executed by the Spanish government. As Ferrer's successor, Portet ran the Casa Editorial Publicaccioners de la Escuela Moderna (Modern School) from Paris, where he lived after leaving Liverpool, when exiled from his native Spain.

Reverend Adam Clayton Powell (1865-1953), in 1908 became pastor of Abyssinian Baptist Church, which grew to become the largest congregation in America. As a member of the NAACP, he organized the Silent Protest Parade of 1917, set up one of the first community recreation centers in Harlem, and worked unstintingly for harmonious race relations.

Lady Dhanvanthi Rama Rau was married in 1919 to the Brahmin banker who was the first Ambassador of India to the United States. She was a past president of the All-India Women's Association. In 1949, she founded and was president of the first voluntary birth control organization in the Far East, the Family Planning Association of India, which hosted the Bombay International Conference in 1952. As one of the cofounders of the International Planned Parenthood Federation, Rama Rau was made chairman and Sanger president. Known for being imperious and high-handed, Rama Rau was also a powerful force, who worked throughout her life for birth control and women's rights in India.

John (Jack) Reed (1887-1920), Harvard graduate, reporter and journalist, one of the Greenwich Village radical circle, became a friend of Lenin and an eyewitness to the 1917 October Revolution, which he covered in *Ten Days That Shook the World* (1919). Reed regularly wrote letters and articles in support of Sanger.

Rev. Karl Reiland (1871-1964), pastor of St. George's Episcopal Church,

Stuyvesant Square, New York City, was a good friend of Noah Slee, with whom he sometimes traveled.

Walter Roberts (1886-1962), Jamaican-born journalist, poet, associate correspondent for the Brooklyn *Daily Eagle*, editor for the *Birth Control Review*, and sometime lover of Margaret Sanger.

Henrietta Rodman (b. 1878), a flamboyant feminist of the Greenwich Village radical circle, a teacher who fought for the right of married women and mothers to continue to hold their teaching positions. She was active in Heterdoxy. Sanger referred to Rodman as "the Feminist of Feminists" (p. 187).

John D. Rockefeller, Jr. (1874-1960), founded the Bureau for Social Hygiene, built Rockefeller Center in New York (1939), and was chairman of the Rockefeller Institute of Medical Research, to which Sanger turned for grants.

John D. Rockefeller, III (1906-1978), became chair of Rockefeller Foundation in 1952, the same year in which he founded the Population Council.

Florence Rose (1889-1987), came to work for Margaret Sanger in 1930 and adored her. Rose had unlimited energy and was a tireless worker, but was finally forced to resign from the Planned Parenthood Federation because of her Sanger sympathies. Rose moved to Los Angeles and managed the Meals for Millions Foundation, which sent inexpensive food to impoverished populations. She kept in touch with Margaret Sanger and in 1951 was responsible for introducing Ellen Watumull of the Watumull Foundation to Sanger.

Juliet Barrett Rublee (1876-1966), a dancer, advocate of the arts and of free thought, heir to a fortune from the Barrett Chicago roofing company, had influential social connections and supported Sanger and the Birth Control movement from its infancy with gifts of money both to Sanger personally and to the Birth Control movement. Rublee was a regular sounding board and was active with the National Birth Control League, Gertrude Pinchot's Committee of 100, the *Birth Control Review*, and the American Birth Control League until Sanger separated herself from it.

Bertrand Russell (1872-1970), Welsh philosopher, mathematician, author, *The Principles of Mathematics* (1903) argues that the whole of mathematics could be derived from logic. *Principia Mathematica* (with Alfred North Whitehead (1910-1913) is a landmark in the study of logic and mathematics. Active pacifist, Nobel prize winner for literature (1950), always a controversial figure, often imprisoned for confronting the government, Russell worked for nuclear disarmament in his last years.

Dr. Johannes Rutgers (1851-1924), Socialist, secretary of Dutch Neo-Malthusian League, was the Dutch physician primarily responsible for establishing the excellent network of mothers' health clinics that served Holland in 1915, the first such organization to offer to the poor information on birth control. Rutgers generously shared information with Sanger when she visited there. "I came to the Hague to study the latest methods adopted by the Dutch League of Neo-Malthusian principles. I found dear little Doctor Rutgers most charming & cordial—He gave me a course of instruction & held a special clinic for my practice. I feel quite set up with the knowledge."

William Sanger (1873-1961), was five years old when he and his parents and sister immigrated from Berlin. William studied art and architecture at New York's Cooper Union and was a draftsman when he met Margaret in 1902 and fell hopelessly and totally in love. The divorce and death of Peggy shattered him completely. He painted for a time in Spain, and in 1919 his Spanish paintings were on exhibit in New York at the Touchstone Galleries. Harold Hersey praised his work, but Bill never achieved serious recognition. Bill remarried and had one daughter and later worked for the City of New York City utilities department.

Olive Schreiner (1855-1920), South African feminist writer, an early lover of Havelock Ellis, whose *Women and Labour* (1911) expressing the need for women's economic, political, and sexual equality impressed Margaret Sanger. Schreiner contributed to the *Birth Control Review.*

George Bernard Shaw (1856-1950), Irish playwright; music, drama, and social critic; Socialist; pacifist; and vegetarian, which he later qualified; Birth Control supporter, member of the Fabian Society, who wrote with irreverent wit many wonderful, wordy plays, including *Man and Superman* (1902), *Mrs. Warren's Profession* (1898), essays, and books, such as *The Intelligent Woman's Guide to Socialism and Capitalism* (1928), all with irreverent wit.

Upton Sinclair (1878-1968), novelist, social reformer, and 1942 Pulitzer prize winner. In his 1906 novel *The Jungle,* he exposed meat packing conditions to a horrified reading public. The outcry led to passage of the U.S. Pure Food and Drugs Act.

Agnes Smedley (1892-1950), journalists and radical, managed the *Birth Control Review* for Sanger in 1918-1919, supported independence for India (for which she was jailed), and lived and worked in Germany and China, where her writings as a foreign correspondent were sympathetic to communist and radical causes.

Lincoln Steffens (1866-1936), a Greenwich Village radical; an investigative journalist, who exposed local government corruption; a Socialist; a founder of the National Birth Control League; supporter of the Free Speech League, who made his name with *The Shame of the Cities* (1904).

Hannah Mayer Stone (1893-1941), gynecologist, connected with the Woman's Lying-In Hospital until becoming medical director of the Clinical Research Bureau, a position she held from 1925 until her untimely death.

Marie Stopes (1880-1958), was the first woman in Scotland to obtain a university certificate, and this experience reinforced her already strong feminist activism. An unfortunate marriage conveyed to her the need for woman's sexual equality, which inspired her book, *Married Love* (1916). When she met Margaret Sanger in 1916, Stopes was immediately converted to the cause of Birth Control, and on March 17, 1921, she opened the first English Birth Control Clinic in Holloway, North London. She was the editor and publisher of *Birth Control News*. Stopes suggested and organized the letter of protest that was sent to President Wilson when Sanger returned to face trial. Sanger, in turn, arranged for publication of *Married Love* in America, where it quickly encountered censorship until attorney Morris Ernst took on the matter.

Rabindranath Tagore (1861-1941), Hindu poet of international renown, was a Nobel Poetry Prize recipient and founder of the great international university Visva-Bharati in Bengal India. His poetry was translated into all European and Asian languages. He was as well a critic of colonialism and a supporter of birth control. A photo and article on him was featured in the *Birth Control Review*, Volume 9, Number 12 [December 1925], pp. 12-14.

Carlo Tresca (1879-1943), an Italian, worked with the Italian Railroad Workers Federation in Italy. In 1904, he came to America, where for twenty years he was editor of the anti-fascist newspaper *Il Martello* (The Hammer). Tresca lived with Elizabeth Gurley Flynn and was an IWW activist in the Pennsylvania coal miners strike and the Lawrence and Paterson strikes. He was assassinated, probably by facists, on a New York City street corner.

Hendrik Willem Van Loon (1882-1944), Dutch-born popular historian, arrived in the United States in 1903, made his name with his bestseller *Story of Mankind* (1922) and subsequent popular histories.

William Vogt (1902-1968), ornithologist and ecologist, began his career with the New York Academy of Sciences and the National Association of Audubon Societies. His first book, *Thirst for Land*, examined the growing scarcity of water. *Road to Survival* (1948) examined the limited amount of all natural resources, the contribution of overpopulation to an oncoming scarcity, and the importance of contraceptives in forestalling unlimited population growth. The book's success inspired Paul Ehrlich to look at population issues and brought Vogt grants to study further and, in 1949, appointment as president of Planned Parenthood Federation of America.

Lillian Wald (1867-1940), nurse and reformer. In 1893, she became a visiting nurse in New York's Lower East Side and in 1895 opened the Nurse's Settlement House, which ultimately became Henry Street Settlement. By 1913, ninety-two nurses were affiliated with Lillian Wald's Nursing Service (Margaret Sanger was one of them), by 1929 two hundred fifty. Her activism was instrumental in the formation of the National Child Labor Committee in 1904 and the U.S. Children's Bureau in 1912. She founded and became president of the National Organization of Public Health Nursing, which supported the new profession that she had pioneered.

Ellen Watumull (1875-1990), The Watumull Foundation was established in 1942 by Gobindram and Ellen Watumull, who had become prosperous through their chain of department stores in Hawaii. Gobindram Watumull, originally from India, was as interested as Sanger in assisting his native country with population control. When Florence Rose introduced Ellen to Margaret Sanger in 1951, as Sanger was organizing the 1952 Bombay Conference, the Watumulls were immediately supportive. It was the beginning of a fifteen-year friendship and one especially beneficial to the startup of the International Planned Parenthood Federation. For the last years of Sanger's life, Ellen Watumull was very close to Sanger, assisting her with administration details and traveling with her in Sanger's failing years. The Watumulls were the source of the papayas that both Sanger and McCormick enjoyed, and Ellen spent much time on an unsuccessful attempt to have Sanger awarded the Nobel Peace Prize.

John Watson (1878-1958), wrote *Behavior—An Introduction to Comparative Psychology* and held that a scientific psychology could study only what was directly observable, i.e., behavior. Watson was professor at Johns Hopkins University, until he resigned to become an advertising executive.

H.G. Wells (1866-1946), ebullient English novelist, short story writer, popular historian, promoter of free love, Fabianism, progressive education, world government, and human rights, wrote over a hundred books, countless articles, pioneered English science fiction, feminist novels, and had great success with his bestseller *The Outline of History* (1920).

Billy Williams (1882-1920), writer and editor of *Woman and the New Race*, was deeply devoted to Sanger, who acknowledged his warmth and generosity and grieved at his unexpected death by nephritis.

Frank Lloyd Wright (1867-1959), American architect, whose daring designs explored modern technology and cubist spatial concepts, built the Guggenheim Museum of Art, New York (1959).

Robert Yerkes (1876-1956), American comparative psychologist, chaired the committee administering Army intelligence tests during World War I, and was known for devising the Yerkes-Bridges Intelligence Test. Yerkes founded the first non-human primate research lab at Yale University.

All unidentified quotes followed by a page number are from *Margaret Sanger, An Autobiography* (1938; reprint, New York: Dover Publications, 1971).

Appendix B

Timeline

PART I: THE REBEL

Year	Margaret Sanger Life and Selected Contemporary Event	Conferences, Publications, and Organizations
1873	March 2 Comstock Law passed by Congress Nov 12 Berlin, Germany, William (Bill) E. Sanger born	
1877	First public telephones in U.S.	
1878	Comstock arrests Morris Glattstine, Madam Restell, Sarah Chase	
1879	Henry George, *Progress and Poverty* **Sept 14 Margaret Louise Higgins born** Henrik Ibsen, *The Doll House*	
1881	Dutch Neo-Malthusian League founded	
1883	Olive Schreiner, *The Story of an African Farm*	
1884	G.B. Shaw, H.G. Wells found Fabian Society	
1885	Galton proves fingerprints are individual	
1886	*Das Kapital* in English translation	
1889	Michael Higgins organizes for Knights of Labor ND, SD, MT, WA become U.S. states	
1890	Henrik Ibsen, *Hedda Gabler*	
1892	Dr. Johannes Rutgers opens Birth Control clinic, Holland Canned pineapple available	
1893	Fall Lillian Wald opens Visiting Nurses Service	
1894	May 4 Robert Ingersoll speaks at Corning, NY	
1895	**MS attends Claverack College and Hudson River Institute** Sigmund Freud, *Studien uber Hysterie*	
1896	**MS attends Claverack College and Hudson River Institute** Robert Ingersoll, *Why I Am an Agnostic*	
1897	**MS attends Claverack College and Hudson River Institute** Havelock Ellis, *Studies in the Psychology of Sex*	
1899	March 31 Anne Higgins dies John Dewey, *School and Society*	
1900	**MS nurse probationer, White Plains Hospital, NY** Ellen Key, *Century of the Child* J.P. Morgan organizes U.S. Steel	
1902	Peter Rabbit stories published	

Aug 18 MS marries Bill Sanger
Oct. 26 Elizabeth Cady Stanton dies

1903 **MS ill with TB**
G.B. Shaw, *Man and Superman*
Nov 28 Stuart Sanger born
Emmeline Pankhurst founds NWSPU

1904 National Child Labor Committee formed
New York woman arrested for smoking

1905 June 27 Big Bill Haywood, Eugene Debs form
    IWW

1906 Upton Sinclair, *The Jungle*
Feb 12 Ramsey MacDonald Labour Party
    Chairman

1908 **Feb 20 Fire damages Hastings house**
New York City population 4 million
July 21 Grant Sanger born
Robert Henri circle dubbed Ashcan School

1909 February 12 W.E.B. DuBois founds NAACP

1910 **May 31 Peggy Sanger born**
Model T Ford mass produced

1911 **Sangers move to NYC join Socialist Party**
MS meets Elizabeth Gurley Flynn
March 25 NYC Triangle Shirtwaist fire

                 March 26 *NY Call* "To Mothers—Our Duty"
              Sept 3, 10 *NY Call* "Impressions of the East Side"
                    Oct 1 *NY Call* "Home Life"
      Oct 29-Dec 17 series *NY Call* "How Six Little Children
                                  Were Told the Truth"
                Dec 24 *NY Call* "Dirt, Smell and Sweat"

1912 Jan 11 Lawrence strike begins

                 Jan 14 *NY Call* "The Women of the Laundry
                                 Workers' Strike"

Feb 10 MS leads strikers' children
Victor Berger demands Lawrence strike investi-
    gation
March 5 MS testifies at Lawrence Hearings
March 5 Mrs. Taft attends Lawrence Hearings
May 6 New York City Woman Suffrage Parade
July MS nurses Mrs. Sachs
July 24-30 London 1st International Eugenics
    Congress
Cellophane invented

        Nov 17-Mar 2, 1913, series *NY Call* "What Every Girl Should
                                  Know"

Rabindranath Tagore, *Gitanjali Poems*

1913 Jan Mabel Dodge holds "Evenings" in Village
    apartment
Feb 9 Comstock censors "What Every Girl
    Should Know"

Timeline

Feb 13 Victor Berger assails Post Office censorship
Feb 15-March 15 Amory Show *Nude Descending*
Feb 24 Paterson strike begins
April 8 Hazelton, PA MS arrested
April 9 Hazelton, PA MS arrested again

April 19 *Solidarity*	"Hazelton Strikers Repudiate A.F. of L."
April 20 *NY Call*	"With the Girls in Hazelton Jail"

June 7 Madison Square Garden, Paterson
  Pageant
Oct 16 Sangers sail to Europe

Fall unpublished manuscript	"Impressions of Glasglow"

Woodrow Wilson U.S. President
Dec 24 MS and children sail Paris-NYC

1914

March first issue	*The Woman Rebel*

April 2 *The Woman Rebel* "unmailable" Sec 211[2]

NY: Rabelais Press 59 pp.	*What Every Mother Should Know*

April 20 Colorado Ludlow massacre
June 28 Archduke Ferdinand assassinated:
  World War I
Aug 25 U.S. District Court MS arraigned
U.S. immigrants since 1905: 10.5 million
Oct 14 MS flees to England

Pamphlet 16 pp.	*Family Limitation*

Oct 17 100,000 *Family Limitation* mailed
Oct 31-Nov 17 First Battle of Ypres
Nov 13 MS arrives Liverpool, England
John Watson, *Behavior: An Introduction*
Dec 22 MS meets Havelock Ellis

1915 Jan 19 Comstock arrests Bill Sanger
Feb 9 MS meets Dr. Johannes Rutgers
May 7 German sub sinks SS *Lusitania*
July 5 Fabian Hall MS meets Marie Stopes

Pamphlet 16 pp.	*Dutch Methods of Birth Control*

Sept 10 Bill Sanger trial

Pamphlet 20 pp.	*Magnetation Methods of Birth Control*

Oct 6 MS arrives NYC

Pamphlet 19 pp.	*English Methods of Birth Control*

Nov 6 Peggy Sanger dies

Dec 5 *NY Call*	"Margaret Sanger Defends Her Battle For the Right of Birth Control"

D.W. Griffith, *Birth of a Nation*
1916 **Jan 18 Hotel Brevoort dinner**
Feb 18 *Nolle Prosequi*

NY: M.N. Maisel, 63 pp.	*What Every Mother Should Know or How Six Little Children Were Told the Truth*

Jazz sweeps U.S.

NY: M.N. Maisel 91 pp. *What Every Girl Should Know*

April 7 MS begins first U.S. lecture tour

May 21 MS starts riot in St. Louis

June 30 Portland, OR MS arrested

Sept 1 Keating-Owen (Child Labor) Act passes

Oct 16 MS opens Brownsville clinic

Woodrow Wilson reelected

Oct 26 Brownsville Clinic raid MS arrested

Dec 1 Gertrude Pinchot forms Committee of 100

1917   Published 251 pp. *The Case for Birth Control: A*
                                                            Supplementary Brief and
                                                            Statement of Facts

Bobbed hair fashionable

Jan 28 Ethel Byrne force-fed

Jan 29 MS begins Brownsville trial

PART II: THE REFORMER

1917   February first issue *Birth Control Review*

Feb 7 MS begins 30 days in jail

April 6 U.S. declares war on Germany

June 15 Espionage Act: Emma Goldman arrested

Aug 28 Suffragists picketing White House
    arrested

Nov 7 Bolshevik Revolution

1918   Jan 8 *Crane Decision*

Feb MS, Rublee incorporate NYWPC New York Women's
                                                 Publishing Company

March 4 Communist Third International

May 16 Sedition Act

Nov 11 Armistice Day

1919   **Feb 8 MS to California with Grant**

Red Scare and Palmer Raids

1920   Prohibition begins

Feb 29 *NY Call* "Woman's New Emancipation"

April 24 England, Scotland lecture tour

NY: Brentano's 234 pp. *Woman and the New Race*

Aug 22-Sept 25 Germany lecture tour

Nov 2 MS returns to U.S.

H.G. Wells, *Outline of History*

1921   **April 5 MS meets Noah Slee**

May 2-Sept London visit

Sept 22-28 NYC 2nd International Eugenics
    Congress

NY: NYWPC 19 pp *Sayings of Others on Birth Control*

Oct 4 Bill Sanger divorce final

Nov 10 MS organizes ABCL American Birth Control League

Timeline

U.S. population 107 million

Nov 11-13, New York City First American Birth Control Conference

Nov 13 Town Hall raid, MS arrested
KDKD Pittsburgh regular radio broadcasts

1922   **Pamphlet 55 pp** *Woman, Morality, and Birth Control*

Feb 21 MS, Grant on *Taiyo Maru* **1st Japan trip**
Feb 21 J. Noah Slee aboard *Taiyo Maru*
U.S. Post Office burns 500 copies James Joyce,
    Ulysses

April-June MS tours Far East, Europe

June NY: Brentano's 284 pp. *The Pivot of Civilization*

Ku Klux Klan gains in power
Eugene O'Neill, *The Hairy Ape*

July 11-14 London, England Fifth International Neo-Malthusian and Birth Control Conference

Sept 18 MS marries Noah Slee
Sept 23 MS sails London-NYC
Oct 29 Mussolini's March on Rome
Oct 30 Carnegie Hall lecture
British edition *Woman and the New Race* retitled *The New Motherhood*
John Dewey, *Human Nature and Conduct*

1923   **Jan 1 MS opens CRB** Clinical Research Bureau
Feb 20 Albany Mayor locks MS out of hall
June-Dec MS tours Canada, U.S. West
Nov 8 Hitler's Munich Beer Hall Putsch fails

1924   2.5 million radios in U.S.
Sept 22 Stuart begins Yale
Oct England visit

1925   Jan 1 Dr. Hannah Stone, Medical Director, CRB
Jan 1 Dr. James F. Cooper, Medical Director,
    ABCL
Jan England visit
Feb. 21 *The New Yorker* begins publication

March 25-31 New York City Sixth International Neo-Malthusian and Birth Control Conference

Adolph Hitler, *Mein Kampf*
Nov 15 MS sails England, Geneva
Charleston fashionable

1926   **NY: Brentano's 231 pp.** *Happiness in Marriage*
U.S. population 115 million

1927   Slow Fox Trot fashionable

Aug 31-Sept 3 Geneva, Switzerland First World Population Conference

First "talkie," Al Jolson, *The Jazz Singer*
Bertrand Russell, *The Analysis of Matter*

Appendix B

What Every Girl Should Know updated   *What Every Boy and Girl Should Know*

	Dec Germany lecture tour, set up clinics
1928	**Feb 9 MS blacklisted by DAR**
	D.H. Lawrence, *Lady Chatterley's Lover*
	MS winters St. Moritz, Switzerland
	June 12 MS resigns presidency ABCL

CRB renamed BCCRB   Birth Control Clinical Research Bureau

Juliet Rublee makes movie *Soul of Mexico*

Oct NY: Brentano's 446 pp.   *Motherhood in Bondage*

	Herbert Hoover elected U.S. President
	Nov-Dec West Coast lecture tour
1929	Feb 14 St. Valentine's Day Massacre
	April 15 BCCRB raid, MS arrested

April 30 Illinois MS launches NCFLBC   National Committee on Federal Legislation for Birth Control

	May 13 MS banned from Boston
	May 15 MS on Fox Movietone News
	Oct 28 NYC Black Friday
	Dec 12 Cleveland lecture & West Coast
1930	**U.S. population 122 million**
	Feb 1 BCCRB opens Harlem Clinic
	Boston bans works by Trotsky
	Since Dec MS spoke to 25,000
	June BCCRB moves to 17 West 16th Street, NYC
	July 23 MS sails Europe
	Lambeth Anglican Bishops sanction Birth Control

Sept 1-5 Zurich, Switzerland   Seventh International Neo-Malthusian and Birth Control Conference

John Maynard Keynes, *Treatise on Money*

London MS, How-Martyn establish BCIIC   Birth Control International Information Center

	Sept 19 MS arrives NYC
	Oct 1 Grant senior year Princeton
1931	

Coedited with Hannah Stone   *The Practice of Contraception*

	Feb 13-14 Senator Gillette Doctors' Bill Hearings
	May 1 Empire State Building dedicated

Sept NY: Farrar & Rinehart 360 pp.   *My Fight for Birth Control*

1932	*Reader's Digest* founded
	Jan 20 Buffalo police try to arrest MS

Jan 27 *The Nation*   "My Answer to the Pope on Birth Control"

	March 3 MS banned from New Haven
	April 20 AWA Award Dinner

April 21 Senator Hatfield introduces Doctors' Bill
Aug 11 MS banned from Rome
Aug 21-23 NYC Third International Eugenics
    Congress
Franklin D. Roosevelt elected U.S. President

1933   Jan 30 Hitler appointed Chancellor
Hitler burns books of Sanger, Ellis, Freud
April 9 MS speaks on radio
Nov 10 Max Ernst files *U.S. v. One Package*

1934   June 13 Senator McCarren recalls Doctors' Bill
July-Aug MS tours Scandinavia, Russia
Male hormone androsterone isolated

1935   Aug 14 FDR signs Social Security Act
Sept 30 Hoover Dam dedicated
**Nov 5 MS sails India and World Tour for
    Birth Control**
Nov 30 MS speaks over Bombay radio
Dec 4 MS meets Gandhi
Rhumba fashionable
Dec 6 MS meets Rabindranath Tagore
Dec 30 All-India Women's Conference

1936   **Feb 21 MS hospitalized in Hong Kong**
Gone With the Wind
Mar 26 MS leaves Hawaii ends World Tour
U.S. population 127 million
Dec 7 *U.S. v. One Package* decision[4]

    **Dec 29-30 NYC Roosevelt Hotel Conference on Contraceptive
    Research and Clinical
    Practice**

1937   **Jan 11 MS radio speech NCFLBC**
Jan 15 Town Hall Award dinner
March 15-30 Pennsylvania tour
June AMA endorses contraception
July 3 MS disbands NCFLBC
**Published World Tour for Birth Control 1935-36 *Round the World for Birth
    Control***

PART III: THE CONSERVATIVE RADICAL

1937   Aug 7 sails from Honolulu
2nd Japan trip
Aug 13 Japan seizes Shanghai
Nov 3 Gall bladder operation
Dec 22 Lincoln Tunnel first tube opens

1938   June 25 Fair (Child) Labor Standards Act
    NY: W.W. Norton & Company 504 pp. *Margaret Sanger: An
    Autobiography*

Nov 9 Austria, Germany Krystallnacht
40-hour work week established in U.S.

1939	**Jan 19 BCCRB and ABCL merge BCFA**	**Birth Control Federation of** America
	MS launches Negro Project	
	Massachusetts Pittsfield Clinic stays closed	
	Connecticut contraceptives remain banned	
1940	**BCCRB renamed MSRB**	**Margaret Sanger Research** Bureau
	Aug 11 Hyde Park MS visits Eleanor Roosevelt	
	Aug 24 Carribean Birth Control tour	
	Sanger joins American Council Against Nazi Propaganda	
	Oct 12-20 Massachusetts lecture tour	
1941	July 10 Dr. Hannah Stone dies	
	Dec 7 Pearl Harbor Day: World War II	
1942	Cambridge Library bans *An Autobiography*	
	Jan 29 BCFA renamed PPFA	**Planned Parenthood** Federation of America
	10,000-ton Liberty ship built in 4 days	
1943	Feb 10 Gandhi begins 21-day fast	
	June 21 Noah Slee dies	
1945	Aug 6 H-bomb ends World War II	
	U.S. population 140.1 million	
	Christmas with Stuart, Grant, families	
1946	Aug Ottesen-Jensen organizes Family Planning Conference	
	Aug 4 MS sails *SS Stockholm*	
	Aug 20 MS addresses Ottesen-Jensen confer-	**"This I Believe"**
1947	ence	
1948	Aug 15 Nehru becomes Prime Minister of India	**International Congress on**
	Jan 1 Cheltenham, England	**Population and World** Resources
		International Committee on
	Jan 2 MS founds ICPP	**Planned Parenthood**
	Jan 30 Gandhi assassinated at age 78	
	April 3 U.S. Congress passes Marshall Plan	
1949	May 12 Berlin blockade lifted	
	June 6 Smith College awards MS Honorary LL.D.	
	Eleanor Roosevelt, *This I Remember*	
	Aug 22 MS hospitalized heart condition	
	Rodgers & Hammerstein, *South Pacific*	
	Dec 31 MacArthur denies MS Japan visa	
1950	**Oct 25 MS receives Lasker Award**	
	U.S. population 150,697,999	
	World Population 2,300,000,000	
1952	George Bernard Shaw, *Don Juan in Hell*	
	August 16,000 escape from East to West Berlin	
	Oct 21 MS sails from Honolulu 3rd Japan trip	
	Nov 24-29 Bombay, India	**Third International Conference** on Planned Parenthood

Timeline

Nov 26 MS addresses conference "The Humanity of Family Planning"

Nov 29 ICPP becomes IPPF International Planned Parenthood Federation

Nov 29 MS President WHR, IPPF Western Hemisphere Region, IPPF

1953 Kinsey, *Sexual Behavior in Human Female*
June 8 Shrewsbury, MA MS meets Katherine McCormick & Gregory Pincus
Dag Hammarskjold UN Secretary-General
Eisenhower inaugurated U.S. President

Aug 17-22 Stockholm, Sweden Fourth International Conference on Planned Parenthood

Aug 17 MS addresses conference "The History of the Birth Control Movement in the English-Speaking World"

Lung cancer tied to smoking
"How Much Is That Doggie in the Window"
1954 **May 18 MS Edward R. Murrow radio broadcast** "This I Believe"
April 4th Japan trip
April 1 MS speaks before Japanese Diet
Dec 2 Senate censures Joseph McCarthy
1955 **Oct 1 MS arrives Tokyo 5th Japan trip**

Oct 25-29 Tokyo, Japan Fifth International Conference on Planned Parenthood

Oct 26 Pincus announces The Pill
Dec 1 Montgomery bus boycott begins
1956 July *Reader's Digest* "Asia Discovers Birth Control"
Dec *Science* announces The Pill
1957 "Beat Generation" emerges
Sept 21 Mike Wallace TV program
U.S. Postmaster bans *Lady Chatterley's Lover*
Oct 4 U.S.S.R. launches *Sputnik*
1959 **Feb 14-21 New Delhi, India** Sixth International Conference on Planned Parenthood

MS resigns as IPPF president
MS titled IPPF Founder and President Emeritus
Feb 25 MS in Tokyo **6th Japan trip**
Fidel Castro, Premier of Cuba
TV covers Britain's General Election
May 21 sails with Margaret, Nancy **7th Japan trip**
Aug 17 Draper Report submitted
Dec 3 Eisenhower repudiates U.S. population assistance
1960 **Jan 3 Tucson, AZ** Letter to Editor, *New York Times*
May 11 FDA approves The Pill

Appendix B

EPILOGUE

1961	Elizabeth Gurley Flynn U.S. Communist Party Chairman
	May 11-12 Waldorf Astoria A World Tribute to MS
	July 25 Ridgefield Park, NJ Bill Sanger dies
1962	**Jan 1 MS moves to nursing home**
1965	**March 22 Tucson, AZ 1,000 guests at MS testimonial dinner: The Woman of the Century**
	May 18 MS awarded Third Class Order of Precious Crown of Japan
	June 7 *Griswald v. Connecticut*
	Malfunctioning relay switch in Ontario leaves 30 million people blacked out in Northeast U.S. Nine months later a sharp increase in births is noted
	U.S. population 205,000,000
	World population 3,860,000,000
1966	President Johnson's Health Message to Congress requests expanded program for birth control under Department of Health, Education and Welfare
	Sept 6 MS dies 8 days short of age 87
	Massachusetts permits legal prescription and sale of contraceptives
1967	Social Security funds family planning
1968	Title X Amendment created
1970	Contraceptives removed from obscene list
1972	March 22 *Eisenstadt v. Baird*
	U.S. fertility rate drops to replacement level for six months
1973	Jan 22 *Roe v. Wade*
1978	Helms Amendment to Foreign Assistance Act forbids U.S. funds for abortion
1984	Reagan institutes Mexico City Policy or Global Gag Rule at UN International Conference on Population
1993	Jan 22 Clinton rescinds Global Gag Rule
1998	Hyde amendment restricting abortion applies to Medicaid
2001	Jan 22 Bush reimposes Global Gag Rule on USAID population programs
2003	**U.S. population 287,400,000**
	World Population 6,215,000,000

Notes

General Introduction

1. James J. Corbett was an aggressive promoter type, a militant who agreed with Sanger that the Planned Parenthood name did not have the connotations of the term "Birth Control" and regarded the Planned Parenthood administration in 1957 as a bunch of "Fat Cats," who were unfortunately ignoring the attacks of the Roman Catholic leadership on contraception. Accordingly, or by coincidence, William Vogt, president of Planned Parenthood Federation of America in 1957, was appalled by the contents of Corbett's *Babies* and wrote Sanger of his concern that such a pamphlet had been endorsed by her. James J. Corbett to Margaret Sanger, February 8 and May 27, 1957; William Vogt to Margaret Sanger, September 4, 1957; Margaret Sanger Papers Microfilm Edition, Smith College Collection Series, Northampton, MA.

2. "Population Union" is the International Union for the Scientific Study of Population with its address on the world wide web at iussp.org.

3. Sanger Papers Microfilm, Smith College Collection.

4. Told to the author by her first granddaughter, Margaret Sanger Lampe.

5. "Informed that the archaeologists meeting in Tucson had received no official welcome, she, who had arranged so many conferences, invited the one hundred and fifty delegates to cocktails in her home and charmed them all." Emily Taft Douglas, *Margaret Sanger: Pioneer of the Future* (Garrett Park, Md.: Garrett Park Press, 1975), p. 260.

6. Ruth Hale, "Profiles: The Child Who Was Mother to a Woman," *New Yorker*, April 11, 1925, p. 11.

7. Helena Huntington Smith, "Profiles: They Were Eleven," *New Yorker*, July 5, 1930, p. 20.

8. "Margaret Sanger Begins to Study Birth Control," *The World*, June 6, 1926, Container 212, The Papers of Margaret Sanger, Manuscript Division, Library of Congress, Washington, D.C., 1977.

9. Harold Brainerd Hersey, "Biography of the Birth Control Pioneer" (Unpublished manuscript, 1938, Rare Books Division, the New York Public Library, New York City), p. 131. Harold A. Content (1887-1944), while assistant district attorney—in later life he was in private practice—was apparently known for his prosecution of radicals. Content's letters to Sanger are politely exasperated, but according to Harold Hersey ("Biography," p. 131), Content had great respect for Sanger. Esther Katz, ed., *The Selected Papers of Margaret Sanger. Volume 1: The Woman Rebel, 1900-1928* (Urbana and Chicago: University of Illinois Press, 2003), pp. 166-167, 181-182.

10. Hersey, "Biography," 1938, p. 270.

11. Lawrence Lader, *The Margaret Sanger Story and the Fight for Birth Control* (Garden City, N.Y.: Doubleday & Company, 1955), pp. 225-226. She turned down many lucrative endorsement offers, including one for a quarter of a million dollars to speak on the radio endorsing a chemical product. But she would not compromise her name or the integrity of the movement. Douglas, *Pioneer of the Future*, 1975, p. 183.

12. Hersey, "Biography," p. 110; Hale, "Profiles," 1925, pp. 11-12.

13. Margaret Sanger, *My Fight for Birth Control* (1931, reprint, Elmsford, N.Y.: Maxwell Reprint Company, 1969), p. 3.

14. Margaret Sanger, *An Autobiography* (1938; reprint, New York: Dover Publications, 1971), p. 107.

15. Harold Hersey, among others, speaks of this. Hersey, "Biography," p. 281.

16. In the early part of the twentieth century, abortion was a dangerous affair, often performed by quacks, to whom lower-class women, having no other contraceptives at that time, turned in desperation. As a nurse, Sanger was acutely aware of this. It was one of the reasons that she always spoke out against abortion and fought so persistently for legal contraception for women.

17. Hersey, "Biography," p. 120.

18. Harold Hersey felt very strongly about this. "The failure to include full details concerning many who have devoted themselves to Birth Control at one time or another is something Margaret Sanger will no doubt correct in later editions of her book. In *My Fight for Birth Control*, she speaks (on page 192) of the 'many friends who dropped in to give a hand' on the work of editing *The Birth Control Review*: 'Billy Williams, Walter Roberts, Harold Hersey, Agnes Smedley, and many others too numerous to mention.' I am sorry to disagree, but these friends are not 'too numerous to mention' and they did vastly more than 'drop in to give a hand.' For example, I was the anonymous Managing Editor for only about a year, from the autumn of 1920 to the autumn of 1921, and was paid for my services, but 'Billy' Williams entered so zealously upon his duties in connection with the *Review*, and with certain writing tasks one might well say are 'too numerous to mention,' that his health was undoubtedly affected by overwork. I have even been told it hastened his death." Hersey, "Biography," p. 127.

19. For instance, she took her younger sister Ethel's birth date as her own, and

Sanger never admits that her sister Mary worked as a maid. Margaret Sanger Lampe feels that her grandmother never got over the shame of having come from such a poor family, especially when she began moving in the circles into which Juliet Rublee introduced her. Revealingly, her grandmother once said, "I can never look back on my childhood with joy." Hersey, "Biography," 1938, p. 43. Margaret Sanger Lampe has said that when Margaret, through Noah's generosity, was able to help her family, she also enjoyed the sense of importance it gave her and the feeling that she had "made it."

20. Quoted in Douglas, *Pioneer of the Future*, p. 194.

Part I: The Rebel
1. Introduction to the Rebel

1. Margaret Sanger, *My Fight*, p. 51.

2. *Ibid.*, p. 55.

3. *Ibid.*, p. 56.

4. *Ibid.*, p. 79.

5. In her earliest radical days, Sanger raged at the living conditions imposed by capitalism on the working class and advocated direct action, but she was concerned for working women only, her concerns ranging from the meager wages to prostitution to wife beating. Thus, *The Woman Rebel* includes but is not devoted exclusively to the issue of Birth Control, as indicated by Sanger's inclusion in the July 1914 issue of the essay "A Defense of Assassination," which triggered the one indictment unrelated to the "obscenities" charges sparked by the Birth Control references.

I. 2. Early Years

1. Hersey, "Biography," p. 47.

2. In his enthusiasm, Michael Higgins (1845-1926) took the family's coal money for the winter and threw a fancy banquet for Henry George; this did not set well with Mrs. Higgins. He invited Robert Ingersoll to speak in Corning, which apparently so enraged the local priest that the Higginses were ever after regarded as outside the pale by the town of Corning, Margaret Sanger, *My Fight for Birth Control* (1931; reprint, Elmsford, NY: Maxwell Reprint Company, 1969), pp. 6-11.

3. Alexander C. Sanger, "Margaret Sanger: The Early Years, 1910-1917," master's thesis, Princeton University, 1969; Hersey, "Biography," p. 29.

4. Hersey, "Biography," pp. 36-40. The Knights of Labor was originally a secret society in Philadelphia, founded by Uriah Stevens for the clothing cutters. In 1879, after Terence V. Powderly became leader, the Knights aggressively opened its organization to all wage earners along with farmers, middle-class workers, and professionals and promoted strikes and boycotts along with their belief that the wage system should be abolished. So successful were Powderly's tactics that in 1885 the Knights won their railway strike against the infamous Jay Gould's Southwest System. After the Haymarket bomb explosion in Chicago in 1886, the Knights, associated as they were in the public mind with anarchism and violence, lost out to

Samuel Gomper's more conservative American Federation of Labor. Michael Higgins was one of the first to join Powderly's Knights and was both a speaker and an organizer for the Knights. The Corning strike never made any headway; three of the strike leaders never went back to their jobs. The Corning owners were implacable. In both the 1889 and a later 1911 strike, owners starved out the strikers, and miserable work conditions remained unchanged.

5. Hersey, "Biography," pp. 39-40.

6. Margaret Sanger, *My Fight*, p. 8.

7. As told to the author by Margaret Sanger Lampe.

8. Hersey, "Biography," p. 15.

9. *Ibid.*, p. 12.

10. Sanger, *My Fight*, p. 24. Margaret's family had four girls, including Margaret. Margaret's two older sisters never married but early on were working to support the family, and Margaret was greatly helped by their generosity. Mary Higgins (1870-1926) worked as a housekeeper for the Houghtons, who owned the Corning Glass Works, and Anna (Nan) Higgins (1874-1943) worked as a governess and later as a secretary. Harold Hersey wrote about Mary, "I only met her once but I had the distinct impression that she exemplified the much abused phrase 'a saint on earth'"; Hersey, "Biography," 1938, p. 29. When Hersey interviewed Bill Sanger, Bill said, "To understand Margaret's early life one must take into consideration the attitude of her sister, Nan. It was Nan who pulled out of the poverty of this Irish family very early. She put Margaret in Claverack school, a coeducational institution of middle-class boys and girls who were taught the elements of social class. Then George Eliot became a 'God' to Margaret. Drawing room manners were also taught . . . Margaret had to undo all this false early training when she began her social research in the slums"; Hersey, "Biography," p. 86. Interestingly, in her later 1938 autobiography, Sanger loses an older sister and conflates Nan and Mary into one older sister named Mary; Margaret Sanger, *An Autobiography*, pp. 14-15.

11. Claverack College was founded in 1830 and in 1854 enlarged and given the name Claverack College and Hudson River Institute. It had about five hundred students and was later destroyed by fire.

12. Harold Hersey interviewed Amelia Stewart Michell (1880-1954) of Schenectady, New York, who attended Claverack and also went through nurses' training in White Plains with Sanger. Michell praised Sanger extensively, saying, "Anything she touched she glorified in some mysterious way…. Given to gales of laughter, she called the place where she had to perform her tasks the 'dish-room.'…She was one of the most popular girls in school; I would be inclined to say the most popular with both the girls and the boys. She is one of those rare women who appealed to both sexes…. She could sew as well as cook, in fact she was to make my uniforms when we were nurses; dance divinely; excel in her classes without becoming a bookworm…. I am only sorry I haven't some of our other schoolmates here to prove I am not biased in her favor…. She told me practically nothing

about her home or her people, then or later, when we were trained nurses and continuing a friendship that has been one of the real comforts of my life.... I don't recall a single boy in school who didn't just adore Margaret, but I do remember the girls went to her with all their sorrows and love affairs.... She attracted confidences without ever asking for them." Hersey, "Biography," pp. 60-64.

13. Sanger was said to have been bitter (possibly refusing to see her father for many years) that her mother, Anne Purcell Higgins (1848-1899), died at fifty, exhausted by eleven pregnancies and at least seven miscarriages, while Michael Higgins lived to be eighty-one.

14. Many of the same incidents are repeated in the later Sanger autobiography, but the language is much changed; see Margaret Sanger, *An Autobiography*.

15. "Memoir," Reel 2, The Papers of Margaret Sanger, Library of Congress.

16. "lung trouble." As noted, Sanger's mother, Anne Purcell Higgins, was ill with tuberculosis throughout most of her married life.

17. "Chimneys" are the glass cylinder-shaped open-ended globes that sit atop kerosene lamps, used for indoor lighting before gas and electricity were available.

18. Sanger refers to her determination, at the age of eight, to see the matinee of *Uncle Tom's Cabin*, which was so overwhelming that she was almost tempted to steal the ten cents needed for the ticket from a nearby open purse. Saved from this by the pushing crowd that swept her into the theater, she saw the desired performance, but took no joy in it, so horrified was she by the deed she had almost committed. Had she been caught stealing, under the laws of that time, she could have been sent to a reformatory or suffered cruelly at the hands of the law. Sanger, *My Fight*, pp. 15-17.

19. Claverack College and Hudson River Institute was an accredited preparatory school that for many years enjoyed an excellent academic reputation.

20. Sanger spent only two years at Claverack.

21. Women were not given the right to vote in the United States until 1920, but suffrage for women was first officially proposed by Elizabeth Cady Stanton (1815-1902) in Seneca Falls, New York, in 1848. Cady Stanton was joined in her lifelong fight by Susan B. Anthony (1820-1906), whom Sanger heard speak and admired. In the first two decades of the twentieth century, debate and protest were intensified as the suffragists maintained a persistent campaign for the vote for women. The American suffrage campaign, however, was not marked by the extreme militancy and violence that was used by the British suffragettes.

I. 3. Socialism

1. "Memoir," Reel 2, The Papers of Margaret Sanger, Library of Congress, p. 19.

2. Esther Katz, ed., *The Selected Papers of Margaret Sanger. Volume I: The Woman Rebel, 1900-1928* (Urbana and Chicago: University of Chicago Press, 2003), p. 7.

3. Harold Hersey describes Sanger's nursing work in paragraphs that bring to life the demands of the nursing student in 1900:
"She soon became accustomed to the odor of disinfectants in a hospital, the smell of corned beef and cabbage (those staple items on the nurses' bill of fare in

the Nineties). She had to learn self-discipline under trying conditions.

"She was taught to read a thermometer and give a hypodermic injection—how to measure doses of medicine—the proper widths to tear bandages of unbleached muslin—the proper way to make those little cloth sponges of cotton that go inside wounds during an operation. She found out how to handle a bedpan—how to heat milk to just the right temperature—fight off sleep during the long watches of the night—remain on duty for twelve hours at a stretch—pacify mothers and newborn, squawking infants—rub backs and follow doctor's orders without question and without thought of self—prepare and serve meals in the diet kitchen—attend operation cases—keep her order book up to the minute—hide her sympathies behind an impassive countenance—fetch and carry hot-water bottles—see that every instrument was interminably boiled—take care of the delirious and dying, and the worst patients of all: those recuperating from illness. She learned the trick of bandaging her eyes when she fell exhausted into bed after coming off night duty—she learned to wash and dress wounds and not turn her head away from the stench of suppuration—to remain on duty when the rest of the world was on a holiday—to stand by when death claimed a soul and the morgue a body." Hersey, "Biography," pp. 71-72.

4. Of all her textbooks, only that on obstetrics was heavily underlined. Sanger, master's thesis.

5. Anna D. Behnke, a coworker at White Plains Hospital, told Harold Hersey in an interview, "Margaret Higgins, as I knew her: very attractive, carried her clothes well, most charming and cheerful manner. Always was interested in the cause she has done so much for. We often, when she got on the subject, laughed and chided her, and asked her what she was going to do about it. A very good student.... Interested in books and art." *Ibid.*, p. 73; "As far back as 1900, I began to inquire of my associates among the nurses what one could tell these worried women who asked constantly: 'What can I do [to prevent conception]?'" Margaret Sanger, *Woman and the New Race* (New York: Eugenics Publishing Company, 1920), p. 213. Margaret Sanger, *An Autobiography*, p. 55.

6. Harold Hersey writes, "Dr. H. Ernest Schmid (assisted by Doctors De Hart and Curtis, with Dr. De Gamo as the attending surgeon) was a physician imbued with great ideals and a strong sense of civic pride. The story of this hospital, now a large and flourishing one . . . is a forty-odd year record of a devoted few who were interested in caring for the sick and the injured." Hersey, "Biography," p. 74. Hersey apparently has the name wrong and must have been referring to Dr. W. H. Sherman. Katz, *Selected Papers*, p. 8.

7. Katz, *Selected Papers*, p. 8. Anna D. Behnke, Sanger coworker at White Plains Hospital, told Harold Hersey in an interview, "[Margaret] had an operation on her neck for T.B. glands. I am sure if she had not had such a fine, considerate Doctor... she would not have gotten on as well as she did." Hersey, "Biography," p. 73; Katz, *Selected Papers*, pp. 8-9 note 7.

8. Interview with Mrs. Julia Emerson House, Hersey, "Biography, p. 87.

9. Sanger: *My Fight*, pp. 40, 44. Margaret Sanger Lampe, oldest daughter of

Stuart, wrote to the author, "She *hated* housework."

10. Hersey, "Biography," pp. 92-93.

11. Bill Sanger had been interested in socialism prior to his marriage to Margaret and probably introduced Haywood to Margaret, for Bill Sanger at one time brought Haywood in as a speaker. Bill Sanger "had always been a Socialist, although not active, and held his friend Eugene V. Debs in high esteem." Sanger, *An Autobiography*, p. 69; Hersey, "Biography," p. 92.

12. As the elected and paid organizer, Margaret was quite successful. Her duties included recruiting women to join the party, supervising the distribution of propaganda, organizing naturalization classes. Alexander Sanger points out that in doing this work, Margaret began to understand how limited were women's freedoms and how great was their need for economic, social, and intellectual freedom. See Sanger, master's thesis.

13. When on July 6, 1892, workers struck the Carnegie Steel plant in Homestead, Pennsylvania, Henry Clay Frick, chairman of the board of Carnegie Steel, hired Pinkerton guards to replace the striking workers. Violence broke out, and three guards and ten workers were killed. Emma Goldman and Alexander Berkman determined on their own to avenge the death of the workers by assassinating Frick. Berkman failed to kill Frick, who was (ironically) saved by nearby workers, and Berkman spent fourteen years in prison, though his sentence was for twenty-two years. Goldman and Berkman, in accordance with anarchist theories, believed their act "to be a flaming call to the men of Homestead to throw off the yoke of capitalism, to use their present struggle as a stepping-stone to the destruction of the wage system, and to continue toward social revolution and anarchism." Emma Goldman, *Living My Life*, 2 vols. (1931; reprint; New York: Dover Publications, 1970), 1:86.

14. Peter Glassgold, ed., *Anarchy! An Anthology of Emma Goldman's* Mother Earth (Washington, D.C.: Counterpoint, 2001), p. xxvi.

15. Goldman first learned of the necessity for birth control after attending a Malthusian Congress in 1900 in Paris on that subject. Working as a midwife in 1906, her personal experiences left her yet more aware of the need for birth control, especially for the poor, though she saw birth control not as the only issue, but as one of many issues to be dealt with if women were to be emancipated. Goldman wrote of her feelings: "Midwifery offered a very limited scope.... But while my work held out no hope of worldly riches, it furnished an excellent field for experience. It put me into intimate contact with the very people my ideal strove to help and emancipate.... Still more impressed was I by the fierce, blind struggle of the women of the poor against frequent pregnancies. Most of them lived in continual dread of conception; the great mass of the married women submitted helplessly, and when they found themselves pregnant, their alarm and worry would result in the determination to get rid of their expected offspring. It was incredible what fantastic methods despair could invent: jumping off tables, rolling on the floor, massaging the stomach, drinking nauseating concoctions, and using blunt instruments. These and sim-

ilar methods were being tried, generally with great injury." Goldman, *My Life*, 1:185-186.

16. Hersey, "Biography," pp. 61, 73, 111.

17. Some of the other lecturers were Leonard D. Abbott, who taught literature; Hutchins Hapgood, American and Russian literature; Lincoln Steffens, muckraking; and George Bellows, art.

18. The importance of the Ferrer Center to Sanger's development as an effective public figure has been generally unacknowledged, no doubt because she herself appeared not to acknowledge the association. After her split with the radical community in the early twenties, Sanger deliberately refuted and/or downplayed those earlier leftist associations. Then in her second 1938 autobiography, she inexplicably wrote at length about those early friends, giving an extensive and intimate portrait of the radical circle of which she had once been a part and describing its members as only an intimate could have, in effect denying her denial. Sanger, *An Autobiography*, pp. 69-76.

19. Sanger, *My Fight*, p. 48.

20. See *New York Call*, Sunday editions. "Impressions of the East Side, Part I," September 3, and "Part II," September 10; and "Home Life," October 1, 1911, all on p. 15.

21. "Autobiographical Sketch," unpublished paper, n.d., Reel 128, The Papers of Margaret Sanger, Library of Congress, p. 1.

22. *New York Call*, Sunday edition, January 14, 1912, p. 15.

23. Priscilla Murolo, and A. B. Chitty, *From the Folks Who Brought You the Weekend: A Short, Illustrated History of Labor in the United States*. (New York: The New Press, 2001), p. 142. Between 1905 and 1914, six of those years had more than a million immigrants entering the United States, four slightly less than a million. *Historical Statistics of the United States: Colonial Times to 1970*, Part I (Washington, D.C., Bureau of the Census, U.S. Department of Commerce, 1975), p. C89-101.

24. Milton Meltzer, *Bread–and Roses: The Struggle of American Labor, 1865-1915*. (New York: Knopf, 1967), p. 53.

25. *New York Call*, March 26, 1911, p. 15.

I. 4. Early Sex Education

1. Harold Hersey interviewed Mrs. Julia Emerson House, whose lot backed on that of the Sangers' when they lived in Hastings-on-Hudson. House recalled that she and Margaret Sanger had many a visit discussing the raising of their children. "The two mothers joined forces in teaching their two sons. Both boys were part of a cooperative of a happy little group of eight boys and one girl who attended a private kindergarten, but the time came when the boys had to start school. It was a long walk down the aqueduct to the public school, so the two mothers decided to teach them at home, taking turns, each laboring faithfully for a week and then turning them over to the other with a sigh of relief.... Finally, when they had arrived at

the stone-throwing age, which it seems all boys must go through, we thought of a club for them which was to meet on Saturday afternoons." Hersey, "Biography," pp. 86-87, 89.

2. According to Lawrence Lader, Bill was a devoted husband. He "encouraged Margaret's efforts to write and often insisted on doing the dinner dishes while she worked on one of her papers." Lawrence Lader, *The Margaret Sanger Story and the Fight for Birth Control* (Garden City, N.Y.: Doubleday, 1955), p. 32.

3. *New York Call*, Sunday edition, October 22, 1911, p. 15.

4. *Ibid.*

5. "Autobiographical Sketch," Reel 128, The Papers of Margaret Sanger, Library of Congress, p. 2.

6. Michael Higgins, Margaret's father, advocated woman suffrage and approved of Amelia Bloomer's Bloomers and sensible dress for women, but he was not a free thinker when it came to sex. Rather he shared his century's prudishness for discussing such matters and was originally appalled at Margaret's involvement with Birth Control and all its concomitant issues.

7. At the turn of the nineteenth century, medical schools taught that masturbation caused physical and mental degeneration, even insanity.

8. *New York Call*, December 17, 1912, p. 15.

I. 5. IWW and the Lawrence Strike

1. *New York Call*, January 15, 1913, p. 1.

2. *New York Call,* January 16, 1913, p. 1. The General Strike was envisioned as the workers' ultimate weapon. If all the wage-earning workers of the world of every industry throughout the world were to go on strike at the same time, the capitalists would be brought to their knees.

3. Margaret Sanger, *The Pivot of Civilization* (New York: Brentano's, 1922), p. 5.

4. Harold Hersey wrote, "The average radical and labor leader was every bit as old fashioned about women in this regard as any conservative.... When [Sanger] appealed for help to a certain leader high in the councils of the Socialist Party, he told her they had enough trouble as it was without bringing down the wrath of the Church upon their heads. The intellectuals merely argued with her and among themselves and did nothing. The Labor politicians were shocked and disturbed by her fight to free their womenfolk from slavery. The IWW and the Anarchists appear to have been the only groups that supported her efforts from the start." Hersey, "Biography," p. 111.

5. Steve Golin, *The Fragile Bridge: The Paterson Silk Strike, 1913* (Philadelphia: Temple University Press, 1988), p. 123.

6. This was not true of all IWW unions in all parts of the United States, but it was true enough and widespread enough to make the IWW exceptional.

7. Golin, *Fragile Bridge*, pp. 118-119.

8. When Haywood was working for the Paterson silk workers' strike (following the Lawrence strike), he advised the strikers to keep "Hands in the Pockets" that the strikers might avoid even the appearance of violence or "direct action," to use the common term. Sanger chides Bill Haywood for this, for not taking direct action, and blames the failure of the Paterson strike on this advice. This seems a strange complaint for her to publish in the late thirties, for Sanger had spent her postradical years downplaying her early radical activity and generally presenting a façade of conservatism and respectability, which ensured continued support from the middle and upper classes that were increasingly approving her work. Margaret Sanger, *An Autobiography*, p. 84.

9. William D. Haywood, *Bill Haywood's Book* (New York: International Publishers, 1929; 1983), p. 247.

10. Those who had invested in the woolen mills included the governor of Massachusetts, the ex-president of Harvard University, and Harvard University itself. Page Smith, *America Enters the World: A People's History of the Progressive Era and World War I, Volume 7* (New York: McGraw-Hill, 1985), 7: 264.

11. This highly dramatic moment, when Sanger arrived with the children, was one Sanger would always remember. It catches the spirit that animated the radical movement before World War I. "As we neared New York, I began to worry about our arrival. We were all weary. Would preparations have been made to feed this hungry mob and house it for the night? But I should have trusted the deep feeling and the dramatic instinct of the Italians. Thousands of men and women were waiting. As my assistants and I left the train, looking like three Pied Pipers followed by our ragged cohorts, the crowd pushed through the police lines, leaped the ropes, caught up the children as they came, and hoisted them to their shoulders. I was seized by both arms and I, too, had the illusion of being swept from the ground. The committee had secured permission to parade to Webster Hall near Union Square. Our tired feet fell into the rhythm of the band. As we swung along singing, laughing, crying, big banners bellying and torches flaring, sidewalks throngs shouted and whistled and applauded." Sanger, *An Autobiography*, p. 82.

12. A very attractive young Margaret Sanger is centered in the photo, surrounded by a group of men and women, and above the picture is the headline, "Mrs. Taft Hears Strike Children Tell Woes to House Rules Committee." Below the photo is another headline: "Wife of the President Remains throughout Morning Session." The *New York Herald*, March 6, 1912, p. 4. On the same day, the *New York Times* published on page 6 a two-column article under the headline, "Mrs. Taft Listens to Strike Charges. Attends Inquiry into Lawrence Police's Treatment of Women and Children in Riots. Babies Torn from Mothers."

I. 6. The Comstock Laws

1. Dr. Mary Halton, Sanger's personal physician, reported that she and Sanger personally took to every hospital and clinic in Manhattan two ill women, one with syphilis and the other having a severe case of tuberculosis, seeking contraception information for them. With one exception, the women were denied help, so com-

pletely was Comstockery in control even after the 1918 Crane decision, which permitted contraception for ill women. "The Investigation of Hospitals," *Birth Control Review*, Volume IV, Number 6 [June 1920], p. 4.

2. Colgate's advertising included a doctor's endorsement of Vaseline as a safe contraceptive, stating that Vaseline, charged with four to five grains of salicylic acid will destroy spermatozoa without injury to the uterus or vagina. Andrea Tone, *Devices and Desires: A History of Contraceptives in America* (New York: Hill and Wang 2001), pp. 28-30.

3. *Ibid.*, pp. 27-28.

4. The Woman's Sphere page, in which Block and Sanger's columns appear, is always on page 15.

5. Sanger might have been happy to have been given the assignment. Possibly she had nursed the real or several Mrs. Sachses and had made her decision to give up nursing late that summer and now needed work.

6. *New York Call*, Sunday edition, November 17, 1912, p. 15.

7. *New York Call*, Sunday edition, December 29, 1912; January 5, 12, 1913, p. 15 in all editions.

8. Quoted in Tone, *Devices*, p. 20.

9. *Volkszeitstung*, February 13, 1913, p. 1; *New York Call*, February 14, 1913, p. 1. *What Every Girl Should Know* was published in treatise form by the summer of 1913 (Sanger sends "a little treatise" to Amelia Michell) and republished as a booklet by Rompapa's Rabelais Press early in 1914. Letter from Margaret Sanger to Amelia Stewart Michell dated July 1913, Katz, *Selected Papers*, pp. 54, 55 note 3.

10. Sanger had an unexpected confirmation of the importance of her information, when she "learned that the section on venereal disease" from *What Every Girl Should Know* was included, "officially but without credit, reprinted and distributed among the [World War I] soldiers going into cantonments and abroad." Sanger, *An Autobiography*, p. 256.

11. *New York Call*, March 9, 1913, p. 15.

I. 7. Life as a Radical

1. Haywood, *Haywood's Book*, p. 255.

2. Carlo Tresca recalled perhaps her first speech, when Sanger was speaking to Paterson strikers. "She started hesitantly, her voice so faint that it barely reached beyond the first few rows. 'Louder! Louder!' shouted the listeners. Displaying the firm willpower that has so often surprised those who meet her and see only a quiet, retiring sort of person, she conquered fear and warmed to her topic. Before it was over, she had the audience in the palm of her hand. Without gestures, nervous, yet gradually getting full control of her faculties, she pounded home the message she had come to deliver by sheer force of personality and a staggering array of facts. When it was over, she almost collapsed." Hersey said that Sanger later took a course in voice instruction. Hersey, "Biography," pp. 108-109.

3. *New York Call*, June 26, 1913, p. 5.

4. Sanger, *An Autobiography*, p. 85.

5. *Ibid.*, p. 84.

6. "finding nothing." "She couldn't have looked very seriously," remonstrated David Kennedy, a determined Sanger detractor, in David M. Kennedy, *Birth Control in America: The Career of Margaret Sanger* (New Haven, Conn.: Yale University Press, 1970), p. 19. But Kennedy missed the point. Regardless of what she may or may not have found, Sanger was searching for contraceptives that put the woman in control and that poor women could afford. Harold Hersey noted that when he was working as a young man at the Library of Congress in 1912, "the few books dealing with contraception in part or in whole were kept under lock and key." Hersey, "Biography," p. 204.

7. In Paris, "I was struck with the motherly attention our femme de chamber gave her one and only child. She came regularly to work at the apartment, but no words could persuade her to come before Jean had been taken to his school, and nothing could prevent her leaving her work promptly at noon to go to fetch him from school for his luncheon. Such considerate care was respected by us all. I compared this attitude of the French mother of one child who, though compelled to work, gave the child her attention and care, with those drunken, slovenly mothers of ten children in Glasgow who dragged their young children through the streets at midnight begging for bread. I began to see the small family as a part of social evolution." Sanger, *My Fight*, p. 72.

8. According to granddaughter Margaret Sanger Lampe, the first Margaret Sanger had many affairs over the course of her life, but none of them and no one was more important to her than her cause: the right of women to birth control.

9. Golin, *The Fragile Bridge*, pp. 43-44.

10. "Local No. 5 of the Socialist Party in Harlem, which William and Margaret Sanger joined, had its headquarters only ten blocks from the Sangers' rambling old apartment on 135th Street. After its meetings, the members would often adjourn for beer to the Sanger living room.... Here were earth-shaking ideas that would change the world.... Margaret Sanger was intrigued by this new political and economic radicalism—yet she was never really a part of it." Lader, *Margaret Sanger Story*, pp. 37-38.

11. Container 209, The Papers of Margaret Sanger, Library of Congress. The Hazelton newspaper has been identified as the *Hazelton Daily Standard*. Katz, *Selected Papers*, pp. 48-49.

12. Sanger, *My Fight*, p. 77.

13. *New York Call*, April 20, 1913, p. 15.

I. 8. Confronting the Government

1. Margaret Sanger, *My Fight for Birth Control*, p. 80.

2. Sanger, master's thesis.

3. The Library of Congress archivist titled Sanger's untitled and unpublished

manuscript "Two Words Changed the Whole Course of My Life," the two words being "Birth Control," and dated the manuscript 1926. Reel 130, The Papers of Margaret Sanger, Library of Congress.

4. "Two Words," *Ibid.*, pp. 1-2.

5. *The Woman Rebel*, March 1914, p. 1.

6. "The New Feminists," *Ibid.*

7. "The Prevention of Conception," *Ibid.*, p. 8.

8. "Humble Pie," *The Woman Rebel*, April 1914, p. 1.

9. Sanger, *An Autobiography*, pp. 109-111.

10. "Suppression," *The Woman Rebel*, June 1914, p. 1.

11. *Ibid.*

12. Sanger, *My Fight*, p. 80.

13. *The Woman Rebel*, May 1914, p. 1.

14. Meltzer, *Bread—and Roses*, p. 194.

15. The United Mine Workers Union was not recognized by Colorado Fuel & Iron until 1933. The labor conditions in Colorado were not unique. According to the 1916 report of the U.S. Commission on Industrial Relations, "In our great basic industries the workers are unemployed for at least one-fifth of the year, and that at all times during the year there is an army of men who can be numbered only by hundreds of thousands, who are unable to find work.... A large part of our industrial population as a result of the combination of low wages and unemployment [is] living in a condition of actual poverty.... It is certain that at least one third and possibly one half of the families of wage earners employed in manufacturing and mining earn in the course of the year less than enough to support them.... Thirty percent of the workers manage to subsist only by keeping boarders and lodgers." Final Report U.S. Commission on Industrial Relations, 1916, I: 22, 23, 34, quoted in Gustavus Myers, *History of the Great American Fortunes* (Modern Library, 1937), pp. 387-388.

16. John D. Rockefeller, Jr. was a devout and most-generous supporter of the Baptist Church. The YMCA, the Young Men's Christian Association, was the original force behind Anthony Comstock and the first to fund him.

17. When John Reed and other investigators visited the Ludlow site after the massacre, they found the charred skulls and skeletons of women and children. The Christian churches at that time taught that the poor were poor because they deserved to be poor. Russell H. Conwell, a Baptist minister preached the gospel of wealth more than six thousand times to audiences all over the country in a lecture titled "Acres of Diamonds," as in, "There are acres of diamonds to be picked up right in your backyard." In his lecture, he stated that success is "an outward sign of inward grace.... While we should sympathize with God's poor—that is, those who cannot help themselves—let us remember there is not a poor person in the United

States who was not made poor by his own shortcomings.... It is all wrong to be poor, anyhow.... To sympathize with a man whom God has punished for his sins, thus to help him when God would still continue a just punishment, is to do wrong, no doubt about it, and we do that more than we help those who are deserving.... Ninety-eight out of one hundred of the rich men of America are honest. That is why they are trusted with money. That is why they carry on great enterprises and find plenty of people to work with them. It is because they are honest men." Meltzer, *Bread—and Roses*, pp. 61-63.

18. In 1913, during the same year that the Colorado Fuel & Iron miners were working under the most unsafe conditions and shameful wages, Standard Oil was reaching its lifetime peak wealth of $900 million—this as a result of the 1911 Supreme Court order for Standard Oil to divest itself of its subsidiaries. During 1913, the Rockefellers were also supporting various philanthropies, including a campaign to end hookworm in the South. In 1913, the Rockefellers gave the Rockefeller Foundation, which had been incorporated "to promote the well-being of mankind throughout the world," the generous sum of $100 million. On June 10, 1914, Rockefeller, Jr., stated, "There was no Ludlow massacre." Ida Tarbell, a radical journalist, took three years to write *The History of Standard Oil* and to expose its corrupt practices. But John D. Rockefeller Jr. had learned at his father's knee. The senior Rockefeller (1839-1937) was a moneylender, who made his money selling lumber and patent medicines. Said he, "I cheat my boys every time I get a chance. I want to make 'em sharp. I trade with the boys and skin 'em. I just beat 'em every time I can. I want to make 'em sharp." Meltzer, *Bread—and Roses*, p. 56.

I. 9. Continuing the Confrontation

1. "Two Words," Reel 130, The Papers of Margaret Sanger, Library of Congress, p. 4. The Birth Control League of America did not survive beyond its announced formation in the July and August *Woman Rebel*.

2. Sanger, *An Autobiography*, p. 117.

3. *Ibid.*, p. 118.

4. Sanger, *My Fight for Birth Control*, p. 93. "If found guilty, I might be sentenced to as much as forty-five years in a federal penitentiary, and fined as much as $45,000!" Whether this was an exaggeration or not, Sanger had no interest in spending time in prison, and certainly she had no means to pay a fine. The law as written provided for five years in jail for each count and/or a five thousand dollar fine for each count. "Two Words," The Papers of Margaret Sanger, Library of Congress, p. 4.

5. Oliver M. Johnson, "Mrs. Sanger's First Visit to England, 1914-1915," Reel 135, The Papers of Margaret Sanger, Library of Congress, pp. 1-2. Oliver M. Johnson is referred to as "Olive Johnston" by Sanger in *An Autobiography* (p. 129) and Oliver M. John elsewhere, but Oliver M. Johnson is the correct name.

6. Douching with Lysol could be safe if the douche was sufficiently diluted, but a woman who put in extra "to make sure" would have injured herself, as complaints to Lysol, which were generally ignored, demonstrated.

7. Because the line drawing of the vagina showed a finger inserted into the vagina, illustrating how to place the pessary, *Family Limitation* was banned in England until the offensive finger was removed.

8. Container 209, The Papers of Margaret Sanger, Library of Congress.

9. *Ibid.*

10. Emma Goldman recognized that "women and children carried the heaviest burden of our ruthless economic system" and saw that available Birth Control was one of the many necessary elements for a transformed society. Goldman's views were shared by Ben Reitman (1879-1942), Goldman's excellent manager and (apparently) equally great lover. Reitman was a doctor, a hobo, and social activist, who freely gave of his services to the poor. Together, Goldman and Reitman distributed surreptitiously their four-page pamphlet, "Why and How the Poor Should Not Have Many Children," which gave sound contraceptive advice, recommending condoms and the womb veil, but, recognizing that the latter had to be fitted by a physician and involved expense, suggested douching and set out formulas for suppositories as a second-best preventative. Reitman and Goldman were arrested in Portland in August 1915 for distributing *Family Limitation*: they were fined and the cases dismissed. In 1916 in New York, they went to jail for distributing Birth Control literature. Reitman was also sent to jail in Ohio, again for distributing such literature. Emma Goldman, *Living My Life*, 2 volumes (1931; reprint, New York: Dover Publications, 1970), I: 187; Candace Falk, *Love, Anarchy, and Emma Goldman* (New York Holt, Rinehart and Winston, 1984) p. 239; James Reed, *The Birth Control Movement and American Society: From Private Vice to Public Virtue* (Princeton, NJ: Princeton University Press, 1978), pp. 48-53; Katz, *Selected Letters*, 2003, pp. 157-158.

11. Joan M. Jensen, "The Evolution of Margaret Sanger's *Family Limitation Pamphlet*, 1914-1921," *Signs* 6 [Spring 1981]: 548-567. With the tenth edition of 1920, references to "working women" and "comrade workers" were dropped.

12. Reel 129, The Papers of Margaret Sanger, Library of Congress.

I. 10. Exile and Europe

1. With the outbreak of World War I in 1914, Germany was attacking all ships, neutral or not, with her submarines; the sinking of the *Lusitania* on May 7, 1915, in which so many civilians died, was an example of the danger that came with crossing the Atlantic at that time.

2. The Fabian Society was a conservative socialist group established in 1884 to support a gradualist approach to social reform. It was closely allied with the British Labour Party, supplying it with socialist ideas. Its founding members included playwright George Bernard Shaw and writer H.G. Wells, who would become so important to Sanger's life. On July 5, 1915, while still in England, Sanger spoke at Fabian Hall. The British Museum in London was established by an act of Parliament in 1753 and in 1757 given the Royal Library by King George II. Since the museum opened in 1759, it has been famous for its holdings and for its library, and its vast central domed reading room was the location where many famous writers and thinkers, including Karl Marx, Charles Dickens, and George Bernard Shaw, worked.

The British Library was moved out of the museum in 1998, and researchers now must go to its new location on Euston Road near the St. Pancras Station.

3. "Two Words," Reel 130, The Papers of Margaret Sanger, Library of Congress, pp. 7-8.

4. Sanger is alluding to a poem by James Thomson (1834-1882), a Scottish poet and essayist. "The City of Dreadful Night," a gothic epic of depressing proportions and equally depressing sentiments, was published in 1880 in *The City of Dreadful Night and Other Poems*. Almost three decades later of that first entry into London, she tailors events rather differently, typical of her ways as she grew older, writing, "I rolled up to London through miles of chimney-potted suburbs; it continued rainy and foggy, but still there was a friendly atmosphere in the air. I seemed to be coming to a second home." Sanger, *An Autobiography*, p.124.

5. Dante's "mandate" refers to the inscription on the Gates of Hell in his *Inferno*.

6. Bloomsbury is the district of London in which the British Museum is located.

7. The Malthusian League was founded in 1861 on the principles of Thomas Malthus, who advocated late marriage and abstinence as a means of birth and population control. With the success of the Besant-Bradlaugh trial in 1876, whereby contraception was no longer deemed obscene under English law, the Malthusian League became the Neo-Malthusian Society–hence the term Neo-Malthusians— the first group in the world to advocate Birth Control and recommend contraception rather than abstinence.

8. Oliver M. Johnson, "Mrs. Sanger's First Visit to England, 1914-1915," Reel 135, The Papers of Margaret Sanger, Library of Congress, p. 2.

9. "Two Words," The Papers of Margaret Sanger, Library of Congress, p. 9.

10. Sanger read Ellis's seven-volume *Studies in the Psychology of Sex* "in one gulp, and had psychic indigestion for several months afterwards." Sanger, *My Fight*, p. 57.

11. Sanger, *An Autobiography*, p. 70.

12. Reel 1, The Papers of Margaret Sanger, Library of Congress.

13. The address of a Mr. Girling who lived in Ipswich was listed in Sanger's address book for that period.

14. Blatchford's *Clarion* was a socialist paper edited by Robert Peel Glanville Blatchford (1851-1943), who cofounded the Independent Labour Party. A number of Clarion Cafes existed as meeting places for *Clarion* readers and party members.

15. The Liverpool Anglican Cathedral, the Cathedral Church of Christ and the largest cathedral in England, was under construction from 1904 to 1978.

16. After the declaration of World War I, America became as violently anti-German as Britain was in 1914, not surprisingly, for Germany was the enemy and the aggressor.

17. Chester is known for its "Rows," double rows of stores, one at street level and the other on the second floor with galleries overlooking the street. The Rows line the junction of the four streets in the old town.

Notes

18. Sanger would naturally have been interested in medical practices in England.

19. Brymbo, Wales, is approximately three miles northwest of Wrexham. Sanger apparently went south from Liverpool to Brymbo, Wales, then west to Wrexham, which is approximately forty miles due south of Liverpool, and then straight north to Chester, which lies midway between Liverpool and Wrexham.

20. Ethel Higgins Byrne, Margaret's younger sister, lived with Robert (Rob) Parker after she left her husband. Jack Byrne, and Ethel and Rob shared living space with a second couple. Robert Parker became Margaret Sanger's excellent and regular ghost-writer. Sanger would give him her rough drafts, and he would polish her prose.

21. Karazza is a tantric technique whereby the man withholds ejaculation during intercourse, a popular contraceptive technique for the free-love followers and one practiced at the Oneida community in America.

I. 11. A European Education

1. Olive Byrne Richard interview with Jacqueline Van Voris, quoted in Ellen Chesler, *Woman of Valor: Margaret Sanger and the Birth Control Movement in America* (New York: Simon & Schuster, 1992), p. 53.

2. Sanger, *My Fight*, p. 43.

3. Sanger, *My Fight*, p. 42.

4. Sanger, *An Autobiography*, p. 23.

5. Sanger, *My Fight*, pp. 43-44, 57-58.

6. "Two Words," Reel 130, The Papers of Margaret Sanger, Library of Congress, p. 9.

7. Sanger, *My Fight*, p. 97; Katz, *Selected Papers*, p. 221.

8. Sanger, *My Fight*, pp. 97-98.

9. Information sent to the author by Margaret Sanger Lampe on September 5, 2002.

10. Margaret Sanger Microfilm Edition, Smith College Collections, Northampton, MA.

11. Sanger uses the bullfight analogy in her later writings.

12. Margaret did not go to Canada, but returned to New York in October 1916 in response to the rising interest of the general public in birth control.

13. Stuart was attending Winnwood School, a Christian Science boarding school in Ronkonkoma, Long Island, at this time, and Mrs. Winn was the school founder.

I. 12. Death and Acclaim

1. Linda Gordon, *Woman's Body, Woman's Right: A Social History of Birth Control in America* (New York: Grossman Publishers, Viking Press, 1976), pp. 225-226.

2. Gordon, *Woman's Body*, p. 226.

3. Lader, *Margaret Sanger Story*, pp. 81-82.

4. Gordon, *Woman's Body*, p. 226.

5. Falk, *Love, Anarchy*, p. 222. Goldman urged a birth strike, telling women to refuse to give birth to children who would only become cannon fodder for the state. Sanger urged a birth strike in 1925 in the *Birth Control Review*.

6. *Pictorial Review*, October 1915, p. 31. In a letter dated January 12, 1916, John Reed wrote to Margaret Sanger, "The [*New York*] Times does not dare use the words 'prevention of conception' in its news columns." Sanger, *My Fight*, p. 136. In the 1980s, the *New York Times* would not accept an advertisement for condoms that referred to them as "contraceptives."

7. "One afternoon I was invited to show myself at a tea arranged by Henrietta Rodman in her Greenwich Village apartment. A group of Feminists and liberals had gathered to decide, evidently, whether I was worthy of their endorsements. Out of that meeting a movement was started to give a dinner in my honor at the Brevoort Hotel on the evening preceding my trial." The group of "Feminists and liberals" was Heterodoxy, and Henrietta Rodman was a flamboyant and powerful activist, a school teacher who fought for, among other things, a woman's right to continue teaching after becoming a mother In this fight, Rodman was assisted by Charlotte Perkins Gilman. Sanger, *My Fight*, 1931, p. 132.

8. Around the time that Sanger began publishing *The Woman Rebel*, she sought support for *Rebel* and for Birth Control from Heterodoxy, the elite feminist group, some of whom were socialists as well as suffragists. The group, which then included Charlotte Perkins Gilman, Mabel Dodge, Henrietta Rodman, Crystal Eastman, and later Elizabeth Gurley Flynn, were not interested in helping Sanger in 1914, regarding Birth Control and frank discussions of sexuality as far too radical for them. Sanger, *Autobiography*, 1938, p. 108.

9. "Two Words," Reel 130, The Papers of Margaret Sanger, Library of Congress, p. 11. Alexander C. Sanger writes that when Peggy was sick, she told Margaret, "I want Aunt Ethel to hold me, not you, Mommy." Sanger, master's thesis.

10. "For two years at least after [Peggy's] death it was impossible for me to sit across from a child in a train, in the New York subway, or in a streetcar. Tears would flood my eyes, and I would move swiftly away to another seat or another car, or even leave the subway at the next station, to the amazement and distress of those who happened to be with me." Lader, *Margaret Sanger Story*, p. 88; Sanger, *My Fight*, p. 128. Margaret and Grant long honored the anniversary of Peggy's death, Grant always with a telephone call or a conversation with Margaret.

11. "Two Words," Reel 130, The Papers of Margaret Sanger, Library of Congress, pp. 11-12.

12. Reel 129, The Papers of Margaret Sanger, Library of Congress.

I. 13. Time in Prison

1. Quoted in Sanger, *My Fight*, p. 138.

2. A letter signed by H.G. Wells, Gilbert Murray, and other distinguished Englishmen had been prepared by Dr. Marie Stopes and sent to President Wilson. Other signators of the Wilson letter included William Archer, Arnold Bennett, Edward Carpenter. Sanger, *My Fight*, pp. 136-138.

3. Never before had there been so many newspaper reporters and photographers at the courthouse as appeared to cover Sanger's trial on the eighteenth. Sanger, master's thesis; Sanger, *My Fight*, p. 139.

4. Sanger, *My Fight*, 1931, p. 134.

5. Sanger, *An Autobiography*, pp. 203, 263.

6. Container 211, The Papers of Margaret Sanger, Library of Congress.

7. *Ibid.*; Sanger, *An Autobiography*, pp. 192-259.

8. "Two Words," Reel 130, The Papers of Margaret Sanger, Library of Congress, pp. 12-13.

9. Container 211, The Papers of Margaret Sanger, Library of Congress, p. 14; Sanger, *My Fight*, p. 150.

10. Ethel actually went on a five-day hunger strike. Katz, *Selected Papers*, p. 208.

11. This protest meeting was organized by Gertrude Pinchot, brought an audience of three thousand and in one night raised one thousand dollars. This is the Carnegie Hall meeting to which Sanger refers in Part I The Rebel, The First Birth Control Clinic and Part II: The Reformer, Introduction to the Reformer.

12. "Two Words," Reel 130, The Papers of Margaret Sanger, Library of Congress, p. 14.

13. An unfortunate wart. When Sanger was old and ill, she asked Ethel to say that she, Margaret, had endured the hunger strike. A Hollywood screenwriter had suggested this would make the better story.

14. Sanger had seen firsthand the power of national publicity in comparing the success of the Lawrence strike to the outcome of the Paterson strike.

15. "Two Words," Reel 130, The Papers of Margaret Sanger, Library of Congress, p. 15.

16. Sanger, *An Autobiography*, p. 237.

17. Sanger, *My Fight*, p. 185; "Doing Time on Prison Reform," *Margaret Sanger Papers Project Newsletter*, Spring 1998: 18: 1-4.

18. Reel 1, The Papers of Margaret Sanger, Library of Congress.

19. "Mother Slattery" was Margaret A. Slattery, head matron of Blackwell's Island workhouse, where Sanger was first taken. *New York Times*, January 24, 1917 in Katz, *Selected Papers*, p. 206.

20. Warden Joseph A. McCann (1885-1937); Matron Whittaker was characterized by Sanger as "kindly and humane person." *New York Times*, March 7, 1917 in *ibid*.

21. Workhouse was Blackwell's Island workhouse; Raymond Street Jail was in Brooklyn. After her first arrest at the Brownsville Clinic, Sanger was put overnight in the Raymond Street Jail, where she "struggled with roaches and horrible-looking bugs" and a rat. "The mattresses were spotted and smelly, the blankets stiff with dirt and grime. The stench nauseated me." Sanger, *An Autobiography*, p. 221.

22. The fingerprints issue became real as Sanger was being released from prison: "The only brutal treatment I received was during the last two hours. Since my fingerprints had not been taken on arrival, Warden McCann first tried to talk me into compliance. His argument that all prisoners' prints must be on file, that not having them was unheard of, got us nowhere. I refused to submit, even though it postponed my release. He then turned me over to two keepers. One held me, the other struggled with my arms, trying to force my fingers down on the inkpad. I do not know from what source I drew my physical strength, but I managed to prevent my hands from touching it. My arms were bruised and I was weak and exhausted when an officer at headquarters, where J.J. [Goldstein, Sanger's attorney] was protesting against the delay, telephoned an order to discharge me without the usual ceremony." Sanger, *Autobiography*, p. 249.

I. 14. The First Birth Control Clinic

1. Reel 131, The Papers of Margaret Sanger, Library of Congress.

2. Sanger is referring to the "Mrs. Sachs story," told in Part I: Introduction to the Rebel.

3. New York state legislators, taking exception to the strictures of the Comstock federal act, in 1881 passed a law that permitted physicians to provide contraception information to prevent the spread of "disease," "disease" being limited to venereal disease. In practice, physicians of the early twentieth century were not comfortable with discussing contraception let alone venereal diseases under any circumstances and certainly would not have considered this authority for advising women on contraception.

4. Black Maria–term for the "paddy wagon," the police vehicle that transports those arrested to jail.

Part II: The Reformer
15. Introduction to the Reformer

1. Sanger, *An Autobiography*, p. 251.

2. I use the term "reformer" drawing on the dictionary definition of "reform": "to abolish abuse…to put an end to (a wrong)." Janice Schuetz categorizes Sanger more scientifically and calls her an "Activist Agitator," based on the definition of C. W. Lomas: "The activist agitator [is] an advocate who defines the social conflict and its moral issues, gives evidence of injustice, and enacts a plan of resistance to alleviate the injustice. C. W. Lomas, *The Agitator in American Society* (Englewood Cliffs, N.J.: Prentice-Hall, 1968), p. 2; quoted in Janice Schuetz, *The Logic of Women on Trial: Case Studies of Popular American Trials* (Carbondale and Edwardsville: Southern Illinois University Press, 1994), p. 91.

3. "Medicus," in the *Medical Review of Reviews*, February 1917, quoted in "Birds of a Feather," *Birth Control Review*, Volume I, Number 2 [March 1917], p. 9.

4. The Drysdales and Ellis advised Sanger against continuing the excesses of rhetoric in *The Woman Rebel*. Havelock Ellis to Margaret Sanger, Reel 3, The Papers of Margaret Sanger, Library of Congress.

Notes

5. Sanger, *My Fight*, pp. 189-190. This attitude of Sanger's is also in keeping with her criticism of Bill Haywood's "Hands in the Pockets" tactics during the Paterson strike (Sanger, *An Autobiography*, 1938, p. 84). The exception to the conservatives was Kitty Marion (1873-1944) who began hawking the *Birth Control Review* on New York street corners in 1917, selling as many as a thousand copies in a month (Sanger to Rublee, August 8, 1920). Marion had been a militant suffragette in England, working for Emmeline Pankhurst, and in London prisons endured "232 compulsory feedings" (Sanger, *Autobiography*, 1938, p. 256). Marion was regularly arrested, even though the arrests were illegal, and as regularly released by attorney Goldstein, but she did spend thirty days in jail for handing over a copy of *Family Limitation*, when she was entrapped, just as Bill Sanger had been. She found herself in jail with Agnes Smedley, and the two of them promoted Birth Control throughout the prison. In 1930, after Sanger had left the American Birth Control League, Marion was summarily dismissed from her "position" by Robertson-Jones, who felt that Marion standing on street corners vulgarized the Birth Control movement. Kitty was one of a kind.

6. February 14, 1917, Reel 7, The Papers of Margaret Sanger, Library of Congress.

7. Sanger, *My Fight*, p. 191. As events would later show, clinics simply disappeared in those cities where well-heeled donors were not available to fund them.

8. In addition to the headstands that Margaret Sanger Lampe describes, the good times included innumerable letters, trips, and visits. The Sanger-Rublee correspondence fairly dances with friendship and delight in life. For confirmation, see Sanger-Rublee correspondence in Margaret Sanger Papers Microfilm Edition, Smith College Collection Series, and, more immediately available, Sanger-Rublee correspondence in Esther Katz, *The Selected Papers of Margaret Sanger. Volume I: The Woman Rebel, 1900-1928* (Chicago and Urbana: University of Illinois Press, 2003), *passim*.

9. Sanger, *My Fight*, p. 190. In Sanger, *An Autobiography*, Sanger omits "agitation" and lists only three steps: "first, education; then, organization; and, finally, legislation," p. 251.

10. Sanger, *My Fight*, p. 196.

11. *The Case for Birth Control: A Supplementary Brief and Statement of Facts* (1917), 251 pages, incorporated statistics, Children's Bureau and other governmental findings, recommendations of health experts, and writings by Ellis, Sanger, and others that downplayed feminist or radical concerns and emphasized the medical and eugenic case for Birth Control.

12. "I just kept going, night and day, visualizing every act, every step, *believing, knowing* that I was working in accord with a universal law of evolution—a moral evolution, perhaps, but evolution just the same. This belief, faith—call it what you will—gave me a feeling of tremendous power. It seemed at times to open locked doors. It attracted the right people; it gave me the physical strength to dictate hundreds of letters through one ill-paid secretary, to interview dozens of people each day, to write articles, to write and deliver lectures, debates—in spite of a daily temperature, low but constant, and a decreasing bank account." *Ibid.*, p. 197.

13. "Birth Control and the Good Old Boys in Congress," *Sanger Papers Project Newsletter*, Number 26 [Winter 2000/2001], *passim*.

14. Sanger, master's thesis.

15. Sanger, *Pivot*, p. 14.

16. Sanger's "goading" was complemented by the work of Robert Latou Dickinson. As a distinguished physician, his advocacy of birth control was slightly more acceptable to the medical community.

II. 16. The *Birth Control Review*

1. Sanger, *An Autobiography*, p. 252.

2. Sanger, *My Fight*, p. 192. Frederick Blossom (1878-1974), librarian and Socialist, left Cleveland's Associated Charities to become managing editor of the *Birth Control Review*. Blossom apparently donated his own money to the movement and to the *Review*. Blossom also founded and was president and treasurer of the New York Birth Control League (not to be confused with the Dennett's National Birth Control League). The New York League was established to administer a defense fund for Sanger. From November 1916 to March 1917, Blossom diligently publicized and promoted Sanger's lectures and the Birth Control movement, but in April a major disagreement arose over control and finances, which dragged on into summer 1918. Esther Katz, ed., *The Selected Papers of Margaret Sanger. Volume I; The Woman Rebel, 1900-1928* (Urbana and Chicago: University of Illinois Press, 2003), *passim*.

3. James Reed, *The Birth Control Movement and American Society: From Private Vice to Public Virtue* (Princeton, N.J.: Princeton University Press, 1978), pp. 109-110.

4. Sanger, *My Fight*, p. 192. The "packing box" story is visually effective. Sanger also says that Blossom took all the files. Sanger writes to Juliet Rublee on December 29, 1917, "The room 2004 is at last free a lock was put on the door & just on time for the gentleman tried to get in after hours for the file etc. He took all the furniture and oh such a desolate looking place. I went out to the second hand furniture place & bought something to sit on—no statement yet." Katz, *Selected Papers*, p. 227.

5. "A Statement of Fact—An Obligation Fulfilled," *Birth Control Review*, Volume 2, Number 6 [August 1918], pp. 3-4.

6. "During the years from 1917 to 1921, the *Review* was the most strenuous work of my already strenuous life." Sanger, *My Fight*, p. 192.

7. "Between 1921 and 1926, I received over a million letters from mothers requesting information. From 1923 on a staff of three to seven was constantly busy just opening and answering them." Sanger, *An Autobiography*, p. 361.

8. *Ibid.*, pp. 251-252.

9. Sanger continued to stay in touch with individual radical friends, corresponding with Eugene Debs, Bill Haywood, and Carlo Tresca. Before Sanger went to California with Grant in the winter of 1919, she hosted a reception for Agnes Smedley to celebrate her release from jail and then hired her to work at the *Review*. Sanger was to be confronted with these acts by the British, who on this basis apparently would not allow her to visit India until 1935.

10. The *Birth Control Review* published pro-radical and anti-war sentiments: on Bill Haywood's IWW, "Let's Have the Truth," Volume 2, Number 7 [August 1918], p. 8; on Max Eastman's *The Masses*, "The New Masses," Volume 2, Number 2 [February/March 1918], p. 10; on Ben Reitman, "Editorial Comment," Volume 2, Number 3 [April 1918], p. 16; on Eugene Debs, "Debs and the Woman's Movement," Volume 2, Number 11 [December 1918], pp. 11-13; anti-war cartoon, "Breed!" Volume 1, Number 3 [April/May 1917], p. 5, set above "Breeding Men for Battle" by Olive Schreiner; on Carlo Tresca, Volume IX, Number 1 [January 1925], p. 4.

11. *Birth Control Review*, Volume VI, Number 1 [January 1922], pp. 4-5.

12. The Bishop of Birmingham. Dr. E.W. Barnes, was Chairman of the English National Birth Rate Commission and President of the National Council of Public Morals. "Famous Churchman Speaks Out," *Birth Control Review*, Volume III, Number 7 [July 1919], p. 15; "An English Bishop on Birth Control," *Birth Control Review*, Volume 4, Number 2 [February 1920], p. 14.

13. "Famous British Health Official Advocates World Wide Birth Control," *Birth Control Review*, Volume 2, Number 9 [October 1918], pp. 8-9.

14. Sanger, *My Fight*, 1931, p. 190. In Margaret Sanger, *An Autobiography* (1938), Sanger omits "agitation" and lists only three steps: "first, education; then, organization; and, finally, legislation" (p. 251).

II. 17. World War I

1. In 1917, many American Federation of Labor affiliates were against intervention, as were other important unions: Amalgamated Clothing Workers; Ladies Garment Workers; United Mine Workers; Mine, Mill and Smelter Workers. Murolo and Chitty, *From the Folks*, p 161. Further evidence of the antiwar sentiment comes from voting returns supporting the Socialists, who in April 1917 were identified with the antiwar sentiment, passing a resolution calling the war "a crime against the people": "In the 1917 municipal elections, Socialists candidates received 22 percent of the vote in New York City, 34 percent in Chicago (where they had received less than 4 percent a year earlier), and 44 percent in Dayton." William E. Leuchtenburg, *Perils of Prosperity* (Chicago: University of Chicago Press, 1958), pp. 41-42.

2. "At the beginning of the war, the Council of National Defense had on its staff 408 persons, only 168 of whom were paid." Smith, *America Enters*, pp. 569, 570-607.

3. Smith, *America Enters*, p. 767. Mitchell Palmer (1872-1936) promoted Wilson's candidacy and was Attorney General (1919-1921) under Wilson. Though previously supportive of progressive demands, such as woman suffrage, as Attorney General with special assistant J. Edgar Hoover, Palmer became zealous in ridding America of communists and reds. Relatively few of Palmer's arrests were justified or sustained conviction. The number actually arrested on the night of the Palmer raids is a variable figure, with as many figures as there are historians. But if only as few as one thousand (as in Hugh Brogan, *The Penguin History of the United States of America* [New York: Penguin Books, 1986], p. 503), the illegality of the sweep is without question, and it is a shameful note in American history.

4. On every side, the most-extreme conservatism seized the day, laying the ground for the rise of the Ku Klux Klan and its control of entire state governments during the twenties, while at the same time any remnant of progressive or radical activity vanished along with workers' rights.

5. "The jury had listened to scores of witnesses. There were hundreds of exhibits to examine. There were 17,500 offenses to consider. There were 40,000 pages of typewritten records, some of which could have been examined. But the jury's verdict was given within an hour." Haywood, *Haywood's Book*, p. 324.

6. The FBI kept a file on Sanger and noted that Sanger had joined the League for Amnesty of Political Prisoners and also linked her to the American Civil Liberties Union. See Chesler, *Woman of Valor*, pp. 161-162.

7. Hersey, "Biography," p. 106.

II. 18. Rightful Causes

1. Markham, Lindsey, and Creel, *Children in Bondage—A Complete and Careful Examination of the Anxious Problem of Child Labor—Its Causes, its Crimes, and its Cure* (New York: Hearst's Intl. Library Co., 1914), quoted on the Web site of the Museum of Early American Childhood.

2. "To Mothers—Our Duty," *New York Call*, (Sunday edition), March 26, 1911, p. 15, herein.

3. "Impressions of the East Side, Part I," *New York Call*, Sunday edition, September 3, 1911, p. 15.

4. "The Child Slave and the Law," *Birth Control Review*, January 1920, pp. 8-10.

5. Sanger, *Pivot*, p. 61.

6. Sanger, *Pivot*, p. 66. Sanger quotes therein from "California the Golden" by Emma Duke, a reprint from *The American Child*, Volume 2, Number 3, November 1920.

7. Sanger, *Pivot*, p. 66-67.

8. Sanger, *Pivot*, p. 70.

9. Sanger, *Pivot*, p. 73.

10. Sanger, *Pivot*, pp. 78-79.

11. *Hammer v. Dagenhart*, 247 U.S. 251 (1918).

12. In 1938, Franklin Delano Roosevelt's Congress passed the Fair Labor Standards Act, which ended child labor in operations affected by interstate commerce. It was challenged, but the Supreme Court declared it constitutional in 1941, and that decision stands to this day (2003).

II. 19. Motherhood

1. Smith, *America Enters*, p. 1,018.

2. *Herald*, Syracuse, New York, April 5, 1926, "Does Marriage Interfere With a Career?" Interview with Margaret Sanger by Hannah Stein, Scrapbook VIII,

Container 212, The Papers of Margaret Sanger, Library of Congress.

3. "Two Words," Reel 130, The Papers of Margaret Sanger, Library of Congress.

4. Sanger, *An Autobiography*, p. 265.

5. Sanger, *An Autobiography*, pp. 265-266.

6. Katz, *Selected Papers*, p. 241.

7. Margaret Sanger to Noah Slee, November 1, 1937. Sanger Microfilm, Smith College.

8. Sanger, *An Autobiography*, p. 431.

9. See II The Reformer: India and World Tour for Birth Control, herein.

10. *Sayings of Others on Birth Control* (New York: New York Woman's Publishing Company, Inc.), 1921, pp. 14-15, Reel 130, The Papers of Margaret Sanger, Library of Congress.

II. 20. Margaret Sanger as Feminist Author

1. Sanger, *My Fight*, p. 192.

2. "Portet died with T.b. of the throat & there is reason to think that deadly germ can play havoc with my throat if it continues." Margaret Sanger to Juliet Rublee, August 25, 1921, Katz, *Selected Papers*, p. 310.

3. Sanger wrote often of her prespeech nervousness, as in this typical comment: "My nervousness ahead of lectures continued to be akin to illness. All through the years it has been like a nightmare even to think of a pending speech. I promised enthusiastically to go here or there, and then tried to forget it. The morning it was to be delivered I awakened with a panicky feeling which grew into a sort of terror if I allowed myself to dwell on it. It was fatal to eat before a meeting." Sanger, *An Autobiography*, p. 263.

4. Katz, *Selected Papers*, pp. 260-261.

5. Katz, *Selected Papers*, pp. 250-251. Friends of Sanger, worried about her health, gave her the money to go to California to rest and recuperate. "Race" was a much-used word in 1920; eugenics was based on "race betterment," and *The Passing of the Great Race* by Madison Grant, an extremely popular book during the twenties, touted his thesis that intermarriage between the "superior" Nordic race with the "inferior" Mediterranean peoples would lead to "mongrelization." Chapter VI of *The Pivot of Civilization* concludes with the phrase "a race of thoroughbreds."

6. Lader, *Margaret Sanger Story*, p. 142.

7. Juliet Rublee to Margaret Sanger, August 6, 1919, Katz, *Selected Papers*, p. 259. Juliet Rublee, speaking of the Roman Catholic leadership, wrote, "It occurs to me that because you tell the truth about the church, many newspapers & magazines may be threatened by the church, with the loss of Catholic advertisements if they advertise your book—Do you think this is possible? Surely the Catholics themselves must see the unanswerable truth of what you say—There must be many fine & able & open, fair minded men among them. Don't you think so? If not, I think it would

be well to offset their activity, by this thought about them, suggested in the preface—or in a letter written to you by some distinguished & well known person, that you could publish."

8. Sanger, *An Autobiography*, p. 299.

9. Sanger, *New Race*, pp. 172-174.

10. Sanger, *New Race*, p. 226.

11. *Ibid.*, pp. 174-175.

12. *Ibid.*, p. 162.

13. *Ibid.*, p. 44.

14. *Ibid.*, p. 62.

15. *Ibid.*, p. 63.

16. *Ibid.*, p. 53.

17. *Ibid.*, p. 229.

18. *Ibid.* "The feebleminded are notoriously prolific in reproduction" (p. 41); "If a child is nursed after it is twelve months old, it is generally pale, flabby and unhealthy...while the mother is usually nervous, emaciated and hysterical" (p. 134); "Those who believe in strictly legal measures . . . are demanding amendments to the obscenity statutes" (p. 194). The mothers who Sanger saw nursing their unspaced infants would have had unhealthy children and would have been unhealthy themselves. In traditional societies where women space their children, maintain their own health, and nurse each child at least through the third year, mother and child remain healthy.

19. *Ibid.*, p. 121.

20. *Ibid.*, p. 182.

II. 21. Appeal to Science

1. In fact, the trip to Ireland with Ellis was apparently not a particularly happy one. Possibly, Sanger was not well, but a sightseeing trip could not have been as exhausting as lecturing. Any flat time with Ellis was more than offset by time spent at Wantley, where lived Hugh de Selincourt, his wife Janet, their daughter Bridget, and Janet's former lover, Harold Child. Child (1869-1945), was a poet, a drama critic for the *Observer* and contributor to the *Times Literary Supplement*, and for a while Sanger's lover. The open marriage that the idyllic sixteenth-century estate of Wantley accommodated was in keeping with its past associations, for it had once been the home of the father of the poet Percy Bysshe Shelley (1792-1882), who, with his good friend the celebrated Lord Byron (1788-1824), advocated and attempted to live relationships uncontaminated by possessive jealousy. Sanger at this time was also being pursued by E.S.P. Haynes (1877-1949), a solicitor and expert on marriage law and vice-president of the Malthusian League. "E.S.P. Haynes is very charming to me very! A friend of H.G.'s," she wrote to Juliet. But enjoy this as she might, none of it mattered to her as much as did her work. As Sanger also wrote to Juliet, "I wonder if man will ever interest me again! . . . Meetings here overcrowd-

ed oh Juliet never was there such a cause—poor pale faced wretched wives—men beat them they cringe before their blows but pick up the baby—dirty & illkempt & return to serve him. 'It's the baby I'm thinking of' She says to explain why she has to endure his blows—I want to talk for a week to you." Margaret Sanger to Juliet Rublee, July 7, 1920, Esther Katz, ed., *The Selected Papers of Margaret Sanger. Volume I: The Woman Rebel, 1900-1928* (Urbana and Chicago: The University of Illinois, 2003), pp. 284-285.

2. Sanger's lengthy travels are much too complicated and should not even be touched on in this volume; however, the temptation wins out occasionally.

3. Katz, *Selected Papers*, pp. 306-307.

4. Sanger, *The Pivot of Civilization*, (New York: Brentano's, 1922), p. 26.

5. Sanger, *An Autobiography*, p. 299.

6. Sanger, *Pivot*, p. 140.

7. Sanger, *Pivot*, p. 1. In 1954, John Rock stated, "The greatest menace to world peace and decent standards of life today is not atomic energy but sexual energy," quoted in Lara V. Marks, *Sexual Chemistry; A History of the Contraceptive Pill* (New Haven, Conn.: Yale University Press, 2001), p. 13, quoted in *Planned Parenthood News*, No. 8 (Summer 1954).

8. Sanger, *Pivot*, p. 23.

9. Smedley goes on to make some additional interesting observations: "I believe [this sexual frustration] finds outlets in a thousand other ways, terrible outlets. If the woman is sensitive, she becomes psychologically if not physically ill. An honest woman brought up in such a manner has no choice before her but to remain an ascetic all her life. Or if she departs from the ways of asceticism, to be broken in health. I often wonder if this national attitude of prudery in America does not find outlet in the lynchings of Negroes, the racial hatred, etc. I don't know." Smedley-McKinnon Collection, MSS 123, Box 1, Folder 4/OV2, University Archives, Department of Archives and Manuscripts, Arizona State University Libraries, Tempe, AZ.

10. A Celtic group active today teaches that sexual energy is sacred and that prayer accompanied by the release of sexual energy ensures the most potent of prayers. Interview with Jon C. Hughes, *Whole Life Times*, August 2002; John C. Hughes, *Celtic Sex Magic* (Inner Traditions, 2002).

11. Freud would have seemed an obvious source to explain the power of sex, but he was not as popular at the beginning of the twentieth century as he was to become later.

12. Candace Pert, Ph.D., served as chief of brain biochemistry at the National Institutes of Health for thirteen years and with Dr. Michael Ruff discovered Peptide T, an antiviral drug that blocks virus receptors on cells. It may be the forerunner of a drug to treat HIV infection. "Physiologically, each chakra is the site of a neuronal plexus, a network of cells dense with neuropeptide transmitters. All are interdependently connected to each other, such that nourishing any one plexus enhances

the effectiveness of the entire system." Candace Pert, "Study Guide: Your Body Is Your Subconscious Mind" (Boulder, Colo.; Sounds True, Inc., 2002), p. 5.

13. Caroline Myss, Chapter Two, "The Second Chakra: The Power of Relationships," *The Anatomy of the Spirit: The Seven Stages of Power and Healing* (New York: Three Rivers Press, 1996), p. 143.

14. Myss, *Anatomy of Spirit*, p. 143.

15. Sanger's adulation of Ellis was complete, as seen in this one of innumerable examples: "Each February it becomes our privilege and honor to offer to Havelock Ellis this humble tribute. Each year it becomes increasingly difficult to express in words the depth of our gratitude. For as time passes we realize that our debt to this serene and solitary spirit becomes heavier and heavier…that the spirit of Havelock Ellis is a radiant one—radiant I mean in the true sense of that overused word: Havelock Ellis radiates light and warmth so that everywhere in the world individuals are the recipients of his miraculous, life-giving influence. How is it possible to repay in the inadequate coinage of mere words, this every increasing debt?…We turn again to Havelock Ellis as a parched traveler turns to a spring. This spring is life-giving. We cannot plumb its depths. We lesser mortals cannot surmise the source of its strange power. But we know that in spite of the apparent passivity, the seeming remoteness of the man from the squabbles and hot controversies of the moment, his beneficent life-giving power is exerting itself day and night." "Radiant," *Birth Control Review*, Volume 9, Number 2 [February 1925], p. 35.

16. From Havelock Ellis, *The Psychology of Sex*, quoted in "Havelock Ellis Speaks," *Birth Control Review*, Volume 8, Number 2 [February 1924], p. 51.

17. Ellis, freethinker that he was, became wildly jealous when his young mistress found herself in love with both Ellis and Hugh de Selincourt. Love within the ménage a trois did not grow exponentially as theory had proposed.

18. Mable Dodge Luhan, *Movers and Shakers. Volume Three of Intimate Memories* (1936; New York: Kraus Reprint Co, 1971), p. 71.

19. *The Woman Rebel*, "The Aim," March 1914, p. 1.

20. Margaret Sanger, "Why the Woman Rebel?" *The Woman Rebel*, March 1914, p. 8.

21. Part I: The Rebel: Exile and Europe, "London Diary" herein.

22. Katz, *Selected Papers*, p. 292.

23. Sanger, *Pivot*, pp. 140-145. This chapter closes with the phrase "a race of thoroughbreds," which sounds to urban dwellers in the twenty-first century a bit strange when applied to humans. But it was a common enough analogy in 1920 when America held a much-larger rural population. At that time, Americans had a more-intimate acquaintance with animal husbandry and were well aware of the importance of careful breeding if their stock were to be healthy, productive, and salable. The cover of the November 1921 issue of the *Birth Control Review* carried the banner "Birth Control: To Create a Race of Thoroughbreds."

II. 22. The Town Hall Raid

1. The Town Hall structure, a Federal Revival design by McKim, Mead and White, was built between 1919 to 1921.

2. On the World Wide Web at *new-york.travelape.com/nightlife/town hall/12/20/2002*.

3. *The Edinburgh Review* was an important literary, political, and historical quarterly, extremely influential, founded in 1802; it ceased publication in 1929. Sanger wrote to Juliet Rublee on August 25, 1921, from Lucerne Switzerland, "I am so glad to tell you dearest that at last I have secured Harold Cox for our conference. Heaven only knows where the money is to be got to pay his expenses.... It's a big card to get him. He is a man of brains & intellect. His standing is on top in the English mind & press. He's almost better than Dean Inge for our purpose." Katz, *Selected Papers*, p. 309. After the conference, Sanger writes to Hugh de Selincourt, November 27, 1921, from Truro, Massachusetts, "Mr. Cox made a splendid impression here, he is so clear & direct in his English." Katz, *Selected Papers*, p. 330.

4. Sanger, *An Autobiography*, pp. 300-301.

5. Sanger, *My Fight*, p. 214.

6. Sanger, *An Autobiography*, p. 304.

7. Mary Winsor (1869-1956) had been one of those arrested in 1919 and sent to the workhouse when the suffragists picketed the White House. Sanger refers to Winsor as "that brave and undaunted suffragist" (*My Fight*, 1931, p. 217).

8. Container 237, The Papers of Margaret Sanger, Library of Congress.

9. Sanger, *An Autobiography*, p. 315.

10. *Ibid.*, p. 315.

11. "The suppression of the Town Hall meeting...had the invaluable effect of revealing and exposing the source of the opposition to Birth Control in this country." "Church Control," *Birth Control Review*, December 1921, p. 3.

12. *New York Times*, December 20, 1921, quoted in Katz, *Selected Papers*, p. 335.

13. Hayes did send a representative, apparently to cover the event, for there is no mention of his speaking. "The Town Hall Raid," *Sanger Papers Project Newsletter*, Number 27 [Spring 2001], p. 3.

14. Container 237, The Papers of Margaret Sanger, Library of Congress.

15. *New York American* clipping dated November 19, 1921. Clippings from the *New York Herald* and *New York Times* claimed that the crowd outside numbered only three thousand. Container 237, The Papers of Margaret Sanger, Library of Congress.

16. During the open forum of the meeting, one opposition statement was presented by the Reverend William Chase, an Episcopal minister, as reported in the *New York Tribune* (November 19, 1921) and the *New York Times* (November 20, 1921). Katz, *Selected Papers*, p. 327.

17. Robert Latou Dickinson to Margaret Sanger telegram, January 15, 1937, quoted in Kennedy, *Birth Control*, p. 217.

18. Sanger, *New Race*, p. 167.

19. Reel 130, The Papers of Margaret Sanger, Library of Congress.

II. 23. First Japan Trip

1. *Birth Control Review*, "Babies and Imperialism in Japan," June 1919, pp. 6-8; "The Awakening of Japan," February 1920, pp. 6-8. Articles on *Kaizo* were published in *Birth Control Review*, June 1921, pp. 5-6 ; July 1921, pp. 5-6; and August 1921, pp. 19-20.

2. "One day in 1920 I had received a visit from a beautiful intelligent young Japanese woman, the Baroness Shidzue Ishimoto, wife of Baron Keikichi Ishimoto, whose father had been Minister of War during the Russo-Japanese conflict. I gave a tea for the Baroness, and naturally the talk came of a visit to the Orient. It seemed at that time a remote possibility; but before the end of the year an invitation had come from the Kaizo group. This group of liberal intellectuals representing young Japan published a radical monthly called Reconstruction, in which four of my articles on birth control had appeared." Sanger, *My Fight*, p. 238.

3. Leane Zugsmith, September 21, 1941, "The East Wind, A Series on the Orient Today," "Japan Puts Birth Control Under Control," copyright 1941 by the Newspaper by PM, PM Exclusive, Container 234, The Papers of Margaret Sanger, Library of Congress.

4. *Birth Control Review,* Volume 6, Number 6 [June 1922], pp. 101-102.

5. Sanger, *My Fight*, p. 246.

6. Sanger, *An Autobiography*, pp. 330-331.

7. "Grant, who was very affectionate, had been accustomed to kiss me when we met, whether it were in a restaurant, hotel, on the street, or anywhere else for that matter. But he had to forego this salute in Japan when we observed that kissing was a shock to Japanese sensibilities, and indeed, was considered immoral." Sanger, *An Autobiography*, p. 323.

8. The Fifth International Birth Control Conference was held in London, July 11 to 14, 1922, and was written of in the *Birth Control Review*, Volume 6, Number 9 [September 1922], p. 174-176.

9. Sanger had originally planned to visit India on this trip: "On April 4th a cablegram was received from Mrs. Sanger stating that she was about to leave Kobe for Hong Kong, calling at points in Korea on the way. According to the plan outlined before she left the United States, she was to go from Hong Kong to Shanghai and Peking, in each of which places lectures had been arranged for her. From China she will go to Manila, and possibly other places in the Philippines. India will be reached from Manila, Calcutta being the first objective. The work in India will include a number of lectures which are being arranged for Mrs. Sanger by Professor Shastri, of the Department of Philosophy in the University of Calcutta." "Margaret Sanger in Japan," *Birth Control Review*, Volume 6, Number 5 [May 1922], p. 78. But the British did not want friends of Agnes Smedley, who might be supporters of India's drive for independence, visiting India, and Sanger did not go to India until 1935.

10. Douglas, *Pioneer of the Future*, p. 176.

11. *Birth Control Review*, Volume 6, Number 5 [May 1922], p. 78; Sanger, *An Autobiography*, pp. 340-342.

12. "Margaret Sanger in China," *Birth Control Review*, Volume 6, Number. 7 [July 1922], p. 124-125; see also Volume 6, Numbers 5 and 6.

13. Katz, *Selected Papers*, p. 373 note 3.

14. Katz, *Selected Papers*, p. 347.

15. Margaret and Juliet surely had a beautiful trip. Leaving Paris for Switzerland. They arrived in Montreux, spent a day in Interlaken, and went to Mürren, where they stayed from August 2 to 22nd. On the 22nd, they began their week-long return trip to Montreux, traveling through the scenic Simmental Valley and stopping on their way at Spiez, Weissenburg, Zweissimmen, and Chateau D'Oex. From Montreux, Sanger returned to London.

16. Katz, *Selected Papers*, p. 354.

17. Reel 128, The Papers of Margaret Sanger, Library of Congress.

18. Baron Kato had been the senior Japanese delegate at the Washington Naval Conference in November and would later become Prime Minister; Masanao Hanihara would become Japanese ambassador to the United States.

19. *Birth Control Review*, Volume 6, Number 9 [September 1922], p. 176.

20. *Birth Control Review*, Volume 9, Number 4 [April 1925], pp. 102, 125-126.

II. 24. The Eugenics Craze

1. A lovely list from a wonderful book that makes the history of eugenics fascinating reading, thanks to Daniel J. Kevles, *In the Name of Eugenics: Genetics and the Uses of Human Heredity* (Cambridge, Mass.: Harvard University Press, 1995), p. 68.

2. *Ibid.*, p. 71.

3. Elof Alex Carlson, *The Unfit: A History of a Bad Idea* (Cold Spring Harbor Laboratory Press, 2001).

4. The final 1932 Eugenics Congress had an attendance of less than a hundred, indicative of its dwindling influence.

5. Kevles, *Name of Eugenics*, p. 62.

6. *Ibid.*, pp. 61-62.

7. In discussing the small size of the British and American eugenics societies, Daniel J. Kevles says, "What the organizations lacked in size they made up for by what an early British member predicted would be 'the advantage of excellent patronage.'" Kevles, *Name of Eugenics*, p. 60.

8. From the scientists' innovations, industry made money; with the backing of scientific reports, the government won its proposals.

9. Working with canaries and poultry, Charles Davenport (1866-1944). made a valid contribution to Mendelian analysis of inheritance in animals, but in attempt-

ing to extend Mendelian laws to human traits, he was governed less by science than by wishful thinking. His later scientific conclusions were definitely refuted by the end of the '30s. At the beginning of his career, between 1910 and 1918, Mrs. Harriman contributed handsomely to Davenport to the tune of approximately half a million dollars—a goodly sum. Kevles, *Name of Eugenics*, p 55.

10. Harry Laughlin (1880-1943) took a six-weeks summer course at Cold Spring Harbor and became enamored of Eugenics. He was appointed Davenport's assistant in 1910 and remained at Cold Spring Harbor for the next twenty-nine years; naturally, his scientific approach was akin to Davenport's. Laughlin earned a D.Sc. in cytology at Princeton University in 1917 and was a prolific writer. His model for sterilization law was used by over thirty states and by Nazi Germany.

11. Italians, in particular, had a tendency to "personal violence." Possibly, the scientists had seen too many Italian operas.

12. In 1938, eugenics was a topic in 376 separate college courses. Between 1914 and 1948, a majority of high school science texts presented eugenics as a legitimate science. *www. eugenicsarchives.org/eugenice.*

13. Indiana had begun sterilizing prisoners in 1899, many believing this was a kindness, and passed the first compulsory sterilization for degenerates in 1907.

14. The Human Betterment Foundation of Pasadena, California, a state with one of the highest sterilization rates in America, listed in its literature the benefits of sterilization: Sterilization prevents parenthood; in no way unsexes the patient; protects, but does not punish; is approved by patients and their families and friends and medical staff, social workers, probation and parole officers; permits many patients who would otherwise be confined to institutions for years to return to their homes; keeps homes together; protects children who might be raised by the mentally diseased from being born; reduces taxpayers' expense; brings about a marked decrease in sex offenses; enables many handicapped persons to marry and to have a normal life; prevents racial deterioration. "The Effects of Sterilization as Practiced in California," Container 221, The Papers of Margaret Sanger, Library of Congress.

15. Kevles, *Name of Eugenics*, p. 114. On the other hand, by the early 1920s, opposition to sterilization was beginning to come from parts of the scientific community, and sterilization laws in a number of states were declared unconstitutional.

16. Chapter IV of Sanger's *Pivot* is titled "The Fertility of the Feebleminded," pp. 80-104.

17. "Editorial Comment," *Birth Control Review*, September 1917, p. 9. Sanger always qualified her discussion of sterilization. In regard to sterilization as a contraceptive, she says, "Sterilization as well as Birth Control has its place as an aim of the American Birth Control League. We do not agree with those Eugenists who would prefer compulsory laws for the unfit, while denying to women generally the right to control their own reproduction. But we recognize the value of sterilization in cases where Birth Control is likely to fail, and we are deeply interested in the work that is being done in this field." *Birth Control Review*, Volume 12, Number 3

[March 1928], p. 74. The Supreme Court upheld state sterilization in *Buck v. Bell* in 1927 by a vote of eight to one, the court's opinion written by the venerable Justice Oliver Wendell Holmes.

18. Karl Pearson (1857-1936), Galton's protégée and successor, founded the Biometric Laboratory at University College, London, and the journal *Biometrika*. "He devised the product-moment formula for the regular coefficient of correlation; established the theory of multiple correlation and regression; developed a general theory of probable errors; and introduced the chi-squared test . . . Pearson laid the foundations of modern statistical methods." Kevles, *Name of Eugenics*, p. 37.

19. "Birth Control and Racial Betterment," *Birth Control Review*, February 1919, p. 12.

20. To list just a few of those on the American Birth Control League advisory council and Clinical Research Bureau board: Roswell Hill Johnson (1877-1967), biologist and psychologist who advocated sterilization for the feebleminded and others; Clarence Cook Little (1888-1973), zoologist and president of University of Maine; Dr. Stuart Mudd (1893-1975), microbiologist and zoologist, University of Pennsylvania, and founder, Pennsylvania Birth Control Federation; Raymond Pearl (1879-1940), biologist and statistician, Johns Hopkins University; Leon Jacob Cole (1877-1948), professor of genetics and animal breeding, University of Wisconsin.

21. "The Eugenic Value of Birth Control Propaganda," *Birth Control Review*, Volume 5, Number 10 [October 1921], p. 5.

22. "Editorial," *Birth Control Review*, Volume 9, Number 6 [June 1925], p. 163.

23. *Ibid.*, pp. 163-164.

24. "The Eugenics Congress," *Birth Control Review*, November 1921, p. 7.

25. "Birth Control and Racial Betterment," *Birth Control Review*, February 1919, p. 12.

26. *Ibid.*

27. "The Eugenic Value of Birth Control Propaganda," *Birth Control Review*, October 1921, p. 5.

28. Fifty-five percent of the world's married women use modern methods of contraception; 21 percent of these women have been sterilized. In Canada and the United States, 71 percent of married women use modern contraceptive methods; 23 percent have been sterilized. In Brazil, India, and China, one-third or more of married women have been sterilized. *Population Reference Bureau 2002 Survey.* According to a United Nations survey, one-fifth of the married women of the world have been sterilized. "Sterilization Most Popular Contraceptive," *Earth Policy News*, October 14, 2002; Betsy Hartmann, Chapter 13, *Reproductive Rights and Wrongs: The Global Politics of Population Control* (Cambridge: South End Press, 1995), pp. 243-267.

29. On December 2, 2002, the governor of the state of Oregon publicly apologized to the twenty-six hundred Oregon residents who had been sterilized between 1917 and 1970 under its laws.

30. "Genes, Embryos and Ethics," *New York Times*, March 3, 2002, p. 6; "Science helps parents design son," *The Tribune-Democrat,* Johnstown, PA, January 20, 2003.

31. "Deoxyribonucleic Acid Trip," review of *Redesigning Human: Our Inevitable Genetic Future* by Gregory Stock, *New York Times Book Review*, August 25, 2002, p. 25.

32. World War I draftees were given extensive testing so that they could be quickly placed in an area of work most appropriate. The testing was headed primarily by Robert M. Yerkes, and his tests showed that the average white draftee had the intelligence of a thirteen-year-old. The test results were later much disputed, particularly by the reform eugenicists.

33. Reel 129, The Papers of Margaret Sanger, Library of Congress.

34. The claim that studies showed two-thirds of the military were unfit to carry a rifle was later refuted. Sanger along with others at that time believed that the feebleminded were especially prolific.

35. William Bateson (1861-1926) British biologist, championed Mendel's laws and wrote *Mendel's Principles of Heredity* (1902).

II. 25. Advice to the Married

1. Agnes Smedley to Margaret Sanger, Jan. 3, Reel 10, The Papers of Margaret Sanger, Library of Congress.

2. Margaret Sanger to Libby Schimmel, October 7, 1953, Reel 7, The Papers of Margaret Sanger, Library of Congress. William Blake (1757-1827), English poet, engraver, and mystic, was known for his *Songs of Innocence* (1789) and *Songs of Experience* (1794). Blake hated materialism and said he was led through his life by angelic visits. Percy Bysshe Shelley (1792-1822), English Romantic poet, was remarkably prolific and a nonconformist to conventional morality. Shelley was convinced that cohabitation without love was immoral, which led to affairs that others regarded as truly immoral. Generous but impractical, Shelley lived by his belief in the power of a nonexclusive, redemptive love that transcended earthly limits. His friend Lord Bryon recalled that Shelley was "the *best* and the least selfish man" he ever knew.

3. Lowell Brentano to Mrs. Noah H. Slee, June 9, 1930, Reel 131, The Papers of Margaret Sanger, Library of Congress.

4. Margaret Sanger, "Chapter I: The First Step," *Happiness in Marriage* (New York: Brentano's, 1926), pp. 13-23.

II. 26. The First World Population Conference

1. The First American Birth Control Conference, November 11-13, 1921, and the Sixth International Neo-Malthusian and Birth Control Conference, March 25-31, 1925, both in New York City.

2. Sanger naively expected the male scientists to make the obvious connection between the contribution birth control could make to limiting population. But such a sensible idea was beneath the notice of the erudite male scientists.

3. Sanger had evidenced her awareness of population pressures as early as 1914,

when in the September-October issue of *The Woman Rebel*, she published an article by B. Liber, M.D., "Birth and the War Machine," which opens with a discussion of Malthus principles and closes despairing that "people continue to produce a surplus of soldiers and laborers for their rulers." Throughout her editorship of the *Birth Control Review*, articles on overpopulation, population growth, and the relation of population to war were in practically every issue. See *Birth Control Review* 1917-1928 *passim*.

4. Katz, *Selected Papers*, p. 456.

5. Birth control, while slowly working toward respectability, continued to be not quite acceptable, and women, as Sanger was to find out, were definitely not welcome within the all-male scientific community.

6. Sanger, *An Autobiography*, p. 387.

7. *Daily Express*, August 30, 1927, Container 233, The Papers of Margaret Sanger, Library of Congress.

8. August 22, 1927, *ibid*.

9. Sir Bernard Mallet (1859-1932) brought in the interest of his friend Sir Eric Drummond (1876-1951), who was secretary general of the League of Nations from 1919 to 1933, then Great Britain's ambassador to Rome (1933-1939), and later deputy leader of the Liberal Party (1947-1951).

10. F.A.E. Crew was a trained physician, a professor of animal genetics at the University of Edinburgh, and a man of good senses. On being asked to define the perfect man, Crew replied, "There isn't any. Define us a heaven and we will tell you what an angel is." Daniel J. Kevles, *In the Name of Eugenics: Genetics and the Uses of Human Heredity* (Cambridge, MA: Harvard University Press, 1983), p. 147.

11. Sanger, *An Autobiography*, pp. 385-386.

12. *Ibid.*, p. 386.

13. Lader, *Margaret Sanger*, p. 348.

14. On the World Wide Web at iussp.org.

15. Katz, *Selected Papers*, p. 481.

16. *Ibid.*, p. 458.

17. On the closing day of the conference, Sir Bernard acknowledged Sanger's work on the conference to the assembled delegates, who gave Sanger a rousing three cheers.

18. "From Geneva to Cairo: Margaret Sanger and the first World Population Conference," *Sanger Papers Project Newsletter*, No. 8 [Fall 1994], pp. 1-2.

19. Reel 123, The Papers of Margaret Sanger, Library of Congress.

II. 27. "Children Troop Down"

1. Sanger, *An Autobiography*, p. 308.

2. *New York Times*, December 20, 1921, Katz, *Selected Papers*, p. 335.

3. Sanger says, "Between 1921 and 1926, I received over a million letters from

mothers requesting information." Sanger, *An Autobiography*, p. 361. Margaret Marsh claims that Sanger received a quarter of a million letters by 1928. Margaret Sanger, *Motherhood in Bondage*. Foreword by Margaret Marsh (Columbus: Ohio State University Press, 2000), p. xi.

4. Linda Gordon, *Woman's Body, Woman's Right: Birth Control in America*, (New York, Penguin Books, 1990), p. 234.

5. "Notes," Reel 130, The Papers of Margaret Sanger, Library of Congress.

6. *Birth Control Review*, June 1918, p. 13.

7. *Ibid.*, June 1921, p. 15.

8. *Ibid.*

9. *Ibid.*, April 1918, p. 12.

10. Sanger Microfilm, Smith College.

11. Reel 134, The Papers of Margaret Sanger, Library of Congress.

12. *Ibid.*

13. *Ibid.*

14. Anna Lifshiz to Noah Slee, November 16, 1929, Reel 134, The Papers of Margaret Sanger, Library of Congress.

15. *Ibid.*

II. 28. The Raid on the Clinical Research Bureau

1. Reel 128, The Papers of Margaret Sanger, Manuscript Division, Library of Congress, Washington, D.C., 1977.

2. "Progress Report," June 1933, Scrapbook D, Container 221, The Papers of Margaret Sanger, Library of Congress.

3. Sanger, *An Autobiography*, p 359. In 1928, the Clinical Research Bureau was renamed the Birth Control Clinical Research Bureau and in 1940 the Margaret Sanger Research Bureau. The bureau was the project most dear to Sanger's heart, the place where women could come for affordable and legal contraception information. In 1920, Sanger wrote of Clinton Chance (d. 1953), "Is to retire & devote all his wealth & time on Birth Control. It is the only cause he believes in doing anything for," (Sanger to Juliet about Clinton Chance. Margaret Sanger to Juliet Rublee, July 7, [1920], Katz, ed. *Selected Papers*, p. 284.) Clinton Chance had made his wealth as an investment consultant. His wife, Janet Chance (1885-1953) founded a sex education center for working class women. Clinton was a member of the Malthusian League and the Eugenics Society and had been a generous contributor to and strong supporter of the First World Population Conference in Geneva in 1927.

4. The Crane decision handed down in 1918 on appeal of Sanger's Brownsville clinic arrest allowed contraceptive advice "for the prevention and cure of disease" in the state of New York. Other states had other restrictions, and Catholic Massachusetts and Connecticut did not allow clinics under any circumstances.

5. Dr. Dorothy Bocker, the first medical director of the Clinical Research Bureau in 1923-24, had good medical credentials, but no experience as a researcher. Her published records were rightly attacked by the medical community. Kennedy, *Birth Control*, p. 191.

6. Quoted in "Margaret Sanger and 'A Glorious Chain of Clinics,'" *Sanger Papers Project Newsletter*, Number 9 [Winter 1994/5], p. 7.

7. Stone's first article appeared in 1928 in *Medical Journal and Record*; additional findings were published in *The Practice of Contraception* in 1931, coedited with Sanger. This volume was the proceedings of the Seventh conference, and the full title is *An International Symposium and Survey. Papers of 38 Contributors to the Proceedings of the 7th International Birth Control Conference, Zurich, Switzerland, 1930*.

8. Hannah Stone worked with Dr. Cooper to devise "a formula for a jelly with a lactic acid and glycerine bases, which was within our means." Sanger, *An Autobiography*, p. 363.

9. *Birth Control Review*, May 1929, p. 139.

10. That arrest apparently precluded Stone's acceptance in 1932 and for long after in the New York County Medical Society. "Margaret Sanger and 'A Glorious Chain of Clinics,'" p. 6.

11. Sanger, *An Autobiography*, p. 405.

12. Sanger, *An Autobiography*, p. 408.

13. "Seventy-Year Anniversary of Legalized Birth Control Services," *Sanger Papers Project Newsletter*, Number 5 [Spring 1993], p. 4.

14. Sanger, *An Autobiography*, p. 406.

15. The composition of the American Birth Control League, on the other hand, was of women predominantly white, Protestant, and middle and upper class.

16. Sanger early on had a vision of what a birth control clinic should include, as many Planned Parenthood clinics do today. "In addition to the usual [clinic] rooms I planned to have a day nursery where children could be kept amused and happy while the mothers were being instructed. A properly chosen staff could enable us to have weekly sessions on prenatal care and marital adjustment. Gynecologists were to refer patients to hospitals if pregnancy jeopardized life; a specialist was to advise women in overcoming sterility; a consultant was to deal with eugenics and, finally, since anxiety and fear of pregnancy were often the psychological causes of ill health, a psychiatrist was to be added. I intended, furthermore, that it should be a nucleus for research on scientific methods of contraception." Sanger, *An Autobiography*, p. 297.

17. Reed, *Birth Control Movement*, p. 117. During the twenties, clinics were opened in Chicago, Los Angeles, San Antonio, Detroit, Baltimore, Cleveland, Newark, Denver, Atlanta, Cincinnati, and Oakland. Funding for clinics other than those close to private wealthy supporters was always problematic. "Margaret Sanger and 'A Glorious Chain of Clinics,'" p. 2.

18. *The New Republic* to Margaret Sanger, April 22, 1929, The Papers of Margaret Sanger, Library of Congress.

19. Sanger, *An Autobiography*, p. 408.

20. Reel 128, The Papers of Margaret Sanger, Library of Congress.

21. During the Prohibition years, 1920 to 1933, organized crime enjoyed the heights of blatant activity.

II. 29. The National Committee on Federal Legislation for Birth Control

1. Container 242, The Papers of Margaret Sanger, Library of Congress.

2. Mrs. Adelaide Archibald was at Place Vendome, Paris, France, when she received this letter. She also had a home in Scarsdale, New York. Adelaide Archibald was a longtime family friend of the Higgins. Her daughter, Helena, had played with Stuart and Grant as children, and Mrs. Archibald had donated sums to Sanger's birth control movement over the years. Stuart invited Helena to at least one function when he was in college, and Grant, while in medical school, was concerned over Mrs. Archibald's health to the extent that Sanger mentioned it in a letter. Miss Anne Morgan, sister of J. P. Morgan, the financier, was president of the American Woman's Association in 1930 and announced Margaret Sanger as recipient of the First Gold Medal Award at the Fifth Annual Friendship Dinner of the Brooklyn Business and Professional Woman's Club in November 1931. Grant was attending Cornell. Reel 2, The Papers of Margaret Sanger, Library of Congress.

3. The American Woman's Association Clubhouse was located at 353 West Fifty-seventh Street, New York City.

4. *New York Herald Tribune,* April 21, 1932, Container 242, The Papers of Margaret Sanger, Library of Congress.

5. April 21, 1932, Container 242, The Papers of Margaret Sanger, Library of Congress.

6. November 16, 1931. Container 242. The Papers of Margaret Sanger, Library of Congress.

7. *Ibid.*, May 3, 1932.

8. *Ibid.*

9. The *Review* evolved into little more than a business organ listing, its size going from its original 11 5/8 x 8 3/4 to 10 1/2 x 7 1/2 inches, a reflection of its shrinking import and influence. The *Review* soon became a quarterly and discontinued publication in 1940. But the *Review* had done its work, reaching many throughout the twenties with the message of birth control and had been an especially valuable tool in the hands of street vendor Kitty Marion in New York City.

10. "Margaret Sanger Outlines the Scope of the New National Committee on Federal Legislation for Birth Control," speech, Tuesday morning meeting, November 19, 1929, American Birth Control League Conference.

"The National Committee on Federal Legislation for Birth Control has the following plans for the amendment of Section 211 of the Penal Code. It has organized the country into regional sections. Eleven Eastern States known as the Eastern Region, Eleven Western States known as the Western Region. Seventeen Midwestern States known as the Midwestern Region, and the Southern States known as the Southern Region. Each of these regions is further divided into the several States which are again subdivided into Congressional Districts, with chairman and vice-chairman at the head of each district. Two regional conferences have already taken place, one in Boston of the Eastern section and the other in Columbus, Ohio, of the Midwestern section. Arrangements have already been made for a Regional Conference in California and a Great National Conference in Washington, D.C.

"On the basis of facts and knowledge gleaned from the [13,000] cases which have received instruction at the Research Bureau in New York, at 48 West 15th Street, the workers of the National Committee are enabled to present to their Congressmen the salient facts at issue and thereby convince these Congressmen of the great necessity for the passage of our bill. The actual drafting of the bill is now in the hands of a legal committee composed of three distinguished attorneys of New York City and in substance will protect the public from commercialism and charlatanism in the matter of the distribution of literature and supplies pertaining to contraception, in that it places the authorization of such activity in the hands of licensed physicians and scientists.

"While there are a few clinics legally operating throughout the United States, we are constantly confronted and hampered by the limitation of the present law which forbids one physician from receiving, or sending, data and supplies to either physicians or clinics by mail or common carriers. Before these restrictions are removed the establishment of clinics on a national scale is impossible. We consider the passage of this law to be the most important and immediate step to be taken in the Birth Control Movement and shall be glad to have the cooperation of all organizations to effect the passage of the federal bill.

"Margaret Sanger is no longer connected with the American Birth Control League but is chairman of the new National Committee on Federal Legislation for Birth Control and is directing the Clinical Research Bureau at 46 West 15th Street." Container 220, The Papers of Margaret Sanger, Library of Congress.

11. "Birth Control and the Good Old Boys in Congress," *Sanger Papers Project Newsletter*, Number 26 [Winter 2000/2001], *passim.*

12. Senator Henry Drury Hatfield, Republican, West Virginia, a licensed physician and former governor of West Virginia; Representative Franklin W. Hancock, Democrat, North Carolina, was in his second term. Ever positive in her professional approach, Sanger sent out a fundraising letter dated September 6, 1932: "Our work in Washington this winter has been stupendous. Our bills were introduced against all odds and I believe that within a very short time—if we can all pull together—that these Bills will be passed." Letter sent to ninety-four Voluntary Parenthood League names, September 6, 1932, Container 221, The Papers of Margaret Sanger, Library of Congress, p. 2.

13. Lader, *Margaret Sanger Story*, p. 300.

14. Sanger, *An Autobiography*, pp. 429-430.

15. Kennedy, *Birth Control*, p. 140.

16. Affirmed *U.S. v. One Package* 86 F 2d 737 (2d Cir. 1936).

17. Sanger, *An Autobiography*, p. 430.

18. Sanger always felt that the law itself should be changed. For some time, the American Medical Association felt similarly and warned its membership against feeling secure in giving contraceptive advice with only the Moscowitz decision to protect them. Learned Hand, one of the three judges who had rejected the government appeal, agreed. "A statute stands until public feeling gets enough momentum to change it." This point was proven by the Catholic leadership, who kept contraception illegal in Connecticut and in Massachusetts, closed down clinics, and made it illegal for physicians to give birth control advice, even to married couples.

19. Reel 128, The Papers of Margaret Sanger, Library of Congress.

II. 30. The New Deal:

1. "America Needs a Code for Babies," *American Weekly*, May 27, 1934, Reel 128, The Papers of Margaret Sanger, Library of Congress. Printed here is the first half of the speech.

II. 31. India and World Tour for Birth Control 1935-36

1. "Several times I had approached the idea of going to India, and always something had prevented me. In 1922 when I was near by, it was the hot season and everybody had gone to the hill stations. In 1928, when I had also made tentative plans, I was not well." In 1922, on her round-the-world trip after leaving Japan, Sanger had plenty of time to visit India. Lectures by her had been announced in Bombay and Calcutta, though Sanger's reply to the British officer who interrogated her in Shanghai was that she knew nothing about such planned lectures. But she did know Agnes Smedley, for whom she had given a reception when Smedley was released from jail in 1917. The British knew about that relationship, about Sanger's support of Smedley, Sanger's support of Debs, of gatherings Sanger had attended that promoted home rule for Ireland and for India. Sanger writes she convinced the British officer that "if the vast millions of India wanted birth control he . . . would visa my passport." It seems more likely that she was told that she would not be allowed to visit India. In December 1927, Sanger was with Agnes Smedley in Berlin. Sanger may have been ill in 1928, but again, the British did not trust Agnes Smedley any more in 1928 than they had in 1922. In an undated letter circa 1927-1928, Smedley writes to Margaret, "I did this because I thought you were going to India." Sanger, *An Autobiography*, pp. 350-351, 461. See also Janice R. and Stephen R. MacKinnon, *Agnes Smedley: The Life and Times of an American Radical* (Berkeley: University of California Press, 1988) and Sanger-Smedley correspondence, Reel 10, The Papers of Margaret Sanger, Library of Congress.

2. "Mrs. John Phillips, who had fought many battles for Birth Control in Pittsburgh, suggested that her daughter, a graduate of Vassar and a newspaper woman, might come along as my secretary. All the way a fine young crowd rallied around the lively Anna Jane, who had as great a capacity for laughter as any human

being I ever knew. Nothing was too hard for her, nothing too big or too small for her to do; altogether she was a perfect companion." Sanger, *An Autobiography*, pp. 461-462.

3. "India and World Tour Diary," Reel 1, The Papers of Margaret Sanger, Library of Congress, pp. 58, 88; Sanger, *An Autobiography*, p. 464.

4. "News from Margaret Sanger. Letter No. 2, December 9, 1935." Reel 17, The Papers of Margaret Sanger, Library of Congress.

5. "India Diary and World Tour Diary," Reel 1, The Papers of Margaret Sanger, Library of Congress, pp. 90-94; "cooks" is Cook's, a large travel agency. Cook's Tours are well known.

6. "Statement by Margaret Sanger Before Her Birth Control Campaign in the East, October 30th, 1935," Reel 17, The Papers of Margaret Sanger, Library of Congress.

7. "India and World Tour Diary," Reel 1, The Papers of Margaret Sanger, Library of Congress, p. 106.

8. "India and World Tour Diary," Reel 1, The Papers of Margaret Sanger, Library of Congress, pp. 110-121.

9. "News from Margaret Sanger. Letter No. 2. For Mrs. Sanger's Intimate Friends and Family. Calcutta, India. December 9, 1935," Reel 138, The Papers of Margaret Sanger, Library of Congress, p. 2.

10. "News from Margaret Sanger. Letter No. 2. December 9, 1935," Reel 138, The Papers of Margaret Sanger. Library of Congress, p. 3.

11. "News from Margaret Sanger. Letter No. 2. December 9, 1935," Reel 138, The Papers of Margaret Sanger, Library of Congress, p. 3.

12. "News from Margaret Sanger. Letter No. 2. December 9, 1935," Reel 138, The Papers of Margaret Sanger, Library of Congress, p. 3. A note in Sanger's hand lists train distances in hours between major India cities: Madras to Calicut 15 hrs, Calicut to Bang[alore] 12 hrs, Bang to Neyne 5 hrs, Bang to Hyder[abad] 24 hrs, Hyder to Madras 22 hrs, Mad to Calcutta 36 hrs.

13. "Indian and World Tour Diary," Reel 1, The Papers of Margaret Sanger, Library of Congress, p. 265.

14. "Indian and World Tour Diary," Reel 1, The Papers of Margaret Sanger, Library of Congress, pp. 134, 136.

15. At the time Sanger visited the Maharshi (Maharshi is a variant of Maharishi), he was in his fifties. At the age of sixteen, the Maharshi arrived in Tiruvannamalai and went into a trance of longstanding. When he came out of the trance state, he was enlightened, but had lost his power of speech. Eventually, his speech returned, and he was recognized as a holy man. He was noted for his rapport with animals. Paul Brunton write of the maharshi, "Once he lived for years in a gloomy solitary cavern high up on [a] hill, plunging his mind ever deeper into profound concentration upon the divine element which hides in man. He sought for the real Self,

THAT infinite Being which invisibly and intangibly supports the lives of all creatures. And he found it.... [Today] he continually 'broadcasts' telepathically the divine atmosphere which has now become his very nature. In effect, he mysteriously communicates his spiritual calm to our troubled souls." *Sunday Times*, Sri Maharishi Supplement, Madras, Sunday January 12, 1936, pp. i, ii. Container 234, The Papers of Margaret Sanger, Library of Congress.

16. Sanger, *An Autobiography*, p. 488.

17. "News From Margaret Sanger. Letter No. 2. December 9, 1935," Reel 138, The Papers of Margaret Sanger, Library of Congress, pp. 2-3.

18. "Edith" is Edith How-Martyn.

II. 32. M. S. Meets Gandhi
1. Sanger, *An Autobiography*, pp. 465-466.

2. "India and World Tour Diary," Reel 1, The Papers of Margaret Sanger, Library of Congress, p. 154.

3. "Copy sent to Mr. Walsh July 9th," Reel 17, The Papers of Margaret Sanger, Library of Congress, p. 2.

4. *Ibid.*, pp. 2-3.

5. *Ibid.*, pp. 3-5.

6. *Ibid.*, p. 9.

7. Gandhi did say to Sanger that he would think about sanctioning the rhythm method for women, but knowing the failure of the rhythm method as a contraceptive, this scarcely seems a concession. Despite his remarkable political victories for India and its people and his espousal of nonviolence, Gandhi, like so many men, had no comprehension whatsoever of the reality of women's lives. See also "Gandhi and Sanger Debate Love, Lust and Birth Control," *Sanger Papers Project Newsletter*, Number 23 [Winter 1999/2000], pp. 1-4.

8. "Self-Control for Gods Only!" *Bombay Chronicle*, Monday, April 18, 1938, Container 234, The Papers of Margaret Sanger, Library of Congress.

9. *The Illustrated Weekly of India*, January 19, 1936, pp. 18-19, Reel 129, The Papers of Margaret Sanger, Library of Congress.

II. 33. Fortunate Support: The Clinical Trials of Clarence Gamble
1. Sanger, *My Fight*, p. 144.

2. Gamble was eminently practical and mindful of details. Once when he found in the men's bathroom of his office a bar of Palmolive soap, he immediately sent a member of the staff out to replace it with a bar of Ivory. Doone and Greer Williams, *Every Child a Wanted Child: Clarence James Gamble, M.D. and His Work in the Birth Control Movement* (Boston: Harvard University Press, 1978), p. 366.

3. Gamble first wanted to do research. His oldest daughter told the author of his experiments on circulation, wherein he would hang himself upside down and then have various measurements taken. He had five children who were wanted and

spaced close to three years apart. This was not inconsistent with his work on birth control, for as he pointed out, his children were wanted.

He was a wonderful father, played games with his children, but always games that taught. Once a month, boxes arrived teaching science, how to make a magnet, etc., that the children would work with. He taught the children how to sail, how to drive, how to build with cement. The family would go on an outing and take a trolley, but the children would have to ask the trolley conductor how to get to where they were going. At the dinner table, after the family had moved to Milton and were new to the city, Gamble would challenge the children and ask who knew the shortest route to get from one place to another. When his oldest daughter was fourteen, the family was living in Michigan, where the age for a driving license began at fourteen. Sally took the test and passed. Gamble then gave his newly licensed daughter the keys to the car and told her he would meet her at home. And so she drove home. Alone. Gamble realized how necessary birth control was for those who could not support and did not want many children. Just as he had chosen medicine over astronomy, he eventually relinquished his dream of himself as researcher and took on the work of seeding clinics and trying to find an inexpensive, simple contraceptive, confident that this was most needed.

4. Dr. Stuart Mudd (1893-1975), was a microbiologist and zoologist at the University of Pennsylvania, and a founder with his wife Emily and others of the Pennsylvania Birth Control Federation. Mudd was both a Princeton and a Harvard classmate of Gamble's, and as Professor of Microbiology at the University of Pennsylvania, he and Gamble were there together as well. Stuart Mudd was the first to become interested in Birth Control after he had heard Margaret Sanger speak: "I was a romantic young man," he recalled, "I was impressed by her experience." Quoted in Williams, *Every Child*, 1978, p. 25. Stuart and Emily were always supportive of Sanger, and in 1927 Stuart went on the board of the American Birth Control League.

5. Much else apparently affected Gamble's decision to devote himself to birth control: his friendship with Stuart Mudd; his earlier acquaintance with the Dr. Philip King Brown, a San Francisco physician and one of the founders of the Arequipa Sanitarium for Wage-Earning Women in Marin County, California; and his sister, Dr. Adelaide Brown, a woman gynecologist interested in birth control. Williams, *Every Child*, pp. 13-19. An important influence was Robert Latou Dickinson, New York City's leading gynecologist, who retired early to devote his life to birth control and started the Committee on Maternal Health in 1923, the same year Sanger opened the Clinical Research Bureau. Gamble visited Dickinson for advice on use of the diaphragm and reported that at a lunch, Dickinson had told Gamble of the need for young doctors to become involved in birth control, asking Gamble, "Don't you want to help me, and keep on with the work when I'm through?" Williams, *Every Child*, p. 91.

Gamble and Dickinson worked together all their lives, and Dickinson had, as well, a complicated relationship with Sanger, first thwarting, then supporting her aims and research. His advocacy for the inclusion of birth control and sexual matters to receive professional treatment by the medical community, at a time when both were considered synonymous with radicalism and superstition, paved the way for just such acceptance. Dickinson, having proven himself superlatively within the medical profession, was able to reach the medical community in a way that Sanger never could, greatly assisting acceptance of the birth control movement. For a good overview of Dickinson's work and life, see Reed, *Birth Control Movement*.

6. Gamble became a member of Dickinson's National Committee on Maternal Health, in 1934 its chairman of field service, and in 1935 its treasurer. Concurrently in 1934, Gamble was president of the Pennsylvania Birth Control Federation and, as Pennsylvania delegate, vice president and member of the board of its parent body, Mrs. F. Robertson-Jones's American Birth Control League.

7. Although Gamble was not one to wait on bureaucracy's blessings, he attempted to cooperate with the various organizations, was unfailingly polite in his dealings, and often urged Sanger to "offer the olive branch" to the America Birth Control League. See for instance, letters from Clarence Gamble to Margaret Sanger dated December 8, 1936, and March 2, 1937, Reel 103, The Papers of Margaret Sanger, Library of Congress.

8. Margaret Sanger to Clarence Gamble, November 23, 1953, Reel 8, The Papers of Margaret Sanger, Library of Congress.

9. Typical of his independent approach, when teaching a course on diagnosis at Harvard Medical School during World War II, Gamble was forbidden under Massachusetts law to teach contraception, so he got the army to sponsor him and took his students to the army center, where he was free to teach as he wished.

10. Quoted in "Margaret Sanger and 'A Glorious Chain of Clinics,'" *Sanger Papers Project Newsletter*, Number 9 [Winter 1994/5], p. 3.

11. Elsie Wulkop was one such worker whom he knew from his intern days at Massachusetts General Hospital. Williams, *Every Child*, p. 116.

12. Reel 23, The Papers of Margaret Sanger, Library of Congress.

13. Williams, *Every Child*, p. 112.

14. *Ibid.*, p. 124.

15. *Ibid.*, pp. 165-168.

16. See Gamble correspondence, Reels 8 and 103, The Papers of Margaret Sanger, Library of Congress.

17. Williams, *Every Child*, p. 220.

18. Sanger's Conference on Contraceptive Research and Clinical Practice was held at the Hotel Roosevelt, New York City, and opened on December 29, 1936. At that time, it was a generally held belief by physicians and others that any kind of contraception was injurious and caused sterility. Reel 127, The Papers of Margaret Sanger, Library of Congress.

19. Clarence J. Gamble to Mr. F. Robertson Jones, June 20, 1934, Reel 22, The

Papers of Margaret Sanger, Library of Congress.

20. Reel 103, The Papers of Margaret Sanger, Library of Congress.

21. Mrs. Sarah Gamble was also a Junior Leaguer and more than five thousand reprints were made of a supportive article on birth control she found in the *Junior League Magazine*. Reels 103 and 56, The Papers of Margaret Sanger, Library of Congress.

22. Williams, *Every Child*, p. 277.

23. *Ibid.*, pp. 273-279.

24. Reel 103, The Papers of Margaret Sanger, Library of Congress.

25. Emily Mudd (1898-1998), was the wife of Stuart Mudd, Gamble's friend. She and Stuart had organized the Southeastern Pennsylvania Birth Control League. Out of the League grew early in 1929 the Maternal Health Clinic at 69th and Market Streets in Philadelphia. Emily Mudd, mother of four, is considered the Margaret Sanger of marriage counseling and was a nationally recognized social scientist, an avid promoter of women's rights and Birth Control throughout her life. She worked with Kinsey and with Masters and Johnson and rewrote abortion laws for the state of Pennsylvania shortly before abortion was legalized by *Roe v. Wade*. *Philadelphia Inquirer*, May 4, 1998.

26. The memorandum with these suggestions was not found, but the reader can be sure that the suggestions were thoroughly thought out and explained in infinite detail.

27. Dr. Abraham Stone, urologist and husband of Dr. Hannah Stone, was medical director of Clinical Research Bureau after Hannah Stone's death in 1941.

28. This may have been Mrs. Thomas Hart of Wayneswood, Pennsylvania.

29. This was probably Henriette (Mrs. Peter L.) Harvie of Troy, New York, secretary of the Association of Junior Leagues of America, also responsible for publicity and the magazine advisory.

30. Mrs. Page, Phillis Bache Page, was one of Gamble's fine fieldworkers, articulate Boston-bred and Smith College graduate, wife of Richmond Page, who was librarian of the Pennsylvania School of Social Work. In later life, she was a gifted teacher of problem children in Winchester, Massachusetts, public schools, Gamble offered her a job as secretary and then sent her as a fieldworker first to Knoxville, later to Berea to line up clinical testing of foam contraceptives. She was instrumental in founding the Mountain Maternal Health League, which eventually affiliated with Kentucky Birth Control League and finally the American Birth Control League. Page's success in Puerto Rico, as mentioned earlier, is not to be overlooked.

31. Florence (Mrs. Bolton J.) Love of Loveton, Frost Hollow Road, Easton, Pennsylvania, wrote long letters to Margaret Sanger, full of praise for Sanger and detailing the great deal of work that both she and Mr. Love were doing for birth control in Easton and the surrounding area. One of her letters details how difficult it was to find a hall where Sanger could speak. To her five-page handwritten letter

dated March 31, 1932, Florence Rose, Mrs. Sanger's personal secretary, appended a note, "Too beautiful a letter to ever destroy—keep! FR." Mrs. Love headed the Maternal Health Society in Easton and organized a committee to support the National Committee on Federal Legislation. Reel 103, The Papers of Margaret Sanger, Library of Congress. Her enthusiastic activity for the Easton clinic paid off handsomely; the *Birth Control Review*, Volume 22, Number 2 [November 1937], reported that the clinics at "Wilkes-Barre, Bethlehem and Easton have just added paid social workers to their staffs."

32. Mrs. Virginia Kitzmiller was executive secretary of the Pennsylvania Birth Control Federation.

PART III: THE CONSERVATIVE RADICAL
34. Introduction to the Conservative Radical

1. Florence Rose, who had gone ahead of Sanger, was in the Cathay Hotel in Shanghai when Japanese bombs fell on it. Rose was evacuated with other refugees.

2 The conference was to be held December 1-4 at the Ambassador Hotel in Los Angeles, but had to be rescheduled because of Sanger's ill health. Reel 127, The Papers of Margaret Sanger, Library of Congress.

3. Stuart had had a longstanding problem with mastoiditis, but a direct hit above his right eye on a squash court in New York City aggravated his sinuses. After twenty-six operations to remove the slivers of bone with tweezers, Margaret drove with him to Arizona, where he could stay while his sinuses dried out. He returned east for additional operations and to finish his residency at Lehey Clinic in Boston. There he met Barbara Peabody, who was chief nurse for the head of the X-ray Department. Stuart and Barbara were married in 1941 and settled permanently in Tucson. Because of the sinus condition and the bombing in Nancy, France, when he was serving overseas, Stuart had problems with his hearing all his life.

4. Tucson was a draw for Margaret, as well, because it was known as the best place for tubercular patients to recuperate. A TB sanatorium was in Tucson when she arrived, and Margaret was instrumental in developing it into the Tucson Medical Center. She is recognized today as one of its founders.

5. The clinic grew to become Planned Parenthood of Southern Arizona. "Margaret Sanger: The Arizona Years," *Sanger Papers Project Newsletter*, Number 9 [Winter 1994/5], p. 4.

6. Container 229, The Papers of Margaret Sanger, Library of Congress.

7. Margaret Sanger to Edith How-Martyn, May 21, 1933, quoted in *Sanger Papers Project Newsletter*, Number 32 [Winter 2002/3], p. 2.

8. *Ibid.*

9. "Margaret Sanger and the 'Refugee Department,'" *Sanger Papers Project Newsletter*, Number 5 [Spring 1993], p. 2.

10 Grant and Edwina eventually had six children. Grant, with Peggy always in mind, wanted a little girl, who came on the sixth try after her five brothers. Margaret blushed at the size of the family, but she acknowledged that at least they

could afford them, and Margaret contributed stock and funds toward their permanent home in Mt. Kisco, New York. Douglas, *Pioneer of the Future*, p. 241.

11. Would that she had for author David Kennedy's sake, who writes, "The 1940s brought a new phase, in which birth control began to enjoy substantial social and official acceptance. Not surprisingly, Mrs. Sanger then slipped quietly from the position of leadership she had enjoyed for twenty-five years." Kennedy, *Birth Control*, p. 271. One wonders what planet Kennedy was on when doing his research for a book published in 1970. Mrs. Sanger may have been less active as a leader at the national level, but on the international level, she was the guiding and animating force—hence, the emergence of the International Planned Parenthood Federation, which she founded and of which she was officially named founder. And this is not leadership? We will not even go into the leadership involved in arranging for research on The Pill.

12. *Sanger Papers Project Newsletter*, Number 9 (Winter 1994/5], pp. 4-5.

13. Sanger's entertaining, more often than not, had the purpose of raising funds for her current project. Douglas, *Pioneer of the Future*, p. 249; Lader, *Margaret Sanger Story*, p. 310.

III. 35. The Negro Project

1. In 1938, both the American Birth Control League and Sanger's newly formed Committee on Public Progress were lobbying Congress for government sponsorship of birth control. It was clear that these efforts were confusing to potential supporters and that a united front was needed, particularly since the Catholic Church was such an effective and well-heeled lobbyist against birth control.

2. To call Sanger a racist would be laughable were it not such a serious charge. Although she may have been autocratic with her peers, never was Sanger less than just with the women and mothers who came to her. As she noted on her visit to Hawaii, "What surprised and pleased me most was the complete absence of race prejudice. I looked out over faces, mostly American but with a liberal sprinkling of Chinese and Japanese in their native costumes and Hawaiian in bright Mother Hubbards. Honolulu was the only place I had found where, class for class, internationalism did exist." Sanger, *An Autobiography*, pp. 317-318, 343-344, 464; "Birth Control in China and Japan," Reel 128, The Papers of Margaret Sanger, Library of Congress.

3. Peter C. Engelman and Cathy Moran Hajo, "Margaret Sanger and the Question of Racism," Margaret Sanger Papers Project, New York University, Department of History, New York, N.Y. 10003, p. 2.

4. Container 221, The Papers of Margaret Sanger, Library of Congress.

5. Katz, *Selected Papers*, pp. 262-263.

6. "Breaking into the South—A Contrast," *Birth Control Review*, Volume III, Number 12 [December 1919], p. 7.

7. Reel 32, The Papers of Margaret Sanger, Library of Congress.

8. Similarly, when Sanger received a letter from Mabel K. Staupers of the National Association of Colored Graduate Nurses, dated August 2, 1935, in which Staupers pointed to the "childish procedures" used by the white women who dealt with the black nurses, Sanger responded immediately and regretfully. By this time, however, the Clinical Research Bureau was not involved with the Harlem Clinic, having turned its management over to the Harlem Advisory Committee. Reel 33, The Papers of Margaret Sanger, Library of Congress.

9. Chesler, *Woman of Valor*, pp. 296-298.

10. Hazel Moore, a savvy professional lobbyist who knew her way around Washington politics, worked for Sanger in the National Committee on Federal Legislation for Birth Control. She was a fieldworker for the Birth Control Federation of America and for Clarence Gamble, for whom she distributed foam and sponges in the North Carolina trials in the late thirties.

11. "Birth Control or Race Control? Sanger and the Negro Project," *Sanger Papers Project Newsletter*, Number 28 (Fall 2001), p. 1.

12. In 1940, Mary Reinhardt Lasker was Secretary and on the Executive Committee and the Board of Directors of the National Birth Control Federation of America. Albert Lasker, who died in 1952, was an innovative advertising executive, who established the Lasker Foundation in 1942 to promote medical research. After his marriage to Mary Rhinehart, they oversaw the work of the Foundation together, and after his death, Mary continued the work.

13. "Birth Control or Race Control? Sanger and the Negro Project," *Sanger Papers Project Newsletter*, Number 28 (Fall 2001), p. 3.

14. Quoted, Engelman and Hajo, "Questions of Racism," Primary Documents, p. 4.

15. The statements of many individuals are attributed to Margaret Sanger, regardless of their source, such as this which follows by W.E.B. DuBois, when he was writing for the June 1932 issue of the *Birth Control Review*. DuBois, founder of the National Association for the Advancement of Colored People, in his discussion of the effects of birth control on quality of life for blacks, says: "The mass of ignorant Negroes still breed carelessly and disastrously, so that the increase among Negroes, even more than the increase among whites, is from that portion of the population least intelligent and fit, and least able to rear their children properly."

16. Going as far back as her studies in Europe with Dr. Rutgers and drawing from many studies on the matter, Sanger proved, as have others, that child spacing reduces infant mortality and that the more closely spaced are the infants, the higher the death rate and the more sickly the infant. See "To Mothers—Our Duty" and "Margaret Sanger as Feminist Author" herein.

17. Some of the Lasker money did go into hiring a few black nurses, who successfully taught contraception in areas of Tennessee and North Carolina.

18. Pressure on Roosevelt and his government by Roman Catholic leadership required that Eleanor Roosevelt keep mute on her support of birth control, as witness the opprobrium she endured when she merely attended the American

Woman's Association dinner honoring Sanger in 1931 with the AWA medal.

19. U.S. Surgeon General Dr. Thomas Parran Jr., who originally refused to supply even condoms to protect against syphilis, under Eleanor Roosevelt-instigated pressure in 1942 finally stated that he would support family planning programs originating with the states. Chesler, *Woman of Valor*, pp. 381, 389-390.

20. Many Catholic hospitals, to which poor women are assigned under government programs, deny contraception. In the state of New York, this has been a contentious matter in the New York State legislature. See, for instance, articles in the *New York Times* under these headlines: "Albany Bill Would Cover Birth Control," February 4, 2002; "Playing Politics with Women's Health: Cardinal Lobbies Against Bill for Contraceptive Coverage," March 13, 2002; "Bishops Sue State to Block Coverage for Birth Control," June 4, 2002. From 1980 to 2000, government spending on family planning and contraceptive services has been cut sixty-five percent. In addition, a maze of state laws make obtaining an abortion both difficult and emotionally wearing. States can require counseling, a waiting period, parental consents or notification; insurance does not cover abortion, even in the case of rape (and often not contraception); and providers are subject to bombings, arson, vandalism, protests, and blockades. Finally, the Hyde amendment forbids federal funds for abortion. Under these conditions, not unexpectedly, abortion providers are steadily declining. In the year 2000, "34% of women aged 15-44 lived in the 87% of the counties with no provider, and 86% of the nation's 276 metropolitan areas had no [abortion] provider." Lawrence B. Finer and Stanley K. Henshaw, "Abortion Incidence and Services in the United States in 2000," Perspectives on Sexual and Reproductive Health, Alan Guttmacher Institute, New York.

21. Daisy Mitchell (1883-1959) was working for J. J. Goldstein, the attorney who handled the Brownsville case, when Goldstein gave a dinner in honor of Sanger and Mitchell was the cook. As Mitchell writes, "I put my best Foot forward, with the Dinner I had taken a liking to Mrs. Sanger & I went to work Part Time for Mrs. S.... [In the year of 1917. or 1916] Mrs. Sanger Went to Europe for a Month or 2. when she return I was here with open arms. Mrs. S. Brought Back a wonderful pair of Shoes. Later on, something Happen so I took them to a Shoe Maker. Not from where Mrs. S. live. I went for them & he told me I did not bring them their. I was so angry with him I was going to hit him with a shoe last but Mrs. S. believe me from then on I love her & Mrs. S. love me I was put in charge of the 2 young boys. In the Summer we went to Turo until the open of their School.... Dr Grant. & they look after me in my aged. I will not say *Old* aged. It really do not seem that I have been with them 42 years in 1958. I go to Mt. Kisco in the Summer for 2 or 3 month to be with Dr & Mrs. Grant Sanger & their family. Still hold My own here is a photo of Me when I came Home from the Hospital 1953. I have been in the Sanger Family for 42 years. May God bless them." In the winters, Mitchell was living in the "Aged Colored Home Brooklyn. NY." Daisy Mitchell to Olive Byrne Richard, February 24, 1958. Courtesy of Margaret Sanger Lampe.

22. As told to the author by Margaret Sanger Lampe.

Notes

23. Lader, *Margaret Sanger Story*, pp. 271-272.

24. "Family Planning, A Special and Urgent Concern," acceptance speech, May 5, 1966.

25. D. Kenneth Rose, a Yale man, took an exceedingly cautious approach in his leadership, apparently believing that in so doing the Catholic hierarchy would tolerate incorporation of contraceptives into federal programs. As part of this strategy, in 1942 he oversaw the name change from Birth Control Federation of America to Planned Parenthood Federation of America and emphasized child spacing.

26. Chesler, *Woman of Valor*, p. 392.

27. Margaret Sanger to Ken Rose, Reel 117, The Papers of Margaret Sanger, Library of Congress.

28. Mrs. Felix Fuld had funded the Harlem Clinic, and Doris Duke, the tobacco heiress, supported Sanger regularly throughout the years.

29. Kathryn Trent was director, Regional Organizational Department of the Planned Parenthood Federation of America.

30. Mildred Delp, a nurse employed by the Farm Security Administration to work in the "Okie" camps on the West Coast, seeing the need for birth control, wrote to Margaret Sanger for information and supplies. Delp was instrumental in spreading birth control services by 1940 into migrant farm worker camps throughout Arizona and California. Lader, *Margaret Sanger Story*, pp. 307-308. Edna Rankin McKinnon, the sister of Congresswoman Jeannette Rankin, worked with Sanger on the National Committee for Federal Legislation, assisted in the field trials of sponges and foam in North Carolina, and was a part of the Bombay conference.

31. Dr. Gamble is Clarence James Gamble, Dr. Dickinson is Robert Latou Dickinson, the prominent gynecologist who founded the Committee on Maternal Health in 1923. Sanger, typically, gathered the most prominent women of Tucson to contribute to founding the Tucson Birth Control Clinic.

32. Mr. Arthur Packard was longtime senior manager of the Rockefeller Foundation charitable staff.

33. Mrs. Henry J. Mali was chairman of the regional committee of the Birth Control Federation of America.

III. 36. Entertaining and Chicken Curry

1. Margaret Sanger to Shinichi Mihara, the Mainichi Newspapers, May 27, 1953, Reel 128, The Papers of Margaret Sanger, Library of Congress.

2. Douglas, *Pioneer of the Future*, p. 187.

3. Reel 2, The Papers of Margaret Sanger, Library of Congress.

III. 37. Marriage and J. Noah H. Slee

1. "Two Words," Reel 130, The Papers of Margaret Sanger, Library of Congress, pp. 17-18.

2. *Ibid.*, pp. 18-20.

Notes

3. Katz, *Selected Papers*, pp. 337-339.

4. "Two Words," Reel 130, The Papers of Margaret Sanger, Library of Congress, pp. 20-21.

5. Sanger's diary shows that in February aboard the *Taiyo Maru*, she fell and hit her head, in late March in Yokahama she became ill and had to cancel her trip to Osaka, and in May on the way to Ceylon aboard the *Penang* she fainted and was again ill.

6. Lader, *Margaret Sanger Story*, pp. 197-198.

7. "Two Words," Reel 130, The Papers of Margaret Sanger, Library of Congress, p. 21.

8. Sanger, *My Fight*, p. 316. The "noble man" of whom Sanger speaks is Noah Slee. Dr. James F. Cooper (1880-1931) became Medical Director of American Birth Control League in January 1925.

9. Sanger, *My Fight*, pp. 316-317; Douglas, *Pioneer of the Future*, pp. 181-182.

10. For the "One Package" decision, see 13 F. Supp. 334 (E.D.N.Y, 1936), affirmed 86 F. 2d 737 (2d Cir. 1936).

11. Katz, *Selected Papers*, p. 414 note 2.

12. Quoted from an interview with Margaret Sanger Lampe in Bernard Asbell, *The Pill: A Biography of the Drug That Changed the World* (New York: Random House, 1995), p. 52.

13. Katz, *Selected Papers*, June 22, 1921, p. 300.

14. Sanger, *My Fight*, p. 297.

15. Katz, *Selected Papers*, January 27, 1922, p. 340.

16. *Ibid.*, January 15, 1922, p. 342 note 12.

17. Lader, *Margaret Sanger Story*, p. 206.

18. Lader, *Margaret Sanger Story*, pp. 197-198.

19. Sanger, *My Fight*, p. 276.

20. *Republican Journal*, Ogdenburg, New York, February 21, 1923, Container 212, The Papers of Margaret Sanger, Library of Congress.

21. Staten Island newspaper, New York, March 17, 1924, Container 212, The Papers of Margaret Sanger, Library of Congress.

22. Reel 8, November 27, 1953, The Papers of Margaret Sanger, Library of Congress.

23. Sanger, *My Fight*, pp. 296-297.

24. Douglas, *Pioneer of the Future*, 1975, p. 188.

25. Lader, *Margaret Sanger Story*, p. 208.

26. As reported to the author by Margaret Sanger Lampe.

27. Quoted in Chesler, *Woman of Valor*, p. 429.

28. Margaret Sanger Microfilm Edition, Smith College.

29. On June 13, 1934, Sanger's Birth Control bill reached the floor and was passed without debate by a voice vote. But Catholic Sen. Pat McCarran of Nevada had been briefly absent. When he returned to the floor, he requested the bill be recalled. In keeping with tradition, the recall received unanimous consent. Hazel Moore, who for an instant in time, believed that their bill had passed, uncharacteristically lost her composure and angrily demanded that McCarren be arrested. Naturally, this only brought laughter from the indifferent male body.

30. Veuve Clicquot Ponsardin Champagne, Reims, France. House founded in 1772.

III. 38. The Birth of The Pill

1. Margaret Sanger to Kan Majima, November 16, 1953, Reel 128, The Papers of Margaret Sanger, Library of Congress.

2. Reay Tannahill, *Sex in History* (Revised and updated, Scarborough House, 1992), p. 32. See also John M. Riddle, *Eve's Herbs: A History of Contraception and Abortion in the West* (Cambridge: Harvard University Press, 1997), *passim*.

3. Riddle, *Eve's Herbs*, pp. 44-46.

4. Riddle, *Eve's Herbs*, p. 257.

5. United States government support for contraceptive research along with the distribution of contraceptives runs counter to the Vatican belief that contraception is against the law of God. In supporting their belief system, the bishops of the Roman Catholic Church have exerted their influence on the United States government to kill the Draper Report of 1959, the Rockefeller Report of 1972, and the National Security Study Memorandum of 1974, all of which included recommendations for contraceptive research and population control. See "Pastoral Plan for Pro-Life Activities," United States Catholic Conference, Publications Office, 1312 Massachusetts Avenue NW, Washington D.C. 20005, 1975.

6. Helena Wright was a London gynecologist, feminist, chairman of the IPPF medical advisory committee, and the IPPF British representative at the Stockholm conference.

7. Williams, *Every Child*, pp. 237-238. Reed, *Birth Control*, p. 289. The *Bombay Sentinel*, April 13, 1938, notes that one trained midwife is available for every 1,072 births, that 45% of registered deaths are among children under five years of age, and that the number of women disabled as a result of pregnancy is as high as 30 per cent. Container 234, The Papers of Margaret Sanger, Library of Congress.

8. Marks, *Sexual Chemistry*, p. 252.

9. The jelly that Sanger brought back from Germany was effective, but too expensive to be produced in America. After experimenting, Drs. Hannah Stone and James Cooper refined the formula and developed a much less expensive and more effective product to be used with the diaphragm. Kennedy, *Birth Control*, p. 183; Douglas, *Pioneer of the Future*, p. 182. In Russia, Dr. Tushnov, who had immunized

twenty-two women out of thirty with his spermatoxin, had been forbidden by the Soviet government to continue his research and could give no information to Sanger. Douglas, *Pioneer of the Future*, p. 227.

10. Williams, *Every Child*, p. 316.

11. Sanyal's pill of the common pea was only 50 to 75 percent effective on humans or it would certainly have been put to use. Williams, *Every Child*, pp. 316-317.

12. McCormick's awareness of the great need for birth control among the poor is documented in her correspondence with Sanger. See Sanger-McCormick correspondence, Sanger Microfilm, Smith College.

13. Quoted in Marks, *Sexual Chemistry*, 2001, p. 13.

14. In this speech, "History of Birth Control in the Western World," given at the 1953 Stockholm conference, Sanger also said, "We have got to have a cheap, simple, harmless contraceptive that can be given to these people in the slums, in the jungles, in every place throughout the world." The Fourth International Conference on Planned Parenthood. Report of the Proceedings 17-22 August, 1953, Stockholm, Sweden (London: the International Planned Parenthood Federation, 1954), p. 9. Container 255, The Papers of Margaret Sanger, Library of Congress, p. 9.

15. Reed, *Birth Control Movement*, pp. 340-341.

16. Dr. John Rock (1890-1984) was a devout Catholic and an infertility specialist. As a clinician, he had success inducing pregnancy by suppressing menstruation for a short time: under a regimen of dosing with estrogen and progesterone in oral pill form, pregnancy would often follow. Pincus suggested large doses of progesterone only from day 5 to 25 of the menstrual cycle, and some pregnancies followed this regimen as well. Rock, a practicing physician, was able to conduct clinical trials, whereas Pincus could not. Rock's initial clinical trials were extremely valuable to Pincus in his development of The Pill, but Rock did his trials under the guise of researching infertility, for research on contraception was illegal in Catholic Massachusetts. Rock's support of The Pill angered the Catholic church, but Rock, who took a balanced view of life, had great sympathy for women and wrote his own view of things in *Voluntary Parenthood* (1949) and *The Time Has Come: A Catholic Doctor's Proposal to End the Battle over Birth Control* (1963).

17. Reed, *Birth Control Movement*, p. 358.

18. Pincus worked in Havana through Dr. Edris Rice-Wray.

19. Reed, *Birth Control Movement*, p. 362. Gamble continued to support the Humacao project in Puerto Rico until his death in 1966. Williams, *Every Child*, p. 327. Though space here does not permit a full discussion, it would be an insult not to salute the splendid work of Dr. Edris Rice-Wray at the Puerto Rico Medical School and Dr. Adaline Pendleton Satterthwaite at the Ryder Memorial Hospital, Humacao, in overseeing the clinical trials so necessary to development of The Pill. For full information, see James Reed, *Birth Control Movement*; Williams, *Every Child*; Marks, *Sexual Chemistry*.

20. Gregory Pincus (1903-1967) earned his M.S. and Sc.D. degrees at Harvard, went to Cambridge for two years as a postdoctoral researcher, and returned to Harvard as an assistant professor, where he established himself as an authority on mammalian sexual physiology. In 1934, he achieved success in his research and attention from the public with *in vitro* fertilization of rabbit eggs, an impressive feat, but one that aroused concern from religionists and envy from his peers. Pincus was a Jew, he was working in an area not quite respectable, and he was successful. But his experiments with "fatherless rabbits" were also cutting edge and difficult to duplicate, and this gave reasons of substance for academia not to support him. When Sanger and McCormick met him, he was a consultant on steroids for pharmaceutical companies.

21. Had Planned Parenthood Federation sponsored and supported Pincus's work, it would also have been entitled to its exclusive use and all profits as the sponsor and patent holder. See Reed, *Birth Control Movement*, p. 343.

22. Pincus was indeed the "Product Champion," as James Reed points out, drawing on the 1967 research of the National Science Foundation, which explains that the scientific breakthroughs that make it into the marketplace do so because they have behind them a champion who is committed to that success. Reed, *Birth Control Movement*, pp. 346-347.

23. "India and World Tour Diary," Reel 1, The Papers of Margaret Sanger, Library of Congress.

24. *Forbes*, December 23, 2002, p. 158.

25. Marks, *Sexual Chemistry*, p. 262.

26. The high estrogen content in the original pills caused in some women serious cardiovascular complications, blood clots, thrombosis, and even death. With reformulation and lowered levels of estrogen and progesterone, the pill in 2001 is considered not only safe, but a protection against ovarian and endometrial cancer. Marks, *Sexual Chemistry*, p. 182. Nevertheless, anecdotal problems with The Pill are still heard of, and women must consider carefully to what extent they can tinker with their individual body chemistry.

27. According to UN figures, 20 percent of the world's married women using contraception have chosen sterilization and 15 percent use the IUD. "Majority of World's Couples are Using Contraception," press release, Department of Public Information, News and Media Service Division, United Nations, New York, May 20, 2002, on the World Wide Web at *un.org*. The desirability of sterilization is enhanced by the less invasive methods than major surgery now available. These include Essure, in which a small metal spring is released into each fallopian tube with a narrow catheter, stimulating the formation of scar tissue, and the extremely inexpensive Quinacrine tablets, which also stimulate the formation of scar tissue when released into the uterus. In both procedures scar tissue prevents the egg and the sperm from meeting, and neither procedure requires anesthesia. The Quinacrine method was invented by Dr. Jamie Zipper of Chile in the early '80s and has been used on over 125,000 women throughout the world with no resulting complications

or deaths. On the world wide web, quinacrine.com, "After Long Hiatus, New Contraceptives Emerge," *New York Times*, December 10, 2002.

28. Marks, *Sexual Chemistry*, p. 244.

29. Since the recall of Norplant, researchers have been zealous in testing for safety. Safer and more convenient contraceptives are constantly coming on to the market, including implants designed to last for three years, skin patches to be worn three weeks out of the month, and IUDs lasting five years. "After Long Hiatus, New Contraceptives Emerge," *New York Times*, December 10, 2002.

30. Interview of Gregory Pincus, *Candide*, 1966, cited in Reed, *Birth Control Movement*, p. 309.

31. Reel 13, The Papers of Margaret Sanger, Library of Congress.

32. Paul Henshaw was the part-time director of research for Planned Parenthood Federation of America until 1954.

33. Dr. C. P. Blacker of Great Britain, London psychiatrist and secretary of the Eugenics Society, became vice chairman of the IPPF. He was instrumental in formation of the IPPF, always respected for his objectivity, diplomacy, and good judgment. Tellingly of the prejudice that yet persists toward Sanger and her work, Kevles (*Name of Eugenics*) mentions that Blacker was a supporter of Birth Control but carefully avoids mention of Blacker's support of Margaret Sanger or her organizations.

34. The friend(s) were G. J. and Ellen Watumull of Honolulu and Los Angeles.

35. The Fourth International Conference of the International Planned Parenthood Federation was held in Stockholm August 17-22, 1953; the Japan conference, the Fifth International Conference, which was held in Tokyo, did not take place until October 1955. Sanger visited Japan in 1954 in part to prepare for the 1955 conference.

36. Between the end of March and the end of October of 1953, Sanger, after spending time in Tucson with Lawrence Lader on her biography, had been to Mount Kisco, New York, to see Grant and his family; back to Tucson in April; returned to New York in June; then to Boston and Shrewsbury in Massachusetts; Stepney, Connecticut; and Mount Kisco. On June 13 she was in Philadelphia and Bryn Mawr. From there it was a short hop back to New York and to Stepney. At the end of June, she visited Juliet Rublee in Cornish, New Hampshire. In July she stayed with Grant in Mount Kisco, went out to Grant's summer place on Fisher's Island, then up to Willowlake to visit Noah Slee's grave. In August, she sailed to Stockholm for the Fourth IPPF Conference and then traveled to Helsinki and Goteberg. She returned to Tucson by way of New York and Tulsa. At the beginning of September, she was in Oslo. She stayed at the Goring Hotel in London, visited Cambridge, and arrived in New York City on September 17 on the *Mauritania*. This was convenient to visiting Grant again in Mount Kisco before returning to Tucson by way of Tulsa. From Tucson, she slipped over to Denmark, and possibly Finland and Norway, at the end of September and was back in Tucson to receive Lady Rama Rau on the twenty-third of October before they both took off to stay in McCormick's guesthouse in Santa Barbara, California. Gracious!

38. International Conference of Planned Parenthood, Report of Proceedings, 24-29 November 1952, Bombay, India (Bombay, India: Family Planning Association of India, 1952), Container 255, The Papers of Margaret Sanger, Library of Congress.

III. 39. Rules for a Life

1. After the removal of her gall bladder in 1937, Sanger faced many more illnesses: appendicitis, coronary thrombosis, pneumonia twice, once with pleurisy. In addition she suffered from recurring pleurisy, lumbago, bursitis, sacroiliac strain, and insomnia. Dorothy Brush said that she "treats her body like a Victorian child...it must be seen and not heard." A doctor tells of listening to Sanger speak for two hours when he knew she was in great pain. Douglas, *Pioneer of the Future*, p. 252. But the angina pain in her later years was very difficult for her. She wrote to Pincus about "the agonizing [pain] in the throat and left side of the chest." Margaret Sanger to Gregory Pincus, February 7, 1957, Sanger Microfilm, Smith College.

2. Herbert and Betty Simonds, who had started the Holland-Rantos contraceptive firm in 1925 with Noah's help, after selling their company to Ortho Pharmaceuticals, had a home in Connecticut.

3. Chesler, *Woman of Valor*, pp. 302, 435.

4. Reel 130, The Papers of Margaret Sanger, Library of Congress.

III. 40. Mainstream Acceptance

1. At the Fifth Conference in Tokyo in October 1955, the Japanese outdid themselves. Visiting delegates from fifteen countries, welcomed by the hospitable Japanese, visited the chrysanthemum show at the Shinjuku Garden; were entertained at Canon Camera Company; attended a Japanese Shinto wedding ceremony; visited a large factory and were given a length of yukata material; went to the Rinnoji Temple for dinner with Japanese dishes, a tea ceremony, and geisha folk dances in the crimsoned gardens; made a day trip along the Tokaido Line; a two-day bus trip to Kyoto and Nara, both ancient capitals of Japan; and an overnight tour of Nikko to see the 330-foot high Kegon Falls and Lake Chuzenji and the extraordinary Toshogu Shrine. Sanger was given a pair of sterling silver candelabra, which she exchanged for a double strand of cultured pearls, and the Margaret Sanger Trophy, a foot-and-a-half high sterling silver chalice, was awarded to Clarence Gamble. *The Japan Planned Parenthood Quarterly*, Volume 6, Number 4 [October-December 1955], *passim*. Reel 128, The Papers of Margaret Sanger, Library of Congress.

2. "The History of Birth Control in the English-Speaking World," *The Fourth International Conference on Planned Parenthood Report of the Proceedings 17-22 August, 1953, Stockholm, Sweden* (London: The International Planned Parenthood Federation, 1954), p. 6-7. Container 255, The Papers of Margaret Sanger, Library of Congress.

3. Chesler, *Woman of Valor*, p. 417.

4. Ted Yates Jr., to Margaret Sanger Slee, June 4, 1957; unsigned memo, Tucson Arizona, August, 12 1957; Margaret Sanger to Anne Kennedy, September 6, 1957.

Notes

All quotes are from the Margaret Sanger-Mike Wallace correspondence, Sanger Microfilm, Smith College.

5. Mike Wallace and Margaret Sanger, transcript of phone conversation, September 5, 1957, *ibid.*

6. Wallace identified the priests as Fathers Donachei and LaFarge and the next day said, one "is a good friend of mine. I talk to him all the time." Mike Wallace and Margaret Sanger, transcripts of phone conversation, September 5 and 6. 1957, *ibid.*

7. Helen Gorelick to Mr. Wallace, September 21, 1957, *ibid.*

8. "The Heart to Go to Japan," *Sanger Papers Project Newsletter*, Number 12 [Spring 1996], p. 4.

9. During one of her trips to the Orient, Sanger was presented in Shanghai with two large and magnificent portraits of someone's Chinese ancestors. When moving her household, she admonished the movers to "be careful with my Japanese ancestors." The movers stared at each other, uncomprehendingly. "She doesn't look Japanese to me," they said to each other. The portraits are clearly Chinese in style, but Sanger always referred to them as Japanese.

10. Shidzue Ishimoto Kato observes that MacArthur, with his own political ambitions in mind, deferred to Roman Catholic pressure in refusing Sanger entrance. Shidzue Kato, *Fight for Women's Happiness*, pp. 87-98, cited in Chesler, *Woman of Valor*, p. 423 note 8.

11. *The Reader's Digest*, July 1956, pp. 36-38, Reel 128, The Papers of Margaret Sanger, Library of Congress.

III. 41. The International Planned Parenthood Federation

1. Douglas, *Pioneer of the Future*, pp. 256-257; Chesler, *Woman of Valor*, p. 450.

2. "The International Planned Parenthood Federation (1952-1962)," *Margaret Sanger Papers Project*, on the World Wide Web at nyu.edu/projects/sanger/ippf/htm. Margaret Sanger is not mentioned, but the chronology of the development of the IPPF is given.

3. The "Our Margaret Sanger" volumes had been compiled by Ellen Watumull.

4. Hugh de Selincourt died in 1951.

5. Chesler, *Woman of Valor*, pp. 417-418.

6. *The Woman Rebel*, September/October 1914, pp. 1-2. The Hugh Moore Fund, organized in 1944 to promote world peace, published *The Population Bomb* in the early fifties and popularized the term "breeding ourselves to death." By 1969, more than 1,500,000 copies had been distributed in America. It was generally agreed to have changed the climate of public opinion regarding overpopulation. Lawrence Lader, *Breeding Ourselves to Death*, 36th Anniversary Edition (Santa Ana, Calif.: Seven Locks Press, 2002), pp. 1, 5-6.

7. Chesler, *Woman of Valor*, pp. 355-356.

8. *Ibid.*, pp. 407-408.

9. Mary and Albert Lasker had set up a prize for pioneering work in family planning. They insisted that Planned Parenthood give the 1950 prize to Margaret Sanger. Chesler, *Woman of Valor*, p. 417.

10. In 1928, the Clinical Research Bureau was renamed the Birth Control Clinical Research Bureau, and in 1940 it was renamed the Margaret Sanger Research Bureau.

11. "The International Committee on Planned Parenthood (1948-1952)," Margaret Sanger Papers Project: International Committee on Planned Parenthood, on the World Wide Web at nyu.edu/projects/sanger/icpp/htm.

12. Chesler, *Woman of Valor*, p. 420.

13. "The International Planned Parenthood Federation (1952-1962)," Margaret Sanger Papers Project: International Planned Parenthood Federation, on the World Wide Web at nyu.edu/projects/sanger/ipff/htm.

14. Chesler, *Woman of Valor*, p. 408. Not discussed here for lack of space is the substantial contribution made by Sanger to the Western Hemisphere Region of the IPPF, one of the four administrative regions into which the IPPF was organized shortly after its formation. Sanger was president of the Western Hemisphere Region until 1955 and thereafter continued as a member of its governing committees until 1959. Just as she had for the international conferences, Sanger also raised substantial funds for the Western Hemisphere Region.

15. *The Fourth International Conference on Planned Parenthood. Report of the Proceedings 17-22 August, 1953, Stockholm, Sweden* (London: The International Planned Parenthood Federation, 1953), p. 7.

16. "Address by Mrs. Margaret Sanger, IPPF President," *The Japan Planned Parenthood Quarterly*, 5th ICPP Pictorial, Volume 6, Number 4 [October-December 1955], p. 65, Reel 128, The Papers of Margaret Sanger, Manuscript Division, Library of Congress, 1977.

17. *The Japan Planned Parenthood Quarterly*, 5th ICPP Pictorial, Volume 6, Number 4 [October-December 1955], p. 82, Reel 128, The Papers of Margaret Sanger, Library of Congress.

18. Not that Gamble foreswore conferences. The 1955 Tokyo conference was paid for in part by him. Reel 128, The Papers of Margaret Sanger, Library of Congress.

19. In carrying on the charitable acts of his parents, who had regularly supported Christian missionaries overseas, Gamble restricted his giving to supplies of contraceptives, using the missionaries also for testing purposes. Gamble never pushed the limitation of children. When asked if he was telling women to limit their families, Gamble always said that that was for the individual to decide. Gamble became very involved in Japan, funding the three-village study in 1950, followed by many gifts over the years to Dr. Yoshio Koya, who founded the Association of Popular Health in Japan. Williams, *Every Child*, pp. 209, 221-226, 228-229.

20. Clarence J. Gamble to the Executive Committee of the International Planned Parenthood Federation, September 28, 1953, Reel 8, The Papers of Margaret Sanger, Library of Congress.

21. Clarence J. Gamble to the Executive Committee of the International Planned Parenthood Federation, September 29, 1953, Reel 8, The Papers of Margaret Sanger, Library of Congress. The IPPF could be approving of Gamble. In its 1954 annual report, it listed respectfully the thirteen countries that Gamble had visited along with the six countries where exploratory visits were made. Quoted in Williams, *Every Child*, p. 240.

22. Lippes loop, a plastic S-shaped loop inserted into the uterus, for unknown reasons interferes with conception.

23. "Meanwhile, from 1962 until 1964, the Population Council restricted its overseas program to Korea, Taiwan, and Pakistan. In 1964 it expanded to thirty countries." Williams, *Every Child*, pp. 358-359.

24. In 1967, a year after Gamble died, the Pathfinder Fund set up by Gamble was serving Africa, Latin America, as well as the Far East and Oceania, Europe, and the Middle East. Williams, *Every Child*, p. 370.

25. The IPPF regularly tried to prevent Gamble from testing contraceptives and did not believe that he should send out fieldworkers, those wonderful women such as Phillis Page, Elsie Wulkop, and Hazel Moore, who would come into a strange town, find the most-important people available, and offer seed money for a birth control clinic in that community. In this manner, clinics were set up all over America, and through similar tactics, only somewhat more arduous, fieldworkers Edna McKinnon, Margaret Roots, and Edith Gates did the same thing in the Far East and Africa.

26. Chesler, *Woman of Valor*, p. 427.

27. Chesler, *Woman of Valor*, pp. 425-427. Research and studies and investigations have their purposes. They consolidate power, confirm the egos of the researchers, and support printing establishments.

28. Chesler, *Woman of Valor*, pp. 425-427.

29. See ippf.org on the World Wide Web.

30. "The Humanity of Family Planning," *The Third International Conference on Planned Parenthood. Report of the Proceedings, 24-29 November, 1952. Bombay, India* (Bombay: The Family Planning Association of India, 1953), pp. 53-55. Container 255, The Papers of Margaret Sanger, Library of Congress.

31. Sir George Sansom [not Samsome] (1883-1965) world renowned specialist on Japan language and culture, began his career in the British Japan Consular Service in 1904. After twenty years of service in Japan consulates, he was appointed Commercial Counsellor for Great Britain. With the outbreak of World War II, he served in advisory appointments at the British Embassy in Washington and continued as advisor to the Americans, who were governing occupied Japan until 1947. He then retired from public service and returned to Columbia University, where he had

been a Visiting Professor in 1935-36, as Professor of Japanese and Director of the East Asian Institute until 1953. His published writings include *Historical Grammar of the Japanese Language* (1928), *Japan, A Short Cultural History* (1931), *The Western World and Japan* (1950), and the three volume *History of Japan* (1958-1964). Sansom died in Tucson, Arizona, on March 10, 1965. *The Times*, London, England, March 10, 1965, p. 16.

III. 42. Overpopulation and the Draper Report

1. Edward O. Wilson, "Book Excerpt," *The Future of Life* (New York: Alfred A. Knopf, 2002), *Scientific American*, February 2002, p. 89.

2. Tina Rosenberg, "The Free Trade Fix," *New York Times Magazine*, August 18, 2002, p. 31.

3. On the World Wide Web at cyberdyaryo.com.

4. Amy Chua, "A World on the Edge," *Wilson Quarterly*, Autumn 2002, p. 64.

5. "The United Nations reported in 1992 that the one fifth of the human race who are the most rich received 82.7 percent of the world's income, leaving the remaining 17.3 percent of income for the remaining 80 percent of the population. The poorest one fifth of the world received 1.4 percent of world income. During the 1980s in America, the bastion of democracy and good living, where the fertility rate does not equal that of the developing countries, the top ten percent of wealthy American families increased their average family income by 16 percent, the top 5 percent by 23 percent, and the top one percent by 50 percent. The bottom ten percent lost 15 percent of their already meager incomes." Daniel C. Maguire, *Sacred Choices: The Right to Contraception and Abortion in Ten World Religions* (Minneapolis, Minn.: Fortress Press, 2001), p. 8.

6. "Well over half the populations of Egypt, Syria, Saudi Arabia, Iran and Iraq are under 25 years old, according to the International Programs Center at the Census Bureau." Elaine Sciolino, "Radicalism: Is the Devil in the Demographics?" *New York Times,* December 9, 2001, p. WK1.

7. Don Collins, "Overabundance of Rogue Males: A Major Contributing Factor in Terrorism," *The Social Contract*, Fall 2001, p. 72; Christian G. Mesquida and Neil I. Wiener, "Population Age Composition and Male Coalitional Aggression," York University, 1997.

8. Male babies have a higher death rate than females, so the slight overage balances out. "John Gittings in Shanghai," *The Guardian*, May 13, 2002, on the World Wide Web at guardian.co.uk.

9. Theodore H. White, "No. 1 American in Europe," *New York Times Magazine*, December 21, 1952.

10. Among the committee members were Eisenhower's special assistant for National Security Affairs, Dillon Anderson; investor John J. McCloy, who headed the World Bank from 1947 to 1949; General Alfred M. Gruenther, former commander of the allied forces in Europe; Admiral Arthur W. Radford, and several former officials of the departments of state and defense.

11. "Oral History Interview with General William H. Draper Jr.," by Jerry N. Hess, Washington, D.C., January 11, 1972, Truman Presidential Museum and Library, p. 60, on the World Wide Web at trumanlibrary.org.

12. On November 25, 1959, the Catholic bishops of the United States released this statement from Washington, D.C.: "United States Catholics believe that the promotion of artificial birth control is a morally, humanly, psychologically, and politically disastrous approach to the population problem.... They will not support any public assistance, either at home or abroad, to promote artificial birth prevention, abortion, or sterilization, whether through direct aid or by means of international organizations." "Statement by Roman Catholic Bishops of U.S. on Birth Control," "Special to the New York Times," New York Times, November 26, 1959, p. 43.

13. Edward O. Wilson, "Book Excerpt," February 2002, p. 85. Assuming a world population of five billion in 1959, the exponential increase at the 1.8 percent figure given by Wilson would bring an additional 369,873,000 four years later, or the equivalent of 1,850 large cities (a large city considered to have a population of 200,000).

14. Martin Luther King Jr., speech on acceptance of Planned Parenthood Margaret Sanger Award, 1966.

15. Reel 129, The Papers of Margaret Sanger, Library of Congress.

16. Nobusuke Kishi (1896-1987) was minister of commerce and industry in Tojo's cabinet and was in prison for three years after World War II. He unified the Liberal Democratic party in 1955 to become party president and prime minister. In 1960, he was forced to resign in the furor over the U.S.-Japanese Security Treaty.

17. December 3, 1958, press conference, *New York Times*.

III. *Finis* and Epilogue

1. Clarence Gamble had died over a month earlier on July 15. In 1967, Gregory Pincus died on August 22 at the age of sixty-four, and Katherine McCormick died on December 28, at ninety-two.

2. "Pastoral Plan for Pro-Life Activities," National Conference of Catholic Bishops, Publications Office, 1312 Massachusetts Avenue NW, Washington, DC 20005, 1975. The success of this public education effort by the Roman Catholic church to dictate the terms used in the abortion debate may be gauged by the recent outcry chronicled in the *Boston Globe*, when the fetus of a pregnant woman received a gunshot and died just after being born. Readers were horrified that the term "fetus" was used, as was the columnist, which is even more disturbing, an illustration of the obeisance with which the media is supporting the pro-life stance of the abortion debate. Christine Chinlund, "Fetus or Baby?" *The Boston Globe*, February 17, 2003.

3. "Title X and the U.S. Family Planning Effort," Facts in Brief, The Alan Guttmacher Institute, March 3, 2003, on the world wide web at guttmacher.org/pubs/ib16.html.

4. Edward O. Wilson, "Book Excerpt," *The Future of Life* (Random House, NY:

Alfred A. Knopf, 2002), in *Scientific American*, February 2002, pp. 84-90. "A recent study...estimated that the human population exceeded Earth's sustainable capacity around the year 1978. By 2000 it had overshot by 1.4 times that capacity" (p. 86). The United States is one of the worst offenders: since the Earth Summit conference at Rio de Janerio in 1992, United States consumption of energy has increased twenty-one percent and greenhouse emissions have increased thirteen percent, this according to United Nations figures. Yet the United States refuses to join in global efforts to protect the environment and withdraws from global accords that attempt to do so.

5. Seventy percent of the married women of the developed world and sixty percent of the married women of the non-developed world use contraception. No figures are available on unmarried women. (Unmarried women apparently do not have sexual relations.) "Majority of World's Couples Are Using Contraception," Press Release, Department of Information, News & Media Service Division, United Nations, New York, May 20, 2002, on the web at un.org.

6. Wilson, "Book Excerpt," 2002, p. 87.

7. "Population Estimates Fall as Poor Women Assert Control," *New York Times International*, March 10, 2002.

Bibliography

Asbell, Bernard. *The Pill: A Biography of the Drug that Changed the World* (New York: Random House, 1995).

Avrich, Paul. *Modern School Movement: Anarchism and Education in the United States* (Princeton, NJ: Princeton University Press, 1995).

Broun, Heywood, and Margaret Leech. *Anthony Comstock: Roundsman of the Lord* (New York: Albert & Charles Boni, 1927).

Cahn, William. *Lawrence, 1912: The Bread and Roses Strike* (New York: Pilgrim Press, 1980).

Chesler, Ellen. *Woman of Valor: Margaret Sanger and the Birth Control Movement in America* (New York: Simon & Schuster, 1992).

Douglas, Emily Taft. *Margaret Sanger: Pioneer of the Future* (Garrett Park, MD: Garrett Park Press, 1975).

Dubofsky, Melvyn. *'Big Bill' Haywood* (New York: St. Martin's Press, 1987).

Falk, Candace. *Love, Anarchy, and Emma Goldman* (New York: Holt, Rinehart and Winston, 1984).

Glassgold, Peter, ed. *Anarchy! An Anthology of Emma Goldman's* MOTHER EARTH (Washington, DC: Counterpoint, 2001).

Goldman, Emma. *Living My Life*, 2 vols. (1931; reprint, New York: Dover Publications, 1970).

Golin, Steve. *The Fragile Bridge: Paterson Silk Strike, 1913* (Philadelphia, PA: Temple University Press, 1988).

Bibliography

Gordon, Linda. *Woman's Body, Woman's Right: A Social History of Birth Control in America* (New York: Grossman Publishing, Viking Press, 1976).

Gordon, Linda. *Woman's Body, Woman's Right: Birth Control in America* (New York: Penguin Books, 1990).

Grant, Lindsey. *Too Many People: The Case for Reversing Growth* (Santa Ana, California: Seven Locks Press, 2000).

Haywood, William D. *Bill Haywood's Book: The Autobiography of William D. Haywood* (New York: International Publishers, 1929; 1938 ed.).

Hershey, Harold Brainerd. "Margaret Sanger; The Biography of the Birth Control Pioneer" (Unpublished manuscript, 1938, Rare Books Division, The New York Public Library, New York City).

Ishimoto, Shadzue. *Facing Two Way: The Story of My* Life (1935; reprint, Stanford, CA, 1984).

Katz, Esther, ed. *The Selected Papers of Margaret Sanger. Volume I: The Woman Rebel, 1900-1928* (Urbana and Chicago: University of Illinois Press, 2003).

Kennedy, David M. *Birth Control in America: The Career of Margaret Sanger* (New Haven: Yale University Press, 1970).

Kevles, Daniel J. *In the Name of Eugenics: Genetics and the Uses of Human Heredity* (Cambridge and London: Harvard University Press, 1985).

Lader, Lawrence. *Breeding Ourselves to Death* (1971; reprint, 30th Anniversary Edition, Santa Ana, California: Seven Locks Press, 2002).

Lader, Lawrence. *The Margaret Sanger Story and the Fight for Birth Control* (Garden City, NY: Doubleday & Company, 1955).

Leuchtenburg, William E. *Perils of Prosperity* (Chicago: University of Chicago Press, 1958).

MacKinnon, Janice R & Stephen R. *Agnes Smedley: The Life and Times of An American Radical* (Berkeley and Los Angeles: University of California Press, 1988).

Mcguire, Daniel C. *Sacred Choices: The Right to Contraception and Abortion in Ten World Religions* (Minneapolis, MN: Fortress Press, 2001).

McLaren, Angus. *Reproductive Rituals: The Perception of Fertility in England from the Sixteenth Century to the Nineteenth Century* (New York: Methuen, 1984).

Bibliography

McLaughlin, Loretta. *The Pill, John Rock, and the Church: The Biography of a Revolution* (Boston: Little, Brown & Company, 1982).

Marks, Lara V. *Sexual Chemistry: A History of the Contraceptive Pill* (New Haven and London: Yale University Press, 2001).

Meltzer, Milton. *Bread-and Roses: The Struggle of American Labor, 1865-1915* (New York: Knopf, NY, 1967).

Murolo, Priscilla, and A.B. Chitty. *From the Folks Who Brought You the Weekend: A Short, Illustrated History of Labor in the United States.* (New York: The New Press, 2001).

Myss, Caroline. *Anatomy of the Spirit: The Seven Stages of Power and Healing* (New York: Three Rivers Press, 1990).

Pert, Candace. "Study Guide. Your Body is Your Subconscious Mind" (Boulder, CO: Sounds True, 2000).

Research Department, Manuscript Division. *Margaret Sanger: A Rester of Her Papers in the Library of Congress* (Washington, DC: Library of Congress: 1977).

Riddle, John M. *Eve's Herbs: A History of Contraception and Abortion in the West* (Cambridge: Harvard University Press, 1997).

Sanger, Alexander C. "Margaret Sanger: The Early Years, 1910-1917" (M.A. thesis, Princeton University, 1969).

Sanger, Margaret. *An Autobiography.* (1938; reprint, New York: Dover Publications, 1971).

Sanger, Margaret. *Motherhood in Bondage.* Foreword by Margaret Marsh. (Columbus: Ohio State University Press, 2000).

Sanger, Margaret. *My Fight for Birth Control* (1931; reprint. Elmsford, NY: Maxwell Reprint Company, 1969).

Sanger, Margaret: The Papers of Margaret Sanger. Manuscript Division, Library of Congress, Washington, D.C., 1977.

Margaret Sanger Papers Microfilm Edition, Smith College Collections Series, Northampton, MA.

Sanger, Margaret. *The Pivot of Civilization* (New York: Brentano's, 1922).

Sanger, Margaret. *Woman and the New Race* (New York: Eugenics Publishing Company, 1920).

Bibliography

Schuetz, Janice. *The Logic of Women on Trial: Case Studies of Popular American Trials* (Carbondale and Edwardsville: Southern Illinois University Press, 1994).

Smith, Page. *America Enters the World: A People's History of the Progressive Era and World War I.* Volume Seven. (New York: McGraw-Hill Book Company, 1985).

Tannahill, Reay. *Sex in History* (Scarborough House, 1992).

Tone, Andrea. *Devices & Desires: A History of Contraceptives in America* (New York: Hill & Wang, 2001).

Williams, Doone and Greer. Edited by Emily P. Flint. *Every Child a Wanted Child: Clarence James Gamble, M.D., and His Work in the Birth Control Movement* (Cambridge, MA: The Francis A. Countway Library of Medicine, Harvard University Press, 1978).

Acknowledgements

Margaret Sanger: Her Life in Her Words owes its complexity to Sarah Epstein and Don Collins, who generously contributed not only ideas and the tonic of critical listening, but their kind home and warm hospitality. In my own small struggle to make sense of life and my subject, I have been fortunate as well in the freely given shelter and assistance of my lifelong friend Emily Kidwell. At the Sophie Smith Archives, my thanks go to Peter Engelman, who kindly gave me a chronology of the life of Margaret Sanger, and Susan Barker, who has dealt so patiently with complicated photo requests. Bruce Kirby and Jeff Flannery at the Library of Congress offered extra helpful research assistance, and—thank you, thank you—they infused good cheer into what could have been a grim grind. My thanks to Doris W. Davis who understands computers. Reimert T. Ravenholt kindly answered endless questions as did Stephen D. Mumford. Most fortunately, Alexander C. Sanger has given permissions and promptly answered questions in the midst of his extremely busy schedule, for which I am most grateful. And after years and years of submitting to questions about her grandmother, Margaret Sanger Lampe continues to have the patience to share insight, memories, and memorabilia with yet another questioner, Finally, my dear thanks to Jeff, who tolerates changes, and to Barricade Books, who does not mind controversy.

Photo and Illustration Credits

All of the line art is from The Papers of Margaret Sanger, Library of Congress

Dr. Clarence J. Gamble photo is courtesy of Sarah Gamble Epstein.

The following photos are courtesy of Margaret Sanger Lampe:
- Margaret Sanger with Stuart 1905 (cover photo)
- William (Bill) Sanger
- Juliet Rublee circa 1920
- Shidzue Ishimoto Kato, circa 1930
- Margaret Sanger in the 30s
- Margaret Sanger with Stuart's daughters, Nancy and Margaret Sanger, Tucson, Arizona, 1946
- Margaret Sanger Lampe, her friend ,and Margaret Sanger at Family Planning Association gathering, Hong Kong, June 20, 1959

The following photos are courtesy Sophie Smith Collection, Smith College, Northampton, Massachusetts:
- Young Margaret Higgins, age 16, December 1899.
- Stuart, Peggy, and Grant Sanger, Paris 1913
- Publicity photo taken after the death of Peggy of Margaret Sanger with Stuart and Grant, 1916
- Margaret Sanger in the U.S. Senate, May 19, 1932
- Pearl Buck, Margaret Sanger, Katherine Houghton Hepburn at a dinner, February 1935
- Mahatma Gandhi with Margaret Sanger at Gandhi's ashram, Wardha, India, December 1935
- Margaret Sanger receiving honorary LL.D. at Smith College, Northampton, Massachusetts, 1949
- Jawaharlal Nehru and Margaret Sanger, International Conference on Planned Parenthood, New Delhi, India, 1959

Index

Index

Index

Index

Index

Index

Index

Index

Index

Index

Index

Index

About the Author

Miriam Reed earned her Ph.D. from the Comparative Literature Department of University of California, Los Angeles, in 1980. She has published *Oscar Wilde's* Vera and has taught English composition and rhetoric from the basis of her textbook, *How to Write Great Prose (almost) Instantly.* Miriam Reed is an actress and the writer of her one-woman shows on powerful women: *Louisa May Alcott: Living* Little Women; *Oscar Wilde's Women; Talking Abortion,* and of course, *Margaret Sanger: Radiant Rebel.*

Margaret Sanger Lampe is the oldest daughter of Stuart Sanger, Margaret Sanger's first child. She was born in Tucson and was Margaret Sanger's first grandchild. For forty years, Margaret Lampe has lived in Arlington, where she has served on the Arlington County School Board, The Virginia Board of Education, The Board of Visitors of Virginia Tech and the National Commission on Education.

Her civic endeavors range from the local and County PTA'S to serving on the Virginia Board of PTA'S. She has chaired the Committee of 100, the Rock Spring Garden Club, and many advisory Boards. She has recently chaired the Arlington County Bicentennial Commission. Arlington will celebrate its 200 anniversary in 2001.

Recently, and much in line with her family tradition, she has begun to fulfill a lifetime dream of painting, and has found great joy in it. She is married to Hank Lampe and is the mother of two daughters and seven grandchildren.